T0266769

The
COMPLETE
LANGUAGE
~ *of* ~
# TREES

The

COMPLETE
LANGUAGE

~ *of* ~

TREES

A Definitive & Illustrated History

S. THERESA DIETZ

wellfleet
press

© 2023, 2024 by Quarto Publishing Group USA Inc.

Text © 2023 by S. Theresa Dietz

This edition published in 2024 by Wellfleet Press an imprint of The Quarto Group,

142 West 36th Street, 4th Floor, New York, NY 10018, USA

(212) 779-4972 www.Quarto.com

Contains content previously published in 2023 by Wellfleet Press, an imprint of The Quarto Group,

142 West 36th Street, 4th Floor, New York, NY 10018, USA.

Wellfleet titles are also available at discount for retail, wholesale, promotional, and bulk purchase. For details, contact the Special Sales Manager by email at specialsales@quarto.com or by mail at The Quarto Group, Attn: Special Sales Manager,

100 Cummings Center Suite 265D, Beverly, MA 01915 USA.

10 9 8 7 6 5 4 3 2 1

ISBN: 978-1-57715-476-1

Library of Congress Control Number: 2024930734

Group Publisher: Rage Kindelsperger
Editorial Director: Erin Canning
Creative Director: Laura Drew
Managing Editor: Cara Donaldson
Editor: Elizabeth You
Interior Design: Verso Design

Front Cover: © The Maas Gallery, London / Bridgeman Images; © Christie's Images / Bridgeman Images
Back Cover: © Natural History Museum, London / Bridgeman Images

Printed in China

This book provides general information on various widely known and widely accepted images of trees and their components, some of which may have been used for culinary or medicinal purposes. However, it should not be relied upon as recommending or promoting any specific diagnosis or method of treatment for a particular condition, and it is not intended as a substitute for medical advice or for direct diagnosis and treatment of a medical condition by a qualified physician. Readers who have questions about a particular condition, possible treatments for that condition, or possible reactions from the condition or its treatment should consult a physician or other qualified healthcare professional.

CONTENTS

INTRODUCTION

I n gathering the information for this book, it came to be that I needed to make a decision about what to include. According to common opinion, a tree isn't a tree until it reaches 20 feet (6 m) tall. The project became too enticing a study to not include that which I found fascinating. So, I included trees much shorter than that. I found myself including an increasingly wider variety of trees with the only criteria being that their maximum potential height is well over my own head. As I am just a smidgen over 5 feet (1.5 m) tall, there was a lot of room overhead for me to look up and consider what I see to be a tree.

There are so many trees that piqued my interest. I found a great deal that I did not know about before I started. My endeavor to find out what I could about the majestic sources of Earth's oxygen has been fruitful for me. I learned so much about some trees that are several hundreds of years old, and a few that have been growing for a thousand years or much, much longer. Their persistent existence in this ever-changing world, for as long as they have been growing within it, is magical and continually energizing.

Most of the magical trees on Earth today are living trees. To simply write that some of them are a thousand years old or much, *much* older, seems too casual of a statement to make. It seems nearly incomprehensible to me, to imagine back *so* far. When the seed of the highly precious *oldest tree in the world* germinated it was sometime back between 3051 and 2833 BCE. What do we know of any parts of our world that far back in time? Not very much. That is how ancient that tree is. There are others.

It is a genuinely awesome consideration to think of time in such a tangible, yet nearly unimaginable way. Trees have not only been on, but have actually been anchored into our planet, creating oxygen and positive energy, for millions of years. They also cleanse our air by absorbing and storing carbon dioxide into their wood. Some trees have the capacity to clean the soil of heavy metals. Trees are tightly integrated into the persistent rhythm of life on Earth. Without trees we will not have sufficient oxygen to sustain life on this planet. Trees provide our next breaths of air.

I have spent a great deal of my life simply paying attention to the trees that I encounter on my way as I pass by them. Seeing what grows in the hedgerows or in the front gardens of homes. Looking off towards the distant horizons, hills, and mountainsides to appreciate the blending of greens. There are a lot of trees to be seen during our lifetime.

Some of the trees nearest to us have been here as saplings that we ourselves planted in our own garden to commemorate a memorable event in our lives, such as a birth or a new home. Many trees have been growing nearby our homes long before we ever showed up. Certain trees that I would find myself near for long periods of time seem to have been the most engaging. Learning about the meanings of trees and the energies they exude, being what they are, growing where they are, has been pleasantly enlightening.

Throughout the course of our lives, many trees in our view are still often thought of as our special trees. We look out a window or walk outside a door, and there they are. Until, suddenly, due to circumstances beyond our control, they have fallen. Be it from wind or a felling that exceeded our own ability to fend off, the tree is no longer upright and its life is over. In some places, such as upon finding a fallen tree in a forest, the fallen tree might be given a new, highly magical purpose. There is a special category of trees that were alive once-upon-a-time, but are no longer. The trees are most usually naturally fallen Ash, Oak, or Sycamore trees that are found in or near a forest. The common connection between them is that most of these very special fallen trees are found in Scotland or England. It is there that it seems that for hundreds of years, wishing coins have been pushed and pounded down into the bark of the fallen trees and their associated stumps. The expectation is that the coin needs to be pushed in past the bark, where the one wishing would gain good fortune and be granted the fulfillment of a wish. Around the beginning of the eighteenth century, there was the additional belief that if someone ill were to push a coin into the Wishing Tree they would be healed. Wishing Trees have been collecting wishing coins and granting wishes long enough for the tree trunks to become encrusted with coins. Fanciful and ominous legends have arisen around these mystical Wishing Trees. The most common is a warning that one should not dare to test: should someone ever remove a wishing coin, illness or some other dire calamity will sweep over the thief.

Regardless of a tree's contribution to the magical invisible world, whether it's a tree's culinary gifts that grace our tables at mealtime, its medicinal benefits that alleviate pain and suffering, its overall usefulness, or if it's something just seriously gorgeous to look at, climb all over, or hang on a branch upside down just for the fun of it in the days when we can, virtually all of our precious trees directly connect all the people and the air-breathing creatures of this world to what we all need to survive: oxygen. The trees absolutely are a vital force of positive energy, providing a life force which is without question, *the* primary source of our continued existence on planet Earth. Let us never forget that.

How to

USE THIS
BOOK

I f you do not know the scientific name of a tree, but you do know one of its common names, you can find that name in the Tree Names Index. There you will find the corresponding number, which you can then refer to in the body of the book. You can also locate the number of a specific tree (or several different trees) by determining which Meaning you are researching.

There may be no specific indication as to what part or parts of the tree are toxic, when they are toxic, if their toxicity is eliminated with ripening, and other such matters. *Please be acutely aware that some trees are so extremely poisonous that simply touching them or breathing in smoke where they may be burning can be fatal.* In no way whatsoever is there a recommendation anywhere in this book that any part of a tree represented should be ingested, inhaled, or put directly on the skin. Please take the time to do further research of your own with regard to what you are going to touch before you dare to touch it. The internet is a wonderful source for that kind of scientific information.

Be informed, stay safe, and feel free to tap into the innate powers of trees. Always let the recipients of your arboreal gifts know what significant thoughts and feelings are in your heart. And please, whatever you do and whenever you do it: *do not* even dare to vex the fairies!

No. 000: (cross-reference number for searching from any index)

Specific primary scientific name

☠ (toxicity symbol)

⚗ (medicinal symbol) •┄┄┄┄┄┄

🍴 (edible part)

🌿 (culinary herb)

🌱 (can be a bonsai)

🕯 (sacred tree)

Note: The medicinal symbol indicates that either currently or at some time in the past, folk healers, herbalist practitioners, or traditional medicine physicians have used this tree or its derivative for medicinal purposes. Further research into its medicinal potential is encouraged.

Primary Common Name
Other Known Scientific Names | Common Names

🌑 **POTENTIAL MAXIMUM HEIGHT:**
Feet [Meters]

✹ **SYMBOLIC MEANING:** Come to me; I am shy; my heart aches for you; and so on.

🎨 **COLOR MEANINGS:** When applicable to particular colors of a flower or leaf.

🌱 **COMPONENT MEANINGS:** Any meanings associated with branches, leaves, seeds, or sprays of a plant.

🌀 **POSSIBLE POWERS:** Healing; love; protection; and so on.

🌍 **FOLKLORE AND FACTS:** Tidbits of factual, fanciful, mystical, magical, or plain silly information.

No. 001

Abies balsamea 🫖 🌰 🌰

Balsam Fir
A'ninandak' | Christmas Tree | Fir Tree | Yule Tree

📷 **POTENTIAL MAXIMUM HEIGHT**
89 feet [27 meters]

✳ **SYMBOLIC MEANINGS**
Elevation; Friendship; Height;
Honesty; Immortality;
Longevity; Manifestation;
Perceptiveness; Progress;
Remembrance; Resilience;
Time.

🌼 **POSSIBLE POWERS**
Abundance; Air element;
Awakening; Change; Chewing
gum; Christmas celebration;
Create oxygen; Dissolving
negativity; Dreaming;
Enlightenment; Feminine
energy; Fertility; Harmony;
Immortality; Insight; Light; Luck; Magic; Masculine energy;
Progress; Protection; Regeneration; Renewal; Resurrection;
Spiritual consciousness; Spirituality; Spiritual love; Strength;
Tan leather; Yule celebration.

🌿 **FOLKLORE AND FACTS**
The *Abies balsamea* Balsam Fir is a fragrant, hardy evergreen
conifer that naturally grows in a conical shape. It has become
the preferred choice for a cut Christmas tree that is displayed
indoors. If the tree is diligently kept watered, it will hold on
to its needles for an extended period. • Balsam Fir essential oil
smells like a fragrant Christmas tree. • Other members of the
Pinaceae family can be set apart from a Balsam Fir by the flat
appearance of Balsam Fir needles and how they attach to the
twig. • The needles of Balsam Fir trees are sharper when they
are young. • Long before it assumed religious significance,
the Balsam Fir was one of the sacred woods burned on a
Sabbath fire. • Balsam Fir is also known as the Yule Tree.
Yule was and still is celebrated in some neopagan religions to
honor the beginning of the winter solstice. A living outdoor
tree is preferred and is decorated with candles hung from its
branches. • The *Abies balsamea* cones will close during the
rain and open to the sunshine. • Balsam Fir cones and sticky
resin-filled blisters in the bark produce a lot of precious,
thick, fragrant resinous sap. • To extract fragrant resin,
swollen bark blisters can be popped open, sometimes with
the pressure of the finger pushing against the blister, but more
often by using a small tool. • Balsam Fir resin is used to make
microscopic slides. Additionally, resin would be chewed like
gum, before it was called as such. The resin-filled bark blisters
were also once ignited to be used as torches. • Balsam Fir
trees cut and sold commercially for use as Christmas trees are
often felled at generationally-owned family tree plantations,
not from the wild. Secrets regarding their cultivation are
handed down through the family. These secrets include how
to beautifully shape the growing trees. • The Balsam Fir has
been used as the Christmas tree at the US Capitol building
several times since 1964. • For thousands of years, Native
Americans of various tribes have utilized the needles, bark,
sap, wood, and root of the Balsam Fir tree for a wide variety
of medicinal remedies. • The bark is rich in tannin, which is
extracted to tan leather. • A Balsam Fir cone on the tip of a
magic wand makes a superior magical "sender."

No. 002

Abies religiosa 🌰

Sacred Fir
Árbol de Navidad | Birth Tree | Oyamel Fir | Pinabete

📷 **POTENTIAL MAXIMUM HEIGHT**
197 feet [60 meters]

✳ **SYMBOLIC MEANINGS**
What is yet to come; Winter refuge.

🌼 **POSSIBLE POWERS**
Abundance; Air element; Awakening; Blessings; Change;
Chewing gum; Christmas celebration; Create oxygen;
Dissolving negativity; Dreaming; Enlightenment; Eternal
life; Feminine energy; Fertility; Harmony; Immortality;
Incense; Insight; Light; Luck; Magic; Masculine energy;
Mother and child; Peace; Progress; Protection; Refuge;
Regeneration; Resurrection; Renewal; See the future;
Spiritual consciousness; Spirituality; Spiritual love; Strength;
Tan leather; Yule celebration.

🌿 **FOLKLORE AND FACTS**
It is in the stands of *Abies religiosa* Sacred Fir evergreen
conifer trees growing in the mountains of central Mexico
that monarch butterflies take refuge during the winter
months. Although the tree is protected, illegal logging of
these trees persists while the stands of trees on which the
monarch depends continue to be depleted. • In Mexico
the Sacred Fir is also known to be a Christmas tree, with
boughs carried into churches and blessed for decorations
during the holiday. • At childbirth, the needles of the
Sacred Fir are burned like incense to protect and bless
mother and child. • The *Abies religiosa* cones will close
during rain and open in sunshine.

A

No. 004
Acacia koa 🪴🌳
Koa Tree
Blue Wattle | Mimosa | Silver Wattle | Thorntree | Wattle

◉ POTENTIAL MAXIMUM HEIGHT
98 feet [30 meters]

✳ SYMBOLIC MEANINGS
Bold; Brave; Fearless; Warrior.

✿ POSSIBLE POWERS
Bravery; Conscious will; Create oxygen; Energy; Fearlessness; Female energy; Fire energy; Male energy; Natural power; Overcome hardships; Protection; Repel demons and ghosts; Sound resonance; Success.

✿ FOLKLORE AND FACTS
Common to all the Hawaiian Islands, the evergreen *Acacia koa* Koa Tree was a favorite choice for making an ancient Hawaiian surfboard or dugout outrigger canoe.
• As a tonewood, Koa wood is a favorite for making acoustic guitars, Hawaiian steel guitars, and ukuleles.

No. 003
Acacia dealbata 🪴🌳
Mimosa
Acacia | Blue Wattle | Silver Wattle | Thorntree | Wattle

◉ POTENTIAL MAXIMUM HEIGHT
20 feet [6 meters]

✳ SYMBOLIC MEANINGS
Chaste love; Concealed love; Elegance; Endurance of the soul; Fortitude; Friendship; Immortality; Platonic love; Purity; Renewal; Resurrection; Secret love; Sensitiveness; Thorny.

✿ POSSIBLE POWERS
Abundance; Advancement; Banishing; Cleansing; Conscious will; Create oxygen; Divination; Energy; Exorcism; Friendship; Growth; Healing; Joy; Leadership; Life; Light; Love; Money; Natural power; Prophetic dreams; Protection; Purification; Repels demons and ghosts; Success.

✿ FOLKLORE AND FACTS
There are approximately 1,200 species of Acacia tree.
• The profusely blooming evergreen *Acacia dealbata* Mimosa originated in Southeastern Australia. • The tree is fragrant when in full bloom. Cut stems laden with its golden-yellow round flowers are sometimes used in floral arrangements. • Mimosa trees can be killed by fire, although mature trees can possibly regrow from any remaining roots. Seeds in the soil can germinate more than five years after a fire. • The essential oil of the flowers is called mimosa or cassie and is used in perfumes.

No. 005
Acacia tortilis 🪴🍴🌳🌰
Umbrella Thorn Acacia
Curly-pod Acacia | Golden Wattle | Israeli Babool | Thorntree

◉ POTENTIAL MAXIMUM HEIGHT
20 feet [6 meters]

✳ SYMBOLIC MEANINGS
Chaste love; Concealed love; Elegance; Endurance of the soul; Friendship; Immortality; Incense; Platonic love; Purity; Resurrection; Secret love; Sensitiveness; Thorny.

✿ POSSIBLE POWERS
Abundance; Advancement; Banishing; Cleansing; Conscious will; Create oxygen; Divination; Energy; Exorcism; Friendship; Growth; Healing; Joy; Leadership; Life; Light; Love; Money; Natural power; Perfumery; Prophetic dreams; Protection; Purification; Repel demons and ghosts; Success; Tan leather.

There are approximately 1,200 species of Acacia tree. The hardy deciduous *Acacia tortilis* Umbrella Thorn Acacia is native to virtually all of Africa and the Middle East. • Legend tells that the Umbrella Thorn Acacia tree could have been the "burning bush" that Moses encountered in Exodus 3:2 of the Bible. • In Egyptian mythology, the Acacia is closely associated with the Tree of Life. • Acacia resin, bark, and roots are used in incense. • Acacia smoke is believed to repel demons and ghosts. • In the Bible's book of Exodus, the Ark of the Covenant and the table that God instructed Moses to build were to be made of Acacia wood. • The crown of thorns that Jesus Christ was forced to wear could have possibly been fashioned from Acacia stems. • The bark is rich in tannin, which is extracted to tan leather. • Acacia wood is hard and was used to make wooden pegs and plows. • Acacia bark fiber has been used to make string. • The gummy substance that is extracted from the raw Acacia pods has been used in the West Indies as a cement that can be used to mend broken pottery. • Useful in the fine arts as a paint extender or glazing additive for watercolors, a gummy substance that is extracted from *Acacia tortilis* bark is considered by many artists to be a better choice than Gum Arabic. • A smoke bath consisting of a mix of Umbrella Thorn Acacia wood and Sandalwood that provides incense-like fragrances while simultaneously tinting the skin a flattering golden shade of orange is known as a *dukhan*, an ancient weekly ritual for many Sudanese women. The woody smoky fragrance will linger strongly on the skin for days. • A magic wand made from Umbrella Thorn Acacia is closely tuned into memories that go back from seed to seed to seed, all the way back to before the time of the pharaohs. • The energy vibration of the Umbrella Thorn Acacia is highly tuned to both thirst and water. It would make a very good dowsing rod to use when searching for a water source. • As the only tree within 100 miles (161 km), an isolated tree in the Sahara Desert known as the Tree of Ténéré became a reliable landmark for caravans. In 1938, when a well was dug next to the tree, the project revealed the tree's roots had reached water that was approximately 118 feet (36 m) deep. The tree was felled when a truck hit it in 1973. A metal sculpture was erected in its place after the remains of the Tree of Ténéré were removed to be exhibited in the Musée National du Niger.

No. 006

Acer palmatum 🐾 🍴 🌿

Japanese Maple

Irohamomiji | Kito | Momiji | Palmate Maple | Smooth Japanese Maple

◐ POTENTIAL MAXIMUM HEIGHT

30 feet [9 meters]

✹ SYMBOLIC MEANINGS

At peace; Balance; Calm; Peace; Practicality; Rest.

✿ POSSIBLE POWERS

Abundance; Air element; Appreciation of others' generosity; Balance; Bright future; Colorful presentations; Create oxygen; Earth element; Feminine energy; Fertility Generosity; Good luck; Hopefulness; Intelligence; Jupiter; Liberation; Longevity; Love; Masculine energy; Money; Offering; Peace; Power; Practicality; Practical magic; Promise; Rebirth; Renewal; Serenity; Success; Transformation; Union; Wealth.

☙ FOLKLORE AND FACTS

The deciduous *Acer palmatum* Japanese Maple is a charming tree for any garden. • The Japanese Maple can be grown from a seed found within the fruit, which is a pair of winged samaras like other *Acer* trees. • There are many different cultivars of the Japanese Maple that present the tree in all its glory, in many different leaf shapes and colors. Depending on the season and the amount of sunshine different tree cultivars receive, the colors of the leaves can be black-red, bronze, cream, dark or light green, purple-red, red, variegated whites, yellow, and yellow-orange. Since the cultivars also have several different forms, the trees can be different shapes, such as umbrella, weeping, vase-shaped, or cascading. • The leaves of the Japanese Maple are considered a delicacy in Minoh, Japan, where they are often dipped in tempura batter then deep-fried. • A wand made from Japanese Maple wood would be useful for spiritual healing and promoting peace.

No. 007

Acer rubrum 🪶🍃

Red Maple

Acer × freemanii 'Jeffersred' | Acer rubrum var. drummondii | Autumn Blaze Maple | Drummond Red Maple | Soft Maple | Swamp Maple | Water Maple

◉ **POTENTIAL MAXIMUM HEIGHT**
90 feet [27 meters]

✸ **SYMBOLIC MEANING**
Reserve.

🌸 **POSSIBLE POWERS**
Air element; Create oxygen; Earth element; Jupiter; Longevity; Love; Masculine energy; Money.

❦ **FOLKLORE AND FACTS**
When the deciduous *Acer rubrum* Red Maple tree is mature, all parts of it, including its flowers, twigs, and seeds, are various shades of red. But in the autumn, the foliage is a deep bright-scarlet color. • Red Maple is one of the first plants that will flower in the spring. • After a tree-killing catastrophe such as fire, disease, or mass felling, the Red Maple is often able to come back even stronger and more plentiful than before. • Fresh or dead Red Maple leaves can be fatally toxic to horses. • The Pennsylvania Dutch use Red Maple's inner bark to dye flax and wool purple. • The Red Maple is the most commonly prolific tree in North America.

No. 008

Acer saccharum 🪶🍁🌿🌰

Sugar Maple

Birdseye Maple | Curly Maple | Hard Maple | Rock Maple | Sugar Tree | Sweet Maple

◉ **POTENTIAL MAXIMUM HEIGHT**
115 feet [35 meters]

✸ **SYMBOLIC MEANINGS**
Endurance; Reserve; Strength.

🌸 **POSSIBLE POWERS**
Air element; Create oxygen; Earth element; Jupiter; Longevity; Love; Masculine energy; Money.

❦ **FOLKLORE AND FACTS**
In the autumn, before the leaves fall from the trees, the deciduous *Acer saccharum* Sugar Maple tree leaves will

change color depending on what kind of light they receive. In the sun they will turn red. In the shade they will be yellow to golden. The result is that all these shades can appear on the tree simultaneously, resulting in a beautifully colored autumn tree. • The seed pods of the Sugar Maple tree are unusual in that they occur connected in pairs that spin as they fall from the tree. • The Sugar Maple's tree seeds are within the fruit, which are connected pods called samaras, maple keys, helicopters, whirlybirds, or poly-noses. The samara is often gilded and worn as jewelry. • The US Army developed an effective carrier based on the shape of the tree's samara. It could hold up to 65 pounds (29 kg) of supplies that were dropped from planes. • In early spring, people tap the Sugar Maple trees to collect the flowing sap in either small buckets or by using tubing and gravity to pull the sap to a collection tank at the bottom of a hill. After the sap is brought into a sugar-shack, it is boiled in order to evaporate the water within it until the sap becomes a viscous syrup, or further on to become Maple sugar. • It is believed that the use of pure Maple syrup as a sweetener is more manageable for diabetics than other glucose sources in their diets. • Sugar Maple tree wood will make a fine centering first magic wand.

No. 009

Acoelorrhaphe wrightii 🪶

Everglades Palm

Botan Palm | Cubas | Cubas Palmetto Palm | Hairy Tom Palmetto | Madeira Palm | Palma Cuba | Papta | Paurotis Palm | Saw-cabbage Palm | Saw Paurotis | Silver Saw Palm | Tasisté | Tique

◉ **POTENTIAL MAXIMUM HEIGHT**
30 feet [9 meters]

✸ **SYMBOLIC MEANING**
Without hollowness.

🌸 **POSSIBLE POWERS**
Create oxygen; Healing; Privacy.

❦ **FOLKLORE AND FACTS**
The evergreen *Acoelorrhaphe wrightii* Everglades Palm grows as a clump in the swampy or flood-prone areas of Central America, the Caribbean, and the Bahamas. Everglades Palm also grows in the southernmost part of Florida where the wild trees are protected by law. Nursery specimens can be obtained and planted elsewhere. • Although it is slow-growing, the Everglades Palm makes a good tree for the garden that can eventually provide an effective privacy screen, since the area of the clump can grow to become approximately 20 feet (6 m) wide. Trimming emerging suckers growing up from the bottom of the cluster can allow more openness between the trees and make for a much more attractive display.

No. 010

Adansonia digitata 🌿🌰

Baobab Tree

Boab Tree | Cream of Tartar Tree | Dead Rat Tree | Monkey-bread Tree | Tree of Life | Upside-down Tree

🔍 POTENTIAL MAXIMUM HEIGHT
82 feet [25 meters]

✳ SYMBOLIC MEANINGS
Old age; Survival.

🌼 POSSIBLE POWERS
Ancient Earth; Create oxygen; Longevity; Survival; Tenacity.

✤ FOLKLORE AND FACTS
The *Adansonia digitata* Baobab Tree is an icon of the African bush lands. Native to the African savanna, with a massively sized and a fabulously round, unique barrel-like trunk shape, the Baobab Tree is a deciduous tree that is able to live to 3,000 years old. Through radiocarbon dating, a Baobab tree in Namibia was discovered to be the oldest flowering tree at 1,275 years of age. • Baobab flowers are pendulous and appear to have a fluffy puff hanging beneath a whirl of petals. They do not have an appealing fragrance at all. The flowers only open at night and are pollinated by bats. • The Baobab fruit is gourd-like and covered over with gray fur, and it hangs by a thin stem. Looking up from the ground, the fruit resembles a deceased rat. • In many regions of Africa, the Baobab Tree is considered to be sacred. This is because it was traditionally believed that the Baobab Tree can hold the spirit of deceased ancestors. • Throughout history, African kings have held meetings under Baobab Trees, believing that its spiritual and magical nature has the power to make wise decisions. • The interior pulp of the tree's trunk is soft and subject to fungus rot, which will leave the trunk hollow. Because the tree trunk is so enormous, the hollow trunk has occasionally been used for such things as a dwelling, a meeting place, and even a jail! • Two ancient Baobab Trees in Western Australia have the unproven legends of once being "prison trees,"

holding prisoners in the ample hollow of its trunk before their trials. One of the trees is 1,500 years old. • The largest Baobab Tree in South Africa is known as the Sagole Baobab or Muri Kunguluwa, which means "tree that roars." It would take approximately twenty people to encircle the tree.

No. 011

Aegle marmelos 🌿🌰🌰

Bael

Bengal Quince | Golden Apple | Japanese Bitter Orange | Shivadruma | Stone Apple Tree | Wood Apple

🔍 POTENTIAL MAXIMUM HEIGHT
32 feet [10 meters]

✳ SYMBOLIC MEANINGS
Creation; Destruction; Preservation; Three eyes of Shiva.

🌼 POSSIBLE POWERS
Create oxygen; Healing; Removal of sins from past lifetimes; Ritual use.

✤ FOLKLORE AND FACTS
The deciduous *Aegle marmelos* Bael tree is a rare tree that is native to Southeast Asia and is usually found growing near Hindu temples or in home gardens. Those who practice Hinduism consider the Bael tree to be sacred and inhabited by the Hindu deity of wealth and prosperity, Lakshmi. It is also believed that the tree itself is the incarnation of the Hindu goddess, Sati. • Lord Shiva is thought to be particularly fond of the Bael tree, especially its fruit and leaves, which are reminiscent of the deity's own trident. • The offering of Bael leaves to Lord Shiva is believed to have the power to remove the sins of one's last three incarnations. • The Bael tree is used in ritual Hindu rites. • The edible fruit of the Bael tree is called a stone apple. Its pulp is often used to make jam, jelly, beverages, and wine.

A

No. 012

Aesculus hippocastanum ☠ ◉

Horse Chestnut Tree

Buckeye | Conker Tree | Spanish Chestnut

◉ POTENTIAL MAXIMUM HEIGHT
80 feet [24 meters]

✹ SYMBOLIC MEANINGS
Good luck charm; Luxury.

❀ POSSIBLE POWERS
Create oxygen; Divination; Fire element; Jupiter; Luck;
Masculine energy; Money; Prosperity; Shade; Wealth.

❦ FOLKLORE AND FACTS
Unlike the Sweet Chestnut, all parts of the deciduous
Aesculus hippocastanum Horse Chestnut Tree are extremely
toxic. • In Bavaria, it is common to see the wide-spreading
thickly canopied Horse Chestnut tree planted in beer
gardens. This practice was initiated prior to refrigeration,
when people relied on the trees to help keep the beer barrels
that were kept in underground caverns cooler during hot
summer days. The shorter roots of the tree would go down
just deep enough to support the tree, but not so much as
to disturb the cavern. The shade overhead that kept the
hot summer sun from beating down onto the cavern's
"rooftop" helped lower the temperature deep down below
in the cavern. • Carrying a Horse Chestnut in a pocket is
supposedly the way to fend off cramps. • Horse Chestnut
seeds, or conkers as they are more commonly known,
are believed to keep away moths and spiders if placed in
household furniture. • Conkers is also the name of an old
British children's game between two players. Horse Chestnut
seeds are threaded onto two pieces of string, then players
take turns hitting the opposing player's seeds until one of the
conkers breaks. • There was a time when Native Americans
used crushed Horse Chestnuts to stun fish.

No. 013

Afrocarpus falcatus ◉ ◉

African Pine Tree

Bastard Yellowwood | Common Yellowwood | Kalander | Mogôbagôba | Outeniekwageelhout |
Outeniqua Yellowwood | Umkhoba | Umsonti | Weeping Yew

◉ POTENTIAL MAXIMUM HEIGHT
197 feet [60 meters]

✹ SYMBOLIC MEANING
Father and son.

❀ POSSIBLE POWERS
Ancestors; Ancient Earth; Awakening; Create oxygen;
Dreaming; Enlightenment; Eternal life; Fertility; Generations;
Harmony; Immortality; Light; Longevity; Magic; Meditation;
Peace; Regeneration; Resurrection; Spiritual consciousness;
Spirituality.

❦ FOLKLORE AND FACTS
In southwest Ethiopia, the *Afrocarpus falcatus* African
Pine Tree is considered to be a sacred tree. Household
heads in parts of Ethiopia will assume the responsibility of
planting and protecting groves of African Pine Trees, which
are closely connected to the father–son relationship from
generation to generation. • Although it is not a threatened
evergreen conifer, the African Pine Tree is a protected tree
in its native South Africa, where some of the largest and
oldest trees can be found in the forests. Some trees have
been estimated to be over one thousand years old. • Potted
African Pine Trees are often brought inside and decorated
to be Christmas trees. • Some South African Yellowwood
antique furniture was made from the wood of the African
Pine Tree. • The tall straight topmasts of some sailing ships
were made from the trunk of the African Pine Tree. • The
ripe fruit is edible, but mostly consumed by bats, fruit-eating
birds, and bush pigs.

A

No. 014

Agathis australis 🍴🥣

Kauri Tree

God of the Forest | Kauri | Lord of the Forest | Tāne Mahuta Kauri Tree

◎ POTENTIAL MAXIMUM HEIGHT
148 feet [45 meters]

✹ SYMBOLIC MEANINGS
Ball of thread; Mysterious wildness.

✿ POSSIBLE POWERS
Create oxygen; Healing.

❦ FOLKLORE AND FACTS
The evergreen *Agathis australis* Kauri Tree is the longest-living tree species on Earth. The largest-living Kauri Tree that is currently known is the iconic ancient tree that is found still growing in the Waipoua Forest of New Zealand. It is estimated to be close to 2,500 years old. • It is the most famous tree in all of New Zealand, having been named Tāne Mahuta, after the Māori god of birds and forests. There is a myth that the marital embrace of Tāne Mahuta's parents, Ranginui the Sky Father and Papatūānuku the Earth Mother, is kept separated by Tāne Mahuta until his father is high above his mother. Tāne Mahuta dresses his mother with Earth's vegetation. The forest trees and birds are Tāne Mahuta's children. The Kauri trees hold Ranginui high above the Earth. • Official efforts to keep this special tree in good health are continuously ongoing. • Kauri Tree resin is fragrant and the fossilized resin, known as kauri gum, is often used to fashion jewelry and other crafts.
• Magnificent upright trees are still growing along streets, in parks, and other interior landscape plans. However, the phenomenally largest Kauri Trees are now few and far between due to extreme logging in the past. • The Kauri Tree does not have true pine needles, rather having leathery leaves. • This enormously tall growing tree is propagated from seed.

No. 015

Agonis flexuosa 🥣

Peppermint Tree

Swan River Peppermint Tree | Wanil | Wannang | Western Australian Peppermint Tree | Willow Myrtle | Wonnow | Wonong

◎ POTENTIAL MAXIMUM HEIGHT
49 feet [15 meters]

✹ SYMBOLIC MEANINGS
Cluster; Full of bends.

✿ POSSIBLE POWERS
Create oxygen; Healing.

❦ FOLKLORE AND FACTS
The evergreen *Agonis flexuosa* Peppermint Tree looks very much like a Weeping Willow. • Peppermint Trees are a common sight in the parks and along roads in Perth, Australia. • The crushed leaves of the Peppermint Tree have the fragrance of peppermint. • The trunks of young saplings have been used for digging sticks and spears by many First Nations Australians.

No. 016

Ailanthus altissima ☠🥣

Tree of Heaven

Ailanthus | Chouchun | Copal Tree | Stinking Sumac | Swingle | Tree of Hell | Varnish Tree

◎ POTENTIAL MAXIMUM HEIGHT
80 feet [24 meters]

✹ SYMBOLIC MEANINGS
Reach for the sky; Tallest.

✿ POSSIBLE POWERS
Create oxygen; Healing; Poisoning.

❦ FOLKLORE AND FACTS
Mentioned in the oldest Chinese dictionary still in existence, the deciduous *Ailanthus altissima* is known as the Tree of Heaven.
• Tree of Heaven's average lifespan is around fifty years, with a tree occasionally reaching to be as old as one hundred years.
• Because of the immense number of seeds produced by a female tree, its cloning habit of reproduction, its ease of sprouting from a stump or any pieces of remaining roots after repeated attempts to remove it . . . *and* its foul-smelling flowers . . . the Tree of Heaven has

A

proven its pesky invasiveness and ongoing reputation as a "Tree of Hell" in the USA. *Ailanthus altissima* is not nearly as invasive in the United Kingdom and in other parts of Europe, where it is commonly used as an ornamental tree. • Tree of Heaven is said to smell terribly of dirty work socks or rancid butter. • The Tree of Heaven is a host for the Ailanthus Silk Moth. As a result, Tree of Heaven is very important in the production of Chinese silk, and more particularly for "Shantung silk," which is also known as "pongee" and "eri silk." • Although native to both Northern and Central China, fossil records clearly show that the Tree of Heaven was present in North America as far back as the Middle Miocene Epoch, about 11.6 to 16 million years ago. • Tree of Heaven is one of the most pollution-tolerant trees, as the leaves can absorb sulfur dioxide and mercury. • The wood from the Tree of Heaven is flexible and steam-able, and thus is often used to make kitchen steamer baskets for food. It is also used for firewood and to produce charcoal.

No. 017

Albizia procera 🕱 🖾 🌳

Karoi Tree
White Siris

🌑 **POTENTIAL MAXIMUM HEIGHT**
82 feet [25 meters]

☀ **SYMBOLIC MEANINGS**
High; Very tall.

🌐 **POSSIBLE POWERS**
Create oxygen; Fish poison; Healing.

☘ **FOLKLORE AND FACTS**
The resin of the deciduous *Albizia procera* Karoi Tree can be used as a substitute for Gum Arabic as an emulsifier for some pharmaceutical products and foods. • *Albizia procera* is an invasive tree in South Africa.

No. 018

Aleurites moluccanus 🕱 🖾

Candlenut Tree
Buah Keras | Candleberry Tree | Godou | Indian Walnut | Kemiri | Kuki | Kukui Nut Tree | Nuez de la India | Rata Kekuna | Varnish Tree

🌑 **POTENTIAL MAXIMUM HEIGHT**
98 feet [30 meters]

☀ **SYMBOLIC MEANINGS**
Enlightenment; Illumination.

🌐 **POSSIBLE POWERS**
Beauty; Create oxygen; Decoration; Enlightenment; Illumination; Light.

☘ **FOLKLORE AND FACTS**
The tropical evergreen tree *Aleurites moluccanus* Candlenut Tree was first cultivated on the islands of southeast Asia and moved outwards from there. • All parts of the Candlenut Tree have been deemed very useful in the day-to-day life of Polynesian peoples. The nutmeats, for example, provided light in ancient times. Hawaiians would open the Candlenut Tree nuts, skewer the oily nutmeats (which are smaller than walnuts), then set them afire. These "candles" burned for close to forty-five minutes. • Native Hawaiians may still use *Aleurites moluccanus* oil for lighting stone lamps. • The unopened Candlenuts can be unpainted, painted, or polished to a gleam, drilled through with a hole, then strung as a beautiful, highly prized Candlenut bead necklace.

A

Alnus glutinosa ☠ ☙ 🌰

Common Alder

Alder | Black Alder | European Alder | European Black Alder

🔍 **POTENTIAL MAXIMUM HEIGHT**

121 feet [37 meters]

✷ **SYMBOLIC MEANINGS**

Giving; King of the Woods; Nurturing.

🌐 **POSSIBLE POWERS**

Air element; Banishing elements; Blocking; Bravery; Charm; Controlling elements; Create oxygen; Decision making; Divination; Earth energy; Education; Feminine energy; Fire element; Healing; Leadership; Music; Poetry; Protection for the dead; Resurrection spells; Spirituality; Teaching; Transformation; Water element; Weather magic; Wind magic.

🜨 **FOLKLORE AND FACTS**

The *Alnus glutinosa* Common Alder is a deciduous tree with large, rounded, dark green leaves. • Common Alder trees can live to be approximately 160 years old. • Common Alder is a choice tree for purifying the water in waterlogged soil, as well as stabilizing riverbanks to manage floods. • Nearly all of the pilings that support the city of Venice, Italy, are made of Alder wood. • Alder bark produces a brown vegetable dye for fabrics. • Include Common Alder in rituals for the dying and the deceased to provide protection as they leave the physical realm. • Common Alder's sticky leaves have been spread out on floors to trap fleas. • Cut Common Alder wood turns from white to red, which inspires awe at the sight of it. • Push the pith out of a young green Alder shoot to make a whistle. Several shoots cut into different lengths, then bound together, can make a serviceable pan-type flute. • It was once unlawful to cut down an Alder tree in Ireland. • Appreciated for its bright tone, Alder wood has been favored to be used for the bodies of Fender Stratocaster® and Telecaster® electric guitars since the 1950s. • Common Alder is strongly connected to both elemental fire and elemental water, making it unusual. As a result, Alder wood is a fine choice for a self-protective healing wand that is gifted in divination and anything regarding the magical elements of fire and water.

Aloidendron barberae

Giant Tree Aloe

African Tree Aloe | Boomaalwyn | Ikhala | Impondonndo | Indlabendlazi | Inkalane-enkulu | Mikaalwyn | Tree Aloe | Umgxwala

🔍 **POTENTIAL MAXIMUM HEIGHT**

54 feet [16 meters]

✷ **SYMBOLIC MEANING**

Spiritually uplift.

🌐 **POSSIBLE POWERS**

Create oxygen; Good luck; Protection; Raise energy; Remove evil spirits; Spiritual cleansing; Spiritually uplifting.

🜨 **FOLKLORE AND FACTS**

Native to South Africa, the iconic and enormous, slow-growing and sculptural evergreen succulent *Aloidendron barberae* Giant Tree Aloe blooms in the winter. The many rose-pink tubular blossoms on the spike-like flowers are pollinated by sunbirds. When the tree's seeds are released, they are dispersed by the wind. • When planted for ornamentation, Giant Tree Aloe should not be planted too close to a building due to the inevitable growth of a hugely wide trunk.

A

Amborella trichopoda

Amborella Tree
Amborella Shrub

◉ POTENTIAL MAXIMUM HEIGHT
25 feet [8 meters]

✸ SYMBOLIC MEANINGS
Beginner; First.

❀ POSSIBLE POWERS
Create oxygen; Holder of secrets; Mystery.

✦ FOLKLORE AND FACTS
The family of *Amborellaceae* and the order *Amborellales* contain only the one species, *Amborella trichopoda*, which is commonly known as the Amborella Tree. • This small evergreen is considered to be the oldest flowering species of plants on the entire Earth. There is ongoing study into the genetics of the small, creamy white, inconspicuous flower of this tree that has bract-like petals that are arranged in a whorl. This is because it is believed that the flowers hold the answer to Charles Darwin's perplexing question asking why flowering plants were able to *suddenly* proliferate millions of years ago. Quite oddly, the Amborella Tree contains something that no other living thing on Earth has: the full DNA code from six other plant species. • Amborella comes from New Caledonia Island, where it is extremely rare. So much so that it is hardly ever seen for sale as nursery stock.

Amelanchier alnifolia 🍲 🍴

Saskatoon
Alder-leaf Shadbush | Chuckley Pear | Dwarf Shadbush | Juneberry | Pacific Serviceberry | Pigeon Berry | Sarvisberry | Saskatoon Berry | Western Juneberry | Western Serviceberry

◉ POTENTIAL MAXIMUM HEIGHT
13 feet [4 meters]

✸ SYMBOLIC MEANING
Everywhere.

❀ POSSIBLE POWERS
Create oxygen; Gathering; Sociability; Sustain.

✦ FOLKLORE AND FACTS
The *Amelanchier alnifolia* Saskatoon is a small deciduous tree. The Saskatoon berry was vital to Indigenous Peoples in Canada, who depended on every part of the entire plant in one way or another. • The fruit is eaten fresh or dried, and added to dried meat for additional flavor. Dried berries are also blended with other ingredients for a trail mix. The berries are juiced, mixed into cider blends, brewed into wine, baked into pies, made into jam, or candied. • The Saskatoon berry was also used by Native Americans, but is now considered a food for emergencies. • Black and purple vegetable dyes for cloth can be made using the Saskatoon berry.

No. 023

Amelanchier canadensis

Canadian Serviceberry Tree

Chuckle-berry | Currant-tree | Downy Serviceberry | Juneberry | Shad-blow | Shadblow
Serviceberry | Shadbush | Shadbush Serviceberry | Sugarplum | Thicket Serviceberry

POTENTIAL MAXIMUM HEIGHT
25 feet [8 meters]

SYMBOLIC MEANING
Passable.

POSSIBLE POWERS
Create oxygen; Indicator.

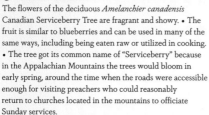

FOLKLORE AND FACTS
The flowers of the deciduous *Amelanchier canadensis*
Canadian Serviceberry Tree are fragrant and showy. • The
fruit is similar to blueberries and can be used in many of the
same ways, including being eaten raw or utilized in cooking.
• The tree got its common name of "Serviceberry" because
in the Appalachian Mountains the trees would bloom in
early spring, around the time when the roads were accessible
enough for visiting preachers who could reasonably
return to churches located in the mountains to officiate
Sunday services.

No. 024

Amentotaxus hatuyenensis

Catkin-Yew

Dẻ Tùng Sọc Nâu Rộng | Hà Tuyên Catkin-yew | Sam Bông Sọc Nâu Rộng

POTENTIAL MAXIMUM HEIGHT
65 feet [20 meters]

SYMBOLIC MEANING
Strap.

POSSIBLE POWERS
Create oxygen; Struggle.

FOLKLORE AND FACTS
The *Amentotaxus hatuyenensis* Catkin-Yew is a rare conifer.
Catkin-Yew is an endangered species. Only a few trees are
still found in the area around Ngoc Linh in the Hà Giang
Province in Northern Vietnam.

No. 025

Anacardium occidentale

Cashew Tree

Acajú | Bibo Tree | Caju | Cashew Apple Tree |
Cashew Nut Tree | Jambu Monyet | Kasui |
Marañon Tree | Mbiba | Mente Tree | Mkanju

POTENTIAL MAXIMUM HEIGHT
46 feet [14 meters]

SYMBOLIC MEANING
Reward.

POSSIBLE POWERS
Create oxygen; Fire element; Job seeking; Masculine energy;
Money; Prosperity; Sun.

FOLKLORE AND FACTS
The *Anacardium occidentale* Cashew Tree is an evergreen
tree that is native to northeastern Brazil and southeastern
Venezuela. • In those regions, the tree is better known as
Maranon Tree or Cashew Apple Tree because the fruit
is more popular than the nut. There, the fruit is available
fresh or juiced. • The Cashew Apple is not a true fruit,
but the swollen stalk to which the Cashew, or nut seed, of
Anacardium occidentale is attached. The seed recognized as
the Cashew "nut" will develop on the tree before the fruit
does. The ripe fruit will fall to the ground to be gathered.
The protruding seed is separated from the fruit, the fruit
is then sent to market, and the multistep processing of the
seed begins. • The seed is baked at a high temperature to
burn off the highly caustic outer husk. Afterwards, the hard
inner shell of the seed is broken open to remove the seed
within it. • The next step is baking the shelled seeds at a low
temperature for twenty-four hours to soften the inner shell
that covers the kernel, which can then be easily removed to
reveal the highly processed Cashew kernel, which is what is
available in markets around the world. • The kernel can be
further processed to produce Cashew "butter" and "milk."
• Eat a few Cashews on Sundays when you want to try to
make some money. • Carry a Cashew sachet as an amulet
to find and secure a well-paying job. • The world's largest
Cashew Tree is known as the Cashew of Pirangi, in Rio
Grande do Norte, Brazil. This one tree, which is 177 years
old, is the size of at least seventy normal-sized trees and
covers over a hectare of land. There is another Cashew tree
in Cajueiro da Praia, Brazil, that is reported to be even larger.

A

Annona cherimola ☠ 🍴 ✂

Cherimoya Tree

Chirimoya | Chirimuya | Custard Apple | Ice Cream Fruit

🔴 **POTENTIAL MAXIMUM HEIGHT**
30 feet [9 meters]

❋ **SYMBOLIC MEANINGS**
Rarity; Sour custard.

✹ **POSSIBLE POWERS**
Create oxygen; Healing; Release from oppression; Unblock desperate emotions.

✷ **FOLKLORE AND FACTS**
The fruit of the evergreen *Annona cherimola* Cherimoya Tree is edible when ripe and considered by many to be the finest of all known fruits. • The flower is especially fragrant in the morning. Cherimoya seeds are inedible and poisonous if they are crushed to open them. • The fruit can be halved and the pulp eaten with a spoon. Its flavor is similar to a blend of apple, banana, pineapple, papaya, peach, and strawberry. When the fruit is ripe, it is soft to the touch and the skin is a yellowish-green color. However, when the skin turns brown, it is inedible. The Cherimoya is eaten fresh as well as added as a flavoring to yogurt and ice cream. • Natural-growing Cherimoya trees rely on wind for pollination, while cultivated trees need to be pollinated by hand. • Make, then carry or wear a sachet that holds a Cherimoya Tree flower and a leaf to help push off and send away the heavy overwhelming sensation of oppression.

Antiaris toxicaria ☠ ✂

Bark Cloth Tree

Ancar | Antiaris | Bark Cloth Tree | Bemu | False Iroko | False Mvule | Ipoh | Jafo | Jiàndú MùKan | Man | Mnguonguo | Poison Arrow Tree | Upas Tree

🔴 **POTENTIAL MAXIMUM HEIGHT**
197 feet [60 meters]

❋ **SYMBOLIC MEANING**
Poison.

✹ **POSSIBLE POWERS**
Cloth making; Create oxygen; Death; Poisoning.

✷ **FOLKLORE AND FACTS**
The balsa-like, lightweight wood of the fast-growing evergreen *Antiaris toxicaria* Bark Cloth Tree can be peeled apart thinly and evenly, making it useful for making wood veneer for furniture and other finely made woodcrafts, as well as for making bark cloth. • The *Antiaris toxicaria* latex sap was used by various southeast Asian island groups as a poison to dip arrows and blow-darts into, which would be used for hunting as well as general weapons. • The poison extracted from the Bark Cloth Tree is considered to be so tremendously deadly that in China it is known to cause a "seven up and eight down nine death," which describes that it would take no more than seven steps uphill, eight steps downhill, or nine steps on level ground before dying. • In the 1700s it was rumored that the poisonous Bark Cloth Tree sap would be gathered by prisoners, with only a few of the many sent to fetch it surviving the venture.

A

Aquilaria malaccensis ☠ ⚱ ▾

Agar-Agar Tree

Agaru | Agarwood | Aloeswood | Eaglewood | Gaharu | Gharuwood | Lignum Aloes | Lolu | Mapou | Oodh | Oud | Wood Aloes | Wood of the Gods

◉ POTENTIAL MAXIMUM HEIGHT
131 feet [40 meters]

✸ SYMBOLIC MEANING
Spirit of life.

✿ POSSIBLE POWERS
Attract good fortune, love, or opportunities; Balance chi; Bring blessings; Clarity; Create oxygen; Enlightenment; Feminine energy; Grounding; Incense; Love; Meditation; Perfumery; Promote joy; Psychoactive energy; Reversing ignorance; Spiritual journeying; Spirituality; Unlocking the subconscious; Venus; Water element.

❦ FOLKLORE AND FACTS
The uniquely fragrant heartwood from the Agar-Agar Tree is the most expensive wood in the world. • Taking into account its religious importance, its fragrance, and its medicinal uses, Agarwood has been a valuable commodity worthy of intensely competitive trade for over two thousand years. • The precious, evergreen *Aquilaria malaccensis* Agar-Agar Tree is so spiritually significant that it is revered in the holy texts of virtually every major religion in the world. • Due to ruthless overharvesting and the consequential loss of its wild habitat, and due to increasing *illegal* harvesting and trade, the Agar-Agar Tree is so highly threatened that it is considered to be virtually extinct in the wild. • Even small Agarwood items that are offered at auction sell for exorbitant amounts. • Anything from the Agar-Agar Tree attracts love if carried or worn. • Agar-Agar is used in the making of perfume and incense. • Carry or wear a sachet of Agar-Agar when you go to the casino, play bingo, or are participating in any chance-type games to promote an advantage of a winner's good luck and success. • Place an amulet of Agar-Agar over the doors and windows of the home to attract blessings into it. • The fragrance of Agarwood has a warm, sweet balsam and woody scent. Burning it as an incense for meditation is not only aromatherapeutic, it can trigger enlightenment. It can also provide the energy to inspire an elevating spiritual experience. • Agar-Agar has been used in magic for centuries to attract good fortune and bring love forward.

Aralia spinosa ☠ ⚱

Devil's Walking Stick

Angelica-tree | Hercules' Club | Pigeon Tree | Prickly Ash | Prickly Elder | Shotbush

◉ POTENTIAL MAXIMUM HEIGHT
25 feet [8 meters]

✸ SYMBOLIC MEANING
Prickly.

✿ POSSIBLE POWERS
Alleviate toothache pain; Create oxygen; Exorcism; Healing; Overcome adversity; Protection.

❦ FOLKLORE AND FACTS
The deciduous *Aralia spinosa* tree is known as Devil's Walking Stick due to the sharp thorny spines that cover the trunk and stems. When the stems are young, they are covered with far more of these spines than when the stem matures. The tree has a cloning habit that sprouts from the roots to grow up into towering thickets. • In the past, the Cherokee people would use the smoke of Devil's Walking Stick to treat paralysis. They did so by blowing or fanning the smoke towards themselves so they could breathe it in, with the unintended consequences of sometimes accidentally getting burnt. • The Iroquois people took advantage of the thorns by planting *Aralia spinosa* saplings near their dwellings and gardens to keep animals away. • The flowers are showy, large, and have a pleasant lemony fragrance. Many Iroquois women would wear them in their hair for their beauty and aroma. The flowers would also be exchanged for money. • *Aralia spinosa* was occasionally planted in Victorian gardens as an interesting specimen.

Araucaria araucana ☠ 🍴 🌰

Monkey Puzzle Tree

Chilean Pine | Monkey Puzzler | Monkey Tail Tree | Pewen | Piñonero

◐ POTENTIAL MAXIMUM HEIGHT
80 feet [24 meters]

✳ SYMBOLIC MEANING
Puzzlement.

◉ POSSIBLE POWERS
Ancient Earth;
Bewilderment; Confusion;
Create oxygen; Protection;
Puzzlement.

✦ FOLKLORE AND FACTS
The *Araucaria araucana*
Monkey Puzzle Tree is
an endangered conifer. It
is sometimes called a living fossil
because it has been determined to be closely related to
Wollemia nobilis, a species that dates back to prehistory.
• The leaves of the Monkey Puzzle Tree are triangular,
have very sharp edges and spiny tips. With the exception
of the oldest branches, the intimidating leaves thickly cover
most of the tree's branches. The leaves have a lifespan of
approximately twenty-four years. • Once the Monkey Puzzle
Tree has matured to be approximately thirty years old, it will
produce cones. The cones will drop when they are ripe.
• The large seeds, or piñones, are gathered from the cones by
indigenous peoples in Argentina and Chile, then roasted and
eaten much like pine nuts. • Once a Monkey Puzzle Tree
reaches full maturity, it can live to be at least one thousand
years old. • It was once believed that the actual devil
would sit in the Monkey Puzzle Tree. To avoid arousing his
attention, people would quietly walk by the tree. Otherwise,
the consequence would be three years of bad luck. • The
common English name for the *Araucaria araucana* tree
is attributed to a noted barrister by the name of Charles
Austin. He was invited to see the unusual tree that had been
planted at Pencarrow Garden, in Cornwall, by Sir William
Molesworth. Charles Austin looked the young tree over, then
said, "It would puzzle a monkey to climb that."

Araucaria bidwillii ☠ 🍴 🌰 🌿

Bunya Pine Tree

Bonye | Bunya | Bunya-bunya | Bunyi | False Monkey Puzzle Tree

◐ POTENTIAL MAXIMUM HEIGHT
164 feet [50 meters]

✳ SYMBOLIC MEANING
Resilience.

◉ POSSIBLE POWERS
Awakening; Create oxygen; Dreaming; Enlightenment;
Eternal life; Fertility; Harmony; Immortality; Light;
Magic; Masculine energy; Patience; Peace; Protection;
Receive strength from Mother Earth; Regeneration;
Resurrection; Sound resonance; Spiritual consciousness;
Spirituality; Strength.

✦ FOLKLORE AND FACTS
The evergreen conifer *Araucaria bidwillii* Bunya Pine
Tree can live for up to seven hundred years. Its cones are
as big as soccer balls. The seeds within it are large, being
approximately 2 inches (5 cm) long by nearly 1 inch (2.5 cm)
wide and are covered over with a tough shell. • When ripe
and either placed in fire or boiled in water, the shell will
split and the edible kernel can be removed. The kernels are
sweet with a flavor of a chestnut or starchy potato. They
are sometimes ground to a paste and made into bread. The
nuts would sometimes be buried in creek mud to ferment
into an Aboriginal delicacy. Once every three years or so the
harvest is especially abundant. • When a harvest of Bunya
Pine Tree seeds was bountiful, people would gather in the
Bon-yi Mountains to feast on the kernels, hold ceremonies,
settle disputes, make trades, arrange marriages, have deep
discussions about important issues, make
decisions, share stories, sing, and
dance. Thousands of First Nations
Australians would travel from afar
in every direction to attend these
events. • Due to the immense
size of the Bunya Pine Tree's
cones, there is a speculative
pondering that it might have
been dinosaurs that moved
the cones to spread its seeds.
• The wood of the Bunya Pine
Tree is valued as a tonewood
for the sound boards of acoustic
guitars. • A wand of Bunya Pine
wood would do well for a wand
with masculine energy.

A

No. 032

Araucaria heterophylla ☠

Norfolk Island Pine

Living Christmas Tree | Polynesian Pine | Star Pine | Triangle Tree

◉ POTENTIAL MAXIMUM HEIGHT
200 feet [61 meters]

✳ SYMBOLIC MEANING
High above.

✤ POSSIBLE POWERS
Anti-hunger; Create oxygen; Protection.

✦ FOLKLORE AND FACTS
Although they are often selected to be grown indoors in containers, the evergreen conifer *Araucaria heterophylla* Norfolk Island Pine will become extremely tall, narrow, and magnificent trees when permitted to grow outdoors in a space that will allow it to fully develop and ultimately attain its potential maximum height. If grown near the home or as a potted houseplant, the Norfolk Pine is believed to offer protection against evil spirits and hunger. • Cutting off the top of the Norfolk Island Pine will surely permanently stunt it while also regretfully, irreparably alter its shape, impeding the future development of the tree.

No. 033

Arbutus unedo ⬥

Strawberry Tree

Apple of Cain | Cain Apple | Cane Apple | Irish Strawberry Tree | Killarney | Texas Madrone | Tick Tree

◉ POTENTIAL MAXIMUM HEIGHT
49 feet [15 meters]

✳ SYMBOLIC MEANINGS
Esteemed love; I love only you; Only love; True love.

✤ POSSIBLE POWERS
Create oxygen; Exorcism; Fidelity; Fire element; Mars; Masculine energy; Protection.

✦ FOLKLORE AND FACTS
Bears have reportedly become intoxicated after eating fermented berries from the evergreen *Arbutus unedo* Strawberry Tree that had been left on or had fallen under the trees. • The ancient Romans used the Strawberry Tree to protect small children since they believed that the tree could chase off any evil lurking around the children. • Strawberry Tree bark is rich in tannin that is used for tanning hides. • When Strawberry Tree berries shrivel 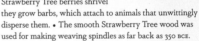 they grow barbs, which attach to animals that unwittingly disperse them. • The smooth Strawberry Tree wood was used for making weaving spindles as far back as 350 BCE.

A

No. 034

Areca catechu ☠ ⚱

Betel Nut Tree

Areca Nut Palm | Areca Palm | Betel Palm | Catechu | Indian Nut | Pinang Palm | Ping Lang | Siri | Supari

⬤ POTENTIAL MAXIMUM HEIGHT
66 feet [20 meters]

✻ SYMBOLIC MEANINGS
Loyalty in love; Strong bond.

❀ POSSIBLE POWERS
Aphrodisiac; Banishing negativity; Create oxygen; Dependability; Fertility; Healing; Intensify; Love; Magnify; Uplift the spirit.

❦ FOLKLORE AND FACTS
In many Asian countries, people have been chewing the nuts that grow on the evergreen *Areca catechu* Betel Nut Tree either whole, or chopped and wrapped with a Betel Leaf, for at least two thousand years. • Betel nuts are addictive and chewing them stains the teeth of heavy consumers red or reddish-black. • When grown in a container, the *Areca catechu* is an extremely popular tree for inside the home or in large areas such as hotels. However, the tree will neither fruit nor reach its potential maximum height.

No. 035

Arenga pinnata ⚱ ◉

Sugar Palm

Aren Palm | Areng Palm | Arengga Palm | Black Sugar Palm | Feather Palm | Gomuti Palm | Irok | Kaong Palm

⬤ POTENTIAL MAXIMUM HEIGHT
65 feet [20 meters]

✻ SYMBOLIC MEANINGS
Eternal life; Peace.

❀ POSSIBLE POWERS
Create oxygen; Fertility; Freedom; Happiness; Healing; Love; Relationships; Resurrection; Reward; Righteousness; Sweetening; Triumph; Victory.

❦ FOLKLORE AND FACTS
The sweet sap of the evergreen *Arenga pinnata* Sugar Palm is collected by tapping before it is converted to sugar by boiling it down, much like Sugar Maple sap. From that point, it can be used as a syrup or fermented into wines, liquors, and vinegars. • In the Philippines, there is an annual festival that celebrates the Sugar Palm. • A tapped Sugar Palm tree can release approximately 30 liters of sap a day. • Traditionally, it is believed that a Sugar Palm will respond to just one tapper who will pray for the tree, recite incantations, chant, and even sing to the tree while tapping once in the early morning and again in the late afternoon.

A

No. 036

Argania spinosa 🪔🍴🌿

Argan Tree

Argania | Bully Tree | Harjän | Skeels

◉ POTENTIAL MAXIMUM HEIGHT
65 feet [20 meters]

✸ SYMBOLIC MEANINGS
Eternity; Iron; Resistance.

❀ POSSIBLE POWERS
Create oxygen; Hair growth; Healing.

❦ FOLKLORE AND FACTS
Thorny and snarled, the evergreen *Argania spinosa* Argan Tree is a favorite food of climbing goats that eat the leaves. • Argan oil is extracted from the hard seed nut found in the pulpy fruit. Selling the vitamin E-rich oil is a source of income to the Amazigh people, who routinely use some of the money to purchase more goats. This is because it is the goats that play a necessary part in gathering the wild nuts. The game wardens do much to try to keep the goats out of the woods until after the dried black fruit falls to the ground. That is when the goats enthusiastically ingest the fruit, both spitting and pooping out the seeds, which are then gathered intact. • An Argan oil enterprise is a venture for some women's co-ops in parts of southwestern Morocco. For them, extracting the seeds from the fruit is arduous work. The seeds are cracked between two rocks. The kernels are removed and roasted before the edible oil is extracted. The roasting lends to the nutty flavor of the oil, which is extracted by hand after grinding. After extracting the oil, the oily leftover paste is used to feed their livestock. Bees will also make a home in some of the Argan Trees, making the honey an additional commodity. • Argan oil is one of the rarest and most expensive oils in the world. • In Morocco, Argan oil is also a favorite wedding gift and used in festive food dishes for celebrations.

No. 037

Artocarpus altilis 🍴

Breadfruit Tree

Beta | Bia | Buco | Bulo | Camansi | Kapiak | Kuru | Meduu | Mei | Mos | Nimbalu | Seeded Breadfruit | Ulu | Uru | Uto

◉ POTENTIAL MAXIMUM HEIGHT
70 feet [21 meters]

✸ SYMBOLIC MEANINGS
Defensive stance; Emotional innocence.

❀ POSSIBLE POWERS
Create oxygen; Prominence; Wealth.

❦ FOLKLORE AND FACTS
In many tropical regions, the prepared and cooked ripe fruit of the evergreen *Artocarpus altilis* Breadfruit Tree is a staple food that can be boiled, roasted, fried, or baked. Once it has been cooked, it can then be added to other foods or used as an ingredient in recipes and soups. • The Breadfruit Tree is one of the most highly productive trees for food, developing and ripening over one hundred grapefruit-size, bumpy-rind fruits without very much attention given to the tree. • The latex that is extracted from all parts of the tree can be used to caulk a boat.

A

No. 038

Artocarpus heterophyllus 🐾 ⚗️ 🍴

Jackfruit Tree

Chakka | Chakka Pazham | Jacaduta | Jaca-manteiga | Jack Tree | Kathal | Langka | Muttomvarikka | Nangka | Sindoor

POTENTIAL MAXIMUM HEIGHT
80 feet [24 meters]

SYMBOLIC MEANING
A good relationship.

POSSIBLE POWERS
Conception; Create oxygen; Fertility.

FOLKLORE AND FACTS
Archeologists have discovered evidence of Jackfruit's cultivation in India dating back six thousand years ago. • The evergreen *Artocarpus heterophyllus* Jackfruit Tree can produce up to five hundred fruits in a year. • The Jackfruit is the largest fruit produced by any tree, growing up to 30 inches (76 cm) long, 20 inches (51 cm) in diameter, and weighing up to 120 pounds (54 kg). • Like the pineapple, it is a multiple or collective fruit, comprised of hundreds or thousands of tiny flowers that develop into a single fruit together. • People eat the fleshy petals of the unripe fruit. The fruit tastes sweeter when it is fully ripe. • Uncut, the fruit has a slightly unpleasant, musty smell. However, when you cut a ripe Jackfruit open, it gives off a sweet, tropical fragrance reminiscent of pineapple, banana, mango, and apple, with a hint of bubblegum. • During religious rituals, Hindu priests sit on seats carved from Jackfruit wood. • Sculptors have carved many Buddhist statues from the wood as well. • People once considered Jackfruit a wonder fruit of the East.

No. 039

Asimina triloba 🐾 ⚗️ 🍴

Paw-Paw

American Pawpaw | Pawpaw | Paw Paw

POTENTIAL MAXIMUM HEIGHT
30 feet [9 meters]

SYMBOLIC MEANING
Abundance and scarcity.

POSSIBLE POWERS
Coping with scarcity; Create oxygen; Preparing for less; Reveling in plentitude; Seasonal great abundance.

FOLKLORE AND FACTS
The fruit of the Paw-Paw tree has a sweet banana-like texture and flavor with hints of pineapple, cantaloupe, and mango. It is usually eaten raw out of hand or blended in a smoothie. • Paw-Paw seeds are poisonous. • The first mention of Paw-Paw in Western writing was in Hernando de Sota's expedition journal in 1541, noting that Native Americans near the Mississippi River were growing Paw-Paw trees.

A

No. 040

$\mathcal{A}$verrhoa carambola 🕊 🍴

Star Fruit Tree

Balimbing | Carambola | Carambolo | Kamaranga | Ma Fen | Starfruit Tree

🔘 **POTENTIAL MAXIMUM HEIGHT**
30 feet [9 meters]

✴ **SYMBOLIC MEANING**
Stars.

✿ **POSSIBLE POWERS**
Call for spiritual forces; Conjure a spirit; Create oxygen.

🜂 **FOLKLORE AND FACTS**
The ridges along the sides of the fruit of the deciduous *Averrhoa carambola* Star Fruit Tree can number five, six, or even seven. • When the five-ridged whole fruit is sliced across, the individual slices of the Star Fruit are in the shape of a star and can be used as a pentagram for magical purposes. A six-ridged fruit will produce a slice with six points that is also known as a magical hexagram or the Seal of Solomon. With it, spirits or spiritual forces for many different purposes can be conjured. • A seven-ridged fruit will produce a slice with seven points that is also known as a magical heptagram as well as the elven star, fairy star, or elf-queen's daughters. Magically, it can mean seven directions implying "north, south, east, west, above, below, and within." It can also represent the seven days of the week. • Regardless of how many star points a slice of Star Fruit can produce, the fruit is magically powerful. • Star Fruit juice can also be used to clean rust and tarnish off brass and most other metals.

No. 041

$\mathcal{A}$zadirachta indica ☠ 🕊

Neem Tree

Arishta | Arya Veppu | Azad Dirakht | Bead Tree | Bevu | Cure Tree | Divine Tree | Dogon Yaro | Elixir of Immortality | Heal All | Holy Tree | Huile de Neem | Indian Lilac | Indian Neem | Kohomba | Lilas de Perse | Lilas des Indes | Margosa | Margousier d'Inde | Muarubaini | Nature's Drugstore | Neeb | Neem Oil Tree | Nim | Nimba | Nimm | Nimtree | Panacea for All Diseases | Persian Lilac | Pride of China | Pride of India | Tamar | Tree of Good Health | Tree of Life | Tree of the Forty | Tree of the Forty Cures | Vempu | Vepa | Vepu | Village Pharmacy

🔘 **POTENTIAL MAXIMUM HEIGHT**
66 feet [20 meters]

✴ **SYMBOLIC MEANINGS**
Complete; the Cure; Freedom; Imperishable; Life; to Live; Noble; Perfect.

✿ **POSSIBLE POWERS**
Create oxygen; Healing; Insecticide.

🜂 **FOLKLORE AND FACTS**
The *Azadirachta indica* Neem tree is deciduous. • Wherever Neem Tree leaves fall to the ground, there are supposedly no pests. • In India, dried Neem Tree leaves are often placed in cupboards to keep insects away from clothing and food. • Neem oil has a very long-lingering, garlicky odor when it gets on fabric. • In Hindu mythology, the divine Devas sprinkled Neem as the Elixir of Immortality on the ground, thereby creating the Earth.

$\mathcal{A}$

No. 042
Backhousia citriodora 🕱 🏺 🍴 ⚘

Lemon Myrtle
Lemon Scented Backhousia | Lemon Scented Ironwood | Lemon Scented Myrtle |
Lemon Scented Verbena | Queen of the Lemon Herbs | Sweet Verbena Myrtle |
Sweet Verbena Tree

📷 **POTENTIAL MAXIMUM HEIGHT**
19 feet [6 meters]

✸ **SYMBOLIC MEANING**
Chaste beauty.

🌀 **POSSIBLE POWERS**
Cleansing; Create oxygen;
Healing; Insect repellent;
Purification; Relaxation;
Relieve anxiety; Relieve stress.

🜂 **FOLKLORE AND FACTS**
The crushed leaves of the evergreen
Backhousia citriodora Lemon Myrtle
emit a strong lemony fragrance.
• The essential oil of the Lemon Myrtle is crisp
and more lemony than Lemon. • In aromatherapy, Lemon
Myrtle is uplifting while simultaneously calming to someone
with anxiety.

No. 043
Bactris gasipaes 🏺 🍴

Peach Palm Tree
Chonta | Chontaduro | Cor Wary | Manaco | Palmito Tree | Peewah | Pejibaye |
Pewa | Pif | Pijibay | Pijiguao | Pijuayo | Pivá | Pixbae | Pupunha | Supa | Tembé

📷 **POTENTIAL MAXIMUM HEIGHT**
79 feet [24 meters]

✸ **SYMBOLIC MEANING**
Fulfilled wishes.

🌀 **POSSIBLE POWERS**
Create oxygen; Healing.

🜂 **FOLKLORE AND FACTS**
The Peach Palm Tree is
a fast-growing evergreen
that is primarily cultivated
as a source of the commercial valuable heart of palm.
• The tree's long plump strands of flowers are pollinated
by insects, gravity, and wind. • The *Bactris gasipaes* Peach
Palm Tree's ripe fruit is edible and nutritious after it has been
cooked for five hours in water. • The texture of the fruit has

been compared to a firm sweet potato when it is both raw
as well as cooked. • The cooked fruit's flavor is similar to
chestnut, squash, or hominy. • The fruit and sap can also be
fermented to make a beer. • Indigenous peoples across South
America have utilized the multi-functional potential of the
Peach Palm Tree as a source of wood to make bows,
arrows, blowguns, fish traps, stirring sticks, and mortars.
• The hollowed trunks are used for such things as irrigation
conduits, water troughs for livestock, and flower planters.

No. 044
Bambusa bambos 🕱 🏺 ⚘

Giant Thorny Bamboo
Indian Thorny Bamboo | Spiny Bamboo | Thorny Bamboo

📷 **POTENTIAL MAXIMUM HEIGHT**
100 feet [30 meters]

✸ **SYMBOLIC MEANINGS**
Endurance; Flexibility; Good fortune; Longevity; Loyalty;
Luck; Protection; Rendezvous; Scientific research;
Steadfastness; Strength; Summer; Suppleness; Youth.

🌀 **POSSIBLE POWERS**
Breaks a hex; Building materials; Classical elements
(Air, Earth, Fire, Water); Construction; Create oxygen;
Furniture; Luck; Masculine energy; New start; Protection;
Sun; Wealth; Wishing.

🜂 **FOLKLORE AND FACTS**
Although *Bambusa* is
botanically a grass, it
is in the realm of being
too tall and genuinely
important not to imagine
it worthy enough to be
thought of as a towering
tree. Most *Bambusa* can
tower over some of the
tallest trees nearby and
is most often thought of
as Bamboo "trees" by
people standing beneath
them. • In honor of the
environmentally sound
and useful contribution
that Bamboo can make
to sustainability, in this
book it is being honored
as a pseudo-tree. After
all, as a very tall grass,
Bamboo is extremely

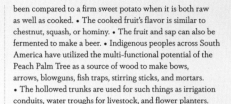

tree-like with unique properties all its own. For all that it is doing for planet Earth, it has earned the right to stand tall next to the true trees of merit. • The *Bambusa bambos* Giant Thorny Bamboo has a running type of root system and can thus very quickly grow to become invasive. Bamboo is the fastest-growing "grass" on the entire planet. Other types of Bamboo have roots that are clumping, and even though they can, over time, spread beyond designated boundaries, they will spread more slowly. • All Bamboo species will grow to their full height and diameter between three to five years to sustainably serve a multitude of easily replenished commercial purposes, which would include those in fabrics, flooring, foods, furniture, and paper. But, because Giant Thorny Bamboo is so strong and the tallest growing of all the *Bambusa*, it is the number one choice to use for Bamboo construction or Bamboo building materials of any kind. • Apart from Common Bamboo, there are several different species of Bamboo that will produce tasty edible shoots, such as *Phyllostachys dulcis*, *Phyllostachys edulis*, *Phyllostachys nigra*, and *Phyllostachys nuda*. In every case, they all require careful preparation and must be boiled before consuming due to the presence of a type of cyanide called taxiphyllin. • Grown, carried, or burned, Bamboo can help break a hex. • *Dracaena sanderiana*, the plant often marketed as "lucky bamboo," isn't Bamboo. • Carve a wish on a piece of Bamboo, then bury it in a quiet place that is unlikely to be disturbed. What is to be will be. • In Japan, during the festival known as Tanabata, or the Star Festival, long strips of mostly red-colored paper holding handwritten dreams and hopes are hung on the Bamboo trees to create Tanabata Wishing Trees. The festival is one of love intended to honor the celestial lovers, the stars Vega and Altair, who are only allowed to meet in the sky once a year.

No. 045

Banksia integrifolia 🍴 🌿

Coast Banksia Tree

Birrna | Coastal Banksia | Honeysuckle Oak | White Banksia | White Bottlebrush

◉ POTENTIAL MAXIMUM HEIGHT
82 feet [25 meters]

✳ SYMBOLIC MEANINGS
New beginnings; Rebirth.

🍃 POSSIBLE POWERS
Create oxygen; Energy boost; Fire element; Happiness; Passion; Protection; Renewal; Saturn; Smoke cleansing; Vitality; Wisdom.

☘ FOLKLORE AND FACTS
The evergreen *Banksia integrifolia* Coast Banksia Tree can be found growing along the east coast of Australia. The tree has a twisted and gnarled trunk and distinctive chubby, bristly flower spikes. The flowers are frequently found as cut flowers in both fresh as well as in dried floral arrangements. • Coast Banksia wood, leaves, and flowers can be burned and used for smoke cleansing. • Coast Banksia wood makes a very good energy or wisdom wand. • Sometimes Coast Banksia flowers are harvested to be eaten by sucking them because they are very rich with nectar. They can also be soaked in water to extract the nectar to produce a non-alcoholic mead-type beverage known as mangite or mungitch that can be fermented to produce an alcoholic drink known as gep.

Beaucarnea recurvata

Ponytail Palm

Bottle Palm | Elefantenfuss | Elephant's Foot Palm | Flaschenbaum | Huiskupullojukka | Maya Palm | Nolina | Ponyschwanz

POTENTIAL MAXIMUM HEIGHT
30 feet [9 meters]

SYMBOLIC MEANINGS
Free spirit; Imperturbability; Strength.

POSSIBLE POWERS
Create oxygen; Love; Optimism; Travel; Warm-heartedness.

FOLKLORE AND FACTS
The distinctive and exceptionally cute evergreen *Beaucarnea recurvata* Ponytail Palm is not a true palm. It is a funky, fun specimen plant for a tropical garden or for growing indoors in a pot. Its bulbous base starts at ground level, growing upwards before narrowing to a longer, much thinner trunk that rises upward, finally topped by long curvy leaves. • When the tree matures to be over ten years old, it can flower a feather-like plume. • No matter how tempting, the ends of the leaves should not be trimmed. When repotting, do not trim back the roots. Allow the tree to grow into what it will become.

Bertholletia excelsa

Brazil Nut Tree

Castañas de Brasil | Castanhas-do-Pará | Nuez de Brasil

POTENTIAL MAXIMUM HEIGHT
165 feet [50 meters]

SYMBOLIC MEANING
Preparing.

POSSIBLE POWERS
Air element; Create oxygen; Fire element; Love; Mars; Masculine energy; Mercury; Moon; Water element.

FOLKLORE AND FACTS
In Brazil it is illegal to cut down the tropical evergreen *Bertholletia excelsa* Brazil Nut Tree.

• The fruit of the *Bertholletia excelsa* tree has a woody hard shell similar to a coconut and it takes fourteen months for the fruit to mature after it has been pollinated. • The Brazil nuts are arranged inside the fruit like citrus segments, but can have up to three whorls of the nuts stacked within the fruit. • The fruit of the Brazil Nut Tree is very large and quite heavy, containing twelve to twenty-five Brazil nuts. When the ripened Brazil Nut fruit falls from the tree it comes down with a loud crash. • Capuchin monkeys have been seen breaking open the hard shell of a Brazil nut with a rock. • The oily kernel found within a shelled seed "nut" of the Brazil Nut fruit is edible. • Carry a Brazil nut as a talisman to have good luck in love. • Brazil nut is an important ingredient in Swiss muesli cereal blends. • The Brazil Nut Tree can live up to seven hundred years.

No. 048

Betula alleghaniensis 🌿🍯🏺🌰

Yellow Birch

Golden Birch | Gray Birch | Silver Birch | Swamp Birch | Tall Birch

◉ POTENTIAL MAXIMUM HEIGHT
39 feet [12 meters]

✹ SYMBOLIC MEANINGS
Growth; New beginnings; Rebirth.

✸ POSSIBLE POWERS
Blessings; Create oxygen; Feminine energy; Happiness.

✿ FOLKLORE AND FACTS
The deciduous *Betula alleghaniensis* Yellow Birch is the largest and most important of the Birch trees, harvested for use as lumber. • The sap of the Yellow Birch can also be tapped and used in a similar way as Sugar Maple sap. It can also be boiled down to syrup. • Native Americans made good use of the Yellow Birch bark to build lodging, dwelling places, buckets, and storage containers of all types.

No. 049

Betula lenta ☠🌿🍯🏺🌰

Black Birch

Cherry Birch | Mahogany Birch | Spice Birch | Sweet Birch

◉ POTENTIAL MAXIMUM HEIGHT
79 feet [24 meters]

✹ SYMBOLIC MEANINGS
Adaptability; Dreams; Elegance; Grace; Gracefulness; Growth; Initiation; Meekness; Pioneer spirit; Renewal; Stability; Transformation.

✸ POSSIBLE POWERS
Astral travel; Create oxygen; Exorcism; Feminine energy; Protection; Protection against infertility, lightning, or the evil eye; Purification; Venus; Water element.

✿ FOLKLORE AND FACTS
The sap of the deciduous *Betula lenta* Black Birch tree can be tapped in the springtime like a much faster-running Sugar Maple sap, thus requiring the sap to be gathered three times

as often. Boiling it down will produce a stronger-flavored syrup with the viscosity of molasses. The syrup can be used to make the very tasty non-alcoholic beverage known as birch beer. • The Vindolanda tablets, some of the oldest handwritten documents found in Britain, date back to around 122 CE, when Roman soldiers were building Hadrian's Wall. They wrote in Latin on pieces of Black Birch about the same size as a modern postcard. Archaeologists have found hundreds of them, and scholars have translated around 750 tablets so far. One tablet, from 100 CE, contains a birthday party invitation and could be the oldest handwritten document in Latin by a woman. • In Russia, people tied a red ribbon around the deciduous Black Birch twig, branch, or tree to repel or expel the evil eye. • In parts of Eastern Europe, Black Birch has a close association with Pentecost. • Black Birch bark helps build lightweight, strong, waterproof canoes. • Norwegian boatbuilders traditionally used Black Birch bark that had been fermented in sea water to season ropes and sails. • Howard Hughes's experimental aircraft, the Spruce Goose, was made mostly of Black Birch wood. • Planting Black Birch close to your home protects it from lightning and the evil eye. • Planting Black Birch near your home also protects against infertility. • The bundled Black Birch twigs form a traditional witch's broom. • Manufacturers used to make cradles from Black Birch to protect the babies sleeping in them from evil. • Black Birch makes a yellow, green, or pale brown dye for fabrics. • A tied bundle of Black Birch twigs is called a switch. A switch's purpose was to impose a physical punishment called a birch. • Use Black Birch gently to strike a person suspected of being possessed to cleanse and heal their spiritually invasive affliction. • Pulp from Black Birch bark makes good paper. In India, the bark alone served as paper for many ancient writings. • In aromatherapy, Black Birch essential oil helps relax an overworked mind.

B

Betula papyrifera 🗡🍴🌱🌰

Paper Birch

American White Birch | Canoe Birch | White Birch

◉ POTENTIAL MAXIMUM HEIGHT
70 feet [21 meters]

✳ SYMBOLIC MEANINGS
Child-like innocence; Wondering.

❀ POSSIBLE POWERS
Create oxygen; Good luck; Protection; Rejuvenation.

❦ FOLKLORE AND FACTS
In Sanskrit the name of deciduous *Betula papyrifera* Paper Birch means "a tree with bark that is used for writing on." • The bark of the Paper Birch is red when it is very young, but it turns white as it matures. The bark peels off the tree easily by hand. At one time it was also used to hold a poultice close to the skin. It was even soaked to wrap around a limb to set a broken bone. After heat was carefully applied to shrink the bark, it sturdily formed around the limb to be a suitable cast. • The inner bark of the Paper Birch tree can be dried and ground into flour to thicken soups or add to wheat flour for use in baking. • The sap can be tapped in the summer like the Sugar Maple's. The syrup can then be used to make syrup or birch beer, or fermented to be a tasty vinegar. • Native Americans made use of the tough, waterproof, and durable outer bark of the Paper Birch in canoe skins, buckets, and many other useful items.

Betula pendula ☠🗡🌱🌰

Silver Birch

Beithe | Bereza | Berke | Beth | Birch | Birch Tree | Bouleau | East Asian White Birch | European White Birch | Lady of the Woods | Warty Birch

◉ POTENTIAL MAXIMUM HEIGHT
75 feet [23 meters]

✳ SYMBOLIC MEANINGS
Adaptability; Dreams; Elegance; Grace; Gracefulness; Growth; Initiation; Meekness; Pioneer spirit; Renewal; Stability; Transformation.

❀ POSSIBLE POWERS
Astral travel; Cleansing; Create oxygen; Exorcism; Feminine energy; Fertility; New beginnings; Protection; Purification; Purifying the property; Shade; Venus; Water element.

❦ FOLKLORE AND FACTS
The deciduous *Betula pendula* Silver Birch is an ancient species that will easily reseed burned land to help establish a new woodland. • Mites or fungus cause deformities called galls or witches' brooms, which resemble bird nests or tangles of twigs on a Silver Birch branch. • A witch's broom, or besom, usually consists of a bundle of Silver Birch twigs bound together. • The Silver Birch wand is a powerful symbol of fertility and new beginnings, as well as cleansing and purification. At one time cradles were made from Silver Birch wood to protect the babies who slept in them from evil. • Use Silver Birch twigs to gently strike a person suspected of being possessed as a means of cleansing them and healing them of the affliction. • In Russia, it was a common practice to tie a red ribbon around a Silver Birch tree or branch, or even a bit of twig that could be worn, in order to repel or expel the evil eye away from themselves. • The Silver Birch is not a tree that lives much longer than seventy years because they too often die from premature old age or a fungus. Even so, during their lifetime they will provide protection and support for slower growing plant species in the woodland that may be growing beneath it in the light shade it provides. • Depending on the fiber and the mordant used, vegetable dye made from Silver Birch can produce red, yellow, or brown colors.

No. 052
Bixa orellana 🐾 🍴 🌱

Achiote Tree
Annatto | Urucum

⬤ POTENTIAL MAXIMUM HEIGHT
16 feet [5 meters]

✳ SYMBOLIC MEANINGS
Blood; Masculinity; Sun.

❀ POSSIBLE POWERS
Create oxygen; Protect against snakebite; Ward off infection.

❦ FOLKLORE AND FACTS
The seed of the evergreen *Bixa orellana* Achiote Tree is edible. However, the fruit is inedible. Achiote seed will transform food to a bright orange-yellow color. • Yellow rice in Latin American recipes is commonly colored with Achiote. • Achiote is a common ingredient in Latin American and Filipino recipes, primarily in Mexico, Central America, and the Philippines. • Nearly all ancient Maya writings used Achiote juice as ink. • In the mythology of the Tupi people of Brazil, a warrior hero climbed an Achiote tree to survive a flood. • Achiote dye is used in many formulas for household polishes, cosmetics, ointments, fabrics, and more.

No. 053
Borassus flabellifer ☠ 🐾 🍴 🌰

Palmyra Palm
Celestial Tree | Doub Palm | Ice Apple | Katpaha Tharu | Panai | Tal Palm | Tala | Toddy Palm | Wine Palm

⬤ POTENTIAL MAXIMUM HEIGHT
98 feet [30 meters]

✳ SYMBOLIC MEANINGS
Creativity; Self-confidence.

❀ POSSIBLE POWERS
Create oxygen; Sensible guidance; Sympathy.

❦ FOLKLORE AND FACTS
The evergreen *Borassus flabellifer* Palmyra Palm is one of the most important trees in India and Cambodia because every part of it is useful in one way or another. • The tree's fruit is similar to a lychee although it is seedless, has a milder flavor, is sugary, and is denser. • Bengali cooks have used the fruit to make artful sweet dishes. The sap can be tapped, then fermented to make alcoholic beverages known as *arrack* and *nam tan mao*. • Sprouted Palmyra Palm seeds are boiled or roasted before eating. These are known as *thegalu*, *gaygulu*, *gengulu*, *panai kizhangu*, *Panangkizhangu*, and *htabin myiqu*. • When the kernel is removed from the shell of the fruit, it is crunchy and much like a sweeter-tasting water chestnut known as *buragunju* and *thavanai*. • It can also be used as a Hindu offering for the religious festival known as Lakshmi Pooja. • Most of Telugu ancient literature was carefully written in cursive on Palmyra Palm leaves.

No. 054

Boswellia sacra

Sacred Boswellia Tree

Boswellia | Frankincense | Incense Tree | Indian Frankincense | Olibans | Olibanum |
Olibanus | Sacred Boswellia

POTENTIAL MAXIMUM HEIGHT
20 feet [6 meters]

SYMBOLIC MEANING
Sanctity.

POSSIBLE POWERS
Abundance; Advancement; Blessings; Conscious will; Create oxygen; Divine energy; Energy; Exorcism; Fertility; Fire element; Friendship; Growth; Healing; Heavenly energy; Holy energy; Incense; Joy; Leadership; Life; Light; Masculine energy; Natural power; Offerings; Petitions; Prayer; Protection; Purification; Spirituality; Success; Sun.

FOLKLORE AND FACTS
Frankincense is the aromatic resinous sap obtained from the small deciduous *Boswellia sacra* Sacred Boswellia Tree. • At one time, *Boswellia sacra* Frankincense was more valuable than gold. • Frankincense is vital for many different magical purposes such as for the bestowing of blessings, as well as for various types of initiation rituals. • Although it is written into the Christian Bible's New Testament as one of the precious gifts given by one of the Three Magi to the newborn Jesus of Nazareth in the stable in Bethlehem, the earliest known written record referring to Frankincense is inscribed on ancient Egyptian tombs. • The charred remains of burned Frankincense is known as the eyeliner called kohl. • Frankincense was discovered within a sealed flask in Pharaoh Tutankhamen's tomb when it was opened in 1922. The Frankincense resin was still viable, releasing scent after being in the vial for 3,300 years. • Frankincense essential oil is particularly soothing and will help lift the downtrodden emotions of one who has been deeply saddened for any reason.
• Frankincense has a very high and powerful vibration which makes it one of the best of all herbs used to drive away any kind of evil.
• Incense has been used in the rituals of many different religions since ancient times, since it was believed that the smoke of the *Boswellia sacra* incense carried prayers and petitions directly upward to waft into Heaven.

No. 055

Bourreria succulenta

Bahama Strongbark Tree

Bahama Strongbark | Bodywood

POTENTIAL MAXIMUM HEIGHT
29 feet [9 meters]

SYMBOLIC MEANING
Rare beauty.

POSSIBLE POWERS
Aphrodisiac; Create oxygen.

FOLKLORE AND FACTS
Highly drought-tolerant and endangered in Florida, the evergreen *Bourreria succulenta* Bahama Strongbark Tree is still fairly common in the Florida Keys and in the Bahamas, but is rare anywhere else. • The shape of the tree is a weeping style with flowers that smell sweetly and are a significant food for the birds, the bees, and the butterflies. • The fruit of the Bahama Strongbark is edible but a bit soapy tasting. A tea can also be made from its bark.

B

Brachychiton rupestris ☠ ❶ ❧

Queensland Bottle Tree
Narrow-leaved Bottle Tree

◉ POTENTIAL MAXIMUM HEIGHT
82 feet [25 meters]

✹ SYMBOLIC MEANING
Sustain.

◉ POSSIBLE POWERS
Create oxygen; Drought tolerance and survival; Memorialize;
Ward off evil spirits.

✾ FOLKLORE AND FACTS
The deciduous *Brachychiton rupestris* Queensland Bottle
Tree trunk has an extremely bulbous swollen base before it
begins branching up and outward. • Between 1918 and 1920
there were ninety-three Queensland Bottle Trees planted
in Roma, Queensland, Australia, to memorialize the local
men who were killed during their military service in World
War I. • Ripe Queensland Bottle Tree seeds are edible after
roasting them. • Many First Nations peoples in Australia
have used the spongy, water-filled tissue of the Queensland
Bottle Tree trunk as fodder during times of severe drought.
• It is possible for a Queensland Bottle Tree to survive up for
to three months after being dug up before replanting it.

Brachylaena huillensis ❧

Silver Oak
Laeveldvaalbos | Low Veld Silver-oak | Mahugu | Mkarambaki | Mkarambati |
Mufhata Thavha | Muhuhu | Mutonzhe | Mvumo

◉ POTENTIAL MAXIMUM HEIGHT
115 feet [35 meters]

✹ SYMBOLIC MEANING
Vulnerable.

◉ POSSIBLE POWERS
Conservation; Create oxygen; Decoration; Income.

✾ FOLKLORE AND FACTS
The quickly growing evergreen *Brachylaena huillensis*
Silver Oak wood is highly valued in Kenya, for its fragrant,
very hard wood. It is used for charcoal and for ornamental
wood carvings.

Brosimum guianense ☠ ❧

Snakewood Tree
Amourette | Bastard Breadnut | Leopardwood | Letterwood

◉ POTENTIAL MAXIMUM HEIGHT
130 feet [40 meters]

✹ SYMBOLIC MEANING
Valuable rarity.

◉ POSSIBLE POWERS
Create oxygen; Feminine
energy; Healing;
Interesting; Masculine
energy; Physical healing;
Snakebite; Sound resonance;
Water element.

✾ FOLKLORE AND FACTS
The unusual speckled, snake-like and
hieroglyphic-patterned dense heartwood of the
deciduous *Brosimum guianense* Snakewood Tree
is highly prized by woodworkers. It is favored for
making such things as furniture inlays, drumsticks,
cabinetry, and umbrella handles. • Snakewood was
once favored for fashioning bow heels, or "frogs," for violin
and cello bows. • The wood of the Snakewood Tree is rare
and one of the most expensive in the world. It is most often
sold based on its weight. Snakewood is the fourth-hardest
and seventh-heaviest of the woods. • As a wand, Snakewood
is the hardest wood and best for one who has already
mastered the darker side of the magical arts and is now fully
intent on manifesting good will. It is believed by some that if
the wand is planted it will grow into a large magical tree.

Broussonetia papyrifera 💀 ⚰ ☠

Paper Mulberry Tree

Aka | Amoreira Do Papel | Gelso Papirifero Del Giappone | Gou Shu | Gul Toot | Hiapo | Kachnar | Kename Kowso | Kku Ji Na Mu | Kodzu | Kowso | Kōzo | Lu-A-Shu | Malaing | Moral De La China | Morera De Papel | Morera Del Papel | Moro Della China | Mûrier à Papier | Papelero | Papermulberry Tree | Papier-Maulbeerbaum | Papiermaulbeerbaum | Papiermoerbei | Papirmorbær | Papirjevka | Pappersmullbär | Po'a'aha | Pokasa | Por-Gra-Saa | Por-Saa | Saeh | Tapa Cloth Tree | Ton-Saa | Wauke

🔍 POTENTIAL MAXIMUM HEIGHT
115 feet [35 meters]

✳ SYMBOLIC MEANING
Slow warmth.

🌀 POSSIBLE POWERS
Cloth; Create oxygen; Dry; Durability; Papermaking; Warm.

🜂 FOLKLORE AND FACTS
Over five thousand years ago, one way or another, the deciduous *Broussonetia papyrifera* Paper Mulberry Tree was brought to Australia and the Pacific Islands. • Ancient Austronesian peoples used the Paper Mulberry Tree bark to make prehistoric bark cloth. Of all the trees capable of being used to make bark cloth, the highest quality is produced by the Paper Mulberry Tree. Although bark cloth is no longer used to make clothing, it is used for artistically decorative purposes. Regalia made from bark cloth is still produced for ceremonial use in some parts of Melanesia and Polynesia. These pieces are passed on from generation to generation. Some of these pieces from the eighteenth and nineteenth centuries are in museums worldwide. • The inner bark of the Paper Mulberry Tree is used to make the elegant, translucent, handcrafted paper in Japan known as washi. • It is also used to make a durable high-quality Korean handmade art paper known as *hanji*. Its waterproof quality makes it especially useful for paper lanterns. • In Tonga and Fiji, bark cloth known as *tapa* is still used to make the elegant, translucent, handcrafted paper in Japan known as washi. • It is also used to make a durable high-quality Korean handmade art paper known as *hanji*. Its waterproof quality makes it especially useful for paper lanterns. • In Tonga and Fiji, bark cloth known as *tapa* is still used to wrap newborn babies as a means of preserving their precious, newly emergent vital energy's connection to the spirit world. In wedding ceremonies, large pieces of the cloth are placed on the ground for the bride and groom to walk upon after they are married. The bodies of the deceased are wrapped in tapa before burial.

Brugmansia arborea 💀

Brugmansia Tree

Angel's Trumpet | Maikoa | Nanahonua | Trumpet of Death

🔍 POTENTIAL MAXIMUM HEIGHT
16 feet [5 meters]

✳ SYMBOLIC MEANINGS
Fame; Gaze downwards; Separation.

🌀 POSSIBLE POWERS
Awaken the dead; Black magic; Create oxygen; Occult use; Shamanism; Sorcery.

🜂 FOLKLORE AND FACTS
The *Brugmansia arborea* Brugmansia Tree is a large evergreen shrub that is commonly grown as a small tree. • It has gorgeous, huge, down-facing, showy, trumpet-shaped flowers that makes it an incredibly beautiful sight when it is in full bloom. • The Brugmansia Tree also has a lovely fragrance during the day that becomes more pleasantly intense as nighttime approaches. • It is considered to be the most beautiful but entirely deadly tree in the world, as every part of the Brugmansia Tree is deadly poisonous. • Brugmansia is not found in the wild.

No. 061

Bursera graveolens 🌿🥜🌰

Palo Santo

Ali A | Bijá | Bursera | Caraño | Chachicen | Crispín | Holy Stick | Holy Wood | Sasafrás |
Tamagaco | Tatamaco | West Indian Sandalwood

◉ POTENTIAL MAXIMUM HEIGHT
50 feet [15 meters]

✱ SYMBOLIC MEANING
Cleanliness.

❀ POSSIBLE POWERS
Cleanliness; Clear
misfortune; Create
oxygen; Dispel evil
spirits or negative
thoughts; Fire element;
Good luck; Incense;
Love; Masculine energy;
Purification; Relaxation;
Soothe nervousness;
Spiritual purification; Sun.

✵ FOLKLORE AND FACTS
The deciduous *Bursera graveolens* Palo Santo is a sacred tree
that grows wild in parts of South America. It is in the same
Burseraceae family as Frankincense and Myrrh. • According
to some local Ecuadorian customs dating back to the Inca
era, Palo Santo is burned like incense to eliminate malevolent
energy and help encourage inner peace. • Palo Santo
charcoal is used for smudging during some ritual customs
that are rooted in the spiritual beliefs of many different
indigenous peoples throughout South America. It is also
sometimes used in various Catholic rituals in some churches
across South America. • Until the rainy season begins, the
Bursera graveolens Palo Santo tree smells like incense, even
though it remains leafless. As soon as the rains commence,
the bare tree begins to quickly sprout leaves. • Palo Santo
essential oil is useful in aromatherapy to help ease insomnia
and stress. It centers the mind for meditation and prayer, and
helps promote compassion whenever it is needed.

No. 062

Butia odorata 🍴

Jelly Palm

Butiá | Butiá-Da-Praia | Pindo Palm | South American Jelly Palm

◉ POTENTIAL MAXIMUM HEIGHT
33 feet [10 meters]

✱ SYMBOLIC MEANINGS
Fragrant fruit; Perfumed fruit.

❀ POSSIBLE POWERS
Create oxygen; Good luck.

✵ FOLKLORE AND FACTS
The fruit of the evergreen *Butia odorata* Jelly Palm has a
simultaneous tartly sweet flavor that tastes like a combined
mix of apricot, pineapple, and vanilla. It is used to make
jams, juice, and liquors. • The Jelly Palm is native to Uruguay
where it is protected by laws that forbid it being either
moved or felled without permission from the Uruguayan
government. • An oil similar to Coconut oil can be extracted
from the seeds of the Jelly Palm.

No. 063

Buxus sempervirens ☠ 🗡 🌲

Boxwood

American Boxwood | Box | Box Tree | Common Box | European Box | Evergreen Boxwood

🌐 **POTENTIAL MAXIMUM HEIGHT**
20 feet [6 meters]

✹ **SYMBOLIC MEANINGS**
Constancy; Constancy in friendship; Determination;
Immortality; Indifference; Longevity; More than enough;
Stature; Stoicism.

🌐 **POSSIBLE POWERS**
Confusion; Create oxygen; Distractions; Frustration;
Interference; Longevity; Plenty; Protection; Protective;
Sound resonance.

🜨 **FOLKLORE AND FACTS**
More than four thousand years ago, the ancient Egyptians
first formally trimmed evergreen *Buxus sempervirens*
Boxwood trees in their gardens. • For centuries,
Mediterranean woodworkers made small, masterfully carved
boxes and musical instruments from Boxwood's fine-grained
wood. • A Boxwood hedge is said to be a distraction to a
witch wanting to steal flowers from a garden. Boxwood
leaves are so small and dense that a challenged witch cannot
count the leaves, losing count and forced to futilely start over
and over again. • To have a Boxwood hedge surrounding the
home is a very powerful protection around the property and
all that is within its boundaries.

No. 064

Byrsonima crassifolia ☠ 🗡 🍴 🌲

Golden Spoon Tree

Chi Tree | Craboo | Golden Cherry | Hogberry Tree | Maricao Cimun | Nance | Nancy Tree | Yellow Cherry

🌐 **POTENTIAL MAXIMUM HEIGHT**
39 feet [12 meters]

✹ **SYMBOLIC MEANING**
Force.

🌐 **POSSIBLE POWERS**
Create oxygen; Healing; Tan leather.

🜨 **FOLKLORE AND FACTS**
The evergreen
Byrsonima crassifolia
Golden Spoon Tree is
drought-tolerant and
ornamental. • The
tree is found in the
wild but is also widely
cultivated for its fruit.
The ripe fruit is edible
raw, rich in vitamin C,
and used to make jams,
ice cream, sorbet,
vinegar, and a drink

that is known as chicha. In Costa Rica and Mexico the fruit
is used to make a popular liquor known as *crema de nance*
and *licor de nance*. • A cut branch tossed into water is used
to poison fish. • Golden Spoon Tree bark can be used to tan
leather while the leaves can be used to make a light-brown
dye for cotton fabrics. • The Golden Spoon Tree fruit is
said to be the food of the mythical Maya false sun deity,
Seven Macaw.

𝓑

No. 065

Calocedrus decurrens 🪔🌳

Incense Cedar
A-Tsi-Na Tlu-Gv | California Incense Cedar | Hō´-tā

🔘 **POTENTIAL MAXIMUM HEIGHT**
195 feet [59 meters]

✳ **SYMBOLIC MEANINGS**
Generosity; Running down.

🕸 **POSSIBLE POWERS**
Air element; Awakening;
Create oxygen; Create space
for the spirits of ancestors;
Dreaming; Enlightenment;
Eternal life; Fertility; Harmony;
Immortality; Incense; Insect repellent;
Light; Love after difficult times; Magic;
Masculine energy; Protection; Regeneration; Resurrection;
Spiritual consciousness; Spirituality.

🜨 **FOLKLORE AND FACTS**
The conifer *Calocedrus decurrens* Incense Cedar can live for
over five hundred years. • When the flat needles have been
crushed, they smell a great deal like shoe polish. • Due to
the Incense Cedar wood being resistant to rot, as well as its
ability to repel insects, it is a favorite for use in blanket and
hope chest cedar linings. • At one time the wood was used
for pencils because it would not splinter when the pencil
was sharpened. • Native American peoples in what is now
known as California used the wood for making hunting bows
and baskets. • Incense Cedar leaves can be placed in a small
bowl or pouch to create or hold a place for the spirits of one's
ancestors within or near to the home. • For use as a fragrant
incense, burn the leaves until they turn into ash.

No. 066

Calophyllum inophyllum ☠🪔🌳🌰

Beautyleaf Tree
Alexandrian Laurel | Balltree | Beach Calophyllum | Beach Touriga | Beauty Leaf | Bintangur |
Bitaog | Borneo Mahogany | Indian Doomba Oiltree | Indian-laurel | Kamani | Laurelwood |
Mastwood | Oil-nut | Red Poon | Satin Touriga | Tacamahac-Tree | Tamanu

🔘 **POTENTIAL MAXIMUM HEIGHT**
60 feet [18 meters]

✳ **SYMBOLIC MEANING**
Beautiful leaf.

🕸 **POSSIBLE POWERS**
Boat building; Create oxygen; Poison.

🜨 **FOLKLORE AND FACTS**
The evergreen
*Calophyllum
inophyllum*
Beautyleaf Tree
is a completely
toxic but very
showy ornamental
with fragrant
white flowers. • The
Beautyleaf Tree is
able to grow to a huge
size. Beautyleaf wood

was used to build large outrigger canoes and outrigger ships.
• The wood from the Beautyleaf Tree is also considered
sacred and the dwelling place of spirits. • The wood has been
favored in Polynesian cultures for carving the deified tiki
statutes that have humanoid features and are often used to
signify sacred sites and their boundaries. • An oil extracted
from the Beautyleaf Tree's seeds was used in the Philippines
for lamp oil and as a substitute for kerosene. It was also used
as a fuel that could help generate electricity that would be
used to power radios during World War II. • The toxic fruit
of the Beautyleaf has been known to be ground up for use as
a rat poison.

No. 067

Camellia japonica 🌳

Japanese Camellia
Fishtail Camellia | Japan Rose | Japanese Camellia | Kingyo-tsubaki | Rose of Winter |
Unryu | Zig-zag Camellia

🔘 **POTENTIAL MAXIMUM HEIGHT**
36 feet [11 meters]

✳ **SYMBOLIC MEANINGS**
Admiration; Deep longing;
Desire; Excellence; Good
luck gift to a man; Gratitude;
Masculine energy; Passion;
Perfect loveliness; Perfection; Pity;
Refinement; Riches; Unpretending.

🎨 **COLOR MEANINGS**
Pink: Desire; Longing; Longing for you; Persistent desire.
Red: Ardent love; In love; You're a flame in my heart.
White: Adoration; Beauty; Loveliness; Perfection; Waiting;
    You're adorable.
Yellow: Longing.

C

🌸 POSSIBLE POWERS

Create oxygen; Luxury; Prosperity; Riches; Romance; Wealth.

🍂 FOLKLORE AND FACTS

The evergreen *Camellia japonica* Japanese Camellia was first introduced to America in 1797 to plant and beautify the Elysian Fields in Hoboken, New Jersey, which is known as the birthplace of organized baseball games in the US.

No. 068

Camellia sinensis 🏺 🍴 🌱

Tea Tree

Black Tea | Green Tree | Oolong Tea | Pu-erh Tea | Tea Tree | White Tea

🔘 POTENTIAL MAXIMUM HEIGHT

15 feet [5 meters]

✹ SYMBOLIC MEANINGS

Change; Constancy; Contentment; Courage; Fire element; Harmony; Mars; Masculine energy; Peace; Refreshment; Rejuvenation; Riches; Spiritual awakening, connection, or enlightenment; Steadfastness; Strength; Sun; Young sons and daughters.

🌸 POSSIBLE POWERS

Courage; Create oxygen; Feminine energy; Fire element; Healing; Mars; Moon; Peace; Prosperity; Rejuvenation; Riches; Spiritual connection; Stress relief; Water element.

🍂 FOLKLORE AND FACTS

All tea comes from the evergreen *Camellia sinensis* Tea Tree. Although most are commonly grown as manageably short bush shrubs to facilitate harvesting within 2 feet (61 cm) from the ground, the Tea Tree can be grown and pruned to be an attractive small tree. • The choice edible part of any *Camellia sinensis* tree are the very new leaf tips, which are harvested by hand twice a year. The second harvest is the most prized collection, known also as "tippy tea," because by then the tips of the leaves are a golden shade that is considered to be a sweeter, more flavorful leaf for tea brewing. • The word "tea" in the common names for *Camellia sinensis* Tea Shrub, *Melaleuca alternifolia* Tea Tree, and *Leptospermum scoparium* New Zealand Teatree imply they are similar plants. However,

they're not related to each other and are not a substitute for each other in any way, for any reason. • Wear a sachet or pouch of Black Tea as a talisman to increase your strength and give yourself a boost of courage. A pre-made store-bought tea bag is not the proper kind of sachet. Even so, the dried tea within it is acceptable, but it should be emptied into a handmade sachet packet. The ideal tea leaves are those that are handpicked from the plant itself. • A hot cup of Black Tea has been the go-to cure-all for nearly every sudden impairment small or great, whether it is lightheadedness, swooning, sadness, or a gloomily slumping spirit, for hundreds, perhaps thousands of years. Who knows? Maybe even millions of years.

No. 069

Cananga odorata 🏺 🌱

Ylang-Ylang Tree

Cananga Tree | Flower of Flowers | Fragrant Cananga | Ilang-Ilang | Kenanga | Mata'oi | Mohokoi | Mokasoi | Mokohoi | Mokosoi | Moso'oi | Moto'oi

🔘 POTENTIAL MAXIMUM HEIGHT

100 feet [30 meters]

✹ SYMBOLIC MEANING

Wilderness flower.

🌸 POSSIBLE POWERS

Aphrodisiac; Create oxygen; Elevate mood; Help alleviate sexual dysfunction; Perfumery; Relieve anxiety and stress.

🍂 FOLKLORE AND FACTS

The evergreen *Cananga odorata* Ylang-Ylang Tree has an unusual, beautifully fragrant blossom, leading to the mistranslation of its common name as "flower of flowers." The name correctly derives from *ilang*, the Tagalog word for "wilderness." • In aromatherapy, there are three grades of

Ylang-Ylang essential oils. The first and earliest oil extracted is called "extra" and is the most potent and expensive version used in upscale perfumery. The next grade, "first through third," is a distillate that continues for several hours after the first "extra" distillate has been completed. This will be a more subtle version. The final distillate is called "complete" and is the most commonly available essential oil. The distillate of the blossoms is processed through each of these steps for ten to twenty hours to fully complete the process. The result is a milder, but still quite fragrant, essential oil. Although it is not used to make high-end perfume, it is still exotically fragrant on its own. • In aromatherapy, Ylang-Ylang's exotically scented essential oil encourages closing your eyes and smelling the air as a means of transporting your imagination to the South Pacific. This helps ease a worried mind, release nervous tension, and relax your body.

No. 070

Canarium luzonicum ☠ ⚓ 🌰

Elemi Canary Tree
Elemi

🔍 **POTENTIAL MAXIMUM HEIGHT**
98 feet [30 meters]

✸ **SYMBOLIC MEANINGS**
Above and below; Calm; New beginning; Peace; Quiet.

🌐 **POSSIBLE POWERS**
Balance; Create oxygen; Emotional plane; Grounding; Healing; Honor the spirits of nature; Initiation; Magic; Rejuvenation; Rites of passage; Spiritual calm; Spiritual plane; Strengthen mental or psychic capacity.

🜊 **FOLKLORE AND FACTS**
The evergreen *Canarium luzonicum* Elemi Canary Tree's essential oil has a citrusy, dill-like minty, lemony fragrance that can be helpful in aromatherapy for balancing and grounding during meditation. • The name "Elemi" means "above and below." That indicates that its energy is active at both the emotional and spiritual levels. • The Elemi Canary Tree's essential oil's thick viscosity is similar to that of Myrrh. • The ancient Egyptians used Elemi essential oil as one of the ingredients to mummify a body. • Put a single drop of Elemi essential oil on a sachet to calm your inner spirit enough to enter the spiritual plane during meditation. • The resin of the Elemi Canary Tree is sacred in the Philippines, where it is known as *pili*.

No. 071

Canella winterana ☠ ⚓

Cinnamon Bark Tree
Canella | White Cinnamon | Wild Cinnamon | Winter Cinnamon

🔍 **POTENTIAL MAXIMUM HEIGHT**
50 feet [15 meters]

✸ **SYMBOLIC MEANING**
Spiced wildness.

🌐 **POSSIBLE POWERS**
Create oxygen; Fish poison; Protection.

🜊 **FOLKLORE AND FACTS**
A piece of the evergreen *Canella winterana* Cinnamon Bark Tree's bark will curl in the same manner as *Cinnamomum cassia* and *Cinnamomum verum*. At one time, the Cinnamon Bark Tree was a common sight in the Florida Keys, where it is native and could be found growing wild under the shade of the taller trees that populate wooded areas. However, that is no longer the case, as it is considered an endangered tree species in Florida and is now legally protected and can be only rarely found. • The Cinnamon Bark Tree has exotically aromatic leaves that are reminiscent of cloves. The presence of the much-appreciated tree and its attractive and pleasantly fragrant attributes were mentioned in many early travel journals to that part of the world. • When the Cinnamon Bark Tree is in bloom, the flowers are purple and white, which make the showy blooming tree even more attractive.

No. 072

Carapa guianensis ⚓

Crabwood Tree
Andiroba | Bastard Mahogany | White Crabwood

🔍 **POTENTIAL MAXIMUM HEIGHT**
114 feet [35 meters]

✸ **SYMBOLIC MEANING**
Protector.

🌐 **POSSIBLE POWERS**
Create oxygen; Insect repellent; Protection.

🜊 **FOLKLORE AND FACTS**
The crab or carapa oil and other fats that are extracted from the deciduous *Carapa guianensis* Crabwood Tree nut are used to make a highly effective repellent that protects premium furniture lumber from damage by wood-chewing insects. • In the Amazon jungle,

C

the elaborately processed dough cakes that are made from crab oil are burned to fend off any flying insects in the vicinity, especially mosquitoes. The crab oil cakes are one of the most popular items to buy or trade. The dough is also used to process soap.

No. 073

Carica papaya 🐞💀🍶🍴💀

Papaya Tree
Caribbean Red Papaya | Lechoza | Maradol | Mugua | Papao | Papaw | Pawpaw | Put | Red Papaya | Sunrise Papaya | Yellow Papaw

◎ POTENTIAL MAXIMUM HEIGHT
39 feet [12 meters]

✹ SYMBOLIC MEANINGS
Bad health; Good health; Inner peace.

✸ POSSIBLE POWERS
Create oxygen; Feminine energy; Love; Moon; Protection; Water element; Wishing.

✿ FOLKLORE AND FACTS
Botanically, the *Carica papaya* Papaya fruit is actually a large berry. • Papaya Trees are male, female, and hermaphrodite. The male never fruits. It will only flower and produce pollen. If the female is pollinated, it will produce fruit. The hermaphrodite will produce both. • A piece of Papaya wood over a door can supposedly keep evil from entering your home. • Tie a ribbon around a Papaya Tree limb and visualize what you want. • Papaya contains papain, an enzyme that can tenderize meat.

No. 074

Carpinus betulus 🍶🌿

European Hornbeam Tree
Ironwood

◎ POTENTIAL MAXIMUM HEIGHT
80 feet [24 meters]

✹ SYMBOLIC MEANINGS
A treasure; Extravagance; Ornament.

✸ POSSIBLE POWERS
Create oxygen; Endurability; Strength.

✿ FOLKLORE AND FACTS
The deciduous *Carpinus betulus* European Hornbeam Tree produces a very hard, nearly white wood that is used where tough, hard wood is required. • Hard European Hornbeam wood is favored for making such things as the gear pegs of windmills, tool handles, horse-drawn carriage wheels, and more.

No. 075

Carya cordiformis 🐞🍶

Bitternut Hickory Tree
Pignut Hickory | Swamp Hickory

◎ POTENTIAL MAXIMUM HEIGHT
154 feet [47 meters]

✹ SYMBOLIC MEANING
Flexible strength.

✸ POSSIBLE POWERS
Create oxygen; Flexibility; Healing; Patience; Strength.

✿ FOLKLORE AND FACTS
The nuts of the deciduous *Carya cordiformis* Bitternut Hickory Tree are inedible. • It is a very large tree with hard wood that is used to make furniture, wall paneling, tool handles, and sturdy ladders.

C

No. 076
Carya illinoinensis 🐿️ 🍶 🌿

Pecan Tree
Nuez de la Arruga

🔎 **POTENTIAL MAXIMUM HEIGHT**
130 feet [40 meters]

✴ **SYMBOLIC MEANINGS**
Southern hospitality;
Wealth.

🌐 **POSSIBLE POWERS**
Air element; Create
oxygen; Employment;
Masculine energy;
Mercury; Money.

☘ **FOLKLORE AND FACTS**
Cultivation of the deciduous *Carya illinoinensis* Pecan Tree began in the 1880s. • Pecan wood is a favorite for grilling and smoking meat. • Thomas Jefferson planted Pecan Trees at his Virginia plantation, Monticello. Jefferson gifted trees to George Washington, who planted them at his own Virginia plantation, Mount Vernon. • A Pecan Tree in San Saba, Texas, that dates to 1850 is believed to be the mother tree of all the Texas Pecan Trees to follow it. • It is a good idea to add a Pecan to all spells concerning money and prosperity if you want them to come to pass as expected.

No. 077
Carya ovata 🐿️ 🍶 🌿 🌰

Shagbark Hickory Tree
Carolina Hickory | Scalybark Hickory | Shellbark Hickory | Upland Hickory

🔎 **POTENTIAL MAXIMUM HEIGHT**
80 feet [24 meters]

✴ **SYMBOLIC MEANING**
Holding.

🌐 **POSSIBLE POWERS**
Create oxygen; Legal matters; Love; Lust; Protection.

☘ **FOLKLORE AND FACTS**
The deciduous *Carya ovata* Shagbark Hickory Tree is native to the state of Pennsylvania, where it is closely connected to the early Algonquin and Seneca tribes who ate the seed nuts raw. The Ojibwe people used the wood to make archery bows. • A light toasting of the Shagbark Hickory nuts intensifies and elevates their flavor significantly. • The nuts are usually foraged, although shelled Shagbark Hickory nuts

can sometimes be found at a farmers' market. The nuts are extremely tedious to open, but worth the effort. • From earliest American times until this day, this exceptionally strong wood has been used to make tools, mostly axe handles. • Shagbark Hickory wood is often used as charcoal for cooking. It is also a favorite wood used to smoke meat, like bacon. • A good charm to make to protect your home against trouble with the law is to burn a piece of the root until it is ash. Mix the ashes with *Argentina anserina* Silverweed Cinquefoil. Put this mixture into sachets and hang them over each entrance door of your home.

No. 078
Caryota obtusa ☠

Giant Fishtail Palm
Black Trunk Fishtail Palm | Fishtail Palm | Thai Giant Caryota | Thai Mountain Fishtail Palm

🔎 **POTENTIAL MAXIMUM HEIGHT**
50 feet [15 meters]

✴ **SYMBOLIC MEANING**
Gentle giant.

🌐 **POSSIBLE POWERS**
Create oxygen; Rapid decline; Slow to flower.

☘ **FOLKLORE AND FACTS**
Native to Thailand, the evergreen *Caryota obtusa* Giant Fishtail Palm is truly a tall and magnificent tree that commands attention. Since it is such a thirsty palm tree, it is not a good choice to plant in a drought-prone area. • Giant Fishtail Palm is a monocarpic plant, which means that after it flowers only one time, it will then rapidly die. • The flower stalk can be over 20 feet (6 m) long! • On the positive side, it will take at least ten years for the Giant Fishtail Palm to flower. There are very few specimens that are older than thirty years old.

Caryota urens 🕱 🍶 🍴

Jaggery Palm

Kitul Palm | Moha-Karin | Sago Palm | Solitary Fishtail Palm | Toddy Palm | Tunsaè | Wine Palm

◉ POTENTIAL MAXIMUM HEIGHT
49 feet [15 meters]

✹ SYMBOLIC MEANINGS
Delusion maker; Stinging.

✹ POSSIBLE POWERS
Create oxygen; Fishing pole.

✺ FOLKLORE AND FACTS
Like the *Caryota obtusa*, the evergreen *Caryota urens*
Jaggery Palm is also a monocarpic plant, which means
that after it flowers only one time it will rapidly die.
• The Jaggery Palm flower stalk can be over 10 feet (3 m)
long! • A Jaggery Palm frond can be stripped of all its leaves
and left to dry, which will transform it into a functional
fishing pole. • The Jaggery Palm is also a type of sugar palm.
In Sri Lanka, the sap of the Jaggery Palm is tapped, collected,
then boiled until it is transformed into thick molasses that
is known as *kithul* treacle, which is used as a sweetener in
Sri Lankan cooking. • The flower stalk is used to make a
powerful wine. • The pulp of the tree is cut into pieces, dried
in the sun, powdered to be a sweet additive to coconut milk,
which is then cooked to make a Sri Lankan specialty known
as *Kithul Thalapa*.

Cascabela thevetia 🕱 🍶

Yellow Oleander

Bee Still Tree | Kaner Flower | Lucky Nut | Mexican Oleander

◉ POTENTIAL MAXIMUM HEIGHT
30 feet [9 meters]

✹ SYMBOLIC MEANING
Snake's rattle.

✹ POSSIBLE POWERS
Create oxygen; Luck.

✺ FOLKLORE AND FACTS
All parts of the deciduous *Cascabela thevetia* Yellow
Oleander are extremely poisonous, most especially the
seeds. There have been many well-documented instances
concerning the accidental poisonings of humans. • The
deadly poisonous seeds of *Cascabela thevetia* are worn as
talismans in Sri Lanka to attract luck.

Cassia fistula 🕱 🍶 🌿

Golden Shower Tree

Amaltas Tree | Bâton Casse | Caneficier | Chacara | Ehela | Faux Sénné | Fleur Cavadee |
Golden Chain Tree | Golden Rain Tree | Indian Laburnum | Lluvia de Oro | Pluie d'Or |
Pudding-pipe Tree | Purging Cassia | Ratchaphruek

◉ POTENTIAL MAXIMUM HEIGHT
40 feet [12 meters]

✹ SYMBOLIC MEANINGS
Disease killer; Forsaken; Pensive beauty; Royalty.

✹ POSSIBLE POWERS
Beauty; Create oxygen; Good luck; Happiness; Healing;
Offerings; Purgative.

✺ FOLKLORE AND FACTS
When the deciduous *Cassia fistula* Golden Shower Tree is
gorgeously in full bloom, it appears to be profusely dripping
long, gold flowering racemes, as if the tree is Nature's
deliberate presentation of natural beauty. The sight of it is
unforgettable. • The Golden Shower Tree has very strong,
long-lasting wood that was used for special spiritually
intended buildings in Sri Lanka. • Although toxic, the
Golden Shower Tree has been used in Ayurvedic medicine
for thousands of years. • In some areas of India, its bark is
processed to be used to artificially tan the skin.

No. 082

Castanea dentata 🥄 🌰 🥄

American Chestnut Tree

Castan-wydden | Châtaigne | Chestnut | Chinkapin | Chinquapin | Gështenjë | Kastanje |
Kistinen | Sweet Chestnut

◉ POTENTIAL MAXIMUM HEIGHT
98 feet [30 meters]

✹ SYMBOLIC MEANINGS
Do me justice; Independence; Injustice; Justice; Luxury.

◉ POSSIBLE POWERS
Abundance; Create oxygen; Energy; Enhance intuition;
Fertility; Fire element; Jupiter; Justice; Longevity;
Love; Masculine energy; Mental acuity; Recognizing
or overcoming difficulties; Stamina; Strength; Success;
Sympathy.

🜊 FOLKLORE AND FACTS
Before being decimated
across North America
by a killing fungus
known as the chestnut
blight, the deciduous
Castanea dentata
American Chestnut
Tree was a very large and
exceptionally important tree.
It was considered to be the finest of all the
Chestnut trees. East Asian Chestnut trees that were brought
to North America carried the fungus with them. Beginning
with the fungus' discovery in 1904, it rapidly spread out
to then kill approximately four billion American Chestnut
Trees across North America. Even though there are still some
American Chestnut Trees growing, they are much smaller in
size and too few and too far between. The number currently
growing in no way represents how many *enormous* trees
there once were. The species is still endangered in the USA
and Canada. • Research is ongoing and quite promising in
an attempt to still find a way to create and then successfully
grow a blight-resistant American Chestnut Tree. • During
the winter holiday season, roasted hot Chestnuts are still
offered for sale on the streets, although they may not be
American Chestnuts, and are more likely Sweet Chestnuts
from Europe. • Large American Chestnut Trees are no
longer felled for lumber, but Chestnut wood from very old,
demolished houses and barns is a prize to reclaim for reuse,
most particularly in cabinetry.

No. 083

Castanea sativa 🥄 🌰 🌰

Sweet Chestnut Tree

Chestnut | Chinkapin | Chinquapin | Gështenjë | Kastanje | Kistinen | Spanish Chestnut

◉ POTENTIAL MAXIMUM HEIGHT
98 feet [30 meters]

✹ SYMBOLIC MEANINGS
Ancient Earth; Chastity; Do me justice; Independence;
Injustice; Justice; Luxury.

◉ POSSIBLE POWERS
Abundance; Create oxygen; Energy; Enhance intuition;
Fertility; Fire element; Jupiter; Justice; Longevity;
Love; Masculine energy; Mental acuity; Recognizing
or overcoming difficulties; Stamina; Strength; Success;
Sympathy.

🜊 FOLKLORE AND FACTS
The edible parts of the long-living deciduous *Castanea sativa*
Sweet Chestnut Tree are the kernels of the seeds.
• People have cultivated the edible and highly versatile
Sweet Chestnut since at least 2000 BCE. • There is a Sweet
Chestnut Tree in Corsica that is one thousand years old.
• Keep Sweet Chestnuts in the house to attract positive
energy into your home. • If you want to conceive, carry or
wear a Sweet Chestnut amulet to boost fertility. • Alexander
the Great began the practice of planting Sweet Chestnuts
wherever his armies traveled. • Although ancient Romans
didn't particularly care for the taste of the Chestnut, the
ancient Roman armies also made it a practice to carry and
plant Sweet Chestnuts wherever the troops traveled. • Carry
or wear a Sweet Chestnut amulet during class to help absorb
and retain information. • Carry or wear a Sweet Chestnut
amulet to court to encourage justice to prevail. • Feed
your heart's desire a Sweet Chestnut to inspire love.
• Do not mistake inedible toxic Horse Chestnut for the
Sweet Chestnut.

C

No. 084

Castanospermum australe 🦴 ⚰ 🍶 🌱

Black Bean Tree

Australian Black Bean Tree | Australian Chestnut | Baway | Bean Tree | Blackbean | Blackbean Tree | Bogum | Ganyjuu | Irtalie | Junggurraa | Mirrayn | Morton Bay Chestnut | Yiwurra

◉ POTENTIAL MAXIMUM HEIGHT
60 feet [18 meters]

✹ SYMBOLIC MEANINGS
Family; Signal; Supply.

✿ POSSIBLE POWERS
Create oxygen; Gathering; Guidance; Life; Migration.

☘ FOLKLORE AND FACTS
For over 2,500 years the evergreen *Castanospermum australe* Black Bean Tree was known to be a gathering place for many First Nations peoples in Australia during ceremonies because of its food value. • Ancient First Nations peoples planted the Black Bean Tree wherever they migrated around the entire Australian continent. It is so much a part of their culture that the tree is included in several dreaming track song cycles. • A staple bush food of many First Nations Australians, the seed is only edible after several long days of processing, which requires many different vital steps carried out by knowledgeable people to remove its extreme toxicity. Days later, the resulting dough is ultimately shaped and fire-baked into a patty called a "damper" that is usually topped with honey before eating it. • All the Black Bean Trees in New South Wales have one tree in common that they have descended from. The tree seeds also spread via water. • Many First Nations Australians used the wood of the Black Bean Tree to fashion throwing spears for use when hunting. • Children often use empty Black Bean Tree seed pods as toy boats.

No. 085

Castilla elastica

Mexican Rubber Tree

Castilloa Rubber | Caucho | Olicuáhuitl | Palo de Hule | Panama Rubber Tree

◉ POTENTIAL MAXIMUM HEIGHT
131 feet [40 meters]

✹ SYMBOLIC MEANINGS
Abundance; Increase.

✿ POSSIBLE POWERS
Abundance; Bounce; Create oxygen; Fortune; Happiness; Increased energy; Luck; Positive energy; Wealth.

☘ FOLKLORE AND FACTS
In ancient Mesoamerica, the latex sap of the invasive deciduous *Castilla elastica* Mexican Rubber Tree was effectively rubberized by mixing it with *Merremia tuberosa* Woodrose sap. This was done with the purpose of vulcanizing the latex to form it into a ball that will readily bounce. The vulcanized rubberized bouncing ball was used to play a ritualized ball game called *ōllamaliztli*, played by pre-Columbian Mesoamerican peoples since at least 1650 BCE. Rubber balls and ancient ball courts have been found by archaeologists that date far back to that time. • Due to the religious nature of the game, after the Spanish conquest of Mexico, the Catholic missionaries would not allow it to be played. Nevertheless, through it all, ōllamaliztli survived that oppression. It is still played today as a ball game called *ulama*. It is the oldest known sport in the world that is played with a rubber ball called a *chichi* or *chivo*.

No. 086

Casuarina equisetifolia 🦴 ⚰ 🌱

Whistling Pine Tree

Agoho Pine | Australian Pine Tree | Beach Casuarina | Beach Oak | Beach Pine | Beach Sheoak | Coast She-oak | Coastal She-oak | Filao Tree | Horsetail Beefwood | Horsetail She-oak | Horsetail Tree

◉ POTENTIAL MAXIMUM HEIGHT
100 feet [30 meters]

✹ SYMBOLIC MEANING
Horsehair.

✿ POSSIBLE POWERS
Cleansing; Compassion; Create oxygen; Family; Fertility; Healing; Intuition; Motherhood; Spirituality; Tranquility; Warmth; Water element; Wisdom.

C

In a strong breeze, the drooping shaggy branches of the deciduous *Casuarina equisetifolia* Whistling Pine Tree give it the appearance of waving horse tails. • The sound made by the swish of the branches is said to be the whispers of the endearing ancient spirits. • Babies would be placed under a Whistling Pine Tree for the sound to lull them to sleep. • In many parts of the world, *Casuarina equisetifolia* wood is considered to be the best firewood there is because its wood will burn long, slowly, and hot. It will also leave very little ash behind. • When growing along coastlines, *Casuarina equisetifolia* does well to help prevent soil erosion. • A legendary 880-year-old Samoan spear known as Kaumaile was cut from *Casuarina equisetifolia* wood for a South Sea Nanumea Island hero known as Tefolaha. Tefolaha used the spear as a fighting weapon during violent conflicts on Samoa and Tonga. The spear was continuously passed down to Tefolaha's heirs for twenty-three generations. • The *Casuarina equisetifolia* tree leaves and bark have the extraordinary ability to provide a remedy for removing textile dyes and their toxins from wastewater via absorption.

No. 087

Catalpa bignonioides 💀 ☕ 🌱

Southern Catalpa Tree

Catawba | Cigar Tree | Indian Bean Tree | Southern Catalpa

POTENTIAL MAXIMUM HEIGHT
60 feet [18 meters]

SYMBOLIC MEANING
Beware the coquette.

POSSIBLE POWERS
Carving; Create oxygen; Express creativity; Purgative; Reveal enchantments; Uncover mysteries.

FOLKLORE AND FACTS
The *Catalpa bignonioides* Southern Catalpa is a very showy ornamental tree with big heart-shaped leaves and very lovely nectar-secreting flowers that resemble orchids. The flowers are followed by long bean-like seed pods. • Southern Catalpa wood is well suited to boatbuilding, as well as for carving. • As the Southern Catalpa's leaves are the only food consumed by the catalpa sphinx moth, if there is an abundance of caterpillars, the trees can be left completely void of leaves. • Make a white sachet of Catalpa flower and leaf to tuck under the pillow to help center one's spirit within the spirit realm.

No. 088

Catha edulis 💀 ☕ 🌱

Khat Tree

African Tea | Arabian Tea | Bushmans Tea | Cat | Qat | Quat

POTENTIAL MAXIMUM HEIGHT
82 feet [25 meters]

SYMBOLIC MEANING
Contrariness.

POSSIBLE POWERS
Additive stimulation; Create oxygen; Heavy depression.

FOLKLORE AND FACTS
For centuries, people have chewed the leaves of the evergreen *Catha edulis* Khat Tree as a euphoric stimulant that can lead to either a decrease or an increase in depression.

No. 089

Cecropia peltata ☕

Trumpet Tree

Ambaiba Negra | Bacano | Duguná | Guarumbo | Guarumo | Snakewood | Trumpet Bush | Yagrumo | Yarumo

POTENTIAL MAXIMUM HEIGHT
82 feet [25 meters]

SYMBOLIC MEANING
Face with a tail.

POSSIBLE POWERS
Create oxygen; Endurance; Fortitude; Healing; Sound resonance; Speed.

FOLKLORE AND FACTS
One of the most invasive trees is the fast-growing evergreen *Cecropia peltata* Trumpet Tree. It can grow 10 feet (3 m) tall in only one year. Its seeds can remain viable for up to five years. Its large leaves are up to 24 inches (61 cm) wide. • In general, a *Cecropia* tree is also considered to be an "ant plant" because of the symbiotic relationship the tree

has with ants. The vigorous *Azteca* ants continually provide unrivaled protection to the trees from vines and insects that would attack the tree. • Local people make use of the wood to fashion it into musical instruments such as guitars and wooden flutes. The bark fibers can be twisted into ropes.

No. 090

Cedrela odorata 🗡️🍄

Spanish Cedar
Cedro | Cuban Cedar

◉ POTENTIAL MAXIMUM HEIGHT
130 feet [40 meters]

✹ SYMBOLIC MEANING
Sweet scent.

✸ POSSIBLE POWERS
Air element; Awakening; Create oxygen; Dreaming; Enlightenment; Eternal life; Fertility; Fragrance stored clothing; Harmony; Immortality; Incense; Insect repellent; Light; Magic; Masculine energy; Protection; Regeneration; Resurrection; Spiritual consciousness; Spirituality.

✤ FOLKLORE AND FACTS
The wonderfully aromatic wood of the deciduous *Cedrela odorata* Spanish Cedar tree is naturally both rot- and termite-resistant. The fragrance of the wood is

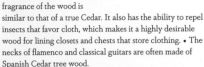

similar to that of a true Cedar. It also has the ability to repel insects that favor cloth, which makes it a highly desirable wood for lining closets and chests that store clothing. • The necks of flamenco and classical guitars are often made of Spanish Cedar tree wood.

No. 091

Cedrus atlantica 🗡️🍄

Atlas Cedarwood Tree
Atlas Cedar | Atlas Deodar

◉ POTENTIAL MAXIMUM HEIGHT
60 feet [18 meters]

✹ SYMBOLIC MEANINGS
Constancy in love; Goals; I live for you; Strength; Think of me.

✸ POSSIBLE POWERS
Air element; Aphrodisiac; Attract love; Awakening; Create oxygen; Cure the tendency to have bad dreams; Dreaming; Fire element; Healing; Incense; Masculine energy; Meditation; Money; Protection; Psychically centering; Purification; Regeneration; Resurrection; Spiritual consciousness; Spiritually grounding; Sun.

✤ FOLKLORE AND FACTS
Place a piece of the evergreen conifer *Cedrus atlantica* Atlas Cedarwood Tree where you usually keep money to attract more. • In 1977 during his residence in the White House, American President Jimmy Carter had a treehouse built for his youngest daughter, Amy Carter, in the Atlas Cedarwood Tree on the South Lawn. It was constructed in such a way as to not cause damage to the tree. • The earthy fragrance of the Atlas Cedarwood essential oil is often used in perfumery. It can also be used as aromatherapy to help ground and center the psyche and spirit throughout a stressful season.

No. 092

Cedrus libani 🗡️🍄🌰

Lebanese Cedar Tree
Cedar of Lebanon | Lebanon Cedar | Taurus Cedar | Tree of the Lord | Turkish Cedar

◉ POTENTIAL MAXIMUM HEIGHT
120 feet [37 meters]

✹ SYMBOLIC MEANINGS
Incorruptibility; Incorruptible.

✸ POSSIBLE POWERS
Air element; Aphrodisiac; Attract love; Awakening; Create oxygen; Cure the tendency to have bad dreams; Dreaming; Fire element; Healing; Incense; Longevity; Masculine energy; Meditation; Money; Power; Protection; Psychically centering; Purification; Regeneration; Resurrection; Spiritual consciousness; Spiritually grounding; Sun.

FOLKLORE AND FACTS

The strength and preciousness of the evergreen *Cedrus libani* Lebanese Cedar Tree's wood have proven its ability to survive for thousands of years. • The Lebanese Cedar Tree has been mentioned in the Christian Bible over seventy times, which has intensified its Christian religious significance. • In Lebanon, the forests of Lebanese Cedar are a constant reminder to the Lebanese people of their great heritage. Time and overharvesting have reduced the great number of forests, with approximately 15 square miles (39 square km) of scattered groves remaining. One famous grove was sectioned off and deemed a preserve in 1876. The grove is known as the Cedars of God. • Push a three-pronged stick of Lebanese Cedar into the ground near your home with the prongs pointed upward to protect your home against all forms of evil. • Place a small piece of Lebanese Cedar wherever you keep your money to attract more.

No. 093

Ceiba pentandra 🌰🌱

Kapok Tree

Balso | Bonga | Bongo | Ceiba | Ceiba Bonga | Ceiba Bruja | Ceiba de Lana | Ceiba Tree | Ceibo | Chivecha | Cumaca | Jabillolano | Java Cotton Tree | Java Kapok | Samauma | Silk-cotton | Silk Cotton Tree | Toborachi | Yuque

📍 POTENTIAL MAXIMUM HEIGHT
50 feet [15 meters]

✴ SYMBOLIC MEANING
Stay afloat.

🌀 POSSIBLE POWERS
Create oxygen; Protection.

🍂 FOLKLORE AND FACTS

The deciduous *Ceiba pentandra* Kapok Tree has seeds that contain an exceptionally buoyant fluff that was once used to stuff life jackets.
• Indigenous groups living along the Amazon use the Kapok Tree's seed fluff to wrap around blowgun darts. This helps thicken the diameter for a better fit and more forceful reactive ejection under pressure.

No. 094

Ceiba speciosa 🌱🌳

Floss Silk Tree

Árbol del Puente | Paineira | Palo Borracho | Samu'ú | Silver Floss Tree | Toborochi

📍 POTENTIAL MAXIMUM HEIGHT
50 feet [15 meters]

✴ SYMBOLIC MEANINGS
Drunken stick; Shelter; Tree of refuge.

🌀 POSSIBLE POWERS
Create oxygen; Healing; Protection.

🍂 FOLKLORE AND FACTS

The pink and white flowers of the deciduous *Ceiba speciosa* Floss Silk Tree are shaped like Hibiscus flowers. The tree's trunk and stems are covered with menacing sharp thorns and prickles which effectively protect it from climbing animals.

No. 095

Celtis occidentalis 🍴🌳

Hackberry Tree

American Hackberry | Beaverwood | Celtis Tree | Common Hackberry | Nettle Tree | Nettletree | Northern Hackberry | Sugarberry

📍 POTENTIAL MAXIMUM HEIGHT
95 feet [29 meters]

✴ SYMBOLIC MEANINGS
Balance; Concert; Unity.

🌀 POSSIBLE POWERS
Balance; Create oxygen; Unification.

🍂 FOLKLORE AND FACTS

The magic of the deciduous *Celtis occidentalis* Hackberry Tree is that it will persuade someone to continuously do their best. • Carry a Hackberry leaf sachet to help balance and unify one's outer and inner selves to help attain one's personal best self. • Hackberry wood will easily rot. • When ripe, the small Hackberries are edible. The berries are highly caloric due to fat, protein, and carbohydrates. They are also easily digestible when raw. • Omaha, Dakota, and Pawnee peoples included Hackberries in their diets either fresh picked or pounded fine and added to other ingredients, such as meat or dried corn.

C

No. 096

Cephalotaxus harringtonia 🐾 🌱 🌿

Plum Yew
Cowtail Pine | Harrington's Cephalotaxus

⚬ **POTENTIAL MAXIMUM HEIGHT**
30 feet [9 meters]

✳ **SYMBOLIC MEANING**
Head.

🌐 **POSSIBLE POWERS**
Create oxygen; Healing.

🜋 **FOLKLORE AND FACTS**
The new shoots of the highly toxic evergreen *Cephalotaxus harringtonia* Plum Yew can stay green for three years. • In 2008, it was discovered that omacetaxine could be extracted from the leaves of the Plum Yew, and since then it has been useful in the development and production of a drug used for treating leukemia.

No. 097

Ceratonia siliqua 🌱 🍴 🌿

Carob Tree
Carob | St. John's Bread

⚬ **POTENTIAL MAXIMUM HEIGHT**
49 feet [15 meters]

✳ **SYMBOLIC MEANINGS**
Affection beyond the grave; Elegance; Love after death.

🌐 **POSSIBLE POWERS**
Create oxygen; Enduring affection; Love; Protection.

🜋 **FOLKLORE AND FACTS**
The evergreen *Ceratonia siliqua* Carob Tree has large, curled pods that will take a year to develop and ripen on the tree. Carob pods are dried and used as a chocolate substitute and as a flavoring. Carob has a somewhat sweet taste and does not contain caffeine. • In Malta and Crete, a Carob syrup known as *gulepp tal-ħarrub* is made from the pods. Carob syrup is also commonly enjoyed in Libya, Portugal, Turkey, Egypt, Spain, and Sicily. Carob liqueur is also made from the syrup. • During ancient times in the Middle East, weighing gold and gemstones against Carob seeds was common. It is the source of the term "carat." • In the nineteenth century it was believed that chewing on Carob pods was a soothing and cleansing throat aid. Thus, it was recommended to singers and sold at British apothecaries. • Wear a Carob seed amulet to guard against evil and maintain good health.

No. 098

Cerbera odollam 🐾

Pong-Pong Tree
Bintaro | Buta-Buta | Famentana | Kattu Arali | Kisopo | Mintolla | Nyan | Othalam | Samanta | Suicide Tree | Tangena

⚬ **POTENTIAL MAXIMUM HEIGHT**
32 feet [10 meters]

✳ **SYMBOLIC MEANINGS**
Final hat; Last hat.

🌐 **POSSIBLE POWERS**
Biofuel; Create oxygen; Death.

🜋 **FOLKLORE AND FACTS**
When it is green, the small fruit of the evergreen *Cerbera odollam* Pong-Pong Tree looks like a small mango. However, the fruit is fatally poisonous. There may be some redemption for its notoriety as a "suicide tree" in that it may be eventually developed and processed as a biofuel for automobiles.

No. 099

Cercidiphyllum japonicum 🌱 🌿

Katsura Tree
Caramel Tree

⚬ **POTENTIAL MAXIMUM HEIGHT**
60 feet [18 meters]

✳ **SYMBOLIC MEANINGS**
God's pathway; Joining of Earth and sky.

POSSIBLE POWERS
Create oxygen; Longevity; Love.

FOLKLORE AND FACTS
The heart-shaped leaves of the endangered deciduous *Cercidiphyllum japonicum* Katsura Tree are edged with the same shade of red as its small flowers. When the leaves fall, they have a sweet caramel or burnt sugar fragrance.
• Although primarily grown for its wood, which is used for woodworking as well as for construction, the Katsura Tree is also a favorite ornamental tree in Japan. • A Katsura Tree growing in Torokawataira, Japan, is over one thousand years old and is known as the "Great Katsura of Wachi."

No. 100

Cercis siliquastrum 🌰🎎

Judas Tree
Betrayal Tree | Judas-tree

🔍 POTENTIAL MAXIMUM HEIGHT
39 feet [12 meters]

☀ SYMBOLIC MEANINGS
Betrayal; Betrayed; Unbelief.

POSSIBLE POWERS
Create oxygen; Enlightenment of deep disappointment.

FOLKLORE AND FACTS
The small deciduous *Cercis siliquastrum* Judas Tree is an exotically beautiful nectar-producing flowering tree.
• Judas Iscariot was said to have hanged himself from this tree, forevermore tagging it with this grim legend.

No. 101

Chamaecyparis obtusa ☠🌰🎎🧒

Hinoki Cypress Tree
Divine Tree | Go-Shin-Boku | Hinoki | Hinoki False Cypress | Japanese Cypress

🔍 POTENTIAL MAXIMUM HEIGHT
75 feet [23 meters]

☀ SYMBOLIC MEANING
Everlasting wisdom.

POSSIBLE POWERS
Create oxygen; Discernment; Emotional; Energy; Everlasting; Incense; Letting go; Longevity; Physical; Purity; Release; Wisdom.

FOLKLORE AND FACTS
The wood of the evergreen *Chamaecyparis obtusa* Hinoki Cypress Tree is of such a high quality that it has been commonly used, among other things, in the construction of special places such as palaces, temples, and shrines in Japan. • It has lemon-scented pinkish-brown lumber and is known to be resistant to bacteria, viruses, fungus, insects, and rot. • One of the Seven Great Temples in Ikaruga, Japan, the Hōryū Gakumonji, or "Learning Temple of the Flourishing Law," was originally constructed in 607 CE from Hinoki Cypress wood. The temple stood for sixty-three years until lightning entirely burned it down. It was rebuilt approximately 1,300 years ago. Its main hall is the remnant of the original temple, which was built from Hinoki Cypress wood. The temple's main hall is the oldest wooden building in the world. • A seven-hundred-year-old Hinoki Cypress can be found growing at the Daichi-ji temple in Gifu, Japan.
• Slivers of the Hinoki Cypress Tree wood are also used as a fragrant stick incense. • Due to the precious nature of and protection given to the sacred Hinoki Cypress Tree, its essential oils can only be extracted after the tree has naturally fallen or died.

C

No. 102

Chilopsis linearis ⚱

Desert Willow

Desert-willow

⬤ **POTENTIAL MAXIMUM HEIGHT**
30 feet [9 meters]

✳ **SYMBOLIC MEANINGS**
Lips; Resemble.

❀ **POSSIBLE POWERS**
Create oxygen; Healing.

❦ **FOLKLORE AND FACTS**
The flower of the deciduous
Chilopsis linearis Desert Willow
tree resembles an orchid. The sweetly
fragrant flowers attract hummingbirds,
butterflies, and bees. • Parts of the Desert
Willow tree are used in traditional medicines that are used to
treat fungal infections.

No. 103

Chionanthus virginicus ☠ ⚱ ⚘

White Fringe Tree

Flowering Ash | Fringe Tree | Grancy Gray Beard | Grandfather Graybeard | Old Man's Beard |
Snowflower Tree

⬤ **POTENTIAL MAXIMUM HEIGHT**
20 feet [6 meters]

✳ **SYMBOLIC MEANING**
Ethereal vision
of spring.

❀ **POSSIBLE POWERS**
Beauty; Create oxygen.

❦ **FOLKLORE AND FACTS**
In early spring, the fragrant
deciduous *Chionanthus*
virginicus White Fringe Tree
blooms the fluffiest, most ethereal-looking flowers, giving
it its name. • The fragrance of the deciduous White Fringe
Tree is similar to lilacs. • The male and female flowers of the
White Fringe Tree are on separate trees.

No. 104

Chiranthodendron pentadactylon ☠ ⚱

Hand-Flower Tree

Árbol de las Manitas | Devil's Hand Tree | Flor de Manita | Hand Flower Tree | Mācpalxōchitl |
Manita Flower Tree | Mexican Hand Tree | Monkey's Hand Tree | Tree of Little Hands

⬤ **POTENTIAL MAXIMUM HEIGHT**
60 feet [18 meters]

✳ **SYMBOLIC MEANINGS**
Five-fingered-hand; Warning.

❀ **POSSIBLE POWERS**
Create oxygen; Hands-on magical proxy.

❦ **FOLKLORE AND FACTS**
The long, thin, pointed petals of open red and yellow flowers
on the evergreen and extremely rare *Chiranthodendron*
pentadactylon Hand-Flower Tree resemble a human or
monkey's hand.

No. 105

Chlorocardium rodiei ☠ ⚱

Greenheart Tree

Bebeeru | Bibiru | Cogwood | Demerara Greenheart | Greenhart | Ispingo Moena | Sipiri

⬤ **POTENTIAL MAXIMUM HEIGHT**
130 feet [40 meters]

✳ **SYMBOLIC MEANING**
Green heart.

❀ **POSSIBLE POWERS**
Create oxygen; Endurance; Power; Strength.

❦ **FOLKLORE AND FACTS**
The wood of the evergreen *Chlorocardium rodiei* Greenheart
Tree is so extremely hard that standard woodworking tools
cannot manage working it. Its extreme durability in water
has made it useful for building docks and bridge pilings.
• Because of its extreme strength, the exteriors of two ships
built to explore the Arctic regions were clad in Greenheart
wood to offer them protection from being crushed by ice.
They were the *Fram*, used by Norwegian explorer Roald
Amundsen, and the *Endurance*, which was used by
Anglo-Irish explorer Ernest Shackleton. They were the two
strongest ships ever built. And yet, Greenheart Tree wood is
so dense that it will not float.

C

No. 106
Chrysobalanus icaco 🪔🍴

Cocoplum Tree
Abajeru | Icaco | Paradise Plum

🔎 **POTENTIAL MAXIMUM HEIGHT**
15 feet [5 meters]

☀ **SYMBOLIC MEANING**
Golden sun fruit.

⚙ **POSSIBLE POWERS**
Create oxygen; Healing; Sea
magic; Water element.

🜨 **FOLKLORE AND FACTS**
The evergreen *Chrysobalanus icaco* Cocoplum Tree can
be found growing near tropical sea beaches. Its ripe fruit is
plump and edible. The fruit can be eaten fresh or cooked,
although it is somewhat tasteless when it is not slightly sweet.
For that reason, it is sometimes used to make jams, jellies, and
syrups. The fruit is sometimes referred to as fat pork. • The
Cocoplum seed within the fruit is dried, then ground into a
powder that is a favored spice in West African cuisine.

No. 107
Chrysolepis chrysophylla 🍴🌱

Giant Chinkapin Tree
Castanopsis | Chechinquamin | Giant Golden Chinquapin | Golden Chinquapin |
Tree Chinquapin | Western Chinquapin

🔎 **POTENTIAL MAXIMUM HEIGHT**
150 feet [46 meters]

☀ **SYMBOLIC MEANING**
Golden leaved.

⚙ **POSSIBLE POWERS**
Create oxygen; Longevity;
Thickening.

🜨 **FOLKLORE AND FACTS**
The evergreen *Chrysolepis chrysophylla* Giant Chinkapin
Tree can live for up to five hundred years. Its flower is white
and smells somewhat musty. Its nut is sweetly chestnut-like
and edible both raw and cooked. The nut looks and tastes
somewhat like a Sweet Chestnut, or even a Hazelnut. It can
be ground into a powder, which can then be used to thicken
soups or mixed with other grains when making breads.
• Giant Chinkapin wood is heavy, strong, and tinged with
pink that is sometimes striped. It is sometimes used for
making furniture.

No. 108
Cinchona officinalis 🪔🍴🌱

Cinchona Tree
Fever Tree | Jesuit's Bark Tree | Jesuit's Powder Tree | Peruvian Bark Tree | Quinine Tree |
Quinquina | Red Cinchona

🔎 **POTENTIAL MAXIMUM HEIGHT**
26 feet [8 meters]

☀ **SYMBOLIC MEANINGS**
Aspiring; Fever breaker.

⚙ **POSSIBLE POWERS**
Boost power to magic working; Break a fever; Create oxygen;
Healing; Luck; Protection; Repels anger or malicious energy;
Resist a spell.

🜨 **FOLKLORE AND FACTS**
The bark of the small, endangered evergreen *Cinchona
officinalis* Cinchona Tree provides quinine, the medicinal
treatment for malaria. Dr. Samuel Hahnemann tested
Cinchona bark, which marked the start of a form of
alternative medicine known as homeopathy around the turn
of the nineteenth century. • The carbonated beverage known
as "tonic water" has the distinctive bitter taste of quinine.
Tonic water originated in British Colonial India by the
British who lived there. They mixed their medicinal-quality,
malaria-preventative and treatment quinine into their gin.
The first tonic water that was available commercially was
made in 1858. It was simply quinine mixed into carbonated
water, with some sugar added to help mask the bitter taste
of the quinine. Nowadays, tonic water is readily available in
public markets to be commonly used as a favorite mixer for
some cocktails. There would be no such thing as a gin and
tonic cocktail without it. Tonic water still contains quinine,
but not as much as it used to, and not for the same malarial
preventative or treatment purposes. • Carry a small piece
of Cinchona Tree bark to protect yourself against evil and
bodily harm.

C

No. 109

Cinnamomum camphora ☠ ⚰ ☠ ❧

White Camphor Tree

Camphire | Camphor Laurel | Camphor Tree | Camphorwood | Chang Nao | Harathi Karpuram | Ho Wood | Kafoor | Kafrovnik Lékarsky | Kapoor | Kapura-gaha | Karpooram | Karpuuram | Kusu No Ki | Nok Na Mu | Paccha Karpoora | Paccha Karpooramu | Pacchaik Karpooram | Pachai Karpuram | Ravintsara | Shajarol-kafoor | Trees of Kafoor | Zhang Shu | Zhangshù

◉ POTENTIAL MAXIMUM HEIGHT
70 feet [21 meters]

☀ SYMBOLIC MEANINGS
Chastity; Divination.

❀ POSSIBLE POWERS
Chastity; Create oxygen; Divination; Emotions; Feminine energy; Fertility; Fumigant; Generation; Insect repellent; Inspiration; Intuition; Moon; Psychic ability; Sea; Subconscious mind; Tides; Travel by water; Water element.

☘ FOLKLORE AND FACTS
During the times of the rampant Black Death in the 1300s, the deciduous *Cinnamomum camphora* White Camphor was valued as a fumigant. • During the fourteenth century, people made infusions of White Camphor with roses and sprinkled them over a corpse before wrapping it within its burial shroud. • White Camphor has been and still is used as an insect repellent to fend off cloth-eating insects from stored clothing.

No. 110

Cinnamomum cassia ⚰ 🍴 ❧

Cassia Tree

Chinese Cassia | Chinese Cinnamon | Wild Cinnamon

◉ POTENTIAL MAXIMUM HEIGHT
60 feet [18 meters]

☀ SYMBOLIC MEANING
Sweet love.

❀ POSSIBLE POWERS
Create oxygen; Encourage self-worth; Healing; Love; Luck; Money; Passion; Power; Prosperity; Protection; Psychic power; Spirituality; Strength; Success.

☘ FOLKLORE AND FACTS
The most common source of cinnamon comes from the evergreen *Cinnamomum cassia* Cassia Tree bark. • When in stick form, *Cinnamomum cassia* is one thick, rolled, hard piece of bark. When finely ground to a powder, it is impossible to discern *Cinnamomum cassia* from *Cinnamomum verum*. • The warm fragrance of Cassia essential oil can encourage healthy feelings of self-worth. • Carry or wear a Cassia sachet to increase spiritual vibrations when meditating. • A Cassia sachet in a gambler's pocket might increase luck at the casino. • A Cassia sachet in a salesperson's pocket can help increase sales. • Carry or wear a Cassia sachet to focus your concentration and stimulate psychic abilities. • Place a pink and red Cassia sachet that you have lovingly made under your mattress to encourage spiritually romantic intimacy and an increase in passionate affection. • Cassia buds resemble cloves and are sometimes used as a seasoning, as well as for brewing tea, adding to marinades, or pickling.

No. 111

Cinnamomum verum ☠ ⚰ 🍴 ❧

Cinnamon Tree

Baker's Cinnamon | Cassia | Ceylon Cinnamon | Chinese Cassia | Chinese Cinnamon | Cinnamon Tree | Sri Lanka Cinnamon | Sweet Wood | True Cinnamon

◉ POTENTIAL MAXIMUM HEIGHT
49 feet [15 meters]

☀ SYMBOLIC MEANINGS
Forgiveness of injuries; Logic; Temptress.

❀ POSSIBLE POWERS
Abundance; Advancement; Aphrodite; Attain higher levels of consciousness; Attract money; Beauty; Business; Conscious will; Create oxygen; Energy; Fire element; Friendship; Good luck; Growth; Healing; Incense; Joy; Leadership; Life; Light; Love; Lust; Masculine energy; Mercury; Moon; Natural power; Passion; Power; Prosperity; Protection; Psychic power; Sanctification; Spirituality; Success; Sun; Uranus; Venus.

☘ FOLKLORE AND FACTS
The edible part of the evergreen *Cinnamomum verum* Cinnamon Tree is the bark, which is used as a flavoring for candies, curries, desserts, pastries, and some meat dishes. It is available as chunked pieces of bark, slivered rolled quills, shorter sticks, or ground. • There is no way to discern

C

whether "ground cinnamon" is inexpensive *Cinnamomum cassia* or the more expensive *Cinnamomum verum* unless it is properly labeled. When in stick form, *Cinnamomum cassia* is one thick, rolled, hard piece of bark. A rolled stick of genuine *Cinnamomum verum* cinnamon is composed of several soft, thin layers of bark. Cinnamon sticks can be easily ground into a fine powder using a spice or coffee grinder. • Ancient Hebrew high priests used Cinnamon oil as a vital ingredient in a holy anointing oil. • The ancient Chinese and Egyptians used Cinnamon to purify their temples. • The ancient Egyptians used Cinnamon as one of their mummification spices. • Cinnamon essential oil can be used for aromatherapy to reduce depression and improve sleeping. • When Cinnamon is used as incense or in a sachet, it provides the power to increase spiritual vibrations, help heal, bring in money, stimulate psychic powers, and provide protection. • The warm fragrance of *Cinnamomum verum* essential oil can encourage healthy feelings of self-worth.

No. 112
Citrus × *aurantiifolia* 🍴 🌿 🌳

Key Lime Tree
Bartender's Lime | Bilolo | *Citrus amblycarpa* | Dayap | *Limonia acidissima* | Mexican Lime | Omani Lime | West Indian Lime

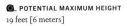

◉ POTENTIAL MAXIMUM HEIGHT
19 feet [6 meters]

✹ SYMBOLIC MEANINGS
Fidelity; Love; Justice.

🌀 POSSIBLE POWERS
Create oxygen; Fire element; Healing; Love; Luck; Marital affection or love; Marriage; Matrimony; Sun; Water element.

☘ FOLKLORE AND FACTS
The evergreen *Citrus* × *aurantiifolia* Key Lime Tree is believed to have originated in Malaysia and eventually carried to the Caribbean, where it became naturalized by the Spanish around the year 1500. • Long before there were other cultivated *Citrus* varieties grown in South Florida, the Key Lime Tree's fruit fulfilled the need for something that was "tart, but not too tart" in cooking. • A ripened-to-yellow Key Lime is still tart but sweeter than a Persian Lime. • Key Lime is the key ingredient in the iconic Key Lime Pie. • Key Lime was also used in beverages for its balanced tartness. The Key Lime flavor shines in the zingy, thirst-quenching Lime Rickey cocktail that became a South Florida favorite among the upper-crust elite in the late 1800s. The rind is also edible, raw or cooked. • Hot Key Lime tea with honey is a worthy home remedy for the sniffles.

No. 113
Citrus × *aurantium* 🍶 🍴 🌿 🌳 🌰

Bitter Orange Tree
Bigarade Orange | Bitter Orange | Daidai | Laraha | Marmalade Orange | Narthangai | Neroli Oil Orange | Raranj | Seville Orange | Sour Orange

◉ POTENTIAL MAXIMUM HEIGHT
29 feet [9 meters]

✹ SYMBOLIC MEANING
Sensual love.

🌀 POSSIBLE POWERS
Aphrodisiac; Attract love; Cleansing; Create oxygen; Deodorize; Fire element; Freshening; Healing; Sun; Water element.

☘ FOLKLORE AND FACTS
The evergreen *Citrus* × *aurantium* Bitter Orange Tree is considered to be a sacred spiritual tree. • Bitter Orange fruit is not usually eaten raw, but it can be and is often juiced. • In Iraq, the Bitter Orange is often juiced to drink as a beverage known as *aseer raranj*. • The juice of a ripe Bitter Orange can also be used in a salad dressing or marinade as a substitute for vinegar. • Bitter Orange is most often used as a flavoring in liqueurs and cooking. The zest can be added to tea. • Dried, powdered Bitter Orange peel is also known as Curaçao orange peel. • In Great Britain the Seville Orange is preferred for marmalade because it has a thicker rind and a high level of pectin. The earliest recipe for marmalade was for "Marmelat of Oranges" that dates back to 1677. • Belgian *witbier* is often spiced with Bitter Orange peel. • The blossoms can be made into a fragrant Persian jam known as *moraba bahar-narenj*. • The wood from a Bitter Orange tree is favored for making Cuban baseball bats. • Bitter Orange essential oil is useful in deodorizing. • The fruit and leaves of the Bitter Orange can lather enough to be used like soap. • Unfortunately, Bitter Orange health food supplements are believed to have been linked to serious cardiovascular side effects.

No. 114
Citrus × *bergamia* 🍶 🍴 🌳

Bergamot Orange Tree
Bergamot | Orange Bergamot | Orange Mint

◉ POTENTIAL MAXIMUM HEIGHT
16 feet [5 meters]

✹ SYMBOLIC MEANINGS
Enchantment; Irresistibility.

C

POSSIBLE POWERS

Air element; Create oxygen; Eliminating interference; Fire element; Healing; Improved memory; Irresistible; Masculine energy; Mercury; Money; Prosperity; Protection from evil or illness; Restful sleep; Success; Sun; Water element.

FOLKLORE AND FACTS

The evergreen *Citrus × bergamia* Bergamot Orange Tree is also known simply as Bergamot. This is not to be confused with *Monarda didyma* Bee Balm, which is also known as Bergamot. • Rub Bergamot Orange leaves on money before spending it to ensure that it comes back to you. • Put a few Bergamot Orange leaves wherever you carry your money, preferably within a wallet, to attract more money to it. • Make a good luck sachet of Bergamot Orange leaves or rind and carry it in your pocket to attract money while gambling at a casino. • Use Bergamot Orange to increase success. • In aromatherapy, Bergamot Orange essential oil helps to lighten a dark mood, especially in times of grief or sadness. • The edible part of the Bergamot Orange is the juice of the fruit, which is very sour and used as a flavoring. • A small amount of the essence that is extracted from its peel is used to lend its distinctive flavor to Earl Grey tea, Lady Grey tea, and the sweet known as Turkish delight. • In Turkey, Bergamot Orange is also used to make a marmalade.

No. 115
Citrus cavaleriei ♉ 🍴 ↙ 🌳

Ichang Papeda Tree
Citrus ichangensis | Shangjuan

POTENTIAL MAXIMUM HEIGHT
15 feet [5 meters]

SYMBOLIC MEANING
Cold will not hinder.

POSSIBLE POWERS
Create oxygen; Fire element; Healing; Sun; Unusual traits; Water element; Withstand cold.

FOLKLORE AND FACTS
The evergreen *Citrus ichangensis*, a variation of Ichang Papeda, is the only other *Citrus* that is as cold hardy as the

Citrus cavaleriei Ichang Papeda Tree. Cold hardiness is an extremely unusual trait for any Citrus. • The fragrant, bumpy-skinned fruit's juice and zest is used as an herb seasoning. Some fruits are so entirely full of seeds that no juice can be extracted from the fruit at all.

No. 116
Citrus hystrix ♉ 🍴 ↙ 🌳

Makrut Lime Tree
Leech Lime | Mauritius Papeda | Thai Lime

POTENTIAL MAXIMUM HEIGHT
19 feet [6 meters]

SYMBOLIC MEANING
Prosperity.

POSSIBLE POWERS
Create oxygen; Fire element; Healing; Leech repellent; Sun; Water element.

FOLKLORE AND FACTS
The evergreen *Citrus hystrix* Makrut Lime Tree's hourglass-shaped leaves and the zest of its fruit's extremely bumpy rind are frequently used as culinary herbs in Asian cuisine whenever acid is needed. • The Makrut Lime's intensely fragrant rind produces an essential oil that is extensively used in perfumery. • There are texts from Sri Lanka dating back to 1868 that indicate Makrut Lime juice was often used as a leech repellent by rubbing it on a person's legs.

No. 117
Citrus × latifolia ♉ 🍴 ↙ 🌳

Persian Lime Tree
Bearss Lime | Page Lime | Pond's Lime | Tahiti Lime

POTENTIAL MAXIMUM HEIGHT
20 feet [6 meters]

SYMBOLIC MEANING
Fornication.

POSSIBLE POWERS
Aphrodisiac; Attract love; Create oxygen; Fire element; Healing; Immortality; Love; Luck; Lust; Protection; Refresh; Refreshment; Sun; Water element.

C

FOLKLORE AND FACTS

The fruit of the evergreen *Citrus × latifolia* Persian Lime Tree will turn yellow as it ripens on the tree. • Persian Lime fruit is harvested and sold as fresh produce while still dark green. • The juice and grated rind are a favorite culinary herb and flavoring ingredient in a variety of foods and beverages. The rind is edible raw or cooked. Limeade is the Persian Lime's version of lemonade. • The Persian Lime Tree's leaf and flower can be used in a love spell. • Carve a good luck charm out of Persian Lime Tree wood. • Citrusy Persian Lime essential oil is used as aromatherapy for invigoration and to uplift a broody mood. • A folk cure for a sore throat was to wrap and tie a string around a whole Persian Lime fruit, to wear as a necklace.

No. 118

Citrus × limon 🐂 🍴 🌿 🌳

Lemon Tree

Bonnie Brae Lemon | Eureka Lemon | Flat Lemon | Four Seasons Lemon | Lemon Tree | Lisbon Lemon | Meyer Lemon | Ponderosa Lemon | Quatre Saisons | Rough Lemon | Sweet Lemon | Ulamula | Variegata Lemon | Volkamer Lemon | Yen Ben Lemon

◉ POTENTIAL MAXIMUM HEIGHT

20 feet [6 meters]

✺ SYMBOLIC MEANINGS

Long-suffering; Patience; Pleasant thoughts; Zest.

🍃 COMPONENT MEANINGS

Blossom: Discretion; Fidelity; Fidelity in love; I promise to be true; Prudence.

🌼 POSSIBLE POWERS

Create oxygen; Feminine energy; Fire element; Friendship; Healing; Longevity; Love; Moon; Protection; Purification; Refresh; Refreshment; Sun; Uplift; Water element.

C. FOLKLORE AND FACTS

The bright yellow evergreen *Citrus × limon* Lemon Tree's fruit, juice, zest, and outer peel are edible raw or cooked. The leaf can be used in recipes like a Bay leaf. • Lemon juice can be used to tenderize meat and as a common substitute for vinegar in recipes. • Meyer Lemons have a sweeter and floral lemony flavor over other Lemons, making it a special favorite for use in baking. The zest of the Lemon rind is frequently used in baking and cooking rice dishes, puddings, and soups. • During a Full Moon, Lemon juice can be added to the bath for purification. • Secret messages can be written in Lemon juice on paper to be revealed later using heat. • Lemon was first referenced in a tenth-century Arabic document on farming. • Christopher Columbus brought Lemon Tree seeds to Hispaniola. • For a lasting friendship, place a slice of Lemon under your friend's chair when they visit your home. • Lemon essential oil has been used for centuries to uplift, energize, and refresh a slumped mood.

No. 119

Citrus × limonia 🐂 🍴 🌿 🌳

Rangpur Tree

Lemandarin | Mandarin Lime | Rangpur Lime

◉ POTENTIAL MAXIMUM HEIGHT

20 feet [6 meters]

✺ SYMBOLIC MEANING

Sturdy foundation.

🌼 POSSIBLE POWERS

Air element; Create oxygen; Fire element; Happiness; Healing; Longevity; Magical energy; Money; Moon; Physical energy; Protection; Purification; Refreshment; Rejuvenation; Stability; Sun; Water element.

C. FOLKLORE AND FACTS

The evergreen *Citrus × limonia* Rangpur Tree's fruit is a cross between the Citron and the Mandarin Orange, which results in an intensely sour, Mandarin Orange-looking fruit that is a perfectly suitable tart substitute for any recipe, cocktail, or beverage that calls for Lemon or Lime. • Rangpur is a common *Citrus* used in Indian cuisine. • The Rangpur was brought to Florida by seed from India in the late nineteenth century.

No. 120

Citrus maxima 🐂 🍴 🌿 🌳

Pomelo Tree

Jambola | Pomélo | Pommelo | Pumelo | Pummelo | Shaddock

◉ POTENTIAL MAXIMUM HEIGHT

20 feet [6 meters]

✺ SYMBOLIC MEANINGS

Biggest; Bless you; Family unity; Largest; Traveler.

🌼 POSSIBLE POWERS

Blessings; Cleansing; Create oxygen; Fire element; Good luck; Happiness; Healing; Moon; Prosperity; Refresh; Status; Sun; Unity; Uplifting; Water element.

FOLKLORE AND FACTS

The fruit of the evergreen *Citrus maxima* Pomelo Tree is the largest *Citrus* fruit. • It is very much like a sweet Grapefruit, and similarly, the Pomelo may adversely affect medication absorption. • Pomelo is a favorite fruit to serve at Chinese celebrations such as the Mid-Autumn Festival. It is also used as a decoration, with two preferred to display, one for good luck and one to represent family unity. Another celebration is during the Lunar New Year when Pomelo fruit is displayed and eaten to bring good luck and money into the household. • One Pomelo can provide several days' worth of vitamin C. • You don't eat the Pomelo membrane along with its juicy segments like you might when you eat a Grapefruit or Orange. • The Pomelo's very large size does not particularly affect the acidity of the juice, but it certainly does provide much more of it. • Pomelo essential oil is helpful in aromatherapy for soothing the flustered mind, relieving stress, and alleviating depression.

No. 121

Citrus medica 🗡️ 🌡️ ☘️ 🌳

Citron Tree
Etrog

⬤ POTENTIAL MAXIMUM HEIGHT
15 feet [5 meters]

✴ SYMBOLIC MEANINGS
Estrangement; Ill-natured beauty; Tradition.

✺ POSSIBLE POWERS
Air element; Create oxygen; Fire element; Healing; Masculine energy; Psychic power; Sun; Water element.

☙ FOLKLORE AND FACTS
The evergreen *Citrus medica* Citron Tree is an original species of three *Citrus* trees from which all other *Citrus* was eventually developed. The others are the Pomelo and the Mandarin Orange. • Citron is an acidic fruit that is edible. Citron peel is often candied. However, the fruit is primarily used as a flavoring. • *Citrus medica* is the most tender of all the *Citrus* species, and it is primarily cultivated in tropical and subtropical home gardens. • Citron is one of the fruits required for rituals during the Jewish Feast of Tabernacles, or Sukkot.

No. 122

Citrus medica var. *sarcodactylis* 🗡️ 🌡️ ☘️

Buddha's Hand Citron Tree
Buddha's Hand | Bushu-Kan | Fingered Citron | Flesh-fingered Citron | Fo Shou Kan | Fou Shou Gan

⬤ POTENTIAL MAXIMUM HEIGHT
15 feet [5 meters]

✴ SYMBOLIC MEANINGS
Happiness; Long life.

✺ POSSIBLE POWERS
Create oxygen; Fire element; Happiness; Longevity; Sun; Water element.

☙ FOLKLORE AND FACTS
The utterly frost-sensitive evergreen *Citrus medica* var. *sarcodactylis* Buddha's Hand Citron Tree can only grow in a completely frost-free area. • The peculiar Buddha's Hand Citron is often considered to be the weirdest fruit of all, as it splits into finger-like sections to resemble a human hand. It has no juice and barely any pulp at all. • The wonderfully aromatic fruit is used for perfuming clothing and rooms in China and Japan. • It is commonly used as a thoughtful sacrifice on temple altars. • The fruit is also eaten as a dessert or used as an herbal ingredient in savory dishes.

No. 123

Citrus × paradisi 🗡️ 🌡️ ☘️ 🌳

Grapefruit Tree
Aranja | Grapefrugt | Grapefrukt | Greibipuu | Greip-Frout | Greipfrut | Greipfrüts | Greippi | Grejp | Grenivka | Grep | Grepfrut | Grépfrút | Greyfurt | Toranja | Toronja

⬤ POTENTIAL MAXIMUM HEIGHT
23 feet [7 meters]

✴ SYMBOLIC MEANINGS
Bitterness; Fire element; Mental problems; Successful independence; Sun; Water element.

✺ POSSIBLE POWERS
Create oxygen; Healing; Independence from a person or thing; Moon; Refresh; Refreshment; Sun; Uplifting; Water element.

C

FOLKLORE AND FACTS

The evergreen *Citrus × paradisi* Grapefruit Tree grows as white, pink, or red varieties. • The fruit is often eaten from a whole, fresh Grapefruit that has been halved, sprinkled over with granulated sugar or drizzled with honey, and the segments scooped out, one by one, with a special serrated grapefruit spoon. • In Costa Rica, Grapefruit is cooked to reduce its sourness to the degree that it becomes confection-like. • Grapefruit rind is edible raw or cooked. • In 1750, Griffith Hughes, a Welsh reverend, first referenced a Grapefruit hybrid called "forbidden fruit" in his book about Barbados. • The fragrance of Grapefruit essential oil in aromatherapy is uplifting. • Grapefruit juice is known to adversely affect the proper absorption of some medications by increasing or decreasing the medication's intended effects within the body.

No. 124

Citrus × reticulata

Mandarin Orange Tree
Clementine | Mandarine

◉ POTENTIAL MAXIMUM HEIGHT
15 feet [5 meters]

✻ SYMBOLIC MEANINGS
Abundance; Fire element; Gold; Good fortune; Life; Money; New beginning; Potential for better experiences; Prayers; Richness; Sun; Water element; Wishes for good fortune.

✼ POSSIBLE POWERS
Abundance; Cheer; Create oxygen; Fire element; Good fortune; Healing; Improvement; Prosperity; Sun; Warmth; Wealth.

C. FOLKLORE AND FACTS
The evergreen *Citrus × reticulata* Mandarin Orange Tree has been cultivated in China for over three thousand years. • The Mandarin Orange was carefully cultivated with cross-pollinations between other *Citrus* varieties to ultimately be what we think of today as the Mandarin Orange. • The Mandarin Orange is a sacred plant in China. • The dried peel of the Mandarin Orange is also used as a spice called *chenpi*. This spice is used in traditional Chinese medicine to regulate the flow of qi, or vital energy which is also spelled in English as chi or ki. • Mandarin Oranges from Japan have become a traditional Christmastime gift in the USA, Great Britain, Canada, and Russia. • It became a tradition to put three Mandarin Oranges in a Christmas stocking instead of the earlier tradition of three gold coins.

• In China during the Lunar New Year celebrations, Mandarin Oranges are traditional decorations and gifts. • Mandarin Orange essential oil can be used for aromatherapy to help reduce nervousness and clear the mind.

No. 125

Citrus × sinensis

Sweet Orange Tree
Apelsin | Apelsinas | Apelsinipuu | Apelsins | Apfelsine | Appelsien | Appelsiini | Appelsin | Blood Orange | Cara Cara | Juice Orange | Navel Orange | Orange Tree | Red-fleshed Navel | Valencia Orange

◉ POTENTIAL MAXIMUM HEIGHT
29 feet [9 meters]

✻ SYMBOLIC MEANINGS
Eternal love; Generosity; Good fortune; Good luck; Innocence; Virginity.

✼ COMPONENT MEANINGS
Blossom: Bridal festivities; Brings wisdom; Chastity; Eternal love; Fruitfulness; Good fortune; Innocence; Marriage; Your purity equals your loveliness.

✼ POSSIBLE POWERS
Create oxygen; Divination; Energizing; Fire element; Good fortune; Healing; Love; Luck; Masculine energy; Money; Protection; Sun; Water element.

C. FOLKLORE AND FACTS
The evergreen *Citrus × sinensis* Sweet Orange Tree was never wild. It is the most cultivated fruit in the world. • During the Victorian era, brides carried fresh Sweet Orange blossoms whenever possible. It was common for a bride to wear a crowning wreath of the flowers, on which her bridal veil was attached. • The Chinese consider the Sweet Orange to be a symbol of good luck and good fortune. • Chinese writings referenced the Sweet Orange Tree in 314 BCE. • France's Louis XIV adored the Sweet Orange and had a fabulous orangery cultivated in the beautiful gardens at his Château de Versailles where potted Sweet Orange Trees grew indoors throughout the entire palace. • The Spanish conquistadores introduced Sweet Oranges to North America. • Beehives placed in fruit groves produce the delicate and orangey delicious Orange Blossom Honey that is sold in just about every souvenir gift shop and grocery store throughout Florida and California. • Sweet Orange blossom petals are

mixed with water to make Orange Blossom Water or Orange Flower water, which is a Sweet Orange version of rosewater. • In Spain, the fallen petals of Sweet Orange blossoms are gathered, dried, and used to brew an herbal tea. • The orangewood sticks that manicurists use are made from wood taken from the Sweet Orange Tree. • Sadly, at least ninety percent of the beloved, iconic Sweet Orange groves that once grew prolifically in South Florida are now either dead or actively dying from a devastating plague brought on by a lethal and incurable bacterium called *huanglongbing*, which means "yellow dragon sickness" and is also called citrus greening disease or yellow shoot disease. All *Citrus* trees are affected by this bacterium. • Huanglongbing was first discovered in China. The disease was introduced to South Florida where it was spread from tree to tree by another invasive species: a tiny insect known as the Asian citrus psyllid that draws the bacteria into its body as it feeds. The bacteria is then carried from tree to tree, leaf to leaf. There has been an intense, concerted effort to find a way to battle this crisis, but sadly, the bacteria and the insect both appear to still be winning the futile war. This crisis with the Sweet Orange Trees is happening not only in Florida, but anywhere Sweet Orange and other *Citrus* trees are cultivated, such as California, Brazil, Cuba, Mexico, and Belize. • In Florida, grove owners were dealt a terrible blow when they lost their *Citrus* trees to huanglongbing. In an effort to recover the *extreme* financial losses, many of the devastated *Citrus* groves have been replanted with Mango trees.

No. 126

Citrus sphaerocarpa 🪵🍴🌿🌳

Kabosu Papeda Tree

Papeda Kabosu

🔴 POTENTIAL MAXIMUM HEIGHT
15 feet [5 meters]

✹ SYMBOLIC MEANING
Coveted.

🌐 POSSIBLE POWERS
Create oxygen; Fire element; Healing; Sun; Water element.

🜨 FOLKLORE AND FACTS
The evergreen *Citrus sphaerocarpa* Kabosu Papeda Tree was brought into Japan at least three hundred years ago. • Its fruit is used in Japanese cuisine as an acidic herb. • There are a few two hundred-year-old trees that are still producing fruit. • Some farm-raised fish food mixes have Kabosu Papeda blended into it.

No. 127

Citrus sudachi 🪵🍴🌿🌳

Sudachi Tree

Sudashi

🔴 POTENTIAL MAXIMUM HEIGHT
9 feet [3 meters]

✹ SYMBOLIC MEANING
Vinegar citrus.

🌐 POSSIBLE POWERS
Create oxygen; Fire element; Healing; Sun; Water element.

🜨 FOLKLORE AND FACTS
The evergreen *Citrus sudachi* Sudachi Tree's fruit is green like a Lime and just as tart. • Sudachi has been used as a Japanese flavoring and condiment for hundreds of years.

No. 128

Citrus tachibana 🪵🍴🌳

Tachibana Orange Tree

Citrus junos | Japanese Lemon | Yamoto Tachibana | Yuzu Citron Tree

🔴 POTENTIAL MAXIMUM HEIGHT
39 feet [12 meters]

✹ SYMBOLIC MEANING
Wild orange.

🌐 POSSIBLE POWERS
Bulk; Create oxygen; Fire element; Healing; Heft; Sun; Water element.

🜨 FOLKLORE AND FACTS
The evergreen *Citrus tachibana* Tachibana Orange Tree grows wild in Japanese forests and is one of the oldest *Citrus* species in Japan. • The common name of the Tachibana Orange was referred to in early Japanese poetry that can be dated back to the sixth century CE. • Fish farmers use Tachibana Orange extract in the water to improve the size and weight of farm-raised fish.

No. 129

Citrus × tamurana 🪵🍴🌳

Hyuganatsu Tree

Konatsu | New Summer Orange | Tosakonatsu

🔴 POTENTIAL MAXIMUM HEIGHT
9 feet [3 meters]

C

※ **SYMBOLIC MEANINGS**
Happy surprise; Summer.

❀ **POSSIBLE POWERS**
Create oxygen; Fire element; Sun; Uplifting; Water element.

🜨 **FOLKLORE AND FACTS**
The evergreen *Citrus × tamurana* Hyuganatsu was first found in a Japanese garden in the 1820s. The surprising hybrid seems to have occurred naturally between a Yuzu and a Pomelo. • The Hyuganatsu is a combination of Hyūga, the ancient name of the place where the tree was discovered, and *natsu*, a word for summer.

No. 130
Citrus × tangelo 🐂🍴🌳

Tangelo Tree
Honeybell Tangelo | Minneola Tangelo | Orlando Tangelo

◗ **POTENTIAL MAXIMUM HEIGHT**
12 feet [4 meters]

※ **SYMBOLIC MEANING**
Uniquely rare.

❀ **POSSIBLE POWERS**
Create oxygen; Fire element; Good fortune; Love; Luck; Masculine energy; Money; Protection; Sun; Water element.

🜨 **FOLKLORE AND FACTS**
The evergreen *Citrus × tangelo* Tangelo Tree is a cross between a Mandarin and a Grapefruit. There has been no evidence that the Tangelo affects medications in the same potentially adverse way as Grapefruit does. • The juicy, easy-to-peel Tangelo fruit looks like a large Mandarin Orange with a characteristic protruding nipple.

No. 131
Citrus tangerina 🐂🍴🌳

Tangerine Tree
Kid Glove Orange | Mandarin | Zipper Skin Dancy

◗ **POTENTIAL MAXIMUM HEIGHT**
25 feet [8 meters]

※ **SYMBOLIC MEANINGS**
Abundant happiness; Fire element; Life; New beginning; Potential for better experiences; Prayers; Sun; Water element; Wishes for good fortune.

❀ **POSSIBLE POWERS**
Air element; Calm nervousness; Cheer; Create oxygen; Fire element; Improvement; Prosperity; Sun; Warmth.

🜨 **FOLKLORE AND FACTS**
The evergreen *Citrus tangerina* Tangerine tree has been cultivated in China for over three thousand years. The child-friendly, easy-to-peel juicy sweet Tangerine is very closely related to the Mandarin Orange, although the Tangerine tends to be sweeter, has much more of a squat shape, and has a peel that is quite a bit looser and comes away with less fuss. Because the Mandarin Orange and Tangerine are so closely related it seems that the Mandarin is the one most available in nearly every market these days. Older people, who as children regularly enjoyed Tangerines, can easily differentiate between the two fruits. • Tangerine essential oil is helpful when used in aromatherapy to help calm nerves and clear the mind of cluttered, nerve-wracking thoughts.

No. 132
Cladrastis kentukea 🌳

American Yellowwood Tree
Kentucky Yellowwood | Virgilia

◗ **POTENTIAL MAXIMUM HEIGHT**
75 feet [23 meters]

※ **SYMBOLIC MEANING**
Fragile.

❀ **POSSIBLE POWERS**
Create oxygen; Rarities.

🜨 **FOLKLORE AND FACTS**
As one of the rarest of the Eastern North American flowering trees, the deciduous *Cladrastis kentukea* American Yellowwood Tree's largest remaining specimen was found in Cincinnati, Ohio, at a national landmark that dates back to 1844, known as Spring Grove Cemetery. • The white American Yellowwood Tree flowers grow on long drooping panicles and are attractive to hummingbirds and bees. • A yellow fabric dye was once extracted from the roots by settlers in the southern Appalachians mountains who would also sometimes fashion their gunstocks from the bright yellow Kentucky Yellowwood. • Wood from long-ago felled Kentucky Yellowwood trees has been used conservatively for special decorative woodworked items.

C

Clusia rosea 🐾☠️🏺

Autograph Tree

Balsam Apple | Copey | Cupey | Gal Goraka | Gal Idda | Pitch-apple | Scotch Attorney

🌑 POTENTIAL MAXIMUM HEIGHT
30 feet [9 meters]

🌟 SYMBOLIC MEANING
Validation.

🍄 POSSIBLE POWERS
Commitment; Create oxygen; Identity; Indelibility; Memories; Validate.

🌿 FOLKLORE AND FACTS
With its seeds easily spread by the birds who readily consume the fruit, the evergreen *Clusia rosea* Autograph Tree is considered the most invasive tree in Sri Lanka and Hawaii. • *Clusia rosea* begins its life as an epiphyte. Where it will grow commences when a bird drops a *Clusia rosea* seed, the seed falls into the crooked branches of any other tree, and then stays there. Once the *Clusia rosea* seed germinates, it will begin to send its own aerial roots down the host tree. As soon as the first root reaches the ground, the root will begin to draw up the nutrients it needs. The *Clusia rosea* will continue to grow. The strangled host tree will not be growing as fast as the *Clusia rosea*, and will eventually become quite constricted by the *Clusia rosea* roots that have become established in the ground. At that point, *Clusia rosea* simply takes over and the host tree weakens until it has completely died. What is left standing is the *Clusia rosea* Autograph Tree. • Uniquely, the *Clusia rosea* is one of the only types of plants that will absorb carbon dioxide throughout the nighttime. • The leaves of the Autograph Tree are paddle-like, leathery, thick, and able to be shuffled in the hands. • In the West Indies, Spanish conquistadores marked the leaves with appropriate symbols and readily used them as playing cards. • The leaves of the Autograph Tree are sometimes signed with a sharp object like a pin, which remains on the leaf while the tree is still growing. • In some places, the tree is deliberately planted on beaches to help thwart erosion.

Coccoloba uvifera 🏺🍴🌱

Sea Grape

Bay Grape | Baygrape

🌑 POTENTIAL MAXIMUM HEIGHT
50 feet [15 meters]

🌟 SYMBOLIC MEANINGS
Grape bearer of the shore; Protector.

🍄 POSSIBLE POWERS
Create oxygen; Light shielding; Protection; Protective; Sea magic; Tan leather; Wishing.

🌿 FOLKLORE AND FACTS
The highly salt- and wind-tolerant evergreen *Coccoloba uvifera* Sea Grape can withstand the trials and tribulations of an extreme seaside existence in South Florida, but will barely survive a shiver of frost. • The male and the female Sea Grape flowers are on completely separate trees. Pollination is achieved with the help of bees.  • Unable to withstand storage, the ripened, purplish-red seeds of the Sea Grape must be planted immediately. • Wherever turtles hatch, all of the taller Sea Grape trees and shrubs along populated coastlines can do much to help block some of the lights that buildings cast onto the sandy beaches. The lights easily confuse baby turtles who are instinctively responding to the full moon's light that has guided newly hatched turtles to the saltwater sea for millions of years. • The Sea Grape plays an integral part in preventing coastal soil erosion and dune stabilization. • Sea Grape wood can make a reddish vegetable dye. • On a day when the sea is calm, wishes can be written on the Sea Grape leaves and floated off into the ocean. The wishing leaves can also be sent out from off a boat. • Sea Grape plant sap has been used in leather tanning and dying. • The edible parts of the Sea Grape are the grape-like clusters of green berries that slowly ripen to a purplish color when they can be eaten raw, made into jelly or jam, or into wine.

No. 135

Cocos nucifera 🌱 🍴

Coconut Palm

Côca | Coco | Cocoanut | Indian Nut | Maypan Coconut | Niyog | Wish Fulfilling Tree

📷 **POTENTIAL MAXIMUM HEIGHT**

100 feet [30 meters]

✴ **SYMBOLIC MEANINGS**

Chastity; Goodness of life; Luster; Purity.

🌸 **POSSIBLE POWERS**

Breaking ego; Chastity; Create oxygen; Exposing purity;
Feminine energy; Life's completeness; Moon; Protection;
Purification; Revelation of purity; Water element.

🍃 **FOLKLORE AND FACTS**

The evergreen *Cocos nucifera* Coconut Palm tree is the
global iconic image that symbolizes the tropics and sparks
the urge to take a get-away vacation to a sunny beach. It is
the only living species of the *Cocos* genus. • The Coconut
fruit is not a huge nut at all. It is a drupe, like a Peach or a
Plum. • For protection, hang a whole Coconut fruit in the
home. Or, cut one in half and fill it with other appropriate
protection such as leaves, seeds, petals, and such. Close the
halves and reseal it by any means. Bury it on your property
and leave it there. • Wherever the Coconut Palm grows it
has often been considered to be one of the trees of life. This
is because, for thousands of years, the Coconut Palm has
been tremendously contributing to human civilization as
food, oil, building materials, weaving fibers, medicine, and so
much more. • Coconut Palm trees can be stricken and killed
by a disease called lethal yellowing, which will occasionally
infect trees and cause the crown of the palm to yellow,
die, and entirely fall off, leaving behind a frond-less trunk
that will never recover. • Coconut oil and Coconut butter
soothes and softens dry, chapped, and chafed skin. • If you
shake a Coconut and there is no splashing to be felt within
it, don't bother to open it. • The outer husk of the Coconut
fruit is very difficult to
remove whether it
is green or dried
brown. Some who
are well practiced
at removing it can
make it theatrically
entertaining. They
can make it look
so easy. It is not.

No. 136

Coffea arabica 🌱 🍴

Arabica Coffee Tree

Arabian Coffee | Charrier Coffee | *Coffea canephora* | *Coffea charrieriana* | *Coffea liberica* |
Coffee Bean Tree | Liberica Coffee | Robusta Coffee

📷 **POTENTIAL MAXIMUM HEIGHT**

15 feet [5 meters]

✴ **SYMBOLIC MEANINGS**

Alertness; Camaraderie;
Friendship; Sociability.

🌸 **POSSIBLE POWERS**

Change; Clearing; Courage;
Create oxygen;
Dispels negative
thinking; Fluctuation;
Grounding; Helps
keep away a nightmare;
Liberation; Make a new
friend; Mercy; Overcomes
a thought blockade; Peace of
mind; Sociability; Victory.

🍃 **FOLKLORE AND FACTS**

The evergreen *Coffea arabica* Arabica Coffee Tree is
believed to be the first species of coffee ever cultivated. The
most gourmet and expensive Coffee beans are almost always
of the *Arabica* variety. • In the twelfth century, coffee was
discovered in Yemen, where scholars wrote how it was made
into a beverage brewed from roasted coffee beans, and that
drinking the beverage helped them work longer. From there,
coffee was introduced to Egypt and Turkey, and then all
around the world. • The trees are pruned to keep them at the
smaller size that will facilitate the unhindered management
and harvest of the berries. • Between two and four years
after planting, the trees will flower. The blossoms are very
sweet smelling and resemble the scent of jasmine flowers.
• When the berries ripen, they are colored a deep glossy
red and are called "cherries." They are then ready to harvest
by hand, because the berries do not ripen all at the same
time. Afterwards, the processing begins, as the interior of
the berries, which are the "seeds" or "beans," are specifically
roasted to attain the desired end result. • Coffee beans can
be made into a confection by coating them in chocolate.
• A method of immediately clearing a scent from the nose is
to sniff coffee beans, either whole or ground. • When feeling
under the weather, the fragrance of coffee essential oil can
be uplifting.

C

No. 137

Cola acuminata ⚷ 🍴

Kola Nut Tree
Bissy Nut | Cola Nut | Kola

◎ POTENTIAL MAXIMUM HEIGHT
65 feet [20 meters]

✹ SYMBOLIC MEANINGS
Friendship; Hospitality;
Respect.

✺ POSSIBLE POWERS
Alertness; Create oxygen;
Diminish fatigue;
Increase stamina.

☙ FOLKLORE AND FACTS
The evergreen *Cola acuminata* Kola Nut Tree's "nut" is not
a true nut, but the seed removed from the center of the Kola
fruit. • Kola nut seeds can produce a caffeinated extract that
is used as a natural food flavoring for some soft drinks and
energy beverages. • The seed nut is sacred to the Igbo people
of southeastern Nigeria. Kola nuts form an integral part in
important social events, such as weddings, baby naming
ceremonies, and funerals. These events always include the
important plate of Kola nuts, where visitors receive a nut
that is blessed with a charm spell. The nut seed is broken
open and the number of the seed's pieces reveal the level of
prosperity in the charm. However, if the nut breaks into
two pieces, something sinister will happen. • The Kola
seeds originally gave Coca-Cola® its unique flavor and
caffeine kick.

No. 138

Combretum micranthum ☠ ⚷

Kinkeliba Tree
Kinkeliba | Sekhew | Tisane de Longue Vie

◎ POTENTIAL MAXIMUM HEIGHT
33 feet [10 meters]

✹ SYMBOLIC MEANING
Health tree.

✺ POSSIBLE POWERS
Create oxygen; Healing; Infuse long life.

☙ FOLKLORE AND FACTS
The deciduous *Combretum micranthum* Kinkeliba Tree
grows on the savannas of southern Africa. • Kinkeliba Trees
are resistant to drought and fire. Its wood is also strong and

useful in building practical items for the home. Regardless of
the practical uses of its wood, the Kinkeliba Tree is primarily
cultivated for medicinal purposes. Its leaf, root, and stem
extracts are considered to be powerful and vital in the
practice of Nigerian folk medicine.

No. 139

Commiphora gileadensis ⚷ 🌿 ☘

Balm of Gilead Tree
Arabian Balsam Tree | Balm of Gilead | Balm of Mecca Tree | Balsam of Gilead Tree | Balsam of
Mecca Tree

◎ POTENTIAL MAXIMUM HEIGHT
13 feet [4 meters]

✹ SYMBOLIC MEANINGS
Healing perfume; Impatience;
Rare perfume.

⚘ COMPONENT MEANINGS
Resin: Cure; Healing;
 I am cured; Love;
 Manifestations;
 Protection; Relief;
 Universal cure.

✺ POSSIBLE POWERS
Binding; Building;
Create oxygen; Death; Feminine
energy; Healing; History; Knowledge; Limitations; Love;
Manifestations; Obstacles; Perfumery; Protection; Relief from
distress after losing a loved one; Time; Venus; Water element.

☙ FOLKLORE AND FACTS
The evergreen *Commiphora gileadensis* Balm of Gilead Tree
is a sacred holy tree that dates back to Biblical times. Balm of
Gilead is a rare perfume that may have first been referenced
in the Bible's Book of Genesis, but it may not have been.
Until proven otherwise, it can be believed to have indeed
been the Balm of Gilead Tree. • There is a legend that the
Queen of Sheba gifted King Solomon with many fantastic
things, one of them a Balm of Gilead root that King Solomon
supposedly personally planted in his garden at Jericho.
• Cleopatra brought Balm of Gilead to Egypt and planted
it in a Cairo district known as Ain-Shams, where it is
believed to have flourished in a garden. The legend about
that particular tree and that particular garden continues,
when, after taking refuge in Egypt, Jesus's mother, Mary,
washed baby Jesus's swaddling clothes in a village spring
at Ain-Shams before returning to Palestine. The legend is
that, from then onward, the Balm of Gilead Trees of Cairo
would only produce secretions if they were growing on land

C

watered by that particular spring. • The soldiers of Rome brought Balm of Gilead Trees home as exotic gifts given to Emperor Vespasian in 79 CE. The emperor considered them a magnificent prize, which they surely were. When two groves of the Balm of Gilead Trees were threatened by an invasion, he placed them under armed guards to protect them from potential destruction. • The best-quality sap from the trees is gathered from slow trickles bleeding from carefully expert-made cuts in the bark before the Balm of Gilead Tree fruits. • In ancient times, Balm of Gilead was also used by young women as a fragrance because it had the proven power to seduce men. • In the Catholic Church's sacrament of confirmation, the anointing oil called chrism is a combination of Olive oil and the sacred holy Balm of Gilead. • Balm of Gilead tears, or drops of dried resin, can be used to help de-stress and heal from the trauma of losing a loved one. • Currently, the *Commiphora gileadensis* Balm of Gilead Tree grows wild in certain areas of Saudi Arabia. • Wear or carry a sachet of Balm of Gilead Tree buds to help mend a broken heart.

No. 140
Commiphora myrrha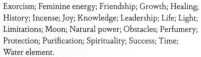
Myrrh Tree
African Myrrh | Common Myrrh | Gum Myrrh | Herabol Myrrh | Somali Myrrhor

POTENTIAL MAXIMUM HEIGHT
16 feet [5 meters]

SYMBOLIC MEANING
Gladness.

POSSIBLE POWERS
Abundance; Advancement; Binding; Building; Conscious will; Create oxygen; Death; Energy; Exorcism; Feminine energy; Friendship; Growth; Healing; History; Incense; Joy; Knowledge; Leadership; Life; Light; Limitations; Moon; Natural power; Obstacles; Perfumery; Protection; Purification; Spirituality; Success; Time; Water element.

FOLKLORE AND FACTS
Throughout history, sacred Myrrh has been treasured as a medicine, an incense, and a perfume. • It is harvested as a sap that is bled from the evergreen *Commiphora myrrha* Myrrh Tree by making multiple cuts into the bark to weep the waxy gum. After it is collected, the gum hardens to a glossy resin that is further processed to extract the viscous essential oil. • According to the Gospel of Matthew in the New Testament, Myrrh was one of the three precious gifts

presented to the newborn Jesus of Nazareth by one of the three Magi who, it was written, had traveled there from some unnamed land far to the east of Bethlehem. • In aromatherapy, Myrrh essential oil creates a relaxing, uplifting atmosphere for meditation and prayer. • The name Myrrh is also applied to *Myrrhis odorata*, which is commonly known as sweet cicely. The two plants are completely unrelated to each other.

No. 141
Conocarpus lancifolius
Qalab Tree
Damas | Ghalab

POTENTIAL MAXIMUM HEIGHT
99 feet [30 meters]

SYMBOLIC MEANING
Button.

POSSIBLE POWERS
Boat building; Create oxygen; Fire making; Protection; Soil cleansing.

FOLKLORE AND FACTS
The evergreen *Conocarpus lancifolius* Qalab Tree is a salt- and drought-resistant tree. It is fast growing, has dense wood and is a favorite for use as firewood and charcoal. • It is also well suited as a durable timber for shipbuilding and for use as adequate windbreaks. • The crushed leaves are sometimes used as a fish poison. • Research into the *Conocarpus lancifolius*'s ability to efficiently remove heavy metals from oil-contaminated soil has been positive and extremely promising.

No. 142
Copernicia prunifera
Brazilian Wax Palm
Carnaúba Palm | Carnauba Wax Palm | Carnaubeira Palm

POTENTIAL MAXIMUM HEIGHT
33 feet [10 meters]

SYMBOLIC MEANINGS
Glaring; Gleaming.

POSSIBLE POWERS
Conservation; Create oxygen; Polish; Protection; Shine; Sustainability.

Because of its immense usefulness, the evergreen *Copernicia prunifera* Brazilian Wax Palm is known as a Tree of Life. • The Brazilian Wax Palm can live for two hundred years. • In the wild, the trees will grow in clustered groups along rivers and streams. • The bees frequent the flowers to gather nectar and pollen. The seeds are spread by the wild creatures of nature that enjoy the fruit. The fruit is a favorite food of birds and bats that can reach them high in the trees. Fallen fruit is enjoyed by wild pigs. • Oil that can be used for cooking is extracted from the seeds, which can also be roasted and used as a coffee substitute. • The fibers from the leaves are utilized for woven goods. The naturally pest-resistant wood is used for making beach tents and construction. The waxy coating on the leaves is better known as carnauba wax. It is carefully extracted, first as a powder and then processed for various medicinal uses as well as for use in all types of polishes for a wide variety of things from shoes to floors, furniture, and cars. It is also used in the manufacture of candles, soap, carbon paper, and soap. • The trees are cultivated on plantations where the leaves are harvested every eighty days, which means each tree is harvested three times per year.

No. 143
Cordia sebestena

Geiger Tree
Kelau | Kopté | Scarlet Cordia | Siricote

POTENTIAL MAXIMUM HEIGHT
30 feet [9 meters]

SYMBOLIC MEANINGS
Oneness; Unity.

POSSIBLE POWERS
Cooperation; Create oxygen; Unification.

FOLKLORE AND FACTS
The small fruit of the evergreen *Cordia sebestena* Geiger Tree is sweet and edible but is not very flavorful. • The leaves are leathery and covered with fine hairs that make them feel a bit like sandpaper. • In full bloom, the Geiger Tree has large showy geranium-like clusters of intensely vibrant red-orange tubular flowers that cover the entire canopy of the tree. • The Geiger Tree is salt-tolerant enough to withstand actual salty sea spray, so it is an outstanding ornamental seaside tree.

No. 144
Cornus florida

Flowering Dogwood
Budwood | Cornel Tree | Dogtree | Dogwood | Florida Dogwood | Flowering Cornel | Green Osier | Virginia Dogwood

POTENTIAL MAXIMUM HEIGHT
30 feet [9 meters]

SYMBOLIC MEANINGS
Durability; Duration.

POSSIBLE POWERS
Create oxygen; Dog loyalty; Fertility; Heroism; Protection; Prowess; Secrecy; Superhuman courageousness; Wishing.

FOLKLORE AND FACTS
The wood from the deciduous *Cornus florida* Flowering Dogwood tree is so hard that it can be used as a splitting wedge to split other woods. • It is believed that placing a drop of Flowering Dogwood sap on a handkerchief on Midsummer's Eve and then faithfully carrying it everywhere will grant you any wish about anything. • For protection, make, then carry or wear a sachet filled with bits of Flowering Dogwood tree bark.

No. 145
Cornus mas

Cornelian Cherry Tree
Cornelian Cherry Dogwood | European Cornel

POTENTIAL MAXIMUM HEIGHT
30 feet [9 meters]

SYMBOLIC MEANINGS
Durability; Duration; Spear.

POSSIBLE POWERS
Create oxygen; Protection; Weaponry; Wishes.

FOLKLORE AND FACTS
The deciduous *Cornus mas* Cornelian Cherry Tree has yellow flowers and will produce dark red or yellow berries that closely resemble coffee berries. When the berries are ripe, they are edible, with a flavor similar to cranberries and Sour Cherries. The

berries are primarily used to make jam. • Unlike so many other known woods, the dense Cornelian Cherry Tree wood will not float. • Starting from the seventh century BCE, the ancient Greeks favored Cornelian Cherry Tree wood to make weapons such as javelins, bows, and spears because it was, in their opinion, better than any other wood for those specific purposes. • In Italy, the traditional stick that is carried by mounted herdsmen is made of Cornelian Cherry Tree wood.

No. 146
Corylus avellana 🗡️🍴🌳🌰

Hazel Tree
Cob Nut | Coll | Common Hazel | Filbert | Hazelnut

🔍 POTENTIAL MAXIMUM HEIGHT
15 feet [5 meters]

✴ SYMBOLIC MEANINGS
Communication; Creative inspiration; Epiphanies; Immortal wisdom; Reconciliation.

✴ POSSIBLE POWERS
Air element; Anti-lightning; Contact spirits; Create oxygen; Divination; Dreams; Dowsing; Fertility; Healing; Heightened awareness; Inspiration; Intelligence; Knowledge; Luck; Marriage; Masculine energy; Meditation; Mercury; Poetic inspiration; Positive change; Prosperity; Protection; Sun visions; Wisdom; Wishing.

✴ FOLKLORE AND FACTS
The deciduous *Corylus avellana* Hazel Tree's nut is believed to have been given the common name of Filbert because the tree's nuts matured on August 20th, which is the Feast Day of Saint Philibert of Jumièges. • Give a Hazelnut to a bride to wish her good fortune, fertility, and wisdom. • Make a wishing crown by weaving Hazel Tree twigs together. Wear this crown when making wishes. • A wand made of Hazel wood can be used to summon fairies. • A forked Hazel Tree branch is the diviner's dowsing rod of first choice. • Eat one Hazelnut before attempting a divination. • For the most opportune effect to be imbued into a brand new divining rod, the cutting must be done after the sun sets on one of the following nights: on the eve of a New Moon, on the first night of a New Moon, Good Friday, Shrove Tuesday, Epiphany, or Saint John's Day. The one who is severing the branch from the tree should be the intended diviner, who would best be the seventh son of a seventh son. He must face east to cut the first branch, which will be the one to catch the first of the morning sunlight. In this way the divining rod will be prepared to perform particularly well for the magically destined operator. The rod can be used to find water or hidden treasure.

No. 147
Corymbia ficifolia ☠️🗑️🌳🌲

Red Flowering Gum Tree
Red-flowered Eucalyptus | Scarlet Gum

🔍 POTENTIAL MAXIMUM HEIGHT
39 feet [12 meters]

✴ SYMBOLIC MEANINGS
Fig-like leaves; Resilience.

✴ POSSIBLE POWERS
Change; Create oxygen; Ease transitions; Fire; Love; Major life changes; Peace; Resilience.

✴ FOLKLORE AND FACTS
The evergreen and very pretty ornamental *Corymbia ficifolia* Red Flowering Gum Tree is the most popular of the ornamental *Eucalyptus* trees. • Composed of a thick tuft of long stamens rather than petals, the fluffy flowers are either bright orange, pink, or red. Because it is best grown from seed, what color the flower will be cannot be determined until the first time the tree blooms. • The Red Flowering Gum Tree is toxic to other plants that are beneath it via an acid that will drip out of some of the living leaves onto the plants beneath it.

C

No. 148

Cotinus coggygria 🌳

European Smoketree

Eurasian Smoketree | Purple Smokebush | Rhus cotinus | Smoke Bush | Smoke Tree | Smoketree | Venetian Sumac | Venetian Sumach

⬤ POTENTIAL MAXIMUM HEIGHT
15 feet [5 meters]

☀ SYMBOLIC MEANINGS
Intellectual excellence; Splendor.

🌸 POSSIBLE POWERS
Create oxygen; Improve quality of carefully considered thoughts; Superior intelligence.

🍃 FOLKLORE AND FACTS
The deciduous *Cotinus coggygria* European Smoketree flowers are very fluffy looking and a greyish-beige color that gives the canopy of the tree a surreal, smoke-like appearance. • Make and carry a sachet of a *Cotinus coggygria* flower when commencing a project that requires a lot of thought.

No. 149

Couroupita guianensis 🏺🌰

Cannonball Tree

Ayauma Tree | Kaman Gola | Lingada Hoovina Mara | Naagalinga | Naagalingam | Nagalinga | Sal Tree | Sala Tree | Shivalingam | Tope Gola

⬤ POTENTIAL MAXIMUM HEIGHT
115 feet [35 meters]

☀ SYMBOLIC MEANINGS
Joy; Radiance.

🌸 POSSIBLE POWERS
Create oxygen; Healing; Joy.

🍃 FOLKLORE AND FACTS
The deciduous *Couroupita guianensis* Cannonball Tree is one of the most beautiful flowering tropical trees in the world. • The Cannonball Tree is considered to be sacred and can often be found growing near both Hindu temples and Buddhist monasteries. • The flowers are orchid-like, showy, large, very fragrant both day and night, and are exceptionally interesting to look at. The flowers appear to be somewhat hooded, which make them appear even more interesting

and mysterious. When the dark pinkish-orange-red flowers bloom, the flowering is so extreme that it appears to cover not only the canopy but also the entire trunk of the tree!

• The name "cannonball" lends itself well to the Cannonball Tree's fruit, since it is brownish, nearly 10 inches (25 cm) in diameter, and has a woody shell. The fruit can take up to almost two years to ripen. The fruit's flesh is white, but when exposed to air it will turn blue. The fruit is edible and the seeds are spread by animals able to break them open, such as pigs. • Bees will gather on the flowers to obtain pollen.

No. 150

Crataegus laevigata 🏺🍶🌳🌰

English Hawthorn Tree

Fairy Tree | Gaxels | Glastonbury Hawthorn | Hagthorn | Halves | Haw | Hawberry Tree | Haweater Tree | Hawthorn | Hawthorn Tree | Huath | Ladies' Meat | May Blossom | May Bush | May Flower | May Tree | Mayblossom | Mayflower | Midland Hawthorn | Shan-cha | Thorn | Thorn Apple | Thornapple Tree | Tree of Chastity | White Thorn | Woodland Hawthorn

⬤ POTENTIAL MAXIMUM HEIGHT
25 feet [8 meters]

☀ SYMBOLIC MEANINGS
Chastity; Contradictions; Duality; Fairy tree; Hope; Purity; Spring; Sweet hope; Union of opposites.

C

⚜ POSSIBLE POWERS

Caution; Charm making; Chastity; Cleansing; Concealment magic; Create oxygen; Defend; Eroticism; Fairies; Female sexuality; Fend off negative energies; Fend off negative magic; Fend off witches and witchcraft; Fertility; Fire element; Fishing magic; Happiness; Hinges; Hope; Inner journeys; Intuition; Lightning energy; Love; Marriage; Mars; Masculine energy; Prosperity; Protection; Purification; Purity; Relaxation; Spark creativity.

⚜ FOLKLORE AND FACTS

In the British Isles, the commonly found deciduous *Crataegus laevigata* English Hawthorn Tree is revered as one of the most sacred trees on Earth. Also known as the Fairy Tree, the fairies of the area live under it as its guardians. The fairies are dedicated to treating the Hawthorn Tree with love, respect, and care, the same as all mortal humans should do. • Because of its correspondence with fertility, English Hawthorn has been added into spring wedding flowers. Respectfully collecting English Hawthorn sprigs and flower blossoms for brides to wear in their hair or to pin up their veils is permitted by the fairies. This is because the act is associated too much with romantic love to deny this pleasure to a mortal human on her wedding day. • There is a legend that while Joseph of Arimathea was in Britain to carry the message of Jesus Christ, he pushed his walking staff into the ground to sleep nearby. When he awoke, he discovered the staff had taken root, grown, and blossomed into what became known as the Glastonbury Thorn. That legend of the English Hawthorn has endured and is deeply rooted in Glastonbury's culture, as is the mystique and symbolism the Glastonbury Thorn has continuously generated. The original tree is believed to have been burned during the mid-1600s when it was declared to be a superstitious relic. The English Hawthorn Trees growing throughout the town of Glastonbury have *all* been propagated from that *one* ancient tree! • As is the pilgrims' custom, it is not uncommon to find English Hawthorn Trees that have been festooned with wishes represented by strips of cloth known as cloots, as well as with colored ribbons and cloth, trinkets, charms, and wishing coins tucked in and around it. • A powerful magic wand can be made from English Hawthorn Tree wood. • Because of its extreme ability to fend off negative forces, English Hawthorn twigs were put in, on, or near baby cradles. • English Hawthorn branches were placed over doors and windows of homes and barns to keep witches from entering the building. It also offers protection from evil, malicious ghosts, storm damage, and lightning. • An English Hawthorn twig was often tucked into the sock of the dead or placed atop the body in the coffin. • Put English Hawthorn under a mattress and around a bedroom to maintain or even enforce chastity. • Tuck an English Hawthorn leaf into your

hat to promote a good catch when fishing. • Wear a sprig of English Hawthorn if troubled, sad, or depressed to help return you to a state of happiness. • An English Hawthorn stake was considered a highly effective instrument to impale a vampire. • One might see fairies where the English Hawthorn, Oak, and Ash trees grow together in a cluster.

No. 151

Cratoxylum formosum 🐄 🌿

Pink Mampat Tree

Derum | Entemu | Geronggang Biabas | Gerunggung | Kemutul | Kemutun | Mampat | Mempitis | Phak Tiu | Pink Mempat | Tew | Thành Ngạnh Đẹp | Thành Ngạnh Vàng

◉ POTENTIAL MAXIMUM HEIGHT

148 feet [45 meters]

✳ SYMBOLIC MEANING

Strong wood.

⚜ POSSIBLE POWERS

Create oxygen; Healing.

⚜ FOLKLORE AND FACTS

The *Cratoxylum formosum* Pink Mampat is a tropical evergreen tree with orchid-like, bright pink flowers that will typically grow to be around 32 feet (10 m) tall. However, in the wild, the tree can grow up to be 147 feet (45 m) tall. • Pink Mampat wood is primarily used for making charcoal. • A brown vegetable dye can be obtained from the bark of the Pink Mampat Tree.

Create oxygen; Healing.

FOLKLORE AND FACTS
The leaves growing on the peculiar narrow spiky branches of the evergreen *Cussonia spicata* Spiked Cabbage Tree are a favorite food of wild African elephants. • The soft Spike Cabbage Tree wood is used for making traps for moles.

No. 152

Cupressus sempervirens ☠ 🥣 🍄 🌰

Italian Cypress
Mediterranean Cypress | Pencil Pine | Persian Cypress | Tree of Death | Tuscan Cypress

POTENTIAL MAXIMUM HEIGHT
60 feet [18 meters]

SYMBOLIC MEANINGS
Death; Despair; Grief; Immortality; Mourning; Sorrow.

POSSIBLE POWERS
Comfort; Create oxygen; Earth element; Ease depression; Eternity; Feminine energy; Healing; Immortality; Jupiter; Longevity; Pluto; Protection; Saturn; Soothe sorrow.

FOLKLORE AND FACTS
Since it is such a strong symbol of immortality, growing the evergreen *Cupressus sempervirens* Cypress conifer tree provides blessings and protection. • Wear a sprig of Cypress for comfort to ease the suffering mind of the grief experienced upon the death of a friend or relative. • Using Cypress essential oil for aromatherapy can provide emotional strength, especially during times of extreme sadness. • The second oldest tree in the world is a *Cupressus sempervirens* called the Zoroastrian Sarv, said to be 4,500 to 5,000 years old and located in Abarkuh, Iran. The legend is that the tree was planted by Zoroaster, possibly sometime around the seventh century BCE.

No. 153

Cussonia spicata ☠ 🥣 🍄

Spiked Cabbage Tree
Common Cabbage Tree | Lowveld Cabbage Tree

POTENTIAL MAXIMUM HEIGHT
30 feet [9 meters]

SYMBOLIC MEANING
Cousins united.

No. 154

Cycas revoluta ☠

King Sago Palm
Japanese Sago Palm | Sago Cycad | Sago Palm

POTENTIAL MAXIMUM HEIGHT
23 feet [7 meters]

SYMBOLIC MEANINGS
Hospitality; Victory.

POSSIBLE POWERS
Create oxygen; Death; Fabric stiffening; Good fortune; Healing; Wealth.

FOLKLORE AND FACTS
The pith of the evergreen *Cycas revoluta* King Sago Palm is *carefully* extracted due to its extreme toxicity, and even more carefully prepared to produce the sago starch that is the reason it is sought out. Sago starch is sometimes used as a sizing starch for textiles. • Because of their primitive nature and connection to antiquity, the study of *Cycad*s, such as *Cycas revoluta*, have yielded interesting discoveries into the natures of the earliest seed plants on Earth.

C

Cydonia oblonga ☠ 🍴 🛡 🌱 🌰

Quince Tree

Apple Quince | Aromatnaya Quince | Jumbo Quince |
Le Bourgeaut | Pineapple Quince | Smyrna Quince

🔍 POTENTIAL MAXIMUM HEIGHT
24 feet [7 meters]

✺ SYMBOLIC MEANINGS
Excellence; Fairy fire; Fertility;
Fidelity; Happiness; Life; Love;
Scornful beauty; Temptation.

🌀 POSSIBLE POWERS
Create oxygen; Earth element; Happiness; Love; Protection;
Protection from evil; Saturn; Venus.

🜨 FOLKLORE AND FACTS
The fruit of the deciduous *Cydonia oblonga* Quince Tree
is yet another fruit that is considered to be the forbidden
fruit found in the Garden of Eden. • Quince fruit is edible
and looks very much like a plump pear. Although some
varieties of Quince produce fruit that when ripe can be
eaten raw, most Quince varieties produce fruit that is too
hard and tart to be eaten raw. It is usually peeled, then
cooked or roasted for use in dishes, or used to make jelly,
jam, pudding, or marmalade. It can even be made into a wine
or liqueur. Because the aroma and flavor of Quince fruit is
strong, small amounts of it can be used as a flavor enhancer
in an applesauce, apple jelly, or pie recipe. • Art seen in
the excavated remains of Pompeii have revealed images of
bears carrying Quince fruit in their paws. • To carry even
one Quince seed is supposed to provide protection against
accidents, evil, and harm to the body. • The Quince is
sacredly associated with the goddesses Aphrodite and Venus.
• In ancient Roman weddings, a Quince fruit was shared
between the bride and groom to guarantee their happiness
together as a married couple. • In many parts of the Balkans,
when a baby is born, a Quince tree is planted to wish the
child a long life, love, and future fertility. • A mother-to-be
eating a Quince along with a coriander seed would assure
that her child in the womb would be born to be clever
and witty.

Cytisus scoparius ☠ 🛡 🌱

Scotch Broom

Banal | Basam | Besom | Bisom | Bizzon | Breeam | Broom Topos | Brum |
Common Broom | English Broom | Genista Green Broom | Hog Weed | Irish Broom |
Irish Tops | Link | Scot's Broom

🔍 POTENTIAL MAXIMUM HEIGHT
24 feet [7 meters]

✺ SYMBOLIC MEANINGS
Sweep; Tidy up.

🌀 POSSIBLE POWERS
Abundance; Collect; Create oxygen; Divination; Gather
up; Plentitude; Protection; Purification; Remove; Strength;
Union; Wind spell.

🜨 FOLKLORE AND FACTS
Hang branches or twig bundles from the deciduous *Cytisus
scoparius* Scotch Broom outside the home to keep evil from
entering. • Scotch Broom will produce a vegetable dye color
that ranges from very pale yellow to beige. • There is an
unproven belief that by holding a nosegay of self-gathered
sprigs of rue, broom, maidenhair fern, agrimony, and ground
ivy that one can gain profound intuition of who is and who
is not a practicing witch. • Make an infusion of rainwater,
natural spring water, or distilled water mixed with the
flowering tops from a stem of Scotch Broom. To sweep out all
the evil that may be lurking around the home, sprinkle this
infusion everywhere inside and all around the entire house.

C

No. 157
Dacrydium cupressinum 🜚

Rimu Tree
Red Pine

◉ POTENTIAL MAXIMUM HEIGHT
164 feet [50 meters]

✺ SYMBOLIC MEANINGS
Destiny; Rarity.

✸ POSSIBLE POWERS
Ardor; Cooperation; Create oxygen; Excitement; Healing;
Luck; Wealth.

✿ FOLKLORE AND FACTS
The evergreen *Dacrydium cupressinum* Rimu Tree is a true
rainforest tree. It is a slow-growing conifer that can live up
to approximately nine hundred years. • The Māori people in
what is now New Zealand traditionally used the Rimu Tree
heartwood for carving hair combs. The wood was also used
for construction and furniture. However, because so many
Rimu Trees have been felled, cutting down the trees in public
forests in New Zealand has been forbidden. The stumps and
remaining Rimu Tree root wood is prized for making smaller
objects. Vintage Rimu wood furniture is highly prized.
• Unripe Rimu Tree fruit stimulates both sexes of the
flightless, nocturnal Kākāpō parrot to breed. The bird is
extremely endangered. • Captain James Cook brewed Rimu
beer when he visited New Zealand. He gave this to his crew
to fend off scurvy.

No. 158
Dalbergia sissoo ☠ 🜚 ✿

North Indian Rosewood Tree
Biradi | Irugudujava | Jag | Seeso | Sheeshan | Sheeshoo | Shewa | Shisham | Sisau | Sisu |
Tahli | Tali

◉ POTENTIAL MAXIMUM HEIGHT
99 feet [30 meters]

✺ SYMBOLIC MEANINGS
Adjoin; Join.

✸ POSSIBLE POWERS
Cabinetry; Create oxygen; Fine
furniture making; Teeth and
tongue cleaning.

✿ FOLKLORE AND FACTS
Large and crooked, the
deciduous *Dalbergia sissoo*

Indian Rosewood Tree is one of the finest woods used for
high-quality cabinetry and furniture. • For centuries, very
thin Indian Rosewood Tree twigs called *datun* were used as
a type of toothbrush and tongue cleaner throughout all of
Pakistan, Africa, and the Middle East. In those same parts of
the world these twigs are still used for the same purpose.
• The sap of the Indian Rosewood Tree is a vital ingredient
in making ancient Indian wall plaster.

No. 159
Davidia involucrata

Handkerchief Tree
Dove Tree | Ghost Tree | Pocket Handkerchief Tree

◉ POTENTIAL MAXIMUM HEIGHT
82 feet [25 meters]

✺ SYMBOLIC MEANING
Illusion.

✸ POSSIBLE POWERS
Create oxygen; Illusions; Magical point of view.

✿ FOLKLORE AND FACTS
In the late spring, the deciduous *Davidia involucrata*
Handkerchief Tree produces small reddish-purple-colored
flower heads that are surrounded by large white bracts. This
blooming gives the illusion of dangling handkerchiefs, doves,
or ghosts on the branches of this exotic shady tree.

No. 160
Delonix regia ✿

Royal Poinciana Tree
Flamboyant | Flame Tree | Flower of Pupil | Gulmohar | Kaalvarippoo | Krishnachura |
Llama del Bosque | Malinche | Peacock Tree | Phoenix's Tail Tree | Phượng Vỹ | Poinciana |
Pupil's Flower | Tabachine

◉ POTENTIAL MAXIMUM HEIGHT
40 feet [12 meters]

D

☀ SYMBOLIC MEANING
The Flower of Calvary.

⦿ POSSIBLE POWERS
Create oxygen; Prosperity; Protection; Sound resonance; Wealth.

☘ FOLKLORE AND FACTS
The evergreen red-orange or the rarer yellow *Delonix regia* Royal Poinciana Tree is one of the most beautiful, spectacularly showy, flowering ornamental trees in the world. • In the Caribbean, when the long seed pods dry, they become woody and the seeds loosen inside of it enough for it to be a maraca-style, shaker percussion instrument.

No. 161

Dendrocnide moroides ☠

Australian Stinging Tree
Gympie-Gympie | Moonlight Plant | Stinging Bush

◐ POTENTIAL MAXIMUM HEIGHT
10 feet [3 meters]

☀ SYMBOLIC MEANING
Beware.

⦿ POSSIBLE POWERS
Create oxygen; Misery; Pain; Suffering.

☘ FOLKLORE AND FACTS
As one of the world's most poisonous trees, the evergreen *Dendrocnide moroides* Australian Stinging Tree is notorious for its long-lasting, excruciatingly painful sting. The pain of such an unfortunate encounter with any part of this tree can last from hours to miserable days long. And then just when the siege of pain seems to have diminished, it can suddenly flare up weeks, even months later. • The entire tree is covered over with tiny, brittle bristle-like hollow thorns called trichomes that will embed themselves in the skin with barely the slightest encounter and stay there for well into a year's time. These hairs are so infinitesimally tiny and embedded so deeply, that the skin will often close over them before any attempt to remove them can even commence. • A great many attempts to find a removal remedy have been tried and tried again and again with little encouragement of success. Topical pain numbing creams offer little relief, and that is, at best, always short-lived. The best thing to do is to avoid going anywhere near this tree.

No. 162

Dillenia indica ❦ ❶ ☘

Elephant Apple
Avartaki | Betta Kangalu | Chalita | Chalta | Chulta | Gimar | Karambel | Karmal | Kurukati | Outenga | Peddakalinga | Pinnay | Punna | Ramphal | Sylitha | Thabyu | Thibuta | Ugakkay | Uva | Uvatteku | Uvav | Vazhapunna | Zinbrun | Zinpyunnga

◐ POTENTIAL MAXIMUM HEIGHT
49 feet [15 meters]

☀ SYMBOLIC MEANING
Reach up high.

⦿ POSSIBLE POWERS
Cleanse; Create oxygen; Healing.

☘ FOLKLORE AND FACTS
The evergreen *Dillenia indica* Elephant Apple is a primary food in India for elephants, as well as deer, monkeys, rodents, and squirrels. As a result, in India, the wild gathering as well as the commercial sale of the edible fruit has been prohibited in order to prevent the potential for over-gathering. • The blossom of the Elephant Apple has an exotically interesting, otherworldly look to it.

No. 163

Diospyros ebenum ❦ ☘

Ebony Tree
Ceylon Ebony Tree | India Ebony

◐ POTENTIAL MAXIMUM HEIGHT
99 feet [30 meters]

☀ SYMBOLIC MEANINGS
Bury me amid nature's beauties; Hypocrisy; Lust.

⦿ POSSIBLE POWERS
Create oxygen; Healing; Luck; Power; Protection; Venus; Water element.

D

FOLKLORE AND FACTS

The prized deciduous *Diospyros ebenum* Ebony Tree wood is black in color and so dense that it will not float. • It is illegal to cut or sell Ebony wood in Sri Lanka. • Polished Ebony wood will feel cold, while its ability to transmit heat is so high that it can cause the metal containers in which the wood is burnt to melt. • Between the sixteenth and the nineteenth centuries, the best furniture was made of Ceylon Ebony. • Ebony wood has been used to fashion all manner of handles, from those on doors to shanks for cutlery and tableware. • The black keys of a grand piano and the fingerboards on string instruments such as guitars, violins, and cellos are frequently made using Ebony wood. • High-quality, lathe-turned pieces such as fancy turned chopsticks and chess pieces have been fashioned from beautiful black Ebony wood. • It is believed that to be rid of the chills, tie one string to a *Diospyros* tree for each chill you've experienced. • The *Diospyros ebenum* fruit is edible, but consumed only under famine conditions. • A magic wand made from the wood of any evergreen *Diospyros* genus tree, such as the *Diospyros ebenum* Ebony Tree, can provide undiluted pure power. • An amulet of Ebony wood offers powerful protection to the wearer.

place the fruit can be stored for several months. • As it is with the Ebony tree, a magic wand made from the wood of any *Diospyros* genus tree, such as the evergreen Oriental Persimmon, can provide undiluted pure power. An amulet made from its wood will offer powerful protection to the wearer. • Bury a green Oriental Persimmon fruit near to the entrance of the home for good luck.

No. 164

Diospyros kaki 🌿🍴🌱

Oriental Persimmon

Black Sapote | Date-plum | Dios Pyros | Ebony | Fruit of the Gods | Gam | Hachiya | Japanese Persimmon | Kaki | Kaki Persimmon | Khormaloo | Lama | Obeah | Ribera del Xúquer | Rojo Brillante | Sharon Fruit | Shi | Triumph

🔴 POTENTIAL MAXIMUM HEIGHT
39 feet [12 meters]

☀ SYMBOLIC MEANINGS
Bury me amid nature's beauties; Hypocrisy; Resistance.

🌼 POSSIBLE POWERS
Create oxygen; Feminine energy; Fertility; Healing; Luck; Lust; Potency; Power; Protection; Resistance; Venus; Water element.

FOLKLORE AND FACTS
The deciduous *Diospyros kaki* Oriental Persimmon tree has been cultivated in China for over two thousand years. The edible ripe fruit is dark orange and very closely resembles a tomato. Although the skin is often removed beforehand, it can be eaten. When ripe, the pulp is soft and often cut into pieces and sprinkled over with sugar before eating. • In Korea, the fruit is often dried to eat over the winter as a special treat that children enjoy. • Persimmon vinegar can also be made from the fruit. • If kept in a cool, dry, dark

---

No. 165

Diospyros lotus 🌿🌱

Date Plum Tree
Date-plum | Fruit of the Gods | Khormaloo | Lilac Persimmon

🔴 POTENTIAL MAXIMUM HEIGHT
29 feet [9 meters]

☀ SYMBOLIC MEANINGS
Deliciousness; God's fruit; Resistance.

🌼 POSSIBLE POWERS
Create oxygen; Fertility; Healing; Luck; Lust; Potency; Power; Protection; Resistance; Venus; Water element.

FOLKLORE AND FACTS
The fruit of the evergreen *Diospyros lotus* Date Plum Tree is usually dried and called amlok. • A sachet of Date Plum seeds tucked under the mattress can help encourage fertilization. • Because of the Date Plum's deliciousness, there are some who believe that it is the fruit that is written of in Homer's *Odyssey* as the fruit that could make all men forget their past and neglect their future. • As with any *Diospyros* genus tree, such as the evergreen *Diospyros lotus* Date Plum, a magic wand fashioned from its wood can provide undiluted pure power, while an amulet offers powerful protection to the wearer.

D

No. 166
Dipterocarpus turbinatus 🍶

Garjan Tree
Ajakarna | Asvakarna | Challaane | Challani | Enney | Enneymaram | India Gurjan | Googe | Gurijun | Gurgina | Jie Bu Luo Xiang | Kalpaini | Karalam | Karccamaram | Mayapis | Teli-Garjan | Tihya-Garjan | Valivara | Vellenney | Yennar

◎ POTENTIAL MAXIMUM HEIGHT
150 feet [46 meters]

✹ SYMBOLIC MEANING
Supportive.

❀ POSSIBLE POWERS
Affordability; Create oxygen; Fortification.

✥ FOLKLORE AND FACTS
The deciduous *Dipterocarpus turbinatus* Garjan Tree is an important source of wood that is primarily used in the manufacture of plywood.

No. 167
Dipteryx odorata ☠ 🍶

Tonka Bean Tree
Brazilian Teak | Coumaria Nut Tree | Cumaru | Kumarú | Tonqua | Tonquin Bean Tree

◎ POTENTIAL MAXIMUM HEIGHT
164 feet [50 meters]

✹ SYMBOLIC MEANING
Wishing for love.

❀ POSSIBLE POWERS
Courage; Create oxygen; Feminine energy; Love; Money; Perfumery; Venus; Water element; Wishing.

✥ FOLKLORE AND FACTS
Some believe that the seed from the evergreen *Dipteryx odorata* Tonka Bean Tree can grant wishes by holding a bean in the hand while whispering the wish to it, then carrying the bean until the wish comes true. Afterwards, bury or stomp on the bean. Another method is to bury the wished-upon bean in a fertile, hospitable location and the wish will come true during the time that the plant is growing. • Radiocarbon dating of large *Dipteryx odorata* stumps left behind by loggers in the Amazon proved that *Dipteryx odorata* is definitely a species of tree that can live to a great age, as several stumps were found to be well over one thousand years old! • The Tonka Bean is sometimes used to flavor pipe tobacco. • *Dipteryx odorata* wood is sometimes used for flooring. • Tonka Bean is high in coumarin. • The Tonka Bean fragrance is similar to sweet woodruff. • Tonka Bean's use in food products is banned in the USA, but not in other countries. • The essential oil of the Tonka Bean is an ingredient in several perfume fragrances.

No. 168
Dracaena arborea ☠ 🌳

Slender Dragon Tree
African Dragon Tree | Cornstalk Tree | Dracaena Tree | Dragon Tree | Ribbon Tree

◎ POTENTIAL MAXIMUM HEIGHT
15 feet [5 meters]

✹ SYMBOLIC MEANINGS
Conflict; Inner strength.

❀ POSSIBLE POWERS
Create oxygen; Inner power; Power.

✥ FOLKLORE AND FACTS
The evergreen *Dracaena arborea* Slender Dragon Tree can have one head, or it can be a multiple-headed dragon on the same trunk. Branching will begin after the first flower spike forms, followed by coral-colored berries. • The Slender Dragon Tree is a small tree that can be adapted to grow indoors wherever the light will support it.

D

No. 169

Dracaena cinnabari ☠

Dragon Blood Tree

Dragon's Blood Tree | Socotra Dragon Tree

POTENTIAL MAXIMUM HEIGHT

33 feet [10 meters]

SYMBOLIC MEANING

Dragon's blood.

POSSIBLE POWERS

Accidents; Aggression; Anger; Blood proxy; Carnal desire; Conflict; Create oxygen; Exorcism; Fire element; Love; Lust; Machinery; Mars; Masculine energy; Potency; Power; Protection; Purification; Rock music; Strength; Struggle; War.

FOLKLORE AND FACTS

As the resinous sap of the evergreen *Dracaena cinnabari* Dragon Blood Tree is crimson red, it was highly prized as dragon's blood in the ancient world. • Dragon's Blood was, and still is, commonly used in ritual magic and alchemy. • Dragon's Blood resin is added to ink to create dragon's blood ink, which is used to officially inscribe magical talismans and seals. • Dragon's blood is used for religious purposes in American hoodoo, New Orleans voodoo, and African-American folk magic. • Like all good things magical, bottled dragon's blood may not be all it is hyped up to be. Take care that a purchase isn't of sap from another type of tree, as that is too often the case. • To quiet a boisterous home and impose peace and quiet, put equal parts of powdered dragon's blood, salt, and sugar in a small, tight-fitting jar and then hide it in the house where it cannot be found.

No. 170

Dracaena draco ☠

Canary Islands Dragon Tree

Drago

POTENTIAL MAXIMUM HEIGHT

50 feet [15 meters]

SYMBOLIC MEANINGS

I'm going to get you; Snare; You are near a snare.

POSSIBLE POWERS

Create oxygen; Protection; Sealant.

FOLKLORE AND FACTS

The evergreen *Dracaena draco* Canary Islands Dragon Tree resin is often used as an ingredient in the production of a specific wood sealer that is used to varnish violins. • The Guanches, the indigenous peoples in what is now known as the Canary Islands, once hollowed out a small space in the trunk of a Canary Islands Dragon Tree that was estimated to be six thousand years old. The small hollow was used as a sanctuary for the worship of the tree. The tree was 70 feet (21 m) tall and 45 feet (14 m) around. The tree was destroyed in a severe 1868 storm. • The oldest-living Dragon Tree in Tenerife, Spain, is named El Drago and is over one thousand years old.

No. 171
Dracaena reflexa

Song of India Tree

Pleomele | Red-edged Dracaena | Song of Jamaica Tree

◉ POTENTIAL MAXIMUM HEIGHT
10 feet [3 meters]

✸ SYMBOLIC MEANING
Singing dragon.

✿ POSSIBLE POWERS
Create oxygen; Healing.

✪ FOLKLORE AND FACTS
If the light is right for it to thrive, the evergreen *Dracaena reflexa* Song of India Tree can be potted and grown entirely inside a home to nearly reach its natural height and span, if it is grown within a large enough pot and there is a high enough ceiling overhead.

No. 172
Drimys winteri

Winter's Bark Tree

Canelo | True Winter's Bark | Wintera | Winter's Cinnamon

◉ POTENTIAL MAXIMUM HEIGHT
24 feet [7 meters]

✸ SYMBOLIC MEANINGS
Good health; Peace.

✿ POSSIBLE POWERS
Create oxygen; Sound resonance; Success.

✪ FOLKLORE AND FACTS
Carry a piece of the evergreen *Drimys winteri* Winter's Bark Tree for success in whatever you do. • Due to its beautiful reddish color and heavy weight, Winter's Bark wood is prized for use in fine furniture and musical instruments.

No. 173
Drypetes deplanchei

Grey Bark Tree

Grey Boxwood | White Myrtle | Yellow Tulip Tree | Yellow Tulipwood

◉ POTENTIAL MAXIMUM HEIGHT
82 feet [25 meters]

✸ SYMBOLIC MEANING
Sociability.

✿ POSSIBLE POWERS
Create oxygen; Protection; Repels sea worms.

✪ FOLKLORE AND FACTS
In the past, the deciduous *Drypetes deplanchei* Grey Bark Tree's wood has been used to make bullwhip handles. • Since the sap of *Drypetes deplanchei* effectively repels sea worms, the wood was once used for the construction of sea piles by the early settlers of Lord Howe Island in the Tasman Sea.

No. 174

Durio zibethinus 🍴🌳

Durian Tree
King of Fruits Tree | Mao Shan Wang | Musang King | Red Prawn Durian | Stinky Fruit Tree

📷 **POTENTIAL MAXIMUM HEIGHT**
98 feet [30 meters]

✳ **SYMBOLIC MEANING**
Mystique.

🌐 **POSSIBLE POWERS**
Aphrodisiac; Create oxygen.

🍃 **FOLKLORE AND FACTS**
The large fruit of the evergreen
Durio zibethinus Durian Tree
did not get tagged with the
common name of Stinky Fruit
for no reason. It is considered the
worst-smelling fruit in the entire world.
• Although some people may consider the smell to be a
pleasant fragrance, most consider the fragrance of the Durian
fruit to be more of a disruptive odor, akin to a disgusting
stench that reeks of sewage mixed with decaying onions,
dirty socks, and rotten eggs with a splash of turpentine
thrown into the stink of it. All of which can linger behind, for
days and days, wherever the fruit has been. • On the other
hand, people who do not find the Durian to be repugnantly
odorous seem to favor eating it and wholeheartedly consider
the fruit to be utterly delectable and unlike any other.
• The texture of the Durian is often described as a smooth,
cheesecake-like, yellow custard, with somewhat of a sweet
banana, almond, vanilla, hazelnut, apricot, and caramel
combination of flavors. It is usually eaten fresh or used to
flavor milkshakes, baked goods, and sweets. It can also be
added to sauces and soups or deep-fried. • In Southeast
Asia, it is forbidden to bring the Durian fruit into many
hotels, airports, restaurants, and subways, or on nearly all
public transportation. • Durian flowers are closed during
the day and open at night to be pollinated by fruit bats.
• The Javanese people have long believed that Durian is a
reliable aphrodisiac.

No. 175

Dypsis lutescens 🥣

Areca Palm
Bamboo Palm | Butterfly Palm | Golden Cane | Yellow Palm

📷 **POTENTIAL MAXIMUM HEIGHT**
30 feet [9 meters]

✳ **SYMBOLIC MEANING**
Gentle calm.

🌐 **POSSIBLE POWERS**
Banish negativity; Create oxygen; Gentleness; Love;
Peacefulness; Uplift.

🍃 **FOLKLORE AND FACTS**
Commonly grown as an ornamental garden tree in
subtropical and tropical areas, the evergreen *Dypsis lutescens*
Areca Palm is also a favorite potted tree for inside the home.
In the right light, this tree with its fluffy, curvy, multiple
bunching fronds and refreshing bright green color will thrive
in the home. • Grown outside, the long fronds will flutter in
the breeze.

No. 176

Elaeis guineensis 🪹 🍴

African Oil Palm

Macaw-fat Tree | Magical Palm Tree Oil | Oil Palm

🔍 **POTENTIAL MAXIMUM HEIGHT**
49 feet [15 meters]

✳ **SYMBOLIC MEANINGS**
Hope; Stature.

✹ **POSSIBLE POWERS**
Create oxygen;
Drives off evil
spirits; Healing;
Hopefulness;
Invulnerability.

✹ **POSSIBLE POWERS**
The stately elegant
evergreen *Elaeis guineensis*
African Oil Palm is grown from
a seed. The fruit seeds produce
the edible palm oil. Palm oil was
discovered in an Egyptian tomb dated
to be from 3000 BCE. • Palm oil is used
for cooking and as an ingredient in
various foods. • It is used for making
soap. • *Elaeis guineensis* oil is also
considered for use as a biofuel.
• Palm oil is an integral ingredient in
most West African rituals. • During
certain Liberian initiation rites calling for scarification
cutting, the healing oil provided by the Oil Palm is applied
to the initiate's wounds with an owl feather. • Throughout
coastal Benin, the oil from the Oil Palm tree is used daily in
personal sacrifices, offerings, and divinations. • One method
of being rid of a problem has been to use the power of the
magical oil to drive off evil spirits by combining it with
something else, like a Kola Nut, then leaving the nut in the
road to be run down by vehicles throughout the day, thus
destroying whatever problem was attached to it. • The seeds
of the Oil Palm tree are regarded as sacred ritual objects
when used for divination involving an oracle, such as when
it was used in secret Beninese oracle divinations from Fa,
the Beninese god of oracles. • In Malaysia and Indonesia,
Oil Palm tree leaves are sometimes woven to make nests for
chickens and to create effective barriers to keep chickens
confined to a particular area. • In parts of Benin and Togo,
woven shields of Oil Palm leaves were worn on the arms
or around the neck to provide a sense of invulnerability to
the wearer. • In Ghana, the flowering branches of the Oil
Palm tree have been burned by the Akan people so that the
smoke can force evil spirits away. • In Liberia, the Mano
people have been known to use Oil Palm oil to try to awaken
someone who was comatose by massaging the unconscious
person's cheeks with the oil in an attempt to force them to
speak. Any other use of the oil in the same Liberian society
might be considered a taboo, because it could be considered
a magical method devised by means of witchcraft to protect
against the negative effect of malicious witchcraft. To them,
the contradiction warrants the taboo.

No. 177

Entandrophraga cylindricum 🪹 🌳

Sapele Mahogany Tree

Aboudikro | Assi | Muyovu | Sapele | Sapelli

🔍 **POTENTIAL MAXIMUM HEIGHT**
164 feet [50 meters]

✳ **SYMBOLIC MEANINGS**
Beauty; Strength.

✹ **POSSIBLE POWERS**
Beauty; Construction; Create oxygen; Sound resonance;
Strength.

✹ **POSSIBLE POWERS**
The deciduous *Entandrophraga cylindricum* Sapele
Mahogany Tree has dark reddish-brown toned wood that
is also rot resistant. The wood has an iridescence of colors
that range from pinks, golds, reds, to browns. • The Sapele
Mahogany Tree wood is used to manufacture furniture,
luxurious flooring planks, veneer, plywood, and boats.
• Sapele Mahogany Tree wood is used to make the back and
sides of acoustic guitars. It is also used to make electric guitar
bodies, ukulele necks, large harps, and a heavy-sounding
Basque wooden percussion type of instrument known as a
txalaparta, which is played by beating it with large sticks.
• Due to an adverse reaction of metal to wood, iron will
discolor and stain Sapele Mahogany wood.

No. 178

Eriobotrya japonica 🌿🍴🌳

Loquat Tree

Chinese Plum | Japanese Plum | Naspli | Nèspera | Nespolo | Nispero | Pipa

POTENTIAL MAXIMUM HEIGHT
30 feet [9 meters]

SYMBOLIC MEANINGS
Gold; Wealth.

POSSIBLE POWERS
Create oxygen; Healing; Luck; Richness; Wealth.

FOLKLORE AND FACTS
Tiny and tartly sweet when ripe, the fruit of the evergreen *Eriobotrya japonica* Loquat Tree has been a trusted favorite in Chinese gardens for several thousand years. • Loquat has been cultivated in Japan for over two thousand years. • The flavor of the Loquat is slightly like that of peach and apricot. • After the large seeds are removed and discarded, the Loquat fruit is often mixed with other fresh fruits in a fruit salad. It is also used in Asian-inspired jams, pies, pastries, sweet confections, and chutney. It is added to smoothies, too. The fruit can be used to make homemade wine. • The Loquat is a favorite in Chinese and home folk medicine, being a trusted thinner and dissolver of lung phlegm, as well as an expectorant. • If your birthday should be on a Sunday, there is a way to increase your good luck on that day that must be carried out *before* sunset. First, tuck a Loquat leaf into your wallet before going to the casino. Preferably go to the one nearest to where you were when you woke up that morning. When you enter the casino, look for a game or a table that shows something gold *on it* or *very near to it*. Intend to gamble no more than your age on that day. Not one penny more. See what comes of it. It is worth a Loquat leaf, a reasonable amount of money to wager, some genuine high hopes, and a birthday wish to find out.

No. 179

Erythrina crista-galli 🐛🌿🌳

Cockspur Coral Tree

Albero di Corallo | Argentininé Rudúné | Ceibo | Common Coral Tree | Coral Tree | Corticeira | Crybaby Tree | Bucaré | Eritrina Cresta de Gali | Erytryna Grzebieniasta | Flor-de-Coral | Korallbusk | Kórarjownik | Kukonkorallipuu | Mulungu | Sananduva | Seibo | Tarajos Korallfa | Vông Móng Gà | Zardénice | Hřebenitá

POTENTIAL MAXIMUM HEIGHT
10 feet [3 meters]

SYMBOLIC MEANINGS
Cock's comb; Rooster.

POSSIBLE POWERS
Create oxygen; Divination; Good luck; Instill bravery; Resist suffering; Ward off evil spirits.

FOLKLORE AND FACTS
The deciduous *Erythrina crista-galli* Cockspur Coral Tree is a tree with vividly bright red orange-colored flowers on spiny branches. It is found in swampy areas and along watercourses in the wild. Because it is so attractive, it is often grown as an ornamental tree in city parks. • The flowers are rich with nectar, attracting insects for pollination.

No. 180

Eucalyptus deglupta

Rainbow Eucalyptus Tree

Mindanao Gum | Rainbow Gum

POTENTIAL MAXIMUM HEIGHT
246 feet [75 meters]

SYMBOLIC MEANINGS
Art; Rainbows.

POSSIBLE POWERS
Artistic; Beauty; Create oxygen; Feminine energy; Rain magic; Uplift a sagging spirit; Water element.

FOLKLORE AND FACTS
The evergreen *Eucalyptus deglupta* Rainbow Eucalyptus Tree has the prettiest, most fascinating bark of any tree. Throughout

the year, as the tree sheds its outer bark, the extremely colorful under-bark layers are revealed to show long vertical streaks of shades and tints of blue, purple, orange, and red blended into the youngest bark of different greens and the oldest bark of various browns. The irregular effect gives the impression that the tree trunks have been artistically and decoratively painted.

No. 181
Eucalyptus globulus 🕱 ✿ ⚱

Tasmanian Blue Gum
Blue Gum | Eukkie | Gum Tree | Maiden's Gum | Southern Blue Gum | Tasmanian Oak | Victorian Blue Gum | Victorian Eurabbie

🔎 POTENTIAL MAXIMUM HEIGHT
180 feet [55 meters]

✳ SYMBOLIC MEANINGS
I watch over you; Loftiness; Prudence; Quiet.

✿ POSSIBLE POWERS
Create oxygen; Feminine energy; Healing; Moon; Perfumery; Protection; Purification; Water element.

☘ FOLKLORE AND FACTS
Out of the 758 species of Eucalyptus, the most common in California and all around the world is the *Eucalyptus globulus* Tasmanian Blue Gum. • To many First Nations peoples in Australia, Eucalyptus is quite sacred because it represents the division of Earth from the heaven above and the underworld below. • The roots of all species of Eucalyptus excrete a toxic chemical that inhibits the growth of any plants that might be growing close by. • Tasmanian Blue Gum has been used for magical purposes, medicines, antiseptics, aromatherapy, and some perfume blends for an uncountably long length of time. • The first mention of there being such a plant with the properties of Eucalyptus were not thought to have been written down until 1642, when Abel Janszoon Tasman journaled his exploration of Tasmania. Later, in 1770, after Captain James Cook arrived in Botany Bay in New South Wales, Australia, he too made a note of Eucalyptus in his journal. • In 1800, the French botanist, Jacques Labillardière, described in his own journal the Tasmanian Blue Gum specimens he had collected in 1792. • Fresh Eucalyptus leaves are the primary diet of that particularly picky Australian marsupial, the iconic, adorable koala. • Due to the volatility of their natural oils making them excessively

flammable and a constant fire threat to the safety of the surrounding area, Eucalyptus trees have been removed in some regions where they grow as a fire safety measure. • The steam from a shower can release the benefits of a small dried or fresh nosegay of Eucalyptus hanging in a thin fabric or net pouch from the shower head. • A drop of Eucalyptus essential oil in aromatherapy may help alleviate stress and anxiety when feeling under the weather. • Carry Eucalyptus leaves to maintain good health. • Hang a piece of Eucalyptus over a sick bed to encourage healing.

No. 182
Eucalyptus regnans 🕱 ✿ ⚱

Swamp Gum
Mountain Ash | Stringy Gum | Tasmanian Oak | Victorian Ash

🔎 POTENTIAL MAXIMUM HEIGHT
374 feet [114 meters]

✳ SYMBOLIC MEANINGS
I watch over you; Loftiness; Prudence; Quiet.

✿ POSSIBLE POWERS
Create oxygen; Feminine energy; Healing; Heights; Moon; Protection; Purification; Water element.

☘ FOLKLORE AND FACTS
Native to Tasmania and Victoria, Australia, the evergreen *Eucalyptus regnans* Swamp Gum is the tallest flowering plant in the world. • Gigantic *Eucalyptus regnans* is the second-tallest tree in the world, with *Sequoia sempervirens* of North America being the tallest. • After a forest fire, unlike many other types of trees, *Eucalyptus regnans* cannot produce ground shoots as a means of recovery, so it must be replenished via growth from a seed. • The lumber from *Eucalyptus regnans* is highly valued. For this purpose, there are many plantations that cultivate the trees to help mitigate overharvesting in the wild.

No. 183

Euonymus europaeus ☠ 🗴

European Spindle Tree
Common Spindle | Spindle Tree

📷 **POTENTIAL MAXIMUM HEIGHT**
33 feet [10 meters]

☀ **SYMBOLIC MEANINGS**
Arrow-wood; Indelible memory; Likeness; Your charms are
engraved on my heart; Your image is engraved on my heart.

🌐 **POSSIBLE POWERS**
Breaks a hex; Courage; Create oxygen; Memorable;
Memories; Remembering; Success.

🜍 **FOLKLORE AND FACTS**
The deciduous *Euonymus europaeus* European Spindle Tree
wood was once used to make spindles for spinning wool.
• Make, then carry or wear a sachet of *Euonymus europaeus*
leaves or bark wood for courage, especially when attempting
to break a hex.

No. 184

Euphorbia pulcherrima ☠

Poinsettia Tree
Bent El Consu | Christmas Eve Flower | Christmas Flower | Consul's Daughter | Crown of the
Andes | Cuitlaxochitl | Easter Flower | Flor de Pascua | Noche Buena | Skin Flower

📷 **POTENTIAL MAXIMUM HEIGHT**
10 feet [3 meters]

☀ **SYMBOLIC MEANINGS**
Be of good cheer; Good cheer; Merriment; Purity.

🌐 **POSSIBLE POWERS**
Create oxygen; Family gathering; Sacrifice;
Spiritual reflection.

🜍 **FOLKLORE AND FACTS**
The flowers of
evergreen *Euphorbia*
pulcherrima Poinsettia
Tree are not flowers
at all, but colored
leafy bracts. • The
Poinsettia Tree
is native to Mexico
and often grown to
be a shapely small
ornamental tree. • The
"flowers" are colorful,
and can be brilliant crimson red, pink,
orange, green, white, or marbled • The
ancient Aztecs used Poinsettia to produce a
crimson vegetable dye. • The association of Poinsettias with
Christmas began in the sixteenth century. • When handling
the Poinsettia, avoid getting the milky sap in the eyes.

No. 185

Euterpe oleracea 🌱 🍶

Açaí Palm

Açaí | Acaí Berry Tree | Açaí d'Amazonie |
Amazon Acai Berry | Asai | Assai |
Baie d'Açaí | Bambil | Berries of Youth |
Black Pearls | Cansin | Extrait d'Açaí |
Naidi | Palmiche

◎ POTENTIAL MAXIMUM HEIGHT
82 feet [25 meters]

✴ SYMBOLIC MEANING
Sad cries.

❀ POSSIBLE POWERS
Create oxygen; Sorrow memorialized.

❖ FOLKLORE AND FACTS
The edible parts of the evergreen *Euterpe
oleracea* Açaí Palm are the berry fruits known as the Açaí
berry. In North America, Açaí berries are used as a topping
for oatmeal or tapioca along with nuts and sweeteners.
• Since its introduction to the wider food market in the early
2000s, Açaí has been central in many internet falsehoods
attributing Açaí berries or juice to such miracle scams as the
cure for cancer, a cure for diabetes, and the only surefire way
of improving the size and stamina of a penis. None of these
particular claims are even remotely true. • A legend among
the people along the Amazon River is that Iaçá, the daughter
of chief Itaqui, gave birth to a child who was sacrificed along
with all other newborns during a terrible famine, by order of
her father. Her sorrow caused her death. Where she died, a
tree grew. The tree provided food for Chief Itaqui's people.
Out of gratitude for their survival, the tribe named the tree
Açaí, as it was the chief's daughter's name spelled backwards.

No. 186

Excoecaria agallocha ☠ 🌱

Blinding Tree

Black Mangrove | Blind-your-eye Mangrove | Buta Buta Tree | Milky Mangrove |
Poisonfish Tree | River Poison Tree

◎ POTENTIAL MAXIMUM HEIGHT
49 feet [15 meters]

✴ SYMBOLIC MEANING
Blinder.

❀ POSSIBLE POWERS
Blinding; Create oxygen;
Healing.

❖ FOLKLORE AND FACTS
The evergreen
Excoecaria agallocha
Blinding Tree received
that pointed common
name as a warning that
this tree can and has
blinded people who got

any of the milky latex sap in their eyes. Even the smoke
from any part of it burning can have the same dire effect,
since slight contact with the eyes can cause temporary
blindness. The sap on the skin can cause painful blistering.
• As so many toxic trees are studied for their potential
benefit as a medicine to counter myriad diseases and
commonly suffered ailments, *Excoecaria agallocha* has
already made a contribution to healing by exhibiting highly
significant antimicrobial potential, which may be beneficial
in the future development of many different medications.
• The powder obtained from dried leaves is used as a fish
poison, as well as tipping poison onto a dart, arrow, or spear.

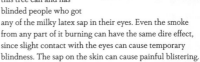

Ɛ

No. 187
Fagraea berteroana ☠ 🥣 🌰

Perfume Flower Tree
Pua-kenikeni | Pua Keni Keni | Pua-Lulu | Ten Cent Flower Tree

🌎 **POTENTIAL MAXIMUM HEIGHT**
50 feet [15 meters]

✹ **SYMBOLIC MEANING**
From Heaven.

🌸 **POSSIBLE POWERS**
Beauty; Create oxygen; Fragrance.

🍃 **FOLKLORE AND FACTS**
According to Tahitian legend, the scent of flowers blooming on the evergreen *Fagraea berteroana* Perfume Flower Tree is heavenly. This is because the tree originated in the Tenth Heaven, where the throne of God can be found and where God's face is seen. • *Fagraea berteroana* yellow flowers are often used to create beautiful, fragrant Hawaiian leis. • The common name of Ten Cent Flower is based on a 1930s selling price of Hawaiian leis made from the *Fagraea berteroana* flowers. • Perfume Flower Tree wood has been used to make drums, furniture, and tool handles. • All parts of the *Fagraea berteroana* tree are poisonous. • In the Solomon Islands, the Perfume Flower Tree is often grown as a living fence.

No. 188
Fagraea fragrans 🥣

Tembusa Tree
Ironwood Tree | Tembusu Tree

🌎 **POTENTIAL MAXIMUM HEIGHT**
82 feet [25 meters]

✹ **SYMBOLIC MEANING**
Hope during uncertain times.

🌸 **POSSIBLE POWERS**
Create oxygen; Euphoria; Hopefulness; Purpose; Resilience; Usefulness.

🍃 **FOLKLORE AND FACTS**
The inedible bitter fruit of the evergreen *Fagraea fragrans* Tembusa Tree is a favorite food of fruit bats. • The tree's very hard wood is often used to make chopping boards. • Tembusa Tree wood is long-lived and can last for over a hundred years. Furthermore, it will not be damaged by either termites or weevils. • Native to Singapore, an image of the Tembusa Tree has graced a Singaporean postage stamp as well as currency. • When the Tembusa Tree is in bloom,

the flowers produce a euphoric fragrance that delightfully perfumes the air, described as somewhat like a fresh lemony jasmine. • The smoothed, stained, and sealed roots of a *Fagraea fragrans* tree are sometimes transformed into plant stands that are most particularly used for bonsai tree specimens.

No. 189
Fagus grandifolia 🥣 🍴 🌰 🌰

North American Beech Tree
American Beech | Beech | Beech Tree | Beechwood | Bok | Boke | Buche | Buk | Buke | Faggio | Fagos | Faya | Haya | Hetre

🌎 **POTENTIAL MAXIMUM HEIGHT**
75 feet [23 meters]

✹ **SYMBOLIC MEANINGS**
Lovers' tryst; Personal finances.

🌸 **POSSIBLE POWERS**
Create oxygen; Creativity; Gambling; Money; Prosperity; Wishes.

🍃 **FOLKLORE AND FACTS**
The wood of the deciduous *Fagus grandifolia* American Beech tree is easily bent with steam, making it a favorite in making furniture that has curves. • Carry American Beech leaves or a piece of its wood to promote and increase creativity. • To make a wish, carve it on an American Beech stick then bury it. If the wish is meant to be, it will be. • The edible beechnuts should not be consumed raw.

F

No. 190

Fagus sylvatica 🌰 🍽 🌿 🌰

European Beech Tree

Common Beech | Copper Beech | Faggio | Fagos | Faya | Haya | Hetre | Queen of the Forest

📍 **POTENTIAL MAXIMUM HEIGHT**
164 feet [50 meters]

✹ **SYMBOLIC MEANINGS**
Ancient wisdom; Lovers'
tryst; Personal finances.

🌐 **POSSIBLE POWERS**
Create oxygen; Creativity;
Divination; Feminine
energy; Gambling;
Guidance from the past;
Happiness; Money;
Prosperity; Revealing
ancient knowledge; Saturn;
Sound resonance; Wishing;
Writing.

🜂 **FOLKLORE AND FACTS**
The deciduous *Fagus sylvatica* European Beech Tree
has a lifespan of up to three hundred years. • The tree
is considered to be native to southern England. • Make,
then carry or wear an amulet or sachet of European Beech
Tree leaves or a piece of its bark to promote and increase
creativity. • To make a wish, carve it on a European Beech
wood stick, then bury it. If the wish is meant to be, it will
be. • Make, then wear or carry a European Beech sachet to
improve your writing skills. • To increase inspiration, put a
European Beech Tree leaf within any two pages of your Book
of Shadows. • Considered to be the Queen of the Forest,
the European Beech Tree is the feminine matched to the
masculine English Oak tree, which is the King of the Forest.
• The smoothed wood of the European Beech Tree was used
as writing tablets. • The fruit of the European Beech Tree
is the unusual triangular-shaped beechnut, which is found
inside the splitting burrs that drop from the tree in autumn.
• European Beech nuts are edible but should not be eaten
raw. • European Beech wood is a favorite addition placed
at the bottom of the tanks used to ferment beer. It is also a
favorite wood used for smoking meats and some cheeses.
• European Beech Tree wood is hard with a straight grain
that is a favorite for cabinetry, furniture, tool handles, and
even musical instruments, such as drums. • When seeking
insight into the future from the past, make a white sachet
of Beech leaves, bits of bark, and nuts to place under
one's pillow.

No. 191

Feijoa sellowiana 🍽 🌿

Feijoa Tree

Brazilian Guava | Fig Guava | Guavasteen | Pineapple Guava

📍 **POTENTIAL MAXIMUM HEIGHT**
15 feet [5 meters]

✹ **SYMBOLIC MEANING**
Perfumed fruit.

🌐 **POSSIBLE POWERS**
Create oxygen; Ease depression;
Lift mood.

🜂 **FOLKLORE AND FACTS**
The evergreen *Feijoa sellowiana* Feijoa
Tree flowers are showy, fancifully frilly,
and have edible petals. It has a distinctly
exquisite fragrance that is strong
and equal to the finest high-quality
perfumes. • Fruiting is usually abundantly bountiful. When
the green plum-like fruit is ripe it will fall from the tree. It is
approximately the size of a chicken egg and rich in vitamin
C. For the fullest flavor, the fruit is most often sold, or most
likely generously shared, close within the vicinity to where
it has been grown. The fruit is usually eaten raw by scooping
out the fruit's pulp with a spoon. It is also used as an
ingredient in pies or desserts that include ice cream, sorbet,
and smoothies. • Feijoa fruit can also be pickled, made into
jam and jelly, or even a fermented beverage.

No. 192

Ficus benghalensis 🌰 🌿 🌰

Banyan Tree

Aalamaram | Arched Fig | Banian | Bargad | Bengal Fig | Borh | Ficus | India Fig |
Indian Fig Tree | Indian God Tree | Nyagrodha | Peral | Strangler Fig | Vada Tree |
Wad | Wish-fulfilling Tree

📍 **POTENTIAL MAXIMUM HEIGHT**
82 feet [25 meters]

✹ **SYMBOLIC MEANINGS**
Eternal life; Meditation; Reflection; Self-awareness.

🌐 **POSSIBLE POWERS**
Air element; Create oxygen; Happiness; Jupiter; Luck;
Masculine energy.

🜂 **FOLKLORE AND FACTS**
To look at or sit under the evergreen *Ficus benghalensis*
Banyan Tree will bring good luck. To be married beneath it

F

brings happiness and good luck to the couple. • Banyan trees represent eternal life in Hindu mythology. • As a strangler fig, the Banyan begins growing on another tree when one of its seeds fall into a crack or crevice in the host tree's trunk. The Banyan Tree will grow and begin enveloping the host tree until there is no more of the other tree left to be seen. • Banyan aerial roots will drop down and touch the ground, grab hold, and eventually grow to become more tree trunks that look separate, but are all still one great big tree that will keep growing and growing to become wider and wider, reaching enormous diameters. Regarding the area occupied by a single tree, which can grow to cover possibly acres of land, *Ficus benghalensis* is, without question, the biggest tree in the world. • The Great Banyan Tree can be found in the Acharya Jagadish Chandra Bose Botanical Garden in Calcutta, India, where it has been growing for at least 250 years. It is the widest Banyan in the world. The one tree system covers 3.5 acres (1.4 ha). The main trunk suffered from a fungus infection and had to be removed, but all the other trunks are still growing. • A very large Banyan Tree at the Jagannath Temple in Puri, India, is considered sacred and is believed to be at least five hundred years old. • Another in Anantapur, known as Thimmamma Marrimanu, is over 550 years old. • At his winter home in Fort Myers, Florida, Thomas Edison planted a little Banyan sapling in 1925 that was 4 inches (10 cm) in diameter. That tree is now 60 feet (18 m) tall and is over an acre (0.4 ha) wide. It is still growing.

No. 193

Ficus benjamina ☠ ◧

Benjamin Fig Tree

Ficus | Ficus Tree | Weeping Ficus | Weeping Fig

🔍 **POTENTIAL MAXIMUM HEIGHT**
98 feet [30 meters]

✸ **SYMBOLIC MEANING**
Peace and abundance.

🌀 **POSSIBLE POWERS**
Create oxygen; Healing; Knowledge; Unity; Universal understanding.

🍃 **FOLKLORE AND FACTS**
The evergreen *Ficus benjamina* Benjamin Fig Tree is a very common sight in the subtropical and tropical parts of the world.
• The fruit is small and enjoyed by birds.
• The bark is relatively smooth.
• The Benjamin Fig Tree can be potted and grown indoors where the light is just right for them. Indoors, they will grow approximately 7 feet (2.1 m) tall.
• Three trees planted together in one pot as saplings can be manually manipulated into an unnatural shape by twisting the trees' trunks into a braid, then coaxing them to slowly grow up together into an interestingly sculpted potted tree. • Given the space to follow its nature growing outdoors, a Benjamin Fig Tree can reach 98 feet (30 m) tall! It is then a gorgeous full tree that tends to lend itself to being the neighborhood "Big Tree" that many parents ultimately warn their children to be careful of when they are climbing all over it. • However, the Benjamin Fig Tree's roots have a bad reputation for invading foundations and pushing up sidewalks and driveways.

F

Ficus carica 🌿🍴🌱

Fig Tree

Common Fig | Doomoor | Dumur | Fico | Mhawa

🔍 POTENTIAL MAXIMUM HEIGHT

30 feet [9 meters]

✳ SYMBOLIC MEANINGS

Argument; Desire; Kiss; Longevity; Long-lived; Prolific.

🌐 POSSIBLE POWERS

Aphrodisiac; Attract love; Create oxygen; Divination; Fertility; Fire element; Jupiter; Love; Love charm; Masculine energy.

🍃 FOLKLORE AND FACTS

The deciduous *Ficus carica* Fig Tree has been cultivated since ancient times.
• In the Jewish text known as the Aggadah, it is written that the Forbidden Fruit grown on the Tree of Knowledge in the Garden of Eden was a fig. • In the Christian Bible's Book of Genesis, the leaves from a Fig Tree

in the Garden of Eden were what Adam and Eve supposedly covered themselves with to hide their newly perceived nakedness from God's eyes. • Fig leaves were often used to modestly cover the genitals of many other nude figures in artworks throughout the ages. • For a yes-or-no divination, write a question on a Fig Tree leaf. If the leaf dries quickly, the answer is no. If it dries slowly, then the answer is yes. • To increase fertility in both men and women and to overcome any sexual impotency or sexual incompetence of any kind, whittle a small phallic carving from *Ficus carica* wood. Then tuck it under the mattress and leave it there. • Figs can be eaten fresh, although they are most often available dried because they do not hold up well once picked. • Figs are a common ingredient in many baked goods, cookies, desserts, jams, beverages, wines, and liqueurs.

Ficus religiosa 🌿🌱🏺

Bodhi Tree

Ashvastha Tree | Bo Tree | Peepal | Pippala | Pippul | Pipul | Sacred Bo Tree | Sacred Fig | Sacred Tree

🔍 POTENTIAL MAXIMUM HEIGHT

98 feet [30 meters]

✳ SYMBOLIC MEANINGS

Awakening; Bright energy; Enlightenment; Fertility; Good luck; Happiness; Inspiration; Longevity; Meditation; Peace; Prosperity; Religiousness; Remembrance; Sacred tree; Sacredness; Ultimate potential; Wisdom.

🌐 POSSIBLE POWERS

Air element; Create oxygen; Enlightenment; Fertility; Jupiter; Masculine energy; Meditation; Protection; Wisdom.

🍃 FOLKLORE AND FACTS

The deciduous *Ficus religiosa* Bodhi Tree has been venerated as an extremely sacred tree for several thousands of years. The Bodhi Tree is believed by Hindu worshippers to be the mythic World-Tree that is the god Brahma himself, with all other gods and goddesses as divine branches of that tree as a canopy over the universe. • Some Biblical scholars believe that the Tree of Life was actually a huge *Ficus religiosa* tree. There is some scripture that could support that hypothesis. • To Buddhist worshippers, the Bodhi Tree appeared at the Buddha's birth. From under its matured branches Gautama Buddha received his first enlightenment, then afterwards went on to receive increasingly illuminated acknowledgements. • Legend tells that Siddhartha Gautama was sitting under the celestial blessed Bodhi Tree in Bodh Gaya, India at the time of his enlightenment. A direct descendant of this particular tree is enshrined within the Mahabodhi Temple in that city. • Another tree was taken as a cutting from the original Bodhi. Cultivated to be a sturdy sapling then hand-carried to Sri Lanka, it was then planted in Anuradhapura, Sri Lanka, in 288 BCE. It is known as the Sri Maha Bodhi Tree. This tree is very well documented to be the oldest known flowering tree planted by a human on Earth. It is still growing and is a frequent destination for Buddhist pilgrims. The Sri Maha Bodhi Tree is 2,300 years old. To this day, Hindu holy men, or Sadhus, meditate beneath it. Every part of the Sri Maha Bodhi Tree is considered to be sacredly holy. • It takes well over at least one hundred years to up to five hundred years for a Bodhi tree to be fully grown. • Walk clockwise around a Bodhi tree several times to make evil flee. • The ritual known as Bodhi Puja means "veneration of the Bodhi tree." It is carried out by chanting a mantra to the tree and offering the tree gifts such as milk, lamps, incense, cakes, sweets, and water. • Whenever a Bodhi Tree dies, whatever the reason, a sapling grown from another blessed Bodhi will be planted and consecrated to take its place. • The distinctive heart-shaped leaves of any Bodhi Tree are regarded as cherished relics when they have fallen underneath the tree. • To simply look directly upon any Bodhi Tree will bring exceptionally good luck and many blessings.

No. 196
Ficus sycomorus 🌱🌿🌰

Sycamore Fig Tree

Fig-mulberry | Mugumo Tree | Sycomore | Sycamore Fig Tree

🌐 POTENTIAL MAXIMUM HEIGHT
66 feet [20 meters]

✺ SYMBOLIC MEANINGS
Curiosity; Grief.

✹ POSSIBLE POWERS
Create oxygen; Divination; Fertility; Love; Luck; Prosperity; Protection; Shade.

✿ FOLKLORE AND FACTS
The deciduous *Ficus sycomorus* Sycamore Fig Tree is as sacred to ancient Egyptians and early nomadic tribes as the Oak was to the ancient Druids. • The ancient Egyptians considered the Sycamore Fig to be the Tree of Life. • Legend tells that Joseph and Mary rested under the shade of a Sycamore Fig when they were fleeing to Egypt from Bethlehem with baby Jesus. • The Sycamore Fig is one of the few trees mentioned in the Bible. It is referred to seven times in the Old Testament, and once in the New Testament.

• King David commissioned a careful watch over the Sycamore Fig Trees for their protection. • Some Egyptian mummy caskets were made from Sycamore Fig wood. • In the Christian Bible, Zacchaeus climbed up a Sycamore Fig Tree to see Jesus over the heads in a crowd. Jesus called for Zacchaeus to climb back down because Jesus wanted to visit his house. The crowd was shocked by that because they considered Zacchaeus too much of a sinner for someone like Jesus. • It is written that *Ficus sycomorus* was killed by frost during the biblical plagues upon the ancient Egyptians. • The fruit of the Sycamore Fig is large, fragrant, and sweet. It has a different flavor than a Common Fig and is edible fresh. Sycamore Figs can be found in Israeli produce markets. • *Ficus sycomorus* is a sacred tree to the Kikuyu people who live in the highlands near Mount Kenya. So much so, that if a Sycamore Fig Tree were to fall, it was considered a very bad omen requiring rituals to fend off the trouble that was coming.

No. 197
Firmiana simplex 🌱🍴🌿

Chinese Parasol Tree

Chinese Parasoltree | Wutong | Wútóng

🌐 POTENTIAL MAXIMUM HEIGHT
50 feet [15 meters]

✺ SYMBOLIC MEANINGS
Fascinating; Happiness; Words.

✹ POSSIBLE POWERS
Create oxygen; Moon; Sound resonance; Water element.

✿ FOLKLORE AND FACTS
Depending on the weather and time of day, when the deciduous *Firmiana simplex* Chinese Parasol Tree is in bloom, the fragrance of the greenish-white flowers will vary between lemony-citronella and lemony-chocolate. The seeds are edible and have been roasted to brew tea. • Chinese Parasol wood is used for the soundboards of the Chinese musical instruments known as the guqin and guzheng. It is also used to make coffins. • In China, there was a time when the Chinese Parasol Tree would be found growing in the gardens of poets and scholars. • It is believed by some that applying the juice of the crushed seeds to the hair will make grey hair fall out and then grow back as black hair.

F

No. 198

Fortunella japonica ☙ ❚❙ ⚘

Kumquat Tree

Cumquat | Gäm-Gwät | Golden Orange | Golden Tangerine | Hong Kong Kumquat | Jangsu Kumquat | Kim Quất | Kinkan | Marumi Kumquat | Meiwa Kumquat | Morgani Kumquat | Muntala | Nagami Kumquat | Oval Kumquat | Round Kumquat | Somchid

◉ POTENTIAL MAXIMUM HEIGHT
15 feet [5 meters]

✹ SYMBOLIC MEANINGS
Fortunate; Good luck; Good luck of the best kind; Prosperity; Prosperous good luck; What glitters may not be gold.

✺ POSSIBLE POWERS
Air element; Create oxygen; Prosperity; Sun; Wealth.

☙ FOLKLORE AND FACTS
In 1846, a collector for the London Horticultural Society introduced the Western world to the evergreen *Fortunella japonica* Kumquat Tree. • Its fruit has an appealing sweet peel with a very tart interior that could imply that which appears golden may not truly be gold. The fruit is mostly eaten fresh, although it can be cooked to make jelly and marmalade. • Kumquats are referenced in imperial Chinese literature dating back to the twelfth century. • Kumquats and Kumquat Trees are often given as much-appreciated gifts during the Lunar New Year celebration in Asian countries. • The Hong Kong Kumquat, which is more often grown as an ornamental tree, is also known as the *Citrus hindsii* or *Fortunella hindsii*. It has large seeds, tastes bitter, and is not much larger than pea-size. What is *most* interesting about the Hong Kong Kumquat is that it is the most primitive of all the Kumquat varieties and is believed to be the species from which *all Citrus* has evolved!

No. 199

Fraxinus excelsior ☙ ⚘ ❚

Ash Tree

Ashe | Asktroed | Beli | Common Ash | European Ash | Fraxinus | Freixo | Jasen | King Tree | King Wood

◉ POTENTIAL MAXIMUM HEIGHT
141 feet [43 meters]

✹ SYMBOLIC MEANINGS
Expansion; Grandeur; Greatness; Growth; Higher perspective.

✺ POSSIBLE POWERS
Create oxygen; Divination; Female mysteries; Fend off fairies; Fire element; Focus; Good singing; Healing; Image magic; Invincibility; Karmic laws; Linking the inner world with the outer world; Love; Luck; Magical potency; Mars; Masculine energy; Neptune; Ocean rituals; Prophetic dreams; Prosperity; Protection; Protection from drowning; Purify soul for resurrection; Sea magic; Sea ritual; Sea spells; Strength of purpose; Sun; Uranus; Willing to repent for our sins.

☙ FOLKLORE AND FACTS
The deciduous *Fraxinus excelsior* Ash Tree was revered by the ancient Greeks, Romans, and Germanic peoples. It is also one of the three highly sacred trees of the Druids. • It is not uncommon to find Ash Trees that have been festooned with wishes represented by strips of cloth known as cloots, as well as with colored ribbons and cloth, trinkets, charms, and wishing coins tucked in and

around it. • The ancient Greeks once believed that the world was born of the clouds, which was believed to be the bower of a great mythical Ash Tree, which in turn was considered the father of all. Oak trees were considered the first mothers. • In Norse mythology an Ash Tree called Yggdrasil is believed to be the greatest and best of all trees and is the actual center of the world. Yggdrasil draws up wisdom and faith via its roots in the underground. Its trunk supports the Earth. Its leaves touch Heaven. All that transpires on Yggdrasil affects life for everyone and everything, everywhere, and in every way on the Earth. Some people still believe that every what, where, when, why, or who can be identified by something that transpired on Yggdrasil, even if it seemingly appears to be only remotely so. To those believers, everything connects to Yggdrasil. • For protection when going out to sea, carry a cross carved from Ash wood that is a cross within a circle, known as the solar cross. • An Ash-wood staff over doors and windows protects against sorcery. • Druid wands are often made of Ash wood because the grain is straight and the wood has a springiness that is favored for fashioning spears. • Burn a Yule log of Ash wood for prosperity. • Make, then carry a sachet of Ash leaves to gain love from the opposite sex and for protection when traveling. • Ash leaves under a pillow may promote prophetic dreams. • As a folk preventative against illness, keep a bowl of water holding fresh Ash leaves by the bed. Empty out the bowl in the morning. • It is believed by some that snakes are repelled by Ash. • Ash wood is strong and favored in woodworking and wooden basketry. • A powerful set of runes can be made from Ash wood. • A *Fraxinus excelsior* Ash Tree can be easily propagated from a seed. • Scatter Ash wood chips, sawdust, or leaves around the perimeter and in all four directions near the home to protect the house and the entire area around the house, or around a barn housing livestock if fairies have become particularly troublesome.

No. 200

Fraxinus ornus 🐚 🌿 🌰

Manna Ash Tree

Flowering Ash Tree | Frassino da Manna | Fresno del Maná | Manna Ash | South European Flowering Ash

POTENTIAL MAXIMUM HEIGHT
82 feet [25 meters]

SYMBOLIC MEANINGS
Grandeur; Higher perspective.

POSSIBLE POWERS
Create oxygen; Divination; Knowledge; Luck; Mystical power; Plenty; Power; Spirituality; Strength; Supply.

FOLKLORE AND FACTS
Around the year 1400, it was assumed that the sugary sap of the deciduous *Fraxinus ornus* Manna Ash Tree was as giving and sustaining as biblical manna. The sap exudes a sugary sap that is gathered by making a cut in the bark. • The tree is often planted as an ornamental because of its beauty when it is in full bloom.

F

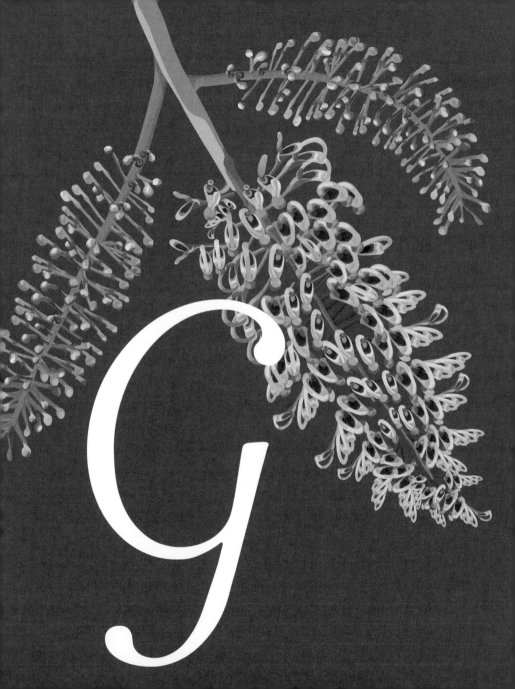

No. 201
Garcinia gummi-gutta ☠ ✿ 🍴 🌿
Garcinia Cambogia Tree
Brindle Berry | Brindleberry | Goraka | Kudam Puli | Malabar Tamarind

📷 **POTENTIAL MAXIMUM HEIGHT**
20 feet [6 meters]

✴ **SYMBOLIC MEANING**
Scouring fruit.

🌸 **POSSIBLE POWER**
Create oxygen.

🍃 **FOLKLORE AND FACTS**
Due to tremendous marketing efforts on the internet, the evergreen *Garcinia gummi-gutta* Garcinia Cambogia Tree fruit became a popular weight-loss supplement, touted as a miraculous and natural way to melt off excess weight. The fact is, the hype was overrated, with no significant evidence of weight loss. However, there was actual evidence of extreme liver toxicity resulting in damage associated with consumption of the Garcinia Cambogia fruit. Some of the commercial preparations were also found to be using too much or too little of the herb, further complicating combinations with any other ingredients that were unsafe for human consumption. • In a Japanese study of overweight rats being fed Garcinia Cambogia, they did lose some weight. However, this resulted in the rats suffering from subsequent testicular atrophy. • In Sri Lanka and other parts of southeast Asia, Garcinia Cambogia is frequently used as an ingredient in curries and other traditional recipes to add a sour taste to a dish.

No. 202
Garcinia indica ✿ 🍴 🌿
Kokum Tree
Kokum Butter Tree | Kundong

📷 **POTENTIAL MAXIMUM HEIGHT**
59 feet [18 meters]

✴ **SYMBOLIC MEANING**
Love for one another.

🌸 **POSSIBLE POWERS**
Cooling; Create oxygen; Healing; Love; Protection from all worldly diseases.

🍃 **FOLKLORE AND FACTS**
The evergreen *Garcinia indica* Kokum Tree produces edible fruit. • The outer covering of the fruit is sun-dried

to be used as a seasoning as well as a substitute for the sour-tasting Tamarind fruit, particularly in curries and soups. The fruit pulp is sweetened with sugar and diluted with water to make sherbet desserts and a beverage that is popular in parts of India. A fatty, butter-like extract called kokum butter is obtained from the seeds and is used in the making of chocolate confections.

No. 203
Garcinia mangostana 🍴 🌿
Mangosteen Tree
Mang-Chi-Shih | Purple Mangosteen | The Queen of Fruit

📷 **POTENTIAL MAXIMUM HEIGHT**
82 feet [25 meters]

✴ **SYMBOLIC MEANING**
Honesty.

🌸 **POSSIBLE POWERS**
Create oxygen; Honesty; Truth.

🍃 **FOLKLORE AND FACTS**
The evergreen *Garcinia mangostana* Mangosteen Tree is cultivated in Southeast Asia and is considered to be the most deliciously luscious of all fruits. For generations, their fragility restricted shipping them, which was disconcerting for yearning fruit lovers. During the ten-week-long Mangosteen season, fresh fruit is most often sold from roadside fruit stands wherever they are grown. • There is an undocumented rumor that the English Queen Victoria offered a hefty reward of a knighthood to anyone who could bring her a fresh Mangosteen fruit. There is no record that she ever received one. • Once a Mangosteen Tree has established itself in a consistently warm climate and has matured to fruiting, which can take between six to twelve years, it can live and produce fruit for at least one hundred years.

G

No. 204
Gardenia brighamii
Hawaiian Gardenia
Forest Gardenia | Nānū | Na'u | Na'u

POTENTIAL MAXIMUM HEIGHT
20 feet [6 meters]

SYMBOLIC MEANINGS
Fragility; Passionate love;
Secret love.

POSSIBLE POWERS
Create oxygen;
Fragrance; Passion;
Romance; Secrets.

FOLKLORE AND FACTS
There is an effort to plant more
evergreen *Gardenia brighamii* Hawaiian
Gardenia trees in Hawaiian gardens as ornamental trees. In
the wild, however, the lovely flowering tree is on the verge of
extinction. There are only two remaining trees on O'ahu and
one tree on the Big Island where their forest habitat has been
diminished, as well as overtaken by invasive species such as
fountain grass. • The leaves of the Hawaiian Gardenia are
very green and glossy. The flowers are white, six-petaled,
intensely perfumed, and have been used to make leis. • The
wood of the Hawaiian Gardenia has been used to make
house posts.

No. 205
Gardenia jasminoides
Common Gardenia
Cape Jasmine | Cape Jessamine | Gardenia

POTENTIAL MAXIMUM HEIGHT
10 feet [3 meters]

SYMBOLIC MEANINGS
Ecstasy; Emotional support; Exhilarating emotions; Good
luck; Healing; I am too happy; I love you in secret; Joy; Love;
Passionate love; Peace; Purification; Purity; Refinement;
Romance; Secret love; Spirituality; Sweet love; Transient joy;
Transport; Transport of joy; You are lovely; You're lovely.

POSSIBLE POWERS
Aphrodisiac; Attraction; Clarity; Create oxygen; Exotic
mood; Healing; Hope; Innocence; Love; Modesty; Peace;
Protection; Renewal; Romance; Sensuality; Sincerity;
Spiritual world; Spirituality; Trust.

FOLKLORE AND FACTS
The leaves of the
evergreen *Gardenia
jasminoides* Gardenia are
large, green, and very
glossy. • The flowers are
white, double-bloomed,
and so intensely fragrant
that they are unforgettable. At sunset and in the early
morning, the flowers are even more fragrant. • The Gardenia
is a member of the *Coffea* family. • The fruit of the Gardenia
can be used as a natural yellow textile dye. • Due to the
extremely high spiritual vibrations of *Gardenia jasminoides,*
float a blossom in a bowl of fresh water or scatter dried
petals around the room to promote a sense of extreme inner
peacefulness and increased spirituality.

No. 206
Gaultheria shallon
Salal Tree
Gaultheria | Lemon Leaf | Shallon

POTENTIAL MAXIMUM HEIGHT
10 feet [3 meters]

SYMBOLIC MEANING
Exuberant.

POSSIBLE POWERS
Create oxygen; Healing.

FOLKLORE AND FACTS
The evergreen *Gaultheria
shallon* Salal Tree is small with
branches and leathery egg-shaped leaves
that can remain attached for up to four years. • The leaves
are a favorite of florists who refer to them as Lemon Leaf.
• The Salal Tree's dark blue berries are edible fresh or dried
and are used in various dishes and as a sweetener. • In some
parts of the world, *Gaultheria shallon* has become invasive.

No. 207

Ginkgo biloba ☠ ✿ 🍴 🌲

Ginkgo Tree

Ginnan | Icho | In Xing | Maidenhair Tree | Tree of Life

📷 **POTENTIAL MAXIMUM HEIGHT**
165 feet [50 meters]

✳ **SYMBOLIC MEANINGS**
Age; Old age; Remembering; Survival; Thoughtfulness;
True Tree of Life.

🌀 **POSSIBLE POWERS**
Aphrodisiac; Attract love; Create oxygen; Fertility; Healing;
Intense concentration; Longevity; Love; Mental acuity;
Survival under the most extreme of all circumstances.

🌙 **FOLKLORE AND FACTS**
The deciduous *Ginkgo biloba* Ginkgo Tree is considered a living fossil because it is the only member of its genus, which is also the only genus in its family, which is also the only family in its order, which is also the only order in its subclass. • Gingko dates from before the time
that dinosaurs roamed the Earth. Ginkgo leaf fossils are very commonly found in the rocks that date back to both the Jurassic and Cretaceous Eras. • Wild *Ginkgo biloba* is rated as critically endangered, with only a few hundred trees remaining due to competition for nutrients, water, and light. • Ginkgo has been used in Chinese medicine since the eleventh century. • The cooked kernels of Ginkgo seeds are valued in Asia and used as an ingredient in special-occasion foods such as Buddha's delight, which has been traditionally prepared for the Lunar New Year, and in some dishes served at weddings.

No. 208

Gleditsia triacanthos ✿ 🌲

Honey Locust Tree

Green Locust Tree | Thorny Honeylocust | Thorny Locust

📷 **POTENTIAL MAXIMUM HEIGHT**
98 feet [30 meters]

✳ **SYMBOLIC MEANINGS**
Affection beyond the grave;
Elegance; Love after death;
Love beyond the grave.

🌀 **POSSIBLE POWERS**
Create oxygen; Puncture.

🌙 **FOLKLORE AND FACTS**
The deciduous *Gleditsia triacanthos* Honey Locust Tree is a very tall and immensely terrifyingly thorny flowering tree that has a wide canopy and can live up to one hundred years. The treacherous thorns that completely cover the trunk and branches are usually 2 to 4 inches (5 to 10 cm) long, with some reaching 8 inches (20 cm) long! • The thorns of the Honey Locust can puncture the thick rubber of a truck tire. • In the era of wooden shipbuilding, the hard thorns of the *Gleditsia triacanthos* were often used as nails.

G

No. 209

Gnetum gnemon 🐄 🍴

Melinjo Tree

Bago | Belinjo | Daeking Tree | Gnemon Tree | Gnetum | Joint Fir | Joint-fir Spinach |
Melinjo Nut | Meminjau | Paddy Oats | Padi Oats | Spinach Joint Fir | Two Leaf

◉ POTENTIAL MAXIMUM HEIGHT
49 feet [15 meters]

☀ SYMBOLIC MEANING
Intuitive.

🌑 POSSIBLE POWERS
Create oxygen; Intuition;
Shade.

🜨 FOLKLORE AND FACTS
The evergreen *Gnetum
gnemon* Melinjo Tree grows
throughout Indonesia,
providing much-needed shade as a pleasant comfort in the
extreme heat of the tropics. • The nuts are edible raw, boiled,
or roasted. The cooked new leaves, flowers, outer flesh of the
fruit, and seeds are commonly used for a sour flavoring in
curries, soups, and stews throughout Indonesia, New Guinea,
Thailand, the Philippines, Fiji, and the Solomon Islands. • A
natural resveratrol, which acts somewhat like an antioxidant,
can be extracted from Melinjo seeds.

No. 210

Grevillea robusta ☠ 🐄 🌿

Silky Oak Tree

Agravilla | Australian Silver Oak | Australische Seideneiche | Bahekar | Bekkar |
Chene d'Australie | Grevillée Robuste | Ha'iku Ke'oke'o | Helecho | Kangiyo | Khadaw Hmi |
Mgrivea | Mukima | Oka-kK | Salamander | Savukkumaram | Shinobu-no-ki

◉ POTENTIAL MAXIMUM HEIGHT
98 feet [30 meters]

☀ SYMBOLIC MEANINGS
Elope with me; Impulsive acts of love.

🌑 POSSIBLE POWERS
Create oxygen; Impulsive love; Impulsivity.

🜨 FOLKLORE AND FACTS
Older than the dinosaurs and referred to as an Oak, the
evergreen *Grevillea robusta* Silky Oak Tree is not an Oak
at all. • Petal-less flowers on a long calyx give them the
stylized appearance of toothbrush bristles. • Due to its
tonal attributes, *Grevillea robusta* wood has been used on
the backs and sides of some acoustic guitars. • The heavily
dripping nectar from the flowers is toxic with cyanide.
• The leaves can produce yellow to green dye for silk.

G

No. 211

Guibourtia tessmannii 🥣

Bubinga Tree

Akume | Binbinga | Buvenga | Essingang | Kevazingo | Lianu | Moubaka | Mouega | Mutenye |
Ovang | Oveng | Waka | Waku

🔍 POTENTIAL MAXIMUM HEIGHT
213 feet [65 meters]

✳ SYMBOLIC MEANING
Intuitive.

🌀 POSSIBLE POWERS
Compassion; Create oxygen; Divination; Enhancement;
Feminine energy; Healing; Influence; Insight; Intuition;
Loving; Nurturing; Positive energy; Sound resonance;
Spirituality.

🜛 FOLKLORE AND FACTS
The evergreen *Guibourtia tessmannii* Bubinga Tree is a
very large, tall tree that grows along streams, near rivers,
and in swamps. • It has very attractive, durably hard,
reddish-brown wood that is streaked with purple. • Wild
harvested, the wood of the Bubinga Tree is intended for
the production of many different things such as furniture,
containers, musical instruments, plywood, flooring, wall
paneling, cabinetry, and veneer. • Its bark is highly
valued for its use in several different traditional medicines.
• Bubinga seeds are a favorite food of monkeys and hornbills.

No. 212

Haematoxylum campechianum 🝆🌿

Logwood

Blackwood | Bloodwood Tree | Bluewood | Campeachy Tree | Campeachy Wood | Campeche Logwood | Campeche Wood | Jamaica Wood

◉ POTENTIAL MAXIMUM HEIGHT
32 feet [10 meters]

✳ SYMBOLIC MEANING
Blood wood.

🌐 POSSIBLE POWERS
Create oxygen; Healing.

☘ FOLKLORE AND FACTS
During the seventeenth century, the deciduous *Haematoxylum campechianum* Logwood tree's wood was highly desired and expensive. It was not uncommon for English, French, and Dutch ships crossing the sea with cargos of Logwood to be attacked by the Spanish, because most of the ships were sailing out of Logwood cutting camps in Central and South America. These were the lands that the Spanish had claimed as their own. The English, French, and Dutch knew they risked being attacked for harvesting where they should not have been, but it was commonly believed that for the valuable Logwood, it was worth taking a chance. In addition to attacks by the Spanish were relentless, attacking pirates who had significantly multiplied when out-of-work Logwood cutters were forced off the land and joined in to become pirates, too. There were also some unemployed cutters who worked on the sly, cutting Logwood that the pirates also took. The bonus for iconic pirate captains, such as Blackbeard, Samuel Bellamy, and others, was that they also gained the captured vessels to add to their pirating fleet. • Logwood is a flowering tree that was used for folk medicinal purposes, but more often to make a versatile dye that was useful for paper and fabrics from the seventeenth through the nineteenth centuries. • The Logwood dye was made using the wood chips from the thorny branches, producing blue, lavender, and dark blue-black colors. The dried-out chips could be stored for long periods and used repeatedly. • An extract that is used to stain blood samples is obtained from Logwood. • Bees favor the nectar of Logwood flowers.

No. 213

Hamamelis virginiana 🝆🌿🌰🔔

Witch Hazel Tree

American Witch Hazel | Common Witch Hazel | Wice Hazel | Winterbloom

◉ POTENTIAL MAXIMUM HEIGHT
30 feet [9 meters]

✳ SYMBOLIC MEANINGS
Changeable; Chastity; a Magic spell; a Spell.

🌐 POSSIBLE POWERS
Chastity; Create oxygen; Divination; Fire element; Masculine energy; Protection; Sun.

☘ FOLKLORE AND FACTS
A forked twig from the deciduous *Hamamelis virginiana* Witch Hazel Tree is the preferred and most commonly used divining rod because it is the most effective. • Many water dowsers, which are also known as water finders, doodlebugs, or water witchers, depend on their Witch Hazel forked divining rod or their dual, L-shaped divining sticks to seek out where to start digging a water well. • Dowsing with a Witch Hazel divining rod is believed to have started in Germany during the fifteenth century in an effort to find ground ores, most particularly gold. • Witch Hazel has been used as a soothing antiseptic and astringent for skin for several hundred years. • The Iroquois people would pour hot water over crushed Witch Hazel leaves to use in poultices that would be applied to reduce the swelling and pain caused by a sprain. • A very fine wand to use for fending off malignant influences and to demand full restoration of positive energy is one made of Witch Hazel wood. • Carry a sprig of Witch Hazel to heal a broken heart.

H

No. 214

Hevea brasiliensis 🐜🗡

Rubber Tree

Pará Rubber Tree | Seringueira | Sharinga Tree | South American Rubber Tree

📷 **POTENTIAL MAXIMUM HEIGHT**
131 feet [40 meters]

✴ **SYMBOLIC MEANINGS**
Fortifier; Resilience; Supporter; Traveler.

🌐 **POSSIBLE POWERS**
Create oxygen; Earth element; Manifestation of shape from liquid.

🌿 **FOLKLORE AND FACTS**
In the past, the production of rubber so strong it could be processed to create a tire tough enough to use on an airplane started out as liquid latex tapped from the trunk of an evergreen *Hevea brasiliensis* Rubber Tree. • The wood of the Rubber Tree is harvested when a tree has outlived its usefulness, between twenty-five to thirty years old, and the tree is removed from an Indonesian plantation to make room to plant another. • When persistent blights were attacking the indigenous Rubber Trees on South American plantations, the plantations were moved to South and Southeast Asia to avoid these blights, although this transition may not have been entirely protective
to the species. • It
takes ten years
of growth to
produce
the first
tapped
harvest of
latex from a
Rubber Tree.

No. 215

Hibiscus rosa-sinensis 🗡🍴🌿

Hibiscus

Astromelia | Bunga Raya | Cañeno | Chemparathy | Chijin | Chinese Hibiscus | Clavel Japonés | Erhonghua | Escandalosa | Flor de Jamaica | Fosang | Fusang | Graxa | Gumamela | Hibiscus | Hongfusang | Hongmujin | Huohonghua | Jaba | Jaswand | Jiamudan | Kembang Sepatu | Kharkady | Mamdaram | Mondaro | Queen of Tropical Flowers | Riji | Rosa de Cayena | Sangjin | Sembaruthi | Shoe Flower | Shoeflower | Songjin | Tuhonghua | Tulipan | Wada Mal | Zhaodianhong | Zhongguoqiangwei

📷 **POTENTIAL MAXIMUM HEIGHT**
12 feet [4 meters]

✴ **SYMBOLIC MEANINGS**
Beauty; Delicate; Delicate beauty; Peace and happiness; Rare beauty.

🌐 **POSSIBLE POWERS**
Ambition; Attitude; Celebration of the simplest joy; Clear thinking; Create oxygen; Divination; Enjoying each step of life's journey; Feminine energy; Harmony; Higher understanding; Logic; Love; Lust; Manifestation in material form; Outward expression of happiness or joy; Seeing hidden and obvious beauty; Spiritual concepts; Thought processes; Venus; Water element.

🌿 **FOLKLORE AND FACTS**
The flower from the evergreen *Hibiscus rosa-sinensis* Hibiscus will bloom to live for only one day. • It is sometimes called a Shoe Flower because the crushed petals can be used to shine shoes. • In the Pacific Islands, a red Hibiscus flower is worn by women as a sign of their interest. If worn behind the left ear, it signals that the woman desires a lover. If behind the right ear, she already has a lover. If a Hibiscus is worn behind both ears, it signals that she has one lover but would welcome another one. • In tropical countries, Hibiscus flowers are tucked into marital wreaths that are used as a marriage ceremony decoration. • In parts of India, the Hibiscus flower is used to venerate the Hindu goddess Kali. • Gifting Hibiscus to someone is an invitation to vacation where it grows. • In Polynesia, the raw petals of the Hibiscus flower are sometimes used in a salad. • The dried Hibiscus petals can be brewed as a tea and to colorize liqueurs.

H

No. 216
Hibiscus syriacus 🌿🍴🌳
Rose of Sharon Tree
Mokkeunhwa | Mugunghwa | Rose of Althea | Shrub Althea | Syrian Ketmia | Syrian Mallow | Tree Hollyhock

🔍 **POTENTIAL MAXIMUM HEIGHT**
12 feet [4 meters]

✳ **SYMBOLIC MEANINGS**
Consumed by love; Eternity; Persistent love; Persuasion.

🌐 **POSSIBLE POWERS**
Create oxygen; Exorcism; Inexhaustible abundance; Love; Protection.

🜨 **FOLKLORE AND FACTS**
After being grown in Korean gardens for thousands of years for both ornamental and edible purposes, the deciduous *Hibiscus syriacus* Rose of Sharon Tree was first brought to Europe during the sixteenth century. • The flowers are five-petaled, large, showy, and can be found in a wide variety of bicolors or solid colors of white, blue, pink, purple, and red. • The leaves are sometimes brewed into a tea.

No. 217
Hippomane mancinella ☠
Manchineel Tree
Little Apple of Death Tree | Machineal Tree | Machioneel | Mancanilla | Mancinella | Manzanilla del la Muerte | Marzanilla

🔍 **POTENTIAL MAXIMUM HEIGHT**
40 feet [12 meters]

✳ **SYMBOLIC MEANINGS**
Betrayal; Falsehood; Falseness.

🌐 **POSSIBLE POWERS**
Create oxygen; Death; Injury; Sorrow.

🜨 **FOLKLORE AND FACTS**
Found on or near coastal beaches, the deciduous *Hippomane mancinella* Manchineel Tree is one of the most toxic trees on Earth. Simply even touching any part of it will cause an excruciating, long-lingering rash. • When explorer Juan Ponce de León was camped near St. Petersburg, Florida, he was wounded by an arrow poisoned with *Hippomane mancinella* sap. He died a few days later. • The ancient Carib and Calusa peoples favored a manner of killing captives by simply tying the victim to the trunk of the Manchineel Tree and letting the poisonous bark do the painful dirty deed. • The smoke from a burning Manchineel Tree can cause blindness. • A Machineel Tree is usually not marked as being deadly poisonous in most places, but in some places you might see a red "X" or a red band on the trunk a few feet up from the ground. Or there might be an actual warning sign to stay away from it because it is an extremely dangerous tree. • Do not touch, eat, or even inhale the air around the Machineel Tree. • The milky sap of the Manchineel Tree can strip paint from cars. • A single drop of the milky sap of the Manchineel Tree mixed with even one drop of rainwater or dew merely falling on the skin will cause serious blistering, so never take cover under it for any reason.

H

No. 218

Hippophae rhamnoides 🪵🍴🌱

Sea Buckthorn
Sallow Thorn | Sea-buckthorn

📷 POTENTIAL MAXIMUM HEIGHT
30 feet [9 meters]

☀ SYMBOLIC MEANINGS
Glowing mane;
Horse shiner.

🌸 POSSIBLE POWERS
Beauty; Create oxygen;
Healing.

🍂 FOLKLORE AND FACTS
The edible berries
that grow on the spiny
deciduous *Hippophae
rhamnoides* Sea Buckthorn
need to be *pulled* from the thorny branches of the plant by
hand, which makes harvesting them labor-intensive and
time-consuming. However, the fruit contains a much higher
level of vitamin C than is present in Oranges, Lemons, or
Limes. • Sea Buckthorn berries are used in some cosmetics
and Russian and Asian folk medicine. It is also used as a food
for livestock.

No. 219

Hopea odorata ☠🪵🌱🌰🌶

White Thingan Tree
Cengal Pulau | Chengal Kampong | Chengal Mas | Chengal Pasir | Kh'e:n | Koki |
Merawan Siput | Merawan Tree | Jantah Mosau | Sao Den | Sao Nghẻ | Sauchi |
Ta-Khian Tree | Takhian Thong | Takhian-Yai | Telshur | Telsur | Tersol | Thingan

📷 POTENTIAL MAXIMUM HEIGHT
131 feet [40 meters]

☀ SYMBOLIC MEANING
Fragrant spirit.

🌸 POSSIBLE POWER
Answer prayers; Create oxygen; Grant wishes.

🍂 FOLKLORE AND FACTS
In Thailand, there is a strong belief that a tree ghost spirit by
the name of Lady Ta-Khian actually inhabits the evergreen
Hopea odorata White Thingan Tree. It is for that reason
that the tree is considered to be immensely sacred and is
generously venerated with offerings of colorful, long silk
ribbons and gifts of all kinds.

No. 220

Hovenia dulcis 🪵🍴🌱

Japanese Raisin Tree
Oriental Raisin Tree

📷 POTENTIAL MAXIMUM HEIGHT
32 feet [10 meters]

☀ SYMBOLIC MEANING
Fisted hand.

🌸 POSSIBLE POWER
Create oxygen; Healing.

🍂 FOLKLORE AND FACTS
The flowers of the deciduous *Hovenia dulcis* Japanese
Raisin Tree are fleshy and look like raisins when they are
dried. They are sweet, fragrant, and edible both raw and
cooked. The flowers can also be brewed as a tea. • The
extract that is taken from the *Hovenia dulcis* leaves, stem,
and seeds is very sweet and used as a substitute for honey in
confections and winemaking.

No. 221

Hura crepitans ☠🪵

Dynamite Tree
Hura | Jabillo | Monkey No Climb Tree | Possumwood | Sandbox Tree

📷 POTENTIAL MAXIMUM HEIGHT
130 feet [40 meters]

☀ SYMBOLIC MEANING
Sudden harm.

🌸 POSSIBLE POWERS
Create oxygen; Injury;
Poison; Treachery.

🍂 FOLKLORE AND FACTS
The evergreen *Hura crepitans*
Dynamite Tree is considered one
of the most dangerous trees in
the world. Every part of the tree is
poisonous. But that is not the worst of it. The trunk is
covered over with hard, sharp, spikelike thorns. The
small pumpkin-shaped dried fruit is woody and will
loudly explode to the touch, sending poisonous seeds up
to 60 feet (18 m) outwards in several different directions,
at a speed of up to 150 miles per hour! • The Dynamite
Tree's poisonous milky sap is used as a fish toxin and for
tipping poisonous arrows and spears.

No. 222

Hymenaea courbaril ♂ ⑪

West Indian Locust Tree

Algarroba | Algarrobillo | Algarrobo | Amami-Gum | Ámbar | Brazilian Cherry |
Brazilian Copal | Copal | Copal Americano | Corobore | Courbaril | Flour Tree |
Guapinol | Mangle Duro | Nazareno | Pecueca | Stink Toe | Stinking Toe

◉ POTENTIAL MAXIMUM HEIGHT

98 feet [30 meters]

✸ SYMBOLIC MEANINGS

Marriage; Sustenance.

✿ POSSIBLE POWERS

Create oxygen; Fire
element; Healing; Incense;
Love; Marriage;
Masculine energy; Sun;
Survival.

☾ FOLKLORE AND FACTS

The evergreen *Hymenaea
courbaril* West Indian Locust Tree
primarily grows in South America.
• It produces large, unpleasantly
smelling pods that are at least 4 inches (10 cm)
long. • The legumes are used to make custards, ice creams,
liqueur, and a tea. If the legume's pulp is eaten raw, it will
cling unpleasantly inside the mouth. If the pulp is dried
and made into a powder, it can be added into soups and
baked goods. • Because of its exceptionally high levels of
proteins and starches, West Indian Locust provides what is
known to be one of the richest vegetable foods on Earth. It
has sustained many indigenous peoples in South America
for millennia. • The genus for the West Indian Locust is
Hymenaea, named after the Greek god of marriage, Hymen,
making it useful to add to love amulets and in the incense
burned at weddings.

H

No. 223

Ilex aquifolium ☠ ✶ ☙

English Holly Tree

Bat's Wings | Christ's Thorn | Christmas Holly | Common Holly | European Holly | Holly |
Holly Bush | Holly Herb | Holly Tree | Holm Chaste | Hulm | Hulver Bush | Ilex | Tinne

◉ POTENTIAL MAXIMUM HEIGHT
29 feet [9 meters]

✸ SYMBOLIC MEANINGS
Am I forgotten?; Courage; Defense; Difficult victory attained;
Domestic happiness; Dreams; Enchantment; Eternal Life;
Fire element; Forecast; Foresight; Good cheer; Good luck;
Goodwill; Looking; Mars; Masculine energy; Protection;
Questioning; Subconscious; Symbol of a human being;
Symbol of Man; Vigilance; Winter's death and rebirth;
Wisdom.

❦ COMPONENT MEANING
Berries: Christmas joy.

❀ POSSIBLE POWERS
Animals; Anti-lightning; Attracts and repels energy;
Consecration; Create oxygen; Directed balance; Dream; Ease
the passage to death; Enhance magic; Good luck; Healing;
Holiness; Immortality; Invulnerability; Luck; Protection;
Protection against harm in a dream; Protection against the
evil eye; Protection against witchcraft; Prophecy; Restfulness;
Sex; Sleep; Vigor; Watchfulness.

❧ FOLKLORE AND FACTS
In England, it is still believed that it is very bad luck to cut
down an evergreen *Ilex aquifolium* English Holly Tree
because the tree represents eternal life. • The ancient Druids
believed that English Holly kept the Earth beautiful during
the time when the Oak trees were leafless. • The Druids
wore English Holly leaves in their hair when their priests cut
the sacred mistletoe from the White Oak trees. • In medieval
Europe, English Holly was planted near homes for good
fortune and to protect them from lightning. • An English
Holly leaf will bring good luck to any person who carries or
wears it. • In England, it was thought that a sprig of English
Holly on a bedpost would invite sweet dreams. • In Wales,
it was believed that bringing English Holly into the home
before Christmas would instigate arguments. • Another
belief is that keeping a piece of English Holly that was used
as a Christmas church decoration will bring about good
fortune throughout the year. • If English Holly is picked on
Christmas Day, it will be very good protection against evil
spirits and witches. • Place tiny candles on English Holly
leaves and float them on water. If the leaves stay afloat, an
endeavor that the seeker has in mind will prosper. If any of

the leaves sink to extinguish a candle, it will not. • Carry
a sachet of Holly leaves and berries to attract the opposite
sex. • The Druids believed that it was an important safety
measure to bring English Holly into their dwellings in the
winter to give shelter to the elves and fairies who would dare
to house with humans to escape the bitter cold. It was also
believed that if English Holly was left around the home as a
decoration *past* Twelfth Night, misfortune would occur.
• The wood of English Holly has a strong protective quality
and makes a fine protective magic wand for the impetuous
practitioner. • A weather divination that was once frequently
taken very seriously is that if the English Holly produced an
overabundance of berries, it was an ominous sign that winter
would be harsh.

No. 224

Ilex guayusa 🌿 🍴

Guayusa Tree

Aguayusa | Guañusa | Huayusa | Wais | Waisa | Wayus | Wayusa

🔍 **POTENTIAL MAXIMUM HEIGHT**
98 feet [30 meters]

✴ **SYMBOLIC MEANING**
Night watchman.

🌸 **POSSIBLE POWERS**
Create oxygen; Dream interpretation; Dreams; Healing;
Insect repellent; Lucid dreaming; Ritual use; Snake repellent;
Stimulation; Wakefulness.

🜂 **FOLKLORE AND FACTS**
The dried leaves of the Amazonian evergreen *Ilex guayusa*
Guayusa Tree have been used to make a caffeinated tea by
indigenous peoples who live in the rainforest. • A bundle
of Guayusa leaves was found in a 1,500-year-old tomb of
a Bolivian shaman that was far from where the Guayusa
Tree grows. • A ritual practiced by the head-hunting,
head-shrinking, upper Amazonian tribe known as the
Jivaro would involve drinking large quantities of a Guayusa
leaf infusion just to forcibly vomit it back out. • Another
Amazonian people known as the Kichua would drink a
Guayusa leaf infusion to provoke lucid dreams to seek clues
before going on a hunt. • The belief that Guayusa leaf tea
is a snake repellent comes from the idea that a snake is too
afraid to bite anyone with the tea within them. • In the
cities outside the Amazonian jungle,
Guayusa leaf tea bags can be
found in many supermarkets.
• A pre-Columbian
plantation of
Guayusa Trees
was discovered
in Baños, Ecuador,
by British plant
explorer Richard
Spruce in 1857.

No. 225

Ilex paraguariensis ☠ 🌿 🍴 🌱

Yerba Mate Tree

Erva Mate | Mate | Paraguay Tea | Yerba | Yerba Maté | Yerva Mate

🔍 **POTENTIAL MAXIMUM HEIGHT**
49 feet [15 meters]

✴ **SYMBOLIC MEANINGS**
Love; Mate; Romance.

🌸 **POSSIBLE POWERS**
Binding; Building; Create
oxygen; Death; Fidelity; History;
Knowledge; Limitations;
Love; Lust; Masculine energy;
Obstacles; Time.

🜂 **FOLKLORE AND FACTS**
The popular tea-like caffeinated
infusion that is brewed with
the leaves of the evergreen *Ilex
paraguariensis* Yerba Mate
Tree and water is known as "mate." It was first consumed
by the Guaraní people in Paraguay, to spread far and wide
from there. • Drinking mate is particularly popular in
Paraguay and Uruguay, where it is a social experience.
People are commonly seen carrying around containers of the
tea. The type of container that the mate is sipped from has
traditionally been a hollowed-out calabash gourd. Although
hollowed gourds are still used to drink mate, nowadays the
symbolic mate cup might be made of ceramic, carved wood,
a bull's horn, or even plastic. • Wear a sprig of Yerba Mate
leaves to attract the opposite sex. • Spill an infusion of Yerba
Mate to break off what was once a romantic relationship.

I

No. 226
Ilex vomitoria 💀 ⚱️

Yaupon Holly Tree
Cassina | Yaupon

◎ POTENTIAL MAXIMUM HEIGHT
30 feet [9 meters]

✳ SYMBOLIC MEANINGS
Expel; Put out.

✾ POSSIBLE POWERS
Alert togetherness;
Create oxygen; Energy
booster; Purge.

✿ FOLKLORE AND FACTS
The evergreen *Ilex
vomitoria* Yaupon Holly
Tree is the only wild, naturally
caffeinated plant that grows in the USA. It has been brewed
by Native Americans to be a ceremonial, tea-like beverage
called Asi, Black Drink, or Big Magic. • The botanical
species *vomitoria* originated when Native Americans
included the poisonous Yaupon Holly stems and leaves with
other ingredients to make a ritualistic, male-only beverage
partaken at unity ceremonies, which included profuse
group vomiting somewhere along the progression of the
male-bonding festivities.

No. 227
Illicium verum 💀 ⚱️ 🍴 🌱

Star Anise
Ba Jiao Hui Xian | Badian | Badian Khatai | Badiana | Badiane | Bunga Lawang | Chinese Anise |
Chinese Star Anise | Eight-horn | Khata | Star Aniseed | Staranise | Thakolam

◎ POTENTIAL MAXIMUM HEIGHT
16 feet [5 meters]

✳ SYMBOLIC MEANINGS
Good luck; Luck.

✾ POSSIBLE POWERS
Air element; Create oxygen; Divination; Good luck charm;
Healing; Incense; Jupiter; Masculine energy; Psychic ability;
Psychic awareness; Psychic power.

✿ FOLKLORE AND FACTS
An enormous percentage of the world's crops of the
evergreen *Illicium verum* Star Anise tree has been dedicated
to making the urgent anti-viral medication oseltamivir,
which is more commonly known as Tamiflu. • Carry one

whole, star-shaped Star Anise dried
fruit pod in a pocket for luck. The
pod and the small seeds
within it are all lucky.
• Make a Star Anise
fruit pod necklace, then
wear it to increase your
psychic power. • A
powerful pendulum
can be made using a Star
Anise pod tied on a string.
• In aromatherapy, Star Anise
essential oil may help calm
unexplainable feelings and sensations resulting from stress.
• A Star Anise pod or seeds can be burned like incense to
increase one's psychic awareness. • Carry an *Illicium verum*
pod in a pocket for luck.

No. 228
Ixora coccinea 💀 ⚱️ 🌳

Ixora
Flame of the Woods | Jungle Flame | Jungle Geranium | Pendkuli | Scarlet Jungle Flame |
West Indian Jasmine

◎ POTENTIAL MAXIMUM HEIGHT
15 feet [5 meters]

✳ SYMBOLIC MEANING
Passion.

✾ POSSIBLE POWERS
Create oxygen; Healing;
Inspiration.

✿ FOLKLORE AND FACTS
Commonly found in
subtropical and tropical
gardens, the evergreen
Ixora coccinea Ixora can be
cultivated and shaped to be a
small ornamental tree with vivid,
bright flower clusters. Ixora
flowers are either red, orange,
yellow, pink, or white.

I

No. 229

Jacaranda mimosifolia 🌳

Jacaranda Tree

Black Poui | Blue Jacaranda | Exam Tree | Fern Tree | Mucakaranda | Nupur | Omosaria

🔎 **POTENTIAL MAXIMUM HEIGHT**
40 feet [12 meters]

✴ **SYMBOLIC MEANINGS**
Imperial; Power.

🌀 **POSSIBLE POWERS**
Beautify; Create oxygen.

☾ **FOLKLORE AND FACTS**
When in full bloom, the deciduous *Jacaranda mimosifolia* Jacaranda Tree is one of the most spectacular blooming trees in the world. Its flowers are long, pendulous, and thickly clustered, in colors ranging from brilliant blue-purple, golden yellow, or vivid red. The tree is highly drought tolerant.

No. 230

Juglans nigra ☠ 🐄 🍴 🌿 🌳

Black Walnut

Eastern American Black Walnut

🔎 **POTENTIAL MAXIMUM HEIGHT**
130 feet [40 meters]

✴ **SYMBOLIC MEANINGS**
Infertility; Intellect; Presentiment; Stratagem.

🌀 **POSSIBLE POWERS**
Access divine energy; Brings forth blessings; Create oxygen; Fertility; Fire element; Infertility; Masculine energy; Mental clarity or power; Shade; Strong mental power; Sun; Wishing.

☾ **FOLKLORE AND FACTS**
Given enough space to fully grow, a deciduous *Juglans nigra* Black Walnut tree can live to be a gorgeously wide shade tree for several hundred years. • The Black Walnut fruit is a drupe, like an Almond or Peach. • The edible part of the Black Walnut tree is the roasted kernel of the corrugated seed or "nut." Once the fruit ripens and drops to the ground, the husk is removed, and the nut's kernel is laboriously removed, then roasted. • Black Walnut is used in pastries and confections, as well as in vegetable, meat, and pasta dishes. • In the spring, the trees can be tapped to collect the sap, which can be drunk, cooked down to a syrup, or distilled into a distinctively flavored liqueur. • The Black Walnut is all about its own self, creating its own best advantage for a substantial establishment that is optimal for maximum growth potential. It accomplishes this by dominating the area where it is growing, exuding overpowering chemicals from its roots. This biological chemical process is known as allelopathy. The chemicals will not allow anything but that tree to grow there. • Black Walnut can produce a brown-colored vegetable dye for fabric. • Ground Black Walnut shells have been used for grit in sandblasting. • Black Walnut lumber is prized for furniture making and cabinetry. • For those persons suffering serious infertility issues, make four Black Walnut sachets or amulets by tucking the leaves into small, white cotton pouches that you, yourself, have made. In your best handwriting, write out your array of prayers, hopes, and dreams for a child on four pieces of paper. Fold each note small enough to tuck into each of the sachets. Hang the first over the head of the bed. Tuck the second under the foot of the mattress. Tuck the remaining two on each side of the mattress. Relax.

No. 231

Juglans regia ☠ ☕ 🍴 🌰 🌰

English Walnut

Allegheny Walnut | Broadview Walnut | Carpathian Walnut | Circassian Walnut | Common Walnut Tree | European Walnut | Gewone Walnoot | Nut Fit for a God | Persian Nut | Persian Walnut | Walnoot | Walnuss

📷 POTENTIAL MAXIMUM HEIGHT

120 feet [37 meters]

✳ SYMBOLIC MEANINGS

Infertility; Intellect; Presentiment; Stratagem.

❋ POSSIBLE POWERS

Attracts lightning; Create oxygen; Family happiness; Fertility; Fire element; Infertility; Mental clarity or power; Sound resonance; Strong mental power; Sun; Wishing.

❦ FOLKLORE AND FACTS

The deciduous *Juglans regia* English Walnut is a very large tree that demands space and full sun to grow to reach its full potential and to live for over two hundred years. • The English Walnut fruit is a drupe with a hull that's seriously difficult to remove in order to reach the hard-shelled seed with its edible kernel within. The kernel is edible after it has been roasted. • English Walnut wood is prized for its strength and lustrous beauty. It is used to make furniture, guitars, flooring, gunstocks, and cabinetry. • Like the Black Walnut, the English Walnut is all about its own self, creating its own best advantage for a substantial establishment that is optimal for maximum growth potential. • It is believed that Alexander the Great introduced the *Juglans regia* to Macedonia and Greece, garnering one of the tree's first common names of Persian Nut and Persian Walnut. • English Walnut will create a brown dye. To get the black color, do the dyeing in an iron pot. • All wishes will be granted if someone is luckily gifted a bag of English Walnuts. • Italian witches supposedly ritually danced under English Walnut trees. • An English Walnut supposedly attracts lightning, so don't carry one in a storm. • If a bride wishes to delay conception for a while, she should tuck as many roasted English Walnuts into the bodice of her wedding gown corresponding to the number of years she wishes to wait before having children. • For those persons suffering serious infertility issues, make four English Walnut sachets or amulets by tucking the leaves into small, white cotton pouches that you, yourself,

have made. In your best handwriting, write out your array of prayers, hopes, and dreams for a child on four pieces of paper. Fold each note small enough to tuck into each of the sachets. Hang the first over the head of the bed. Tuck the second under the foot of the mattress. Tuck the remaining two on each side of the mattress. Relax.

No. 232

Juniperus communis ☕ 🍴 🌿 🌱 🌰

Juniper Tree

Gin Berry | Gin Plant | Juniper Berry

📷 POTENTIAL MAXIMUM HEIGHT

50 feet [15 meters]

✳ SYMBOLIC MEANINGS

Bless; Cleanse; Protect.

❋ POSSIBLE POWERS

Abundance; Advancement; Anti-theft; Aphrodisiac; Binding; Blessing; Break a hex; Building; Cleanse; Conscious will; Create oxygen; Curse breaking; Death; Drive off snakes; Energy; Exorcism; Fire element; Friendship; Growth; Healing; History; Joy; Knowledge; Leadership; Life; Light; Limitations; Male sexual potency; Masculine energy; Natural power; Obstacles; Protection; Psychic power; Purification; Success; Sun; Time.

❦ FOLKLORE AND FACTS

The berries from the evergreen conifer *Juniperus communis* Juniper Tree are used in several Scandinavian and Northern European dishes, most particularly as a flavoring for wild game and wild birds. • Juniper is also used to flavor gin and some other beverages. • Juniper berries can be strung together and hung over a door to help protect the home from evil forces, evil people, intruding ghosts, sickness, snakes, and theft. • Men can make, then carry or wear a red sachet or amulet of a Juniper sprig to hopefully increase their sexual potency. • Juniper berries can enhance psychic power. • Juniper essential oil can create a peaceful atmosphere for aromatherapy. Juniper essential oil can also increase prosperity. • Make an amulet of Juniper to keep near the center of the home to continually help to banish anything that will harm the health of those who live there. • The ancient Greeks believed that Juniper berries gave the Olympian athletes their stamina. • Take care which type of Juniper berries you eat. Some species of Juniper will produce inedible, toxic berries.

No. 233

Juniperus virginiana 🐦 🌳

Virginian Juniper Tree

Aromatic Cedar | Baton Rouge | Eastern Juniper | Eastern Red Cedar | Pencil Cedar |
Red Cedar | Red Juniper | Savin | Virginia Juniper | Virginian Cedarwood Tree

🔎 POTENTIAL MAXIMUM HEIGHT
50 feet [15 meters]

☀ SYMBOLIC MEANING
Constancy.

🌐 POSSIBLE POWERS
Art; Communication;
Create oxygen; Fire element;
Masculine energy; Sun.

🜨 FOLKLORE AND FACTS
The evergreen conifer
Juniperus virginiana
Virginian Juniper Tree
got the name Pencil
Cedar because, up
until the 1940s, it was used to make pencils. • The Virginian
Juniper Tree can live for over 300 years. The oldest that was
once located in the state of Virginia was 940 years old.
• When in need to dig bait worms to go fishing, you will
most likely find all you need under a Virginian Juniper
Tree. • Virginian Juniper heartwood can be used to make a
lovely dark-red dye. • The Virginian Juniper essential oil is
usually marketed as Virginian Cedarwood. In aromatherapy,
it is considered to promote a sense of oneness with
woodsy nature.

No. 234
Kalmia latifolia 🕱 ⬛ 🌳

Mountain Laurel
Calico Bush | Clamoun | Ivybush | Lambkill | Sheep Laurel | Spoonwood

◉ POTENTIAL MAXIMUM HEIGHT
40 feet [12 meters]

✳ SYMBOLIC MEANINGS
Ambition; Ambition of a hero; Glory; Perseverance;
Treachery; Victory; Words though sweet may deceive.

✿ POSSIBLE POWERS
Ambitious endeavors; Create oxygen; Death; Perseverance.

✤ FOLKLORE AND FACTS
As beautiful as the flowers are, be warned that all parts of
the evergreen *Kalmia latifolia* Mountain Laurel are deadly
poisonous, including any honey
that might be produced from
its pollen. • Branches of
Mountain Laurel can
be used to make sturdy,
long-lasting wreath
forms. The wood
is sometimes used
to make ornamental
railings and
furniture, as well as
other moderately-
sized wooden objects.

No. 235
Kalopanax septemlobus ⬛ 🍴

Prickly Castor Oil Tree
Castor Aralia | Ciqiū | Eumnamu | Harigiri | Tree Aralia

◉ POTENTIAL MAXIMUM HEIGHT
82 feet [25 meters]

✳ SYMBOLIC MEANINGS
Beautiful.

✿ POSSIBLE POWERS
Calming; Create oxygen;
Divination; Protection.

✤ FOLKLORE AND FACTS
The large, slow-growing,
deciduous *Kalopanax
septemlobus* Prickly Castor
Oil Tree is often grown as

a cold-hardy, broad-leaved ornamental shade tree. This is
because it has such an overall tropical appearance. • When
cooked, its tender young shoots are edible. • The tiny white
flowers are found in large clusters, followed by tiny black
berries that are enjoyed by birds.

No. 236
Kigelia africana 🕱 ⬛ 🍴 🌳 🌰 🏺

Sausage Tree
Cucumber Tree | Kigeli-Keia | Modukguhlu | Muvevha | UmFongothi | Um Vunguta | Worsboom

◉ POTENTIAL MAXIMUM HEIGHT
66 feet [20 meters]

✳ SYMBOLIC MEANINGS
A lost loved one; Ingenuity.

✿ POSSIBLE POWERS
Create oxygen; Healing;
Portability; Tan leather;
Usefulness.

✤ FOLKLORE AND FACTS
The evergreen *Kigelia africana*
Sausage Tree flowers are huge,
deep-dark red, trumpet-shaped,
and dripping with nectar. • The unusual fruit of the Sausage
Tree looks like long sausages hanging all over it. The fresh
green fruit is highly toxic. The ripe fruit requires drying and
roasting to make it edible. It is then covered with honey and
fermented to make an alcoholic sweet beer known in Central
Kenya as both *muratina* and *kaluvu*. • Sausage Tree bark has
been used for tanning hides. • The Sausage Tree fruit can be
dried, hollowed out, and converted into sturdy containers,
cups, ladles, and mouse traps. • A black dye can be made
from the Sausage Tree fruit. A yellow dye can be made from
the roots. • The Luo and Luhya people in Kenya will bury
a Sausage Tree fruit as a proxy body for someone who has
been missing and is believed dead. • The huge woody fruit of
the Sausage Tree can grow up to 39 inches (99 cm) long,
8 inches (20 cm) around, and can weigh between 11 and
26 pounds (5 and 12 kg). Considering the size and overall
weight of the Sausage Tree fruit, it is easy to imagine the
extent of damage that the fruit can cause to vehicles and
people who may happen to be under a tree when a dangling
"sausage" suddenly falls.

K

No. 237
Koelreuteria paniculata ☠ ♂ ♣

Golden Rain Tree
China Tree | Goldenrain | Pride of China | Pride-of-China | Pride of India | Pride-of-India | Varnish Tree

◉ POTENTIAL MAXIMUM HEIGHT
40 feet [12 meters]

✻ SYMBOLIC MEANINGS
Agreement; Dissension.

🌼 POSSIBLE POWERS
Create oxygen; Peace between differences.

🍃 FOLKLORE AND FACTS
Once mature enough to flower, usually in the summer, the beautiful, *Koelreuteria paniculata* Golden Rain Tree blooms will cover the tree to transform it into a spectacle of long sprays of golden blossoms. • The flowers of the Golden Rain Tree can be used to make a yellow dye. • Wherever you should encounter a Golden Rain Tree, leave it in peace. Give the tree your most sincere blessing. In return for your blessing, the nature spirits will bless you.

No. 238
Kokia drynarioides ♂

Hawaiian Cotton Tree
Hau Hele'ula | Hawai'i Tree Cotton | Hawaiian Tree Cotton | Koki'o

◉ POTENTIAL MAXIMUM HEIGHT
35 feet [10 meters]

✻ SYMBOLIC MEANINGS
Blushing heart.

🌼 POSSIBLE POWERS
Create oxygen; Dye; Happiness; Healing; Love.

🍃 FOLKLORE AND FACTS
Found wild only on the Big Island of Hawai'i, the deciduous *Kokia drynarioides* Hawaiian Cotton Tree, with its star-shaped leaves and large scarlet flowers, is perhaps the most spectacularly beautiful tree in all of the Hawaiian Islands. • It is also classified as critically endangered. Consequently, the Hawaiian Cotton Tree is one of the world's rarest trees. Although seeds have been gathered, planted, and cultivated in botanical gardens around the world, not to mention in home gardens as an ornamental specimen, there are less than a half dozen trees known to be still growing wild in Hawai'i. • The bark from the Hawaiian Cotton Tree was used to dye fishing nets red. • The honeycreeper, a tropical American songbird, is dependent on the Hawaiian Cotton Tree as its main source of food.

K

No. 239

Koompassia excelsa

Tualang Tree

Bangris | Mangaris | Tapang

◉ POTENTIAL MAXIMUM HEIGHT

282 feet [86 meters]

✳ SYMBOLIC MEANINGS

Elegantly tall; Honey holder; Majestic elegance.

🌐 POSSIBLE POWERS

Create oxygen; Protect then provide honey.

✿ FOLKLORE AND FACTS

The *Koompassia excelsa* Tualang Tree is the tree that
is usually towering over the other trees in the tropical
rainforest. It is the tallest deciduous rainforest tree in Borneo.
• The Tualang Tree is usually bare of branches up until
approximately 98 feet (30 m) up the trunk. • The roots of the
Tualang Tree are huge buttress roots that bulge and spread
around the base of the tree to provide ample support for
such a high, relatively narrow tree. • The Tualang Tree is
a favorite dwelling place for giant *Apis dorsata* honeybees,
which hang valuable combs from the branches that are heavy
with honey. They also scare potential loggers who would
rather avoid the trees than deal with enraged giant bees.
• In Jambi, Sumatra, the collection of the honey involves
traditional magical love songs that are sung to the bees and
to the spirit of the Tualang Tree. This is done to ensure that
those climbing up the tree to gather the honeycombs will not
be harmed or stung by bees.

K

No. 240
Laburnum anagyroides ☠ ⬢ ☠ ⬢

Common Laburnum

False Ebony | Golden Chain | Golden Rain

◉ POTENTIAL MAXIMUM HEIGHT
20 feet [6 meters]

✳ SYMBOLIC MEANINGS
Forsaken; Pensive beauty.

⬢ POSSIBLE POWERS
Beauty; Complications; Confused messaging; Create oxygen; Death; Life's pattern; Luck.

☾ FOLKLORE AND FACTS
Every single part of the deciduous *Laburnum anagyroides* Common Laburnum tree is deadly poisonous. And yet, for the short time that the tree is in full bloom, it is a living tribute to beauty. The golden yellow, orchid-like flowers are sweetly scented and hang down as long, pendulous clusters from the blooming tree. The overall effect is an exquisite sight to behold. So, just look. Never touch! • Be aware: there is a great concern that children might tragically mistake the deadly Common Laburnum seeds to be edible because garden peas and the poison Common Laburnum tree pods and seeds look much too similar. • The Common Laburnum tree is also quite commonly known as a Golden Chain Tree.

No. 241
Lagerstroemia indica ⬢ ☠ ⬢

Crape Myrtle

Astromelia | Common Crape Myrtle | Crepeflower | Crêpe Myrtle | Escandalosa | Flower of The Gods | Indian Lagerstroemia | Júpiter | Queen's Crape Myrtle

◉ POTENTIAL MAXIMUM HEIGHT
35 feet [11 meters]

✳ SYMBOLIC MEANING
Eloquence.

⬢ POSSIBLE POWERS
Chastity; Create oxygen.

☾ FOLKLORE AND FACTS
The flowering deciduous *Lagerstroemia indica* Crape Myrtle was greatly favored by China's emperors for many centuries. • In areas where it

easily grows, the lovely *Lagerstroemia indica* is used to line the streets with flowering trees that range in color from pink to deep red or white to a light purple. • In medieval times *Lagerstroemia indica* was often used in bridal garlands. • There is a legend that if Crape Myrtle appears in a dream it signifies a long life with good fortune. • Bring peace and love into a home by growing Crape Myrtle on each side of the front door.

No. 242
Lagunaria patersonia ☠ ⬢ ⬢

Pyramid Tree

Cow Itch Tree | Itchy Bomb Tree | Itchy Powder Tree | Lagunaria | Norfolk Island Hibiscus | Primrose Tree | Queensland White Oak | Sally Wood | White Oak |

◉ POTENTIAL MAXIMUM HEIGHT
30 feet [9 meters]

✳ SYMBOLIC MEANING
Inconstancy.

⬢ POSSIBLE POWERS
Create oxygen; Misery; Pain.

☾ FOLKLORE AND FACTS
The evergreen *Lagunaria patersonia* Pyramid Tree is a flowering tree that is native to Australia. When it is in full bloom, it is beautiful. However, its pods and itchy fibers can quite painfully penetrate the skin. These fibers are *extremely difficult* to remove. It is best to completely avoid the tree and admire its beauty from a safe distance. • Because the Pyramid Tree will quickly sprout new shoots, it is very difficult to remove the tree by simply cutting it down. Furthermore, when the seed pods fall from the tree they will pop open, releasing the needle-like thorns within them to blow loosely all over the vicinity. They would be unavoidable to encounter in the most unpleasant of ways. • Bees love *Lagunaria patersonia* flowers.

No. 243
Larix decidua ⬢ ☠ ⬢

European Larch

◉ POTENTIAL MAXIMUM HEIGHT
130 feet [40 meters]

✳ SYMBOLIC MEANINGS
Audacity; Boldness.

⬢ POSSIBLE POWERS
Anti-fire; Anti-theft; Create oxygen; Fend off evil energy; Induce visions; Protection; Protection against the evil eye.

L

Beautiful and strong, *Larix decidua* European Larch wood can be fashioned into a wand that is considered to be particularly blessed, since it can be used to cast powerful protection spells with the intent to keep people and animals safe from harm. • A European Larch wood amulet can be made, then carried or worn to help offer protection against enchantment from the evil eye. • Unlike conifers, *Larix* is deciduous and will lose needles in the autumn. • European Larch can be used to make a green vegetable dye for fabric.

No. 244

Larix gmelinii 🐾 🎋

Dahurian Larch
Gmelin Larch

📷 POTENTIAL MAXIMUM HEIGHT
131 feet [40 meters]

🌿 SYMBOLIC MEANING
Glory in the extremes.

🌼 POSSIBLE POWERS
Cold hardiness; Create oxygen.

🌀 FOLKLORE AND FACTS
The deciduous conifer *Larix gmelinii* Dahurian Larch is capable of forming huge forests in eastern Siberia. It is the most extraordinarily cold-hardy tree in the world, able to withstand temperatures that dip deeply down to –94° F in Oymyakon, Siberia, the coldest permanent settlement on Earth. • The tree does not adapt well to places where the winters are milder. • The *Larix gmelinii* Dahurian Larch is known as the northernmost tree found in the world.

No. 245

Larix laricina 🐾 🎋

Tamarack Tree
Akemantak | American Larch | Eastern Larch | Hackmatack | Red Larch

📷 POTENTIAL MAXIMUM HEIGHT
95 feet [29 meters]

🌿 SYMBOLIC MEANINGS
Audacity; Boldness.

🌼 POSSIBLE POWERS
Anti-fire; Anti-theft; Create oxygen; Fend off evil; Induce visions; Masculine energy; Protection against the evil eye.

🌀 FOLKLORE AND FACTS
The deciduous *Larix laricina* Tamarack Tree wood is soft. The Tamarack needles are also soft and will turn golden and then fall off in the autumn. • When the cones on the Tamarack Tree first develop, they will be pink, turn red, then brown in the autumn.

No. 246

Laurus nobilis 🐾 🍴 🌿

Bay Laurel Tree
Bay Tree | Grecian Laurel | Laurel Tree | Sweet Bay

📷 POTENTIAL MAXIMUM HEIGHT
55 feet [17 meters]

🌿 SYMBOLIC MEANINGS
Fadeless affection; Fame; Glory; I change but in death; Immortality; Love; No change till death; Notability; Poets; Praise; Prosperity; Renown; Resurrection of Christ; Strength; Success; Victory.

🌿 COMPONENT MEANINGS
Leaf: I change but in death.
Wreath: Fame; Glory; Reward of merit.

🌼 POSSIBLE POWERS
Abundance; Advancement; Attract romance; Clairvoyance; Cleansing; Conscious will; Create oxygen; Energy; Fire element; Friendship; Good fortune; Good luck; Growth; Healing; Induces prophetic dreams; Joy; Leadership; Life; Light; Masculine energy; Natural power; Physical and moral cleansing; Prosperity; Protection; Protection against black magic; Protection against evil spirits; Protection during

an electrical storm; Psychic power; Purification; Ritual purification; Strength; Success; Sun; Wards off evil and evil magic; Wards off lightning; Wards off negativity; Wisdom.

🜊 FOLKLORE AND FACTS
The edible parts of the evergreen *Laurus nobilis* Bay Laurel Tree are the berry-like fruit and the leaf. • The fruit is harvested, dried or pressed, then marketed as the seasonings called "Laurel Berry" and "Laurel Oil," but it is the "Bay Leaf" that is most commonly used to flavor many dishes, especially in Mediterranean cuisine. • The wood is sometimes used for smoking foods. • In ancient Greece, poets, heroes, winning athletes, and esteemed leaders were crowned with wreaths made from Bay Laurel leaves. The term "Poet Laureate" is a result of the custom of crowning an honored poet with wreath crowns woven from leafy Bay Laurel twigs and English Ivy. • In ancient Rome, Bay Laurel leaf garlands were hung over the doors of the sick to protect them. As a result of its affiliation and correspondence with the protection and healing of the sick, in the fifteenth century, newly qualified doctors were garlanded with Bay Laurel and sent on their way to be professional healers. • Bay Laurel leaves were especially used to protect emperors and warriors going off into battle. • Put a whole undamaged Bay Laurel leaf in every corner of the home to protect all who live there. • To ensure lasting love, a couple would break off a twig of Bay Laurel and then break it in half, with each retaining a piece. • Wishes written on Bay Laurel leaves, which are then buried in a sunny spot, help make the wishes come true. • Bay Laurel leaves placed under a pillow can induce prophetic dreams. • According to legend, if you stood by a Bay Laurel Tree you could not be struck by lightning or be affected by the evil of witches. • Write a wish on a Bay Laurel leaf, then burn the leaf to make the wish come true. • In ancient Rome, Bay Laurel leaf was forbidden to be burned at an altar because its loud crackling and sputtering signaled the plant's repulsion at being used in such a lowly manner. This led to ancient Roman beliefs that Bay Laurel protected itself from fire and lightning. • Wear a Bay Leaf for protection against evil.

Lawsonia inermis ☠ 🜶 🜏

Henna Tree
Camphire | Egyptian Privet | Hina | Hinna | Mignonette Tree

🔍 POTENTIAL MAXIMUM HEIGHT
20 feet [6 meters]

✹ SYMBOLIC MEANINGS
Artifice; You are better than handsome.

🌐 POSSIBLE POWERS
Blessings; Create oxygen; Emotions; Fertility; Generation; Headache relief; Healing; Inspiration; Intuition; Love; Moon; Protection from the evil eye; Protection from illness; Psychic ability; Romance; Romantic love; Sea; Sea magic; Subconscious mind; Tides; Travel by water; Water element.

🜊 FOLKLORE AND FACTS
The evergreen *Lawsonia inermis* Henna Tree leaves are used as a dye for skin, fingernails, fabrics, and leather. • A Henna rinse over shades of blonde hair will transform it into a vivid red-orange color. • In Europe during the 1800s, Henna-colored red hair became popular with the Aesthetic and the Pre-Raphaelite artists who fancied painting red-haired women with flowing hair into their artistic visions. This inspired young bohemian European women to color their own hair red, popularizing personal beautification via Henna all the more. • In India, it is often believed that the person with Henna on their palms can receive and offer blessings. • The Henna symbolism painted on the tops of the hands is placed there for protection. • Every culture that includes the use of Henna does so in its own way. In Morocco, Henna is used to paint symbols to fend off the evil eye. In India, a bride's hands are covered with intricate Henna tattoos as a blessing to her on her wedding day to grant her joy, the beauty of love, the commitment of marriage, and as an offering of herself to be spiritually awakened into her future as a wife and mother. • Wear a sprig of Henna leaves near your heart to attract romantic love to you.

L

No. 248

Lecythis zabucajo 🏺🍴🌳

Paradise Nut Tree

Castanha-de-Sapucaia | Cream Nut | Monkey Pot Tree | Sapucaia Nut

◎ POTENTIAL MAXIMUM HEIGHT
98 feet [30 meters]

✹ SYMBOLIC MEANING
Monkey pot.

⊛ POSSIBLE POWERS
Create oxygen; Entrapment; Temptation.

⊛ FOLKLORE AND FACTS
The seeds, or nuts, of the deciduous *Lecythis zabucajo* Paradise Nut Tree are coconut-sized and take eighteen months to fully mature and ripen after the tree has flowered. The creamy nut seed oil is primarily used in cosmetics.
• The highly unusual, hard, wooden Paradise Nut Tree "fruits" have been used as monkey traps. The fruit has a lid that falls off when it ripens, releasing the seeds and an empty fruit behind. A monkey hunter will put bait inside an empty fruit, which entices a monkey to reach in to fetch it. The monkey is unable to remove its hand from the fruit trap unless it drops the bait and withdraws empty-handed. The hunter will reach the trap before that occurs.

No. 249

Leptospermum scoparium 🏺🌳🌰

Mānuka Tree

Broom Tea Tree | Creeping Tea Tree | Jelly Bush | Kāhikatoa | Mānuka Myrtle | Manuka Tea Tree | New Zealand Teatree | Tea Tree

◎ POTENTIAL MAXIMUM HEIGHT
49 feet [15 meters]

✹ SYMBOLIC MEANING
Like a broom.

⊛ POSSIBLE POWERS
Connects oneself to the divine; Create oxygen; Healing.

⊛ FOLKLORE AND FACTS
The evergreen *Leptospermum scoparium* Mānuka Tree is primarily cultivated for the famous Mānuka honey that bees produce from it, with all the honey's legendary health benefits. • To capitalize on Mānuka honey's popularity due to its global reputation and value, it is one of the food items that has been subject to counterfeit and adulteration schemes galore. Always look at the labeling. Genuine Mānuka honey is produced in New Zealand and is certified as authentic.
• The small green New Zealand kākāriki parakeets use the bark and leaves of the Mānuka Tree to treat themselves when affected by certain parasites. • The sawdust from the Mānuka Tree is a favorite wood used in New Zealand for smoking fish and meat.

No. 250

Libidibia punctata 🌳

Bridalveil Tree

Bridal Veil Tree

◎ POTENTIAL MAXIMUM HEIGHT
35 feet [11 meters]

✹ SYMBOLIC MEANING
Alluring hidden strength.

⊛ POSSIBLE POWERS
Create oxygen; Feminine energy; Strength.

⊛ FOLKLORE AND FACTS
During the summer and early autumn, the clusters of yellow flowers on the evergreen *Libidibia punctata* Bridalveil Tree appear to be delicate with its tiny leaves. And yet, the tree's wood is extremely dense and hard. In the summer, the dark bark sheds to reveal a much lighter new bark, which gives the trunk an interesting bicolor look.

No. 251

Ligustrum lucidum ☠🏺🌳

Chinese Glossy Privet

Broad-leaf Privet | Chinese Privet | Glossy Privet | Tree Privet | Wax-leaf Privet | White Wax Tree

◎ POTENTIAL MAXIMUM HEIGHT
32 feet [10 meters]

✹ SYMBOLIC MEANINGS
Bad luck; Invasion; Mildness; Prohibition; Youth.

POSSIBLE POWERS

Clarify energy; Create oxygen; Promotes communication; Soothes arguments.

FOLKLORE AND FACTS

The evergreen *Ligustrum lucidum* Chinese Glossy Privet is very often the tree of choice for topiary artists to reshape into fanciful shapes and garden figures. • Planted near the home, Chinese Glossy Privet can promote and support communication. • Impress a sprig of *Ligustrum lucidum* with your intention to promote harmony between yourself and someone whom you are in conflict with, then place it somewhere among this someone's belongings to resolve the argument within one day.

No. 252

Ligustrum vulgare ☠ ⚱ ♣

European Privet
Common Privet | Wild Privet

POTENTIAL MAXIMUM HEIGHT
40 feet [12 meters]

SYMBOLIC MEANINGS
Bad luck; Prohibition.

POSSIBLE POWERS
Clarify energy; Create oxygen; Promotes communication; Soothes arguments.

FOLKLORE AND FACTS
The evergreen *Ligustrum vulgare* European Privet is the only commonly used hedging "Privet" that is native to the British Isles. • The European Privet has been featured in the designs of many Elizabethan-style gardens.

No. 253

Lindera benzoin ⚱ 🍶 ♣

Spicebush Tree
Benjamin Bush | Common Spicebush | Northern Spicebush | Wild Allspice Tree

POTENTIAL MAXIMUM HEIGHT
13 feet [4 meters]

SYMBOLIC MEANINGS
Arable land; Growth potential.

POSSIBLE POWERS

Air element; Create oxygen; Crop worthiness; Masculine energy; Success in the field; Sun.

FOLKLORE AND FACTS

During the pioneer years in North America, land surveyors used the small, deciduous *Lindera benzoin* Spicebush Tree as a tangible sign that the land could sustain cultivated crops. • The *Papilio troilus* butterfly favors the Spicebush Tree so much as a host plant to feed its developing caterpillars, that one of its common names is spicebush swallowtail. • A tea can be made from the buds and leaves of the Spicebush Tree. The fruits are dried for use like Allspice.

No. 254

Liquidambar styraciflua ⚱ ♣

Sweetgum
Alligator Wood | American Storax | Gum Tree | Incense Tree | Liquid Amber | Liquidambar | Redgum | Satin-walnut | Star Gum | Voodoo Witch Burr | Witch Burr

POTENTIAL MAXIMUM HEIGHT
75 feet [23 meters]

SYMBOLIC MEANINGS
Flowing; Fluid.

POSSIBLE POWERS
Blessings; Create oxygen; Fire element; Holiness; Incense; Masculine energy; Protection; Spirituality; Sun.

FOLKLORE AND FACTS
The deciduous *Liquidambar styraciflua* Sweetgum tree is native to southern North America. • Its resinous sap is called liquidambar. The spiky round seed pods of the Sweetgum tree are known as witch balls or witch burr. • The botanical name, *Liquidambar*, refers to the Sweetgum's sweet resin that is tapped for many different uses. • The Sweetgum tree's liquidambar resin is one of the primary sources for ritual copal incense resin that is required for many different religious ceremonies, most especially in the Roman Catholic church. • The Sweetgum witch burr seed pod can be carried or worn as a powerful protection amulet against magic or evil intentions aimed toward the wearer. • Arrange a small bowl with Sweetgum tree seed pods and keep it on a table in the home for powerful protection. • The resin of the Sweetgum tree is sometimes marketed under the name young amber. It can also be processed under the pressure and heat of an autoclave to create industrialized amber, which is used in some jewelry.

L

No. 255

Liriodendron tulipifera 🪓🌰

Tuliptree

American Tulip Tree | Apollo of the Woods | Canoewood Tree | Fiddle Tree |
Ko-Yen-Ta-Ka-Ah-Tas | Oonseentia | Saddle Leaf Tree | Tulip Poplar | Tulip Tree | Tulipwood |
Whitewood | Yellow Poplar

◉ POTENTIAL MAXIMUM HEIGHT

200 feet [61 meters]

✹ SYMBOLIC MEANINGS

Fame; Lily tree; Rural
happiness.

❀ POSSIBLE POWERS

Ancient Earth;
Connection to
the ancient past;
Create oxygen; Ease
transitions; Healing;
Practical thinking;
Sound resonance; Utility;
Utilitarian planning.

❦ FOLKLORE AND FACTS

The *Liriodendron tulipifera* Tuliptree is one of the tallest
deciduous trees in eastern North America. The tallest
specimen on Earth is approximately 200 feet (61 m) tall.
• The Tuliptree flowers are very large and tulip-shaped.
When the tree is in full bloom, its blossoms are upright. It is a
majestic sight to behold. • This enormous tree is easily grown
from a seed. • Tuliptree wood is used for the construction
of musical instruments such as organs and pianos. It is also
used for wide flooring, bowls, decorative boxes, and much
more, including long passenger canoes. According to Captain
John Smith in 1612, long dugout canoes could transport forty
passengers. • Morel mushrooms can often be found growing
under or near a Tuliptree. • There have been Tuliptree fossils
discovered that are from the Upper Cretaceous period, dated
to be one hundred million years old.

No. 256

Litchi chinensis ☠🪓🍴

Lychee Tree

Cây Vải | Lichee | Litchi

◉ POTENTIAL MAXIMUM HEIGHT

39 feet [12 meters]

✹ SYMBOLIC MEANINGS

Beauty; Good fortune; Good luck; Happiness; Love;
Romance; Summer; Wishing for children.

❀ POSSIBLE POWERS

Create oxygen; Love; Luck; Romance; Wishing.

❦ FOLKLORE AND FACTS

The cultivation of the evergreen *Litchi chinensis* Lychee
Tree in China dates back to 1059. • Lychee was the fruit
favored as a delicacy by ancient Chinese emperors and
empresses. The edible part of the Lychee Tree is the interior
flesh found under the thin but tough-skinned, pink-red fruit.
• Some species of Lychee grow wild in parts of Asia, but
the only commercialized variety is *Litchi chinensis* subsp.
chinensis. • Only ripe Lychee should be eaten. • It was not
until 1962 that it was discovered that the Lychee seeds found
within the fruit's flesh contained a chemical that can cause
hypoglycemia. In India and in North Vietnam, a mysterious
outbreak of very ill children with dangerously low blood
sugar was traced back
to eating a lot of
Lychees, including
unripe fruits, on
an empty stomach
earlier in the
day. • Lychee Tree
wood is supposedly
indestructible.

L

Litsea cubeba

May Chang Tree

Aromatic Litsea | Maqaw | Mountain Pepper

◎ POTENTIAL MAXIMUM HEIGHT
23 feet [7 meters]

✹ SYMBOLIC MEANINGS
Interested; Renewed.

❋ POSSIBLE POWERS
Create oxygen; Diminishes a painful memory; Mental clarity;
Optimism; Renewal; Spiritual love.

❀ FOLKLORE AND FACTS
The slightly lemony fragrance of the evergreen *Litsea cubeba*
May Chang Tree lifts the mind, body, and spirit from a heavy
sense of overall weariness. • To help step further and further
away from a bad memory, put a few drops of May Chang
essential oil on a cotton ball to tuck into a pocket to wear
throughout the day. • Make, then carry or wear a sachet of
May Chang flower and leaf to seek love that is spiritual.
• May Chang essential oil is often used to scent bar soap.

No. 258

Litsea garciae

Engkala Tree

Beva' Mali | Borneo Avocado | Bua Talal | Engkala | Kalangkala | Kangkala | Kayu Mali |
Kelima | Kelimah | Kelime | Kelimie | Lan Yu Mu | Malei | Pangalaban | Pong Labon | Tebulus |
Wi Lahal | Wuru Lilin

◎ POTENTIAL MAXIMUM HEIGHT
85 feet [26 meters]

✹ SYMBOLIC MEANING
Interested.

❋ POSSIBLE POWERS
Create oxygen; Healing; Renewal.

❀ FOLKLORE AND FACTS
Although it is cultivated more for its medicinal uses, the fruit
of the evergreen *Litsea garciae* Engkala Tree has an
avocado-like flavor and is edible raw, cooked, or pickled.
• The oil extracted from the Engkala fruit seeds is used for
making soaps and candles.

No. 259

Lodoicea maldivica

Coco de Mer Palm

Coco-de-mer | Coco Fesse | Double Coconut | Love Nut | Sea Coconut | Seychelles Nut

◎ POTENTIAL MAXIMUM HEIGHT
112 feet [34 meters]

✹ SYMBOLIC MEANING
Beautiful buttocks.

❋ POSSIBLE POWERS
Aphrodisiac; Beauty;
Create oxygen; Sensuality.

❀ FOLKLORE AND FACTS
The enormous fruit of the
evergreen *Lodoicea maldivica* Coco
de Mer Palm looks like a double coconut or a heart. It will
take from six to ten years to ripen. Its seed is the largest
seed of a plant, and it will take an additional two years to
germinate. Its contents are edible. • In the sixteenth century,
wealthy Europeans coveted the highly polished Coco de Mer
Palm nuts. • Now a rare protected species, there was a time
when it was believed that the Coco de Mer Palm fruit was a
seed adrift or a sea bean that was intended to be distributed
via sea currents. But research revealed the nut does not float
well and will rot in the sea water. This research pointed
out why the trees are only found on two adjacent islands.
• The Coco de Mer Palm holds eight records: two of them
include being the largest wild fruit and the world's heaviest
seed. Another pertains to the fact that, when the seed does
finally germinate, the embryonic first leaves, known as the
cotyledon, can be up to 13 feet (4 m) long, which are by
far the longest known. • Up until 1768, it was commonly
believed that the Coco de Mer nut grew on a mythical tree
that grew up from the bottom of the sea.

L

No. 260

Macadamia integrifolia 🐿 ✂️ 🍴 🌱

Macadamia Tree

Bauple Nut | Bush Nut | Gympie Nut | Hawaii Nut | Maroochi Nut | Nut Oak | Prickly Macadamia | Queensland Nut | Rough-shelled Macadamia | Small-fruited Queensland Nut | Smooth-shelled Macadamia | Smooth-shelled Queensland Nut

🔍 POTENTIAL MAXIMUM HEIGHT
32 feet [10 meters]

✴️ SYMBOLIC MEANING
Ingenuity.

🌼 POSSIBLE POWERS
Aphrodisiac; Attract love;
Create oxygen; Earth element;
Fertility; Jupiter.

⚗️ FOLKLORE AND FACTS
The evergreen *Macadamia integrifolia*
Macadamia Tree is native to Australia and was introduced
to Hawaii in 1882. • Low in protein but high in
monounsaturated fat, the kernel of the seed is edible raw, but
not every variety of Macadamia is edible. • After growing
for ten years, the Macadamia Tree can produce a bounty of
nuts for more than one hundred years. • Macadamia oil is
also extracted for use in salad dressings and in frying. • The
nuts have extremely hard shells that must be cracked with
a hammer or notched with a saw, then popped open with a
tool that looks like a steel guitar pick and functions like a key.
• The hyacinth macaw is one of the very few birds capable of
shelling the Macadamia nut, using only its powerful beak.

No. 261

Maclura pomifera ⚗️

Osage Orange Tree

Bodark | Bodock | Bois-D'Arc | Hedge Apple Tree | Horse Apple | Mock Orange | Monkey Ball | Monkey Brains | Osage-Orange | Yellow-Wood

🔍 POTENTIAL MAXIMUM HEIGHT
40 feet [12 meters]

✴️ SYMBOLIC MEANING
Bow wood.

🌼 POSSIBLE POWERS
Create oxygen; Living fence; Windbreak.

⚗️ FOLKLORE AND FACTS
The thorny *Maclura pomifera* Osage Orange Tree is not
related to *Citrus*. • The Osage Orange Tree is not edible
by humans, and animals choose not to eat it. All of the
prehistoric creatures that may have consumed the fruit to
help distribute its seeds are extinct. • The Osage Orange's
highly rot-resistant wood is a bright orange color. The
coarsely bumpy, textured fruit is large, round, hard, and dry.
It also has a milky latex sap. • The Osage Orange is a
fast-growing deciduous tree that can reach its full height very
quickly. Because it can create a dense canopy, it is useful as a
windbreak across the Great Plains of North America. • The
Osage Orange Tree was useful before the invention of barbed
wire, because when the trees were trimmed back, they could
grow shoots up from the base that intertwined and created
a defining dense hedge. • Because the Osage Orange Tree
wood is flexible and strong, it was a favored choice by the
Comanche people, as well as several other Native American
peoples, to make highly prized durable hunting bows. • The
wood is also a choice selection in making duck calls as well
as high-quality woodwind instruments.

M

No. 262
Madhuca longifolia 🥣 🍴 🌰

Me'ee Tree

Arbre à Beurre | Bassie | Butter Tree | Honey Tree | Illipe | Iluppai | Indian Butter Tree | Madhuca | Mahula | Mahwa | Mee Tree | Mohua | Mohulo | Oil-nut Tree | Vippa Chettu

◎ POTENTIAL MAXIMUM HEIGHT
66 feet [20 meters]

✹ SYMBOLIC MEANING
Always there.

✺ POSSIBLE POWERS
Create oxygen; Imbalance of thinking; Lunacy.

✺ FOLKLORE AND FACTS
The evergreen *Madhuca longifolia* Me'ee Tree is a sacred tree in South India, where the tree can be found growing very near to temples. • The *Madhuca longifolia* flower is edible. • Fermented Madhuca flower wine is written of in some Buddhist and Hindu literature. • Me'ee Tree flower wine and liquor has been a necessary element in the cultural celebrations of various peoples in Southern India. • The flowers are also dried, then ground into a flour that is used in breadmaking. • The fruit is also made into jam. Oil is extracted from the seeds. • For many of those who live in the western part of Odisha, India, the *Madhuca longifolia* fruit is considered to be an essential food.

No. 263
Magnolia acuminata 🥣

Cucumber Magnolia

Blue Magnolia | Cucumber Tree | Cucumbertree

◎ POTENTIAL MAXIMUM HEIGHT
60 feet [18 meters]

✹ SYMBOLIC MEANINGS
Determination; Dignity.

✺ POSSIBLE POWERS
Ancient Earth;
Create oxygen;
Earth element;
Endurance;
Feminine energy;
Venus.

✺ FOLKLORE AND FACTS
The deciduous *Magnolia acuminata* Cucumber Magnolia is the cold-hardiest of the *Magnolia* trees as well as one of the largest. • The trees in the *Magnoliaceae* family have been growing on Earth for over one hundred million years. There are Cucumber Magnolia tree fossils that date back to twenty million years ago. • Cucumber Magnolia flowers are small, greenish-yellowish, somewhat tulip-shaped, and relatively unimpressive. Unlike most other *Magnolia* species, Cucumber Magnolia flowers have no fragrance. • The unripe fruit of the Cucumber Magnolia is shaped like a small cucumber. And yet, like any other Magnolia species' fruit, when they ripen and split they will have the same type of fleshy red seeds within them.

No. 264
Magnolia champaca 🥣 🌰

Champak Tree

Bai Lan Tree | Cempaka Putih | Champaca | Chempaka | Himalayan Champaca | Joy Perfume Tree | Pak Lan | White Jade Orchid Tree | White Sandalwood | Yellow Jade Orchid Tree | Yü Lan Hua

◎ POTENTIAL MAXIMUM HEIGHT
164 feet [50 meters]

✹ SYMBOLIC MEANINGS
Happiness; Love.

✺ POSSIBLE POWERS
Aphrodisiac; Attract love; Cleanse; Create oxygen; Divine beauty or love; Earth element; Feminine energy; Love; Perfumery; Romance; Sensuality; Unconditional love; Universal love; Venus.

✺ FOLKLORE AND FACTS
In India, the deciduous *Magnolia champaca* Champak Tree is considered to be an immensely sacred tree to Krishna, the Hindu god of love and romance. • Ceremonial wedding garlands of Champak and Jasmine flowers are strung together to be worn by Indonesian brides and grooms. • Because it is believed that the fragrance of Champak is pleasing to the gods, Champak is grown in temple gardens and near dwelling places to bring joy to all who come near to it. • Considered one of the greatest fragrances ever created, the iconic French fragrance Joy contained the essential oil of the Champak flower. The perfume was created for fashion designer Jean Patou by perfumer Henri Alméras in 1929.

No. 265
Magnolia grandiflora
Southern Magnolia
Bull Bay Magnolia | Evergreen Magnolia | Large-flower Magnolia

POTENTIAL MAXIMUM HEIGHT
70 feet [21 meters]

SYMBOLIC MEANINGS
Ancient Earth; Beauty; Determination; Dignified; Dignity; Love of nature; Magnificence; Nobility; Peerless and proud; Perseverance; Sweetness; You are a lover of nature.

POSSIBLE POWERS
Continuity; Create oxygen; Earth element; Feminine energy; Fidelity; Longevity; Venus.

FOLKLORE AND FACTS
Fossils discovered of the evergreen *Magnolia grandiflora* Southern Magnolia reveal that this tree was around during the time of the dinosaurs, making it among the oldest flowering plants in the world. • The magnificent Southern Magnolia is iconic of and native to the Southeastern USA. • The very large, creamy white blossoms have fleshy petals and are very fragrant. • Southern Magnolia wood is heavy, hard, and has been used to make fine furniture and veneers. • Make an amulet of a flower, leaf, and seed pod of the Southern Magnolia and put it under the bed to assure faithfulness.

No. 266
Magnolia officinalis
Houpu Magnolia
Chinese Magnolia | Hou Po | *Houpoea officinalis* | Magnolia-bark Tree | Spice Magnolia

POTENTIAL MAXIMUM HEIGHT
70 feet [21 meters]

SYMBOLIC MEANINGS
Love of nature; Natural; Purification.

POSSIBLE POWERS
Ancient Earth; Control over addiction; Create oxygen; Earth element; Faithfulness; Feminine energy; Loyalty; Reduces obsessive behavior; Venus.

FOLKLORE AND FACTS
A magic wand fashioned from the wood of the deciduous *Magnolia officinalis* Houpu Magnolia will bring its user closer to working the core magic and spirits of ancient Earth. • Houpu Magnolia wood wand is good for psychic development. • Fashion a useful pendulum out of a small piece of Houpu Magnolia wood. • Houpu Magnolia bark is used in traditional Chinese medicine.

No. 267
Magnolia × soulangeana
Saucer Magnolia
Chinese Magnolia

POTENTIAL MAXIMUM HEIGHT
25 feet [8 meters]

SYMBOLIC MEANINGS
Love of nature; Natural.

POSSIBLE POWERS
Ancient Earth; Create oxygen; Earth energy; Earth magic.

FOLKLORE AND FACTS
A wand fashioned from the wood of the evergreen *Magnolia × soulangeana* Saucer Magnolia will bring the magician closer to working the core magic and spirits of ancient Earth. • When in bloom, the flowers of the Saucer Magnolia are large, saucer-shaped, and fragrant.

M

No. 268

Magnolia splendens

Laurel Magnolia

Laurel-leaved Magnolia | Laurel Sabino | Shining Magnolia

POTENTIAL MAXIMUM HEIGHT
76 feet [23 meters]

SYMBOLIC MEANING
Dignity.

POSSIBLE POWERS
Create oxygen; Fidelity.

FOLKLORE AND FACTS
The evergreen *Magnolia splendens* Laurel
Magnolia has exceptionally showy white flowers and fragrant
wood. • Place a sachet of the Laurel Magnolia's leaf and
flower, as well as a piece of its wood, under the bed to
assure faithfulness.

No. 269

Magnolia virginiana 🌿🌱

Sweetbay Magnolia

Beaver Tree | Laurel Magnolia | Magnolia | *Magnolia glauca* | Swamp Magnolia | Swampbay |
Sweetbay | Whitebay

POTENTIAL MAXIMUM HEIGHT
50 feet [15 meters]

SYMBOLIC MEANINGS
Love of nature; Perseverance.

POSSIBLE POWERS
Ancient Earth; Beauty; Calm anxiety; Create oxygen; Earth
element; Feminine energy; Love; Loyalty; Manage obsessive
behavior; Marital harmony; Overcome addiction; Peace;
Venus.

FOLKLORE AND FACTS
The deciduous *Magnolia virginiana* Sweetbay Magnolia
flowers are very big, creamy white, and beautifully scented.
• The Sweetbay Magnolia tree was the first of the *Magnolia*
trees to be cultivated in England in the late 1600s. • A
Sweetbay Magnolia leaf under the mattress will do much
to help encourage marital harmony by calming
obsessive anxieties.

No. 270

Malpighia emarginata 🌿🍾

Acerola Cherry Tree

Barbados Cherry | Guarani Cherry | West Indian Cherry | Wild Crepe Myrtle

POTENTIAL MAXIMUM HEIGHT
13 feet [4 meters]

SYMBOLIC MEANINGS
Fertility; Innocence; Love; Youthfulness.

POSSIBLE POWERS
Create oxygen; Fertility; Love; Love energy.

FOLKLORE AND FACTS
The edible part of the small evergreen *Malpighia emarginata*
Acerola Cherry Tree is the fruit-berry. It is considered to be
a high source of natural vitamin C. • It is believed that the
Acerola Cherry was spread from one West Indies Island to
the next by birds. It was introduced to Florida from Cuba in
the late nineteenth century. • The Spanish explorers named
the fruit *cereza*, after the Spanish word for cherry, because
 it reminded them of the cherries they remembered from
their homeland.

No. 271

Malus domestica ☠🌿🍾🍎

Common Apple Tree

Apple | Fruit of the Gods | Fruit of the Underworld | King of Fruits | Manzana | Orchard Apple |
Silver Bough | Silver Branch | Tree of Love

POTENTIAL MAXIMUM HEIGHT
17 feet [5 meters]

SYMBOLIC MEANINGS
Art; Breasts; Death; Divination; Earth element; Fall of man;
Feminine energy; Immortality; Joy; Knowledge; Lingering
love; Love; Luxury; Motherhood; Peace-loving; Perpetual
concord; Perpetual peaceful agreement; Poetry; Presence
of love; Purity; Self-control; Sexuality; Sin; the Soul;
Temperance; Temptation; Transformation; Virtue; Vulva;
Water element; Well-wishing; Wisdom.

POSSIBLE POWERS
Attract love; Choice; Create oxygen; Earth energy; Feminine
energy; Fertility; Friendship; Garden blessing; Garden magic;
Healing; Healing magic; Immortality; Longevity; Love; Love
magic; Mutual happiness; Passionate good nature; Sensuality;
Transformation; Venus; Water element; Water energy.

M

☙ FOLKLORE AND FACTS

The edible parts of a deciduous *Malus domestica* Common Apple Tree are the fleshy fruit and skin. • Apple fruit is enjoyed fresh, dried, juiced, as well as fermented for use as liqueur, wine, and vinegar. The fruit is also enjoyed as ingredients in baked goods or cooked down to apple butter and applesauce • Apple blossoms are thought to have the ability to attract angels who send happiness and love within us, while offering guidance on finding continued happiness and love in life. • Up until the seventeenth century, in religion, folk stories, and mythology the word "apple" was actually a generic term used to describe *all* fruits other than berries and nuts. • It is believed that the Apple is capable of projecting hidden . . . *occult* . . . magical power from the core of its fruit. Supposed evidence of this capability is the star pattern formed at the center of the fruit that is revealed after it has been sliced open crosswise. That hidden star inspired the centuries-old habit of rubbing out any evil spirit that might be hitchhiking within it before eating it. • Druids fancied magic wands they had cut for themselves from the Common Apple Tree, because they *knew* these would positively respond to them magically. It is also the right wood for a magic wand that is intended to generate the steady flow of intense positive energy needed to enter into the realm of the fairies. • Apple wood can be whittled into a lucky charm for a long life. • Apples are thought to be the food of the dead. • It has been speculated that the statue of Venus de Milo may have been holding an Apple in one of her two missing hands. • The Wiccan faith's Samhain is sometimes referred to as the Feast of Apples. • A divination using an Apple involves cutting the fruit in half, then examining and counting what seeds are visible. If it is an odd number, the inquirer will remain unmarried in the near future. If the total is an even number, there will be a marriage sooner rather than later. If one of the seeds has been cut, that relationship will be volatile. If two seeds have been cut, widowhood is the foretelling. • To offer healing during the waning of the moon, cut an Apple into three pieces. Rub each of the pieces wherever illness is perceived to be. Then immediately bury the Apple pieces. • Bury thirteen Apple leaves in the soil after harvesting the fruit to guarantee a bountiful crop for the following season. • Johnny Appleseed, whose legend involves the tale that he planted Apple seeds wherever he traveled, was a real American missionary, gardener, and bachelor pioneer named John Chapman. Some believe that Chapman's Apple seeds were of a wild variety that produced tall trees with fruit that was only suitable for cider. Which was fine, because nearly everyone loves Apple cider. • As part of a house-blessing ritual, cut an Apple in half, put one half outside to leave as an offering, then eat the other half. • Apple cider vinegar has been used as a home remedy for a wide variety of ailments for hundreds of years. • A cider Apple is always used to make cider. Cider apple varieties have been sorted into the definitive categories of a "cooker" or an "eater," which is good enough for dessert. Or it will be a "spitter" if it is deemed to be good for nothing else but adding to the cider-making blend. • In the annual January orchard ritual known as wassailing to the trees, which occurs in the west of England and has its origins in pre-Christian Britain, bread and the best-tasting cider from the current year are offered to the trees for good luck, along with serenades to the spirits of the trees and to the fairies of the orchard. • A teacher who has been honored for achievement is often gifted a trophy or keepsake in the form of a decorative golden Apple. Traditionally, a shiny fresh Apple was a common gift from a student. • In a roundabout way, Paris of Troy caused the Trojan War. Eris, the Greek goddess of discord, was not invited to the wedding of Peleus and Thetis because she was such a predictably troublesome troublemaker. Utterly upset about that, Eris inscribed a golden Apple with the worlds *"to the most beautiful one"* before tossing it to the guests in attendance at the wedding. Athena, Hera, and Aphrodite claimed it! Paris was to decide who should get to keep the Golden Apple. Each of the goddesses stripped naked in his presence, offering Paris massive bribes. A kingship from Hera. Wisdom and battle skills from Athena. Aphrodite tempted Paris with Helen of Sparta's love. Paris awarded the Golden Apple to Aphrodite, which ultimately led to the Trojan War, the ruin of Paris, and the total destruction of the city of Troy.

No. 272

Malus × floribunda 🌿🌱

Japanese Flowering Crabapple Tree

Chokeberry | Flowering Crabapple | Japanese Crab | Ornamental Crabapple | Snowy Crabapple

◎ POTENTIAL MAXIMUM HEIGHT
25 feet [8 meters]

✳ SYMBOLIC MEANINGS
Ill nature; Ill-tempered.

❀ POSSIBLE POWERS
Announcement of springtime; Beauty; Create oxygen.

❦ FOLKLORE AND FACTS
In the spring, before a deciduous *Malus floribunda* Japanese Flowering Crabapple Tree will begin to fully leaf out, it is covered with a spectacular show of huge masses of pink blossoms that gradually lighten to the palest tint of pink.

No. 273

Malus sylvestris 🌿🐛🍎🌱

European Crabapple Tree

Crab Apple | Crabtree | European Crabapple | Forest Apple | Wild Apple | Wild Crab Apple

◎ POTENTIAL MAXIMUM HEIGHT
30 feet [9 meters]

✳ SYMBOLIC MEANINGS
Beguiling; Crabby; Ill nature; Ill-tempered.

❀ POSSIBLE POWERS
Create oxygen; Healing.

❦ FOLKLORE AND FACTS
The deciduous *Malus sylvestris* European Crabapple Tree that is fully wild will have thorns. • A Wild European Crabapple Tree can live to be one hundred years old. • The European Crabapple is the only ancient Apple tree indigenous to Great Britain.

• The fruit of the European Crabapple Tree is called a pome. • European Crabapple bark can produce a yellow dye for fabrics. • European Crabapple features in the Nine Sacred Herbs healing charm written in Wessex, England, around 900 CE. • In the early spring, many European Crabapple Trees bloom with exquisite white blossoms. But there are also some varieties that will flower fully with blossoms that are a bright rosy pink, very slowly lightening daily, until the flowers are the palest pinkish-white, to turn even whiter before the petals flutter off the tree. • When you cut across a European Crabapple, the same symbolic star shape of the core and seeds can be seen, as is the case with any *Malus* Apple.

No. 274
Mangifera indica ☠ 🍴 🌿

Mango Tree

Common Mango | Indian Mango | King of Fruits | Manga

⊙ **POTENTIAL MAXIMUM HEIGHT**
100 feet [30 meters]

✳ **SYMBOLIC MEANINGS**
Happiness; Life.

✺ **POSSIBLE POWERS**
Conversion; Create oxygen; Fire element; Grant a wish;
Happiness; Love; Romance; Sensual romance;
Sound resonance.

✦ **FOLKLORE AND FACTS**
The evergreen *Mangifera indica* Mango Tree was introduced
to Asia around 500 BCE. • There are more than two hundred
different Mango cultivars and their fruit all have different
tastes and textures. Nearly all varieties are sweet, but some
will produce fruit that is soft and juicy, while others will be
firm and fibrous. • Cutting a Mango can be a challenging
effort. The large, flat seed or stone clings tenaciously to the
very slippery fruit flesh. The easiest way to cut and remove
the fruit is using a cross-cutting grid method. • Juicy, sweet,
ripe Mangoes can be cut up and eaten fresh, juiced, or dried,
or used in curries, jelly, smoothies, milkshakes, sauces, and
pastries. Unripe and sour Mangoes can be used to make
jam, chutney, daal, confections, and Mango pickles. • In the
Philippines, dried Mango strips are combined with Tamarind
to make a very popular treat known as mangorind. • A
popular spicy street treat in Mexico is a peeled Mango on a
stick that is cut to appear like a pinecone, which is seasoned
with fresh-squeezed lime juice and hot pepper. • A mixture
of Mango and sweetened condensed milk can be used as a
topping for cake, ice cream, and shaved ice. • Mango Tree
wood is frequently used to craft ukuleles, fine furniture, and
wood flooring. • During the blooming season, the airborne
flower pollen can also trigger allergies. For those who are
especially allergic, any contact with any part of the Mango
tree can trigger an allergic reaction. • Mango blossoms are a
favorite effective ingredient in a love potion. • A pink Mango
blossom sachet that is made,
then carried or worn, can
attract romance.

No. 275
Manilkara zapota 🍴 🌿

Sapodilla Tree

Chikoo | Sapota | Sapoti

⊙ **POTENTIAL MAXIMUM HEIGHT**
98 feet [30 meters]

✳ **SYMBOLIC MEANING**
Fortitude.

✺ **POSSIBLE POWERS**
Chewing gum; Create oxygen;
Fertility; Peace.

✦ **FOLKLORE AND FACTS**
The edible and nutritious ripe fruit of
the evergreen *Manilkara zapota* Sapodilla Tree is
brown-colored with a rough, fuzzy feeling that is soft when
pressed with the fingers. It is also sweet and juicy with a
flavor similar to that of a pear. The unripe fruit is unpleasant
to touch. The tree bark contains chicle, which has a texture
similar to latex that is used to make a natural chewing gum.

No. 276
Medusagyne oppositifolia

Jellyfish Tree

Cây Sứa | Medusagyne | Medusagynaceae | Meduuspuu | Quallenbaum

⊙ **POTENTIAL MAXIMUM HEIGHT**
50 feet [15 meters]

✳ **SYMBOLIC MEANING**
Umbrella-shaped.

✺ **POSSIBLE POWERS**
Create oxygen; Moon; Sea magic; Water element.

✦ **FOLKLORE AND FACTS**
The unusual evergreen *Medusagyne oppositifolia* Jellyfish
Tree is extremely rare and critically endangered. Over the
past century, it was announced on two different occasions
that it had gone extinct. Unfortunately, no young trees
have been observed. It is a protected species that has only
been found within two miles from the sea on Mahé, in the
Seychelles. • The flowers of the Jellyfish Tree are small and
white, and turn bright red with age. The fruits have a surreal
appearance of floating jellyfish.

M

Melaleuca alternifolia ☠☙♣

Melaleuca Tree

Honey-myrtle | Paperbark Tree | Punk Tree | Tea Tree | Tea Tree Oil Tree | White Bottlebrush Tree

◉ POTENTIAL MAXIMUM HEIGHT
19 feet [6 meters]

✳ SYMBOLIC MEANING
Communication.

❀ POSSIBLE POWERS
Antibacterial; Black and white;
Create oxygen; Harmony;
Healing; Odor removal;
Protection; Water
element; Wisdom.

☙ FOLKLORE AND FACTS
The evergreen *Melaleuca alternifolia* Melaleuca Tree is the
source of the Tea Tree oil that is used in aromatherapy and
for medicinal purposes due to its antibacterial and antiseptic
properties. It has been used commercially since the 1920s
as a remedy for an overly wide variety of ailments that
have yet to be validated, and can be extremely dangerous if
used incorrectly. Medicinally, Tea Tree oil is thought to be
legitimately helpful in treating the common maladies of lice,
acne, and dandruff. It has been added into a wide array of
products and personal toiletries all around the world. • An
endocrinological study presented in 2018 overtly suggested
that a previously rare occurrence was becoming increasingly
less so. There had been a disconcerting and growing number
of cases involving young boys who had exhibited prepubertal
male gynecomastia, which is a swelling of the breast tissue
in a prepubescent male child. The study indicated that the
common denominator that linked these young boys was the
repeated topical use of a combination of Tea Tree oil with
Lavender essential oil. A further study by researchers at the
National Institute of Environmental Health Sciences found
laboratory evidence that these two essential oils appear to be
endocrine disruptors, having estrogen-like and testosterone
inhibiting-like properties, and should not be used in
combination. • Melaleuca Tree pollen has been attributed to
the exacerbation of severe hay fever symptoms. • Melaleuca
Tree bark has been used as an emergency bandage.

Melaleuca leucadendra ☠☙♣

Cajeput Tree

Long-leaved Paperbark | Weeping Paperbark | White Paperbark | White Tea Tree

◉ POTENTIAL MAXIMUM HEIGHT
98 feet [30 meters]

✳ SYMBOLIC MEANINGS
Sense of flow; Strong inner-self.

❀ POSSIBLE POWERS
Ability to move through a contrary experience; Break
compulsive habits; Clean ritual objects; Create oxygen; Expel
intruding energy; Focus mind or willpower; Healing; Heals;
Insect repellent; Protection; Soothes; Soothes sunburn;
Stimulant.

☙ FOLKLORE AND FACTS
In Malaysia, the evergreen *Melaleuca
leucadendra* Cajeput Tree is considered
to be an entire apothecary in one tree.
• Cajeput is one of
the ingredients in the
iconic ointment known
as Tiger Balm. • Cajeput is
used in traditional Indonesian
medicine. • Cajeput
is used to treat
fish suffering from
bacterial and fungal
infections such as fin rot
and velveting. • Many
First Nations Australians
have used the peeled bark
from the Cajeput Tree to
cut into long strips to use as ties. It is also used to make
waterproof canoes and huts. Cajeput bark has been used to
wrap food that would then be placed in a hole that would act
as an oven. • The bark was also used to wrap the bodies of
the deceased prior to burial.

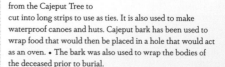

Melia azedarach 🪱🫚🌳

Chinaberry Tree

Bead Tree | Cape Lilac | Chinaball Tree | Indian Lilac | Japanese Bead Tree |Paradise Tree |
Persian Lilac | Pride of India | Syringa | Syringa Berrytree | Texas Umbrella Tree | White Cedar

◉ POTENTIAL MAXIMUM HEIGHT
39 feet [12 meters]

✹ SYMBOLIC MEANING
Beaded.

🌼 POSSIBLE POWERS
Create oxygen; Insecticide.

🜍 FOLKLORE AND FACTS
All parts of the deciduous *Melia azedarach* Chinaberry Tree are toxic. The ripe fruit is the most poisonous part of all. • The dried seeds of the Chinaberry Tree have five grooves that make them a common choice of beads to craft a Catholic rosary. • Florists use cut branches of the fruit as well as the leaves in floral arrangements to add a different shape and texture to the design.

Melicoccus bijugatus 🪱🫚🍷🌳

Guinep

Bajan Ackee | Canepa | Chenet | Genip | Genipe | Ginepa | Huaya | Kenép | Kenepa | Kinnip |
Limoncillo | Mamón | Mamoncillo | Quenepa | Quenepe | Quenette | Skinip | Skinup | Spanish
Lime | Talpa Jocote

◉ POTENTIAL MAXIMUM HEIGHT
59 feet [18 meters]

✹ SYMBOLIC MEANING
Soothing calm.

🌼 POSSIBLE POWERS
Calming; Create oxygen;
Sleep.

🜍 FOLKLORE AND FACTS
The fruit of the evergreen *Melicoccus bijugatus* Guinep tree is bittersweet, juicy, and edible. • The pulp is often prepared to be used in both non-alcoholic and alcoholic beverages. • The seed can be consumed fresh or roasted. • The wood of the Guinep tree is used for fine indoor cabinetmaking.

Mesua ferrea 🫚🌳🥜🫚

Ironwood Tree

Ceylon Ironwood | Cobra's Saffron | Indian Rose Chestnut | Lenggapus | Nagacuram |
Nagasari | Penaga | Penaga Lilin | Poached Egg Tree

◉ POTENTIAL MAXIMUM HEIGHT
99 feet [30 meters]

✹ SYMBOLIC MEANINGS
Extravagance; Ornament.

🌼 POSSIBLE POWERS
Create oxygen; Heals snake bite; Invincibility; Strength.

🜍 FOLKLORE AND FACTS
The slow-growing, evergreen *Mesua ferrea* Ironwood Tree is propagated by seed. • The Ironwood Tree is grown near ancient Sri Lankan Buddhist temples because the tree is very sacred to Buddha Maitreya. • Four different Buddhas are believed to have reached their enlightenment underneath an Ironwood Tree. It was considered to be the bodhi tree for the Buddhas Mangala, Sumana, Revatha, and Sobhitha. • The Ironwood Tree's deep, dark-red lumber is very hard, strong, heavy, and extremely difficult to saw, making it entirely suitable to use for railroad ties. • Before the British brought kerosene lighting to Eastern India, Ironwood Tree seed oil was used in evening lamps. • The pillars of the fourteenth-century Embekke Shrine in Sri Lanka are made of Ironwood Tree timber. • The roots of the Ironwood Tree are believed by some to have the power to heal a snake bite.

M

No. 282

Metasequoia glyptostroboides

Dawn Redwood

Dwarf Redwood

🔍 **POTENTIAL MAXIMUM HEIGHT**

120 feet [37 meters]

🌸 **SYMBOLIC MEANINGS**

Like a sequoia; Subtle survivalist.

🌼 **POSSIBLE POWERS**

Abundance; Air element; Ancient Earth; Awakening; Create oxygen; Dreaming; Enlightenment; Fertility; Harmony; Immortality; Light; Longevity; Luck; Magic; Masculine energy; Protection; Regeneration; Renewal; Resurrection; Spiritual consciousness; Spirituality; Spiritual life; Spiritual love; Survival.

🍂 **FOLKLORE AND FACTS**

The fast-growing *Metasequoia glyptostroboides* was named the Dawn Redwood because it is an ancient tree that comes to us all the way from the dawn of time. • In 1941, the first studies of the endangered deciduous conifer *Metasequoia glyptostroboides* Dawn Redwood were made from fossils from the Mesozoic Age. There were none that were younger than 150 million years old. At that time it was noted via leaf impressions that there was something different about it when compared to other Redwood trees. In the 1940s, a living *Metasequoia* tree was discovered in a village in west central China. It seemed to fit the specific description of the presumed extinct tree. That tree was the first of three *Metasequoia glyptostroboides* found in the Szechuan province. Since then, the Dawn Redwood has become a worldwide favorite ornamental tree planted in parks and botanical gardens wherever they will grow. • The Dawn Redwood is the shortest of the Redwood trees.

No. 283

Metrosideros excelsa 🌰🌿🌰

Pōhutukawa Tree

Iron Tree | New Zealand Christmas Bush | New Zealand Christmas Tree

🔍 **POTENTIAL MAXIMUM HEIGHT**

80 feet [24 meters]

🌸 **SYMBOLIC MEANINGS**

Highest; Iron; Sublime.

🌼 **POSSIBLE POWERS**

Beauty; Cheeriness; Create oxygen; Longevity; Support.

🍂 **FOLKLORE AND FACTS**

The naturally curvy wood of the evergreen *Metrosideros excelsa* Pōhutukawa Tree was used in shipbuilding as joint supports known as "knees" because it is dense and strong. • A Pōhutukawa Tree in Auckland, New Zealand, is named Te Waha o Rerekohu. This sacred tree is estimated to be six hundred years old and was an integral element in ancient Māori burial practices. • As it gets closer to Christmas, the Pōhutukawa Tree will begin to bloom the cheerful brush-like red flowers that have hundreds of bristling stamens instead of petals.

Milicia excelsa 🌿🐾🥜

African Teak Tree

Intule | Iroko Tree | Kambala | Moreira | Mvule | Odum | Tule

🔍 **POTENTIAL MAXIMUM HEIGHT**
164 feet [50 meters]

✹ **SYMBOLIC MEANINGS**
Made of stone; Turn to stone.

❀ **POSSIBLE POWERS**
Birth; Create oxygen; Durability; Fends off witchcraft; Fends off witches; Fertility; Protection; Resist rot; Strength.

🍂 **FOLKLORE AND FACTS**
The deciduous hardwood timber tree *Milicia excelsa* African Teak Tree is resistant to termites. • For pollination, there needs to be both female and male trees. The difference between the two trees is determined by the direction in which the smaller branches hang. In males they curve upward; in females they hang down. • African Teak Tree lumber is used for boat building, furniture, construction, floors, and other carpentry applications. • African Teak Tree wood has an ability to convert carbon in the atmosphere into land carbon. • In Ghana and other parts of Africa, the African Teak Tree is revered as a highly sacred tree, where it is fiercely protected by the villagers who live near one because the tree is feared by witches. • In West Africa, ceremonies, most especially those relating to fertility and birth, are held beneath an African Teak Tree.

Mimusops elengi 🌿🍴🐾🥜

Tanjong Tree

Bakula | Bullet Wood | Medlar | Spanish Cherry

🔍 **POTENTIAL MAXIMUM HEIGHT**
49 feet [15 meters]

✹ **SYMBOLIC MEANING**
Unwavering devotion.

❀ **POSSIBLE POWERS**
Beauty; Create oxygen; Healing; Love; Protection; Shade.

🍂 **FOLKLORE AND FACTS**
The evergreen *Mimusops elengi* Tanjong Tree is sacred to Buddhists and Jains. • The Tanjong Tree provides fragrant, comforting shade as an escape from the hot rays of the sun. • The flowers of the Tanjong Tree are dried in the sun before they are used to make infusions that are then mixed into green tea. • The extremely hard Tanjong Tree wood is deep red and is used in furniture making and for floors that will polish brightly. • Fallen Tanjong Tree flowers can retain their fragrance for many days. • The small, star-shaped, fragrant flowers of the Tanjong Tree are traditionally strung with a needle onto thread to make flower leis and lovely floral garlands for decoration.

M

No. 286
Moringa oleifera ☠ ✂ 🏺 🌰

Moringa Tree

Ben Oil Tree | Benzolive Tree | Drumstick Tree | Horseradish Tree | Miracle Tree | Oil of Ben Tree

◉ POTENTIAL MAXIMUM HEIGHT
53 feet [16 meters]

☀ SYMBOLIC MEANINGS
Cadence; Never die.

🌐 POSSIBLE POWERS
Create oxygen; Endurance; Eternal;
Nourishment; Perfumery.

ℂ FOLKLORE AND FACTS
The deciduous *Moringa oleifera* Moringa Tree can also be
called Drumstick Tree, so-called because the tree's seed pods
are shaped like drumsticks. • Even though the flowers are
fragrant, the essential oil has no scent. The ancient
Egyptians made a perfume called *kyphi* that included the
Moringa Tree's essential oil, which is known as Oil of Ben.
• Several parts of the Moringa Tree are edible and commonly
consumed in Southeast Asia, such as the flowers, leaves,
immature seed pods, the seeds, and the clear odorless oil that
also resists rancidity. • The tree's young fruit is shaped like a
drumstick with an outer skin that is tough and fibrous. The
fruit is usually cut up, then stewed until tender. It has a flavor
similar to a sweeter asparagus. The seeds are often fried and
eaten as a snack, added to sauces, or used as a condiment.
They are dried and ground into a nutritional fortifying
powder that is added to wheat flour. The leaves are also dried
and powdered to make a nutritious dietary supplement that
is added to soups, smoothies, sauces, yogurt, soft cheeses,
bread, and pastries. • The oil of the Moringa Tree can be
used to help purify water through a chemical process known
as flocculation.

No. 287
Morus alba ☠ ✂ 🏺 🌰 🍷 ▮

White Mulberry Tree

China Mulberry | Russian Mulberry | Sang Shen Tzu | Silkworm Mulberry | Tuta | Tuti

◉ POTENTIAL MAXIMUM HEIGHT
50 feet [15 meters]

☀ SYMBOLIC MEANINGS
Kindness; Prudence; Strength; Wisdom.

🌐 POSSIBLE POWERS
Air element; Balance; Cosmic knowledge; Courage; Create
oxygen; Earth element; Female energy; Fire element; Mars;
Masculine energy; Mercury; Metamorphosis; Positive energy;
Protection; Psychic dreaming; Strength; Transformation;
Venus; Yin and Yang.

ℂ FOLKLORE AND FACTS
For the specific intention of using the leaves as the preferred
food needed for raising healthy, productive silkworms,
careful cultivation of the deciduous *Morus alba* White
Mulberry Tree began in China more than four thousand
years ago. • In ancient times, a forest area that was thick
with White Mulberry Trees was considered the most sacred
of all places. • White Mulberry fruit is edible if it is ripe,
and is more often made into wine. • White Mulberry is an
herb used in traditional Chinese medicine. • The White
Mulberry is a multiple fruit, as is the Pineapple and Jackfruit,
with each cluster of fruits resembling a single Raspberry or
Blackberry. Each minuscule segment in the cluster is actually
an individual seed-bearing fruit that has grown from its own
individual flower, with all the fruits aggregating together to
form the appearance of one whole berry. • Tuck a sachet
of White Mulberry leaves under the pillow to help induce
psychic dreams. • Use a feng shui compass to determine the
northern planting for a White Mulberry Tree. • A wand
made from White Mulberry Tree wood would be useful in
boosting the magician's willpower.

M

No. 288
Morus nigra ☠ ☙ ❶ ❧

Black Mulberry Tree
Black Berry Tree | Gelso | Morera | Shahtoot | Toot | Tut

📷 **POTENTIAL MAXIMUM HEIGHT**
32 feet [10 meters]

✳ **SYMBOLIC MEANINGS**
Devotion; I shall not survive you; Wisdom.

🌐 **POSSIBLE POWERS**
Air element; Centering oneself; Cosmic knowledge; Courage; Create oxygen; Earth element; Female energy; Fire element; Mars; Masculine energy; Mercury; Protection; Strength; Venus; Yin and Yang.

🍂 **FOLKLORE AND FACTS**
The deciduous *Morus nigra* Black Mulberry Tree will supposedly protect your property from lightning. • Since Black Mulberry wood is powerfully protective against evil, it makes an excellent  wood for a magic wand. • Black Mulberry Trees were introduced into England in the seventeenth century with the intention of using them to feed silkworms. However, silkworms prefer White Mulberry. Even so, the Black Mulberry was often used in folk medicine. • The fruit of the Black Mulberry Tree is edible when it is ripe to make delicious jams, sherbets, and wine. • The Black Mulberry is a multiple fruit, as is the Pineapple and Jackfruit, with each cluster of fruits resembling a single Raspberry or Blackberry. Each minuscule segment in the cluster is actually an individual seed-bearing fruit that has grown from its own individual flower, with all the fruits aggregating together to form the appearance of one whole berry.

No. 289
Morus rubra ☠ ☙ ❶ ❧

Red Mulberry Tree
Red Mulberrytree

📷 **POTENTIAL MAXIMUM HEIGHT**
72 feet [22 meters]

✳ **SYMBOLIC MEANINGS**
Faith; Growth; Nature.

🌐 **POSSIBLE POWERS**
Air element; Cosmic knowledge; Courage; Create oxygen; Earth element; Female energy; Fire element; Mars; Masculine energy; Mercury; Protection; Strength; Venus; Yin and Yang.

🍂 **FOLKLORE AND FACTS**
The ripe fruit of the deciduous *Morus rubra* Red Mulberry Tree is edible, very sweet, and a favorite to use for making jam, pastry fillings, sherbets, and wine. • Since Red Mulberry Tree wood is powerfully protective against evil, it makes an excellent wood for a magic wand. • The Choctaw people once used the inner bark of the Red Mulberry Tree as a fiber that would be processed and woven into fabric for clothing.

No. 290
Murraya koenigii ☙ ❶ ✿ ❧

Curry Leaf Tree
Curry Bush | Curry Leaves | Curry Tree | Sweet Neem

📷 **POTENTIAL MAXIMUM HEIGHT**
20 feet [6 meters]

✳ **SYMBOLIC MEANING**
Pungent.

🌐 **POSSIBLE POWERS**
Create oxygen; Fire element; Mars; Masculine energy; Protection.

🍂 **FOLKLORE AND FACTS**
The fresh leaves of the evergreen *Murraya koenigii* Curry Leaf Tree are edible and commonly known as "curry leaves," which are a fundamental ingredient in Indian cuisine. They are often used in curries, fried with onions, added to soups, or stewed in sauces.

M

No. 291

Musa acuminata 🌿 🍴 🥄

Banana Tree

Cavendish Banana | Dessert Banana | Dwarf Cavendish | Manzano Banana | *Musa balbisiana* |
Musa ingens | *Musa × paradisiaca* | Mysore Banana

🔘 **POTENTIAL MAXIMUM HEIGHT**
20 feet [6 meters]

✳️ **SYMBOLIC MEANINGS**
Brilliance; Goodness.

🌼 **POSSIBLE POWERS**
Brilliance in education; Create oxygen; Feminine energy;
Fertility; Good work; Money; Potency; Prosperity; Venus;
Water element.

🜨 **FOLKLORE AND FACTS**
Cultivated for its huge, heavy clusters of fruit that hang from
the top of the plant, the evergreen *Musa acuminata* Banana
Tree's "Cavendish" Banana is the most commonly
cultivated Banana found in markets around the world.
• Banana trees grow up from the base of the trunk as shoots.
The one tree can increase in number over time. Fruit
development commences with the maroon "heart," which
is a huge, inverted tear-drop-shaped pod that opens to
reveal individual petal-like leathery bracts at the top.
The clusters of small flowers revealed under the opened
bracts profusely drip with nectar. • When prepared and
eaten as a vegetable, the exotic flower heart tastes similar to
an artichoke. The other edible parts of the tree will be the
elongated, fully developed and ripened individual fruits.
• It becomes increasingly and recognizably fragrant as the
fruit ripens from an unripe green color, remaining on or
removed from the tree. The ripe peel or rind of varieties
other than Cavendish may be yellow, red, purple, or brown.
• The small-fruited Mysore Banana is the most popular
Banana in India. • The Manzano Banana is the favorite in
Latin America. • The large Banana leaf is often used much
in the same way that parchment paper or aluminum foil is
used for steaming, grilling, or poaching food. • The species
that are known as *Musa × paradisiaca* and *Musa balbisiana*
is the starchy Plantain Cooking Banana, which has a thicker,
tougher skin than any dessert banana. A Plantain is used
when it is at its ripest, as indicated by a very dark brown,
nearly black colored peel. At that point it will be sweet like a
Banana, but without the characteristic Banana-like flavor of
one. • Ripe Plantains can be sliced and deep-fried, used as an
ingredient in casseroles, or dried and ground to make a flour.
• The world's largest Banana Tree species is the incredible
Musa ingens Great Highland Banana, which reaches nearly
50 feet (15 m) in height with leaves that are 16 feet (5 m)

long. Its long starchy fruits
are prepared in the
same ways as Plantains,
having a similar
taste and texture.
• In ceremonial
sacrifices to the
gods by Tahitians and
Hawaiians, a stalk of Bananas
would be used as a proxy
for a human being. • To be
married beneath any Banana
Tree is lucky. • In Hawaii until 1819,
certain species of Banana were so
strictly forbidden to women that the
punishment for violating this taboo
was death. • There are some scholars
who believe that the Biblical Tree of Life
could have been the species of Banana known as
Musa × paradisiaca, and the Tree of Knowledge a different
species known as *Musa sapientum*. • The leaves, flowers, and
fruit of the Banana Tree are used in money and prosperity
spells because the Banana Tree is such a fruitful plant and the
fruit turns a golden color.

No. 292

Myrica cerifera 🌿 🪴

Southern Wax Myrtle Tree

Southern Bayberry | Wax Myrtle

🔘 **POTENTIAL MAXIMUM HEIGHT**
25 feet [8 meters]

✳️ **SYMBOLIC MEANINGS**
Discipline; Instruction.

🌼 **POSSIBLE POWERS**
Create oxygen; Love; Love
magic; Poise; Youthfulness.

🜨 **FOLKLORE AND FACTS**
Carry a small piece of the
evergreen *Myrica cerifera*
Southern Wax Myrtle Tree
wood or place it in an
amulet to wear or carry in
order to promote a youthful
presence and demeanor.
• Prepare and wear a cap of Southern Wax Myrtle leaves
when preparing a love charm. • Put a leaf of Southern Wax
Myrtle in an amulet you wear to draw love towards you.

No. 293

Myrica pensylvanica ☠ ♉ ⑪ 🌳

Northern Bayberry Tree

Candle Tree | Candleberry | Candlewood | Tallow Bayberry | Waxberry

◉ POTENTIAL MAXIMUM HEIGHT
25 feet [8 meters]

☀ SYMBOLIC MEANINGS
Fragrant illumination;
Love; Peace.

❀ POSSIBLE POWERS
Cleanliness; Create
oxygen; Fertility;
Illumination.

☡ FOLKLORE AND FACTS
The berries of the deciduous *Myrica pensylvanica* Northern
Bayberry Tree are said to be the original cleanly-burning
wax source of the first old-fashioned Christmas Bayberry
candles. The fragrant waxy Bayberries inspired the pleasant
Bayberry soap the early North American colonists enjoyed.
Their pleasure in soap-making inspired them to make the
Bayberry candles. • Burn a fragrant Bayberry candle when
celebrating events, carrying out a magical ritual, or working
on anything pertaining to peace and love in any positive
manner. • The leaves and fruit of the Bayberry Tree have
been used in soups.

No. 294

Myrica rubra ♉ ⑪

Yangmei Tree

Chinese Bayberry | Japanese Bayberry | Red Bayberry | Yamamomo | Yumberry

◉ POTENTIAL MAXIMUM HEIGHT
49 feet [15 meters]

☀ SYMBOLIC MEANING
Mountain peach; Slow to age.

❀ POSSIBLE POWERS
Anti-aging; Create oxygen; Earth
element; Good fortune; Healing;
Jupiter; Luck; Protection.

☡ FOLKLORE AND FACTS
The succulent fruit of the evergreen Chinese *Myrica rubra*
Yangmei Tree is most often eaten fresh, but it is also very
often used to make alcoholic beverages such as wines and
beers, as well as jam. The fruit can also be dried and added
to recipes. • Yangmei berries are often soaked in an alcoholic
beverage known as *baijiu*. An infusion of the berries in the
baijiu is also consumed for medicinal purposes.

M

No. 295

Myristica fragrans ☠ ☗ 🍴 ⬇ ✿

Nutmeg Tree
Mace Tree

🌀 **POTENTIAL MAXIMUM HEIGHT**
60 feet [18 meters]

✺ **SYMBOLIC MEANING**
Clarity of thought.

🌐 **POSSIBLE POWERS**
Air element; Aphrodisiac; Attract
love; Break a hex; Create oxygen;
Earth element; Fidelity; Incense;
Increase clarity of thought;
Intellect; Jupiter; Luck; Masculine
energy; Mental power; Mercury;
Money; Protection; Psychic power;
Purification; Sun.

🜨 **FOLKLORE AND FACTS**
It is the grated or ground seed that is used as a seasoning
and is one of the edible parts of the evergreen *Myristica
fragrans* Nutmeg Tree. • The reddish covering of the seed
tastes similar but is the more delicately flavored seasoning
known as Mace. The whole Nutmeg seed is grated as needed
or ground to a powder. Dried powdered Mace is available
under the names of both Nutmeg and Mace. It is used as
a seasoning to flavor baked goods, pastries, meats, fish,
vegetables, fruits, and beverages. • Mace can be burned
like incense to purify and consecrate a ritual area, as well as
increase one's psychic powers. • Make, then carry a Mace
sachet to improve one's intelligence prior to taking exams.
• Sprinkle Nutmeg on a lottery ticket for good luck. • Make
an amulet of a whole Nutmeg to carry as a good luck charm
and to increase clarity of thought. • If you want a lover to
be faithful, cut a whole Nutmeg into four pieces. Bury one
piece. Burn one piece. Toss one piece off a cliff. Then boil
the last piece in water. Drink one very small sip of the water,
then carry that boiled quarter piece of Nutmeg with you
wherever you go, putting it under your pillow when you
sleep. • Due to the medicinal properties and popular use
of Nutmeg in the Middle East, Saudi Arabia has banned
it, classifying it as an intoxicant and a hallucinogenic drug.
Apparently, very small amounts of Nutmeg have been
permitted to flavor food. • Nutmeg has been banned in most
prisons because of its routine theft from prison kitchens to be
bartered for money and cigarettes.

No. 296

Myroxylon balsamum var. pereirae ☠ ☗ 🍴 ⬇

Balsam of Peru Tree
Balsam Tree | Peru Balsam | Santos Mahogany

🌀 **POTENTIAL MAXIMUM HEIGHT**
148 feet [45 meters]

✺ **SYMBOLIC MEANING**
Calm.

🌐 **POSSIBLE POWERS**
Create oxygen; Healing; Relaxation; Shade.

🜨 **FOLKLORE AND FACTS**
The evergreen *Myroxylon balsamum* var. *pereirae* Balsam
of Peru Tree is a very tall, spreading tree that is most often
used to provide shade on coffee plantations. • Balsam of
Peru's sweet fragrance smells like Vanilla with a hint of
Cinnamon. It is useful in aromatherapy to calm nervous
tension and help promote a tranquil environment in which
to relax. • The Balsam of Peru resin from the *Myroxylon
balsamum* var. *pereirae* tree is obtained by stripping the bark
off the tree and wrapping rags around the wounded trunk to
soak up the resin. The resin is extracted when the rags are
boiled and the fragrant, oily, brown balsam resin sinks to the
bottom of the vessel, where it is collected. One of its many
uses is for flavoring a wide range of beverages and foods
that includes, but is not limited to, barbecue sauce, beer,
candy, chewing gum, chili sauce, chocolate, vanilla, citrus
fruit peel, coffee, cola, flavored teas, gin, ice cream, juice,
liqueurs, apéritifs, marmalade, pickled fruits and vegetables,
puddings, soft drinks, tomato products, and wine. Needless
to say, Balsam of Peru is extremely versatile and immensely
useful. • Balsam of Peru has been identified as one of the top
five most common allergens.

M

No. 297

Myrtus communis ☠ ♥ 🍶 ⚱ 🌰

True Myrtle Tree

Common Myrtle | Corsican Pepper | Myrtle | Myrtus | Sweet Myrtle

🔍 POTENTIAL MAXIMUM HEIGHT

16 feet [5 meters]

✳ SYMBOLIC MEANINGS

Beauty; Chastity; Friendship; Generosity; Good deeds;
Happiness; Heartfelt love; Honor; Hope; Immortality; Joy;
Justice; Love; Marriage; Memory of the Garden of Eden;
Mirth; Modest worth; Money; Peace; Prosperity; Sacred
love; Scent of the Garden of Eden; Souvenir of the Garden of
Eden; Symbol of the Garden of Eden; Weddings; Youth.

🌐 POSSIBLE POWERS

Assistance; Create oxygen; Feminine energy; Fertility; Fond
memories; Friendship; Harmony; Independence; Love;
Material gain; Money; Peace; Peace of mind; Persistence;
Purification; Recovery; Restoration; Stability; Strength;
Tenacity; Venus; Water element; Youth.

🜨 FOLKLORE AND FACTS

The evergreen *Myrtus communis* True Myrtle can be
cultivated and pruned to grow into a small tree. • True
Myrtle is considered to be the sacred symbol and the
fragrance of the Garden of Eden. • A sprig of True Myrtle
in Queen Victoria's bridal bouquet was planted on the Isle
of Wight. Since then, sprigs of that same plant have been
included in many different royal bridal
bouquets. • Carry True Myrtle
wood to preserve youthfulness.
• Carry or wear a True Myrtle
flower to preserve love. • Grow
True Myrtle on each side of a
house to promote that peace and
love will be within the home.
• If a woman plants True
Myrtle in a window box, it will
become lucky. • According to
Arabian traditions, when Adam
was forced to leave the Garden
of Eden, he took three plants
with him. One was the True
Myrtle so that he could
replant it, as it is considered
the foremost of all sweetly
scented flowers. • According
to the Talmudic Jewish tradition,
the bough with leaves of a True
Myrtle is one of the four species of plants

lovingly tied together to be waved in the festival of Sukkot.
The other three are the fruit of a Citron tree, a ripe, green
closed frond of a Date Palm, and the leafy branches from a
Willow tree. • True Myrtle Tree flowers are often made into
a pleasantly fragrant toilet water called *eau d'ange*. • True
Myrtle is occasionally used in a bride's floral head wreath
and bouquet to symbolize her chastity. • Sleep on a pillow
filled with True Myrtle leaves to attain peace of mind.
• Make, then carry or wear a sachet of True Myrtle leaves
to attract what one hopes to be a true friend. • The fruit of
the True Myrtle is aromatic and has been used to flavor some
Middle Eastern dishes. The berries can be a milder-flavored
replacement for Juniper berries. The leaves can be used to
flavor soups. In Sardinia and Corsica, the ripe berries are
used to make a popular liqueur.

M

No. 298

Nectandra membranacea 🪑🌳

Nectandra Tree

Black Cedar | Canela Branca | Ishpingo | Laurelillo | Sweet Myers | Sweetwood Tree

◉ POTENTIAL MAXIMUM HEIGHT
75 feet [23 meters]

✹ SYMBOLIC MEANING
Restorable.

✹ POSSIBLE POWERS
Create oxygen; Restoration.

✦ FOLKLORE AND FACTS
The evergreen *Nectandra membranacea* Nectandra Tree is fast growing and would be especially useful for the restoration of a woodland. • Nectandra Tree wood has been used to make furniture.

No. 299

Nerium oleander ☠🪑🌳

Oleander

Adelfa | Ceylon Tree | Dog Bane | Rose Bay

◉ POTENTIAL MAXIMUM HEIGHT
20 feet [6 meters]

✹ SYMBOLIC MEANINGS
Beauty; Beware; Caution; Danger; Distrust; Grace; I am dangerous.

✹ POSSIBLE POWERS
Create oxygen; Death; Explosive; Love.

✦ FOLKLORE AND FACTS
In Italy it is believed that bringing any part of the beautiful evergreen *Nerium oleander* Oleander tree into the home will surely bring disgrace, sickness, and misfortune of all types. • A clumping perennial plant, the Oleander can be coaxed to form living borderline fences and barriers. • Oleander produces trees that have either single or double flowers colored cream, pink, purple, red, yellow, or white. • Images of the *Nerium oleander* have been recognized in some of the wall art uncovered in Pompeii. • As all parts of the plant are deadly poisonous, the sap has been used as a rat poison.

No. 300

Newbouldia laevis ☠🪑🌰🌿

Boundary Tree

Ewe Akoko | Ogilisi

◉ POTENTIAL MAXIMUM HEIGHT
49 feet [15 meters]

✹ SYMBOLIC MEANING
Chief seed.

✹ POSSIBLE POWERS
Create oxygen; Drive away a bad spirit; Luck; Protection; Repels witches and wizards.

✦ FOLKLORE AND FACTS
The evergreen flowering *Newbouldia laevis* Boundary Tree is planted near shrines and in household gardens because it is considered to be a highly sacred tree. • It is believed by some that witches or wizards flying over a Boundary Tree will fall from the sky to crash to the ground and disappear.

No. 301

Nothofagus antarctica ☠🪑🌳

Antarctic Beech Tree

Ñire | Ñirre

◉ POTENTIAL MAXIMUM HEIGHT
80 feet [24 meters]

✹ SYMBOLIC MEANING
Adapted language.

✹ POSSIBLE POWERS
Adaptation; Create oxygen; Endurance; Flexibility; Regeneration; Tolerance.

✦ FOLKLORE AND FACTS
Prior to the 2019 discovery of the *Nothofagus betuloides* Magellan's Beech as the southernmost tree in the world, the deciduous *Nothofagus antarctica* Antarctic Beech Tree had that distinction. • The waxy leaves of the Antarctic Beech Tree have a sweet fragrance. • The tree has been planted in Great Britain and the North Pacific Coastal area of the USA, where it thrives.

No. 302

Nothofagus betuloides

Magellan's Beech
Coihue de Magallanes | Guindo | Guino Beech | Oigue de Magallanes

POTENTIAL MAXIMUM HEIGHT
82 feet [25 meters]

SYMBOLIC MEANING
Southernmost tongue.

POSSIBLE POWERS
Cold-resistant; Create oxygen; Endurance; Regeneration; Wind-resistant.

FOLKLORE AND FACTS
The evergreen *Nothofagus betuloides* Magellan's Beech was observed during Ferdinand Magellan's expedition in 1520. A specimen of the tree was collected on Captain Cook's first voyage to Tierra del Fuego, Patagonia, in 1769 by botanist Sir Joseph Banks. • Easily propagated from seed and able to withstand cold temperatures, *Nothofagus betuloides* has been grown in some coastal parts of the Pacific Northwest. • Setting out in search of the world's most southernmost tree, a National Geographic expedition in 2019 discovered that one tree growing on the southeastern tip of Hornos Island, close to Cape Horn, is a Magellan's Beech. That enduring tree has the distinction of being known as the tree at the end of the world.

No. 303

Nothofagus dombeyi

Dombey's Beech Tree
Coigue | Coigüe | Coihue

POTENTIAL MAXIMUM HEIGHT
148 feet [45 meters]

SYMBOLIC MEANING
Adapted language.

POSSIBLE POWERS
Adaptation; Create oxygen; Endurance; Flexibility; Regeneration.

FOLKLORE AND FACTS
Fast-growing and able to thrive in many different climates, the evergreen *Nothofagus dombeyi* Dombey's Beech Tree is cultivated as a leathery-leafed ornamental tree as well as for its excellent quality lumber. • The fruit is small and only barely larger than the 1½-inch (4 cm) flowers. The tree is large and extremely hardy. Grown from seed, it has the capacity to produce dense forests when its requirements for soil and water are amply met. • Desired for the construction of floors, furniture, and barrels, the Dombey's Beech Tree wood is hard, heavy, strong, durable, and resistant to decay. • The tree can become very tall. A tree that fell during a Patagonian storm in 1954 was reported to be 285 feet (87 m) tall.

No. 304

Nothofagus pumilio

Lenga Beech Tree
False Beech | Lenga | Southern Beech

POTENTIAL MAXIMUM HEIGHT
100 feet [30 meters]

SYMBOLIC MEANINGS
Language; Tongue.

POSSIBLE POWERS
Create oxygen; Regeneration.

FOLKLORE AND FACTS
The deciduous *Nothofagus pumilio* Lenga Beech Tree will easily regenerate from seed after a forest fire. • In the spring, the inner bark is edible when scraped, dried, ground into a powder for use as a thickener in soups, or added to grains when making bread. The sap is also edible. • Lenga Beech wood is used in construction and to make furniture. It is also occasionally used as a substitute for Black Cherry or English Walnut wood in cabinetry.

No. 305
Notholithocarpus densiflorus 🌰 🍄 🌿

Tanoak Tree
Chishkale | Tanbark-oak

📷 POTENTIAL MAXIMUM HEIGHT
208 feet [63 meters]

✺ SYMBOLIC MEANING
Beautiful tree.

🌼 POSSIBLE POWERS
Create oxygen; Healing; Tan leather.

🜾 FOLKLORE AND FACTS
At one time in southwestern Oregon, the evergreen *Notholithocarpus densiflorus* Tanoak Tree was considered the second most abundant and strong hardwood harvested for timber. • A Tanoak Tree can be grown from an acorn seed and live up to 250 years. • Tanoak flowers are a yellow-green color and bloom in the spring. • Some Native American peoples in California, such as the Pomo, use the Tanoak acorn to make bread, biscuits, pancakes, hot cereal, and soup. The roasted acorns are sometimes used as a substitute for coffee. • Tanoak bark is very rich in tannin which, up until approximately the early 1960s, was once commonly used to tan leather in California. The bark can also be used to make a dye. • Tanoak leaf mulch has the ability to repel slugs. • In 1995, a mysterious disease was first discovered in California when many Tanoak Trees suddenly suffered wilting, dark sap, bark splitting, and then death. The disease was named Sudden Oak Death, which is also known as SOD. Studies have revealed that the spread of this disease has both natural and human-related behaviors.

No. 306
Nothotsuga longibracteata 🌰

Bristlecone Hemlock
Chang Bao Tie Shan | *Tsuga longibracteata*

📷 POTENTIAL MAXIMUM HEIGHT
98 feet [30 meters]

✺ SYMBOLIC MEANING
Big old tree.

🌼 POSSIBLE POWERS
Create oxygen; Healing.

🜾 FOLKLORE AND FACTS
The genus *Nothotsuga* contains one species, the evergreen *Nothotsuga longibracteata* Bristlecone Hemlock. • At one time it was found throughout China. However, due to extensively overharvesting the Bristlecone Hemlock for its timber, it is now very rare and finally protected.

No. 307
Nyssa sylvatica 🌰 🌿

Tupelo Tree
Beetlebung Tree | Black Gum | Black Tupelo | Pepperidge Tree | Sour Gum

📷 POTENTIAL MAXIMUM HEIGHT
50 feet [15 meters]

✺ SYMBOLIC MEANING
Swampy.

🌼 POSSIBLE POWERS
Attract honeybees; Create oxygen; Resistance; Strength.

🜾 FOLKLORE AND FACTS
The deciduous *Nyssa sylvatica* Tupelo Tree flowers are a favorite of honeybees that collect the nectar and pollen that ultimately becomes the famous Tupelo honey. • Sections of hollow Tupelo Tree trunks are sometimes used as beehives by beekeepers. • Tupelo Tree wood is extremely hard and very difficult to split, making it a good choice for constructing pulleys and even weaving shuttles. Its strength and resistance to acids has also made Tupelo wood a favorite for factory flooring. Since Tupelo Tree wood can be coated with creosote, it is a favored wood for railroad ties.

N

No. 308

Ochroma pyramidale

Balsa Tree
Balsa Wood Tree

📷 **POTENTIAL MAXIMUM HEIGHT**
98 feet [30 meters]

✸ **SYMBOLIC MEANING**
Raft.

🌕 **POSSIBLE POWERS**
Aloft; Create oxygen;
Flotation; Lightness; Moon;
Softness; Water element.

🍂 **FOLKLORE AND FACTS**
The deciduous *Ochroma pyramidale*
Balsa Tree is fast growing. Its wood is
the softest of the commercial woods, having a lower density
than cork. A Balsa Tree will live for only around forty years.
• The spongy, water-saturated wood of the living tree is just
barely able to float. Once the kiln-drying of the cut lumber
extracts all the water from the wood's cells, its floatability
increases substantially. It is often used as a core material with
other less-absorbent products such as fiberglass or carbon
plastic providing a full coating around it. • Kiln-dried Balsa
wood is a favorite material for crafting hobby boats. It is also
the wood of choice for building competitive free-flight model
sport aircraft. • Balsa wood is used in a great many break-
away types of theatrical props. • Balsa wood is a favorite
choice when first starting to learn the art of wood whittling.

No. 309

Olea europaea 🪔🍴🏺🌰🕯

Olive Tree
Common Olive

📷 **POTENTIAL MAXIMUM HEIGHT**
30 feet [9 meters]

✸ **SYMBOLIC MEANINGS**
Abundance; Fertility; Glory;
Holiness; Peace; Power;
Purity; Sacredness;
Wisdom.

🌿 **COMPONENT MEANINGS**
Branch: Peace.
Leaf: Peace.

🌕 **POSSIBLE POWERS**
Abundance; Air element; Ancient Earth; Benediction;
Consecration; Create oxygen; Fertility; Fire element;
Healing; Longevity; Lust; Masculine energy; Nourishment;
Peace; Potency; Protection; Purification; Sun; Survival in
harsh conditions.

🍂 **FOLKLORE AND FACTS**
The fruit of the evergreen *Olea europaea* Olive Tree is a
drupe, as is a Peach or a Plum. • It is the source of the Olive
oil that has long been considered sacred. Olive oil is used
in the sacred rituals of several different world religions
from birth to death. Some of these rituals include anointing
solemn blessings on people, places, and things. Another is
consecrating world monarchs at their coronations. And yet
another is anointing the infirm with prayers for healing.
Olive oil has also been presented as offerings to a wide
variety of deities. It has also been utilized in some magical
workings that focus on the promotion of peace. • There
is fossilized evidence discovered in what is now Italy that
Olive Trees existed nearly forty million years ago. • Olive
Trees were cultivated in parts of the Mediterranean seven
thousand years ago. • Olive seeds and pieces of Olive Tree
wood have been found in many ancient tombs. • The Olive
Tree is one of the first plants mentioned in the Bible's Book
of Genesis, when a dove returned bringing an Olive Tree
branch to Noah to prove to him that the Great Flood had
ended. • According to Jewish law, the Olive is one of the
Seven Species that require a blessing before being eaten.
• Some traditional methods of extracting Olive oil date
back thousands of years. • In ancient times, Olive oil was
commonly used as fuel for lamps. • Brides in ancient Greece
would traditionally wear Olive leaf crowns as their visible
hope and wish for fertility. • Hang an Olive branch over the
front door to fend evil away from entering the home. • Wear
an Olive leaf as a good luck charm. • The eternal flame at the
original Olympic games in Greece was fed by Olive oil.
• Some of the Olive Trees around the Mediterranean Sea
that are still producing fruit have been dated to be up to
3,500 years old. • An Olive Tree in Portugal known as
Oliveira do Mouchão was planted sometime near the start
of the Bronze Age. • A very special Olive leaf crown, or
kotinos, was placed on the heads of the winners of the
ancient Olympic games. Wood for each crown was ritually
cut from sacred Olive trees that grew near the Temple of
Zeus in ancient Olympia before being fashioned into the
champions' crowns on an ivory and gold table in the Temple
of Hera nearby. • According to local folklore, a small grove
of sixteen Olive Trees in Bcheale, Lebanon, could possibly
be six thousand years old. Perhaps older. • Raw, unprocessed
Olives are inedible but not toxic. • Scatter Olive leaves to
create a vibration of peace.

O

No. 310
Pachira aquatica ☠ 🪴 🍴 🌱
Malabar Chestnut Tree
Carolinea | French Peanut | Guiana Chestnut | Money Plant | Money Tree | Pochota | Provision Tree | Pumpo | Saba Nut

⬤ POTENTIAL MAXIMUM HEIGHT
70 feet [21 meters]

✳ SYMBOLIC MEANINGS
Good financial
fortune; Good fortune;
Good luck.

❋ POSSIBLE POWERS
Create oxygen; Luck;
Money.

☙ FOLKLORE AND FACTS
The evergreen *Pachira aquatica* Malabar Chestnut Tree is most often referred to as a Money Tree. It is sold as a small tree or shrub houseplant that has a five-stemmed braided trunk, with each stem representing one of the five Chinese elements in feng shui. It is also often decorated with red ribbons and other Chinese symbols of good fortune.
• The nuts of the Malabar Chestnut Tree have been known to be roasted, ground, and then used to brew a hot chestnut-flavored beverage.

No. 311
Paeonia × *suffruticosa* ☠ 🪴 🌱
Tree Peony
Beauty of The Empire | King of Flowers | Rose of Spring

⬤ POTENTIAL MAXIMUM HEIGHT
10 feet [3 meters]

✳ SYMBOLIC MEANINGS
Affection; Aristocracy;
Bashfulness; Beautiful;
Beauty; Blessed herb; Feminine
beauty; Honor; Love; Most beautiful;
Riches; Romantic love; Shame;
Wealth.

❋ POSSIBLE POWERS
Adaptability; Ambition; Create oxygen; Determination; Happy marriage; Harmonious union; Healing; Prosperity; Protect pregnant woman; Protection of harvests; Protection of shepherds and their flocks; Thriving; Virility; Ward off demons; Ward off evil eye; Ward off nightmares; Ward off storms.

☙ FOLKLORE AND FACTS
In China, the deciduous *Paeonia* × *suffruticosa* Tree Peony holds a place of honored cultural significance as King of Flowers. • The *Paeonia* × *suffruticosa* has been depicted in Chinese art and literature more than any other flower in the country's long history. • Tree Peony seeds that have been gathered at night, then soaked in rainwater, can be strung or placed in a sachet to carry or wear for protection against malicious witchcraft and the Devil.

No. 312
Palaquium gutta
Gutta-Percha Tree
Getah Merah | Karet Oblong | Taban | Taban Merah

⬤ POTENTIAL MAXIMUM HEIGHT
65 feet [20 meters]

✳ SYMBOLIC MEANINGS
Good gum; Sap.

❋ POSSIBLE POWERS
Create oxygen; Elasticity; Flexibility; Healing.

☙ FOLKLORE AND FACTS
The evergreen *Palaquium gutta* Gutta-Percha Tree has been particularly productive and immensely useful in many important ways. • Gutta-Percha Tree seeds are used to make candles, soap, and because of its low toxicity, it is also the material used for dental root canal fillings.
• The tree sap is used to make what was an innovatively phenomenal latex product, also called Gutta-Percha, which is an electrically nonconductive thermoplastic latex that was eventually surpassed by polyethylene in 1940. Prior to that time, it is astonishing to note how many ways it was used. Telegraph wires, including the early ones under the sea, as well as the first transatlantic telegraph cable, were all insulated with Gutta-Percha Tree latex. The first guttie golf ball had a solid Gutta-Percha center, and it changed the game. Gutta-Percha was used on pistol grips and even made into mourning jewelry because it was black and could be easily rolled into beads. Gutta-Percha was also made into such things as walking sticks and medical devices. All this prior to the invention of Bakelite plastic, which was superior to the Gutta-Percha properties of the day. • For approximately two years, strange cutting-board-size blocks of Gutta-Percha washed ashore in parts of northern Europe that were engraved with the name of a Dutch plantation that had long since vanished in what is now Indonesia. They are believed to have come from a Japanese ocean liner that sank back in 1917 off the coast of Cornwall, England.

P

No. 313
Pandanus edulis 🍴

Bakong
Knob-fruited Screwpine

⬤ **POTENTIAL MAXIMUM HEIGHT**
33 feet [10 meters]

✦ **SYMBOLIC MEANINGS**
Comfort; Devotion.

✿ **POSSIBLE POWERS**
Create oxygen; Protection; Protection from the elements.

✾ **FOLKLORE AND FACTS**
The fruit of the evergreen *Pandanus edulis* Bakong looks like a perfectly round pineapple-like fruit hanging prettily from a fancy decorative palm tree. • In Guam, the flesh of the fruit is cooked and eaten. • The seeds can be eaten and taste like coconut. • The leaves of the Bakong are commonly harvested for use in making handicrafts and weaving mats. The root fibers are made into twine. • Fold, then tuck a Bakong leaf into a sachet to wear or carry for personal protection.

No. 314
Pandanus odorifer

Fragrant Screw-Pine
Adan | Al-kādi | Kaithai | Ketaki Tree | Kewda | Kewra | Pandan Flower | Pandan Leaf | Screw Tree | Screwpine | Thatch Screwpine | Thazhai | Umbrella Tree

⬤ **POTENTIAL MAXIMUM HEIGHT**
13 feet [4 meters]

✦ **SYMBOLIC MEANING**
Aromatic.

✿ **POSSIBLE POWERS**
Create oxygen; Perfumery.

✾ **FOLKLORE AND FACTS**
Only the male evergreen *Pandanus odorifer* Fragrant Screw-Pine flowers are used to make *keorra-ka-arak*, which is the pleasantly rose-like aromatic essential oil used in the making of some perfumes. • Although many of the trees have been destroyed by the onslaught of massive tourism that provoked the overharvesting of the leaves for their use as woven souvenirs, Fragrant Screw-Pine still grows widely on St. Martin Island, off the coast of Bangladesh. • The Fragrant Screw-Pine flower is never offered to the Hindu god Shiva because he cursed the flower, blaming the tree for helping Brahma lie to him.

No. 315
Pausinystalia yohimbe ☠ ⚗

Yohimbe Tree
Johimbe | Johimbi | *Pausinystalia johimbe*

⬤ **POTENTIAL MAXIMUM HEIGHT**
82 feet [25 meters]

✦ **SYMBOLIC MEANING**
Erotic love.

✿ **POSSIBLE POWERS**
Aphrodisiac; Create oxygen; Fertility; Impotence remedy; Love; Lust; Virility.

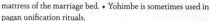

✾ **FOLKLORE AND FACTS**
To spice up marital love life, place a small piece of the evergreen *Pausinystalia yohimbe* Yohimbe Tree bark in a small red pouch and tuck it under the mattress of the marriage bed. • Yohimbe is sometimes used in pagan unification rituals.

No. 316
Peltogyne purpurea 🌳

Purpleheart Tree
Nazareno | Violet Wood

⬤ **POTENTIAL MAXIMUM HEIGHT**
164 feet [50 meters]

✦ **SYMBOLIC MEANINGS**
Survival; Veteran.

✿ **POSSIBLE POWERS**
Beauty; Create oxygen; Love; Sound resonance; Survival; Veteran.

✾ **FOLKLORE AND FACTS**
When the deciduous *Peltogyne purpurea* Purpleheart Tree's heartwood is cut and exposed to air, it quickly turns a highly desirable purple tone. • Purpleheart Tree wood is highly water-resistant. Even though the wood is challenging to work with, an experienced woodworker can produce beautiful inlay using the valuable, unusual wood for musical instruments, cabinets, fine furniture, flooring, and staircases, as well as luxurious coffins and small items such as jewelry boxes and bowls. • In Panama and Costa Rica, harvesting the Purpleheart Tree is prohibited.

No. 317

Pennantia baylisiana

Three Kings Kaikōmako Tree

Kaikōmako Manawatāwhi | The World's Loneliest Tree

◉ POTENTIAL MAXIMUM HEIGHT
26 feet [8 meters]

✹ SYMBOLIC MEANING
Independent survival.

❀ POSSIBLE POWERS
Coping skills; Create oxygen; Survive loneliness.

✿ FOLKLORE AND FACTS
At the time it was discovered in 1945, there was only one large cluster-leafed female specimen of *Pennantia baylisiana* Three Kings Kaikōmako Tree to be found in the wild. The tree is only found in New Zealand on Manawatāwhi, in the Three Kings Islands. There have since been several other trees propagated from cuttings of that one lonely tree.
• At one time, the *Guinness Book of World Records* listed the *Pennantia baylisiana* as the rarest tree in the world.

No. 318

Persea americana ☠ 🍴

Avocado Tree

Abacate | Alligator Pear | Butter Fruit | Butter Pear | Hass Avocado | Persea Testicle Tree

◉ POTENTIAL MAXIMUM HEIGHT
49 feet [15 meters]

✹ SYMBOLIC MEANINGS
Love; Relationship; Romance; Sexual romance.

❀ POSSIBLE POWERS
Aphrodisiac; Attract love; Beauty; Create oxygen; Feminine energy; Fertility; Love; Lust; Sex magic; Sexual vigor; Testicles; Venus; Water element.

✿ FOLKLORE AND FACTS
The evergreen *Persea americana* Avocado Tree can be grown from a seed. • Carry an Avocado pit to promote beauty. • A magic wand made from Avocado Tree wood is believed to be very powerful for any reason. • An Avocado pit dating between nine and ten thousand years ago was discovered in Coxcatlan Cave, located in Puebla, Mexico. • The first time the word "avocado" was recorded in English was in an index of Jamaican plants written in 1696. • The Great Avocado Panic and Guacapocalypse of 2019 was precipitated by an idle stock market prediction that expected a clash between the skyrocketing obsessive neediness for

Avocado toast in the morning and guacamole at night. That, along with the USA on one side of the Rio Grande River and Mexico on the other side, would lead to a shortage in the fruit based on some imaginary principle. The rest is history that didn't actually happen. Although the price of the Avocado fruit did go up and then down again, an effort to meet the expanded demand for Avocados resulted in a surplus of more Avocados than could be reasonably consumed. • The fruit-like berry from the Avocado Tree is edible and will not ripen until after it has been removed from the tree. • It is better to purchase a hard, underripe Avocado and ripen it to the desired softness at home than to buy a softer Avocado and wait another day to eat it. • Avocado oil and Olive oil have similar monounsaturated fat profiles. Both unrefined and refined Avocado oil can be safely heated for high-heat cooking that includes stir-frying. • To grow an Avocado plant in the house from the seed of a fruit that you have consumed will bring love into the home. • A magic wand made from Avocado Tree wood is believed to be very powerful for any reason.

No. 319

Phoenix dactylifera ✥ ❶ ✿

Date Palm

Date | Deglet Noor | Halawy | Medjool | Thoory

◉ POTENTIAL MAXIMUM HEIGHT
99 feet [30 meters]

✺ SYMBOLIC MEANINGS
Abundance; Fertility; Prosperity; Triumph; Victory.

✾ POSSIBLE POWERS
Abundance production; Air element; Create oxygen;
Fertility; Masculine energy; Potency; Spirituality;
Strength; Sun.

⊕ FOLKLORE AND FACTS
In some parts of the world, the majestic evergreen *Phoenix
dactylifera* Date Palm has been cultivated for over forty-eight
thousand years. • Dates are referenced in the Bible more
than fifty times. They are referenced in the Quran twenty
times. • According to Arabian traditions, when Adam was
forced to leave the Garden of Eden, he took three plants with
him, one of them being the seeds to regrow the Date Palm,
which is the foremost producer of all fruits. • The ancient
Babylonians ate dried Dates like we now consume candy
and other sweets. • In ancient Mesopotamia, Date wine
and syrup were both considered to be sacred foods. • Dates
presented upon Olive oil–soaked bread was given as offering
to the ancient Babylonian deities Anu, Ea, Shamash, and
Marduk. • It is believed by some that if a piece of the Date
Palm frond is carried as an amulet, it will increase fertility.
• A Date Palm frond placed near the door of the home
will keep evil from all sources from entering the premises.
• Carry a Date pit to regain waning or lost virility. • The
Phoenix dactylifera Date Palm has separately sexed trees.
The females bear fruit. The male plants are only pollinators
and are assisted in
accomplishing their
task with the
help of the
wind. On
plantations
where there
is a limited
number of
males, human manual
intervention takes place
from atop tall ladders.
• The Date Palm's fruit
will continue ripening
after it has been picked.

• Dates can be dried, ground, and even brewed like coffee.
Dates are eaten out of hand, stuffed, added to a wide variety
of sweet and savory dishes, made into a paste, pressed and
turned into syrup, dried and powdered into date sugar,
juiced, made into wine and liqueur, and also transformed
into vinegar. • A two thousand-year-old *Phoenix dactylifera*
Date Palm seed, found in Israel during the excavation
of Masada in the mid-1960s, successfully sprouted after
being planted.

No. 320

Phyllanthus emblica ☠ ✥ ❶ ✾ ✿

Amla Tree

Amalaki | India Gooseberry | Indian Gooseberry | Malacca Tree | Myrobalan Plum

◉ POTENTIAL MAXIMUM HEIGHT
49 feet [15 meters]

✺ SYMBOLIC MEANINGS
Enlightenment; Sustainer.

✾ POSSIBLE POWERS
Abundance; Create oxygen;
Enlightenment; Healing;
Powerful healing; Prosperity.

⊕ FOLKLORE AND FACTS
Sacred to Hinduism, the evergreen
Phyllanthus emblica Amla Tree fruit
is referenced in the *Ashokavadana*.
• According to legend, half of an
Amla fruit was the last gift by the
emperor, Ashoka the Great, to a Buddhist community
of religious devotees, monks, and nuns. • The Amla Tree
bark can be peeled off into thin flakes, then used in making
an amulet or a sachet that can be carried or worn to heal any
malady of body, mind, or spirit. • Use a gold string or ribbon
to tie together a small bundle of Amla twigs that have the
leaves still attached to be used as a talisman for the home.
Place the Amla talisman in a position of honor at or near to
the center of the house to radiate beneficial physical, mental,
and spiritual energy to all within the home. • The fruit of
the Amla Tree is edible and can be eaten raw, cooked, or
added into other dishes such as daal. • One dish, called *amle
ka murabba*, is a sweet dessert made by soaking the Amla
berries in a sugary syrup to candy them.

No. 321
Picea abies 🪴🍴🍂🌰🕯

Norway Spruce
European Spruce

🔍 **POTENTIAL MAXIMUM HEIGHT**
100 feet [30 meters]

✺ **SYMBOLIC MEANINGS**
Divine light; Mother Earth.

🌀 **POSSIBLE POWERS**
Abundance; Air element;
Awakening; Childbirth;
Create oxygen; Dreaming;
Enlightenment; Feminine
energy; Fertility; Harmony;
Immortality; Light;
Luck; Magic; Masculine
energy; Moon; Mothers;
Protection; Regeneration;
Renewal; Reproduction;
Resurrection; Spiritual
consciousness; Spirituality;
Spiritual life; Spiritual love.

🜨 **FOLKLORE AND FACTS**
The evergreen conifer *Picea abies* Norway Spruce can live
to be four hundred years old. • The Norway Spruce will
produce plump citrusy stem tips in the spring. These are
considered a delicacy for making spruce sugar and tea.
• The fragrant Norway Spruce is a popular choice for a
Christmas tree. It is also the species selected for the big
Christmas tree erected at Rockefeller Center in New York
City. • The Norway Spruce is the most popular tree in
Europe. • A branch of Norway Spruce in the home will
attract the positive energy of generous nature spirits. • At
one time, a treatment for scurvy was to drink the rustic
beer that is sometimes prepared using young Norway
Spruce spring stem tips. • The oldest Norway Spruce
was discovered at a nature preserve in Buskerud County,
Norway. It was planted in 1480. However, the oldest Norway
Spruce *clone* is 9,550 years old. It is located in Dalarna,
Sweden, and is known by the name Old Tjikko.

No. 322
Picea laxa 🪴🍴🍂🌰🕯

White Spruce
Alberta White Spruce | Black Hills Spruce | Canadian Spruce | Cat Spruce | Porsild Spruce |
Skunk Spruce | Western White Spruce

🔍 **POTENTIAL MAXIMUM HEIGHT**
100 feet [30 meters]

✺ **SYMBOLIC MEANING**
Bring new things.

🌀 **POSSIBLE POWERS**
Abundance; Air element; Awakening; Childbirth; Create
oxygen; Dreaming; Enlightenment; Feminine energy;
Fertility; Harmony; Immortality; Light; Luck; Magic;
Masculine energy; Moon; Mothers; Protection; Regeneration;
Renewal; Reproduction; Resurrection; Spiritual
consciousness; Spirituality; Spiritual life; Spiritual love.

🜨 **FOLKLORE AND FACTS**
The evergreen conifer *Picea laxa* White Spruce is a
dependably cold-hardy tree that has been known to survive
extremely low temperatures in the range of –58°F (–50°C)
and even lower. • The White Spruce can thrive for three
hundred years. • White Spruce is a favorite choice for a
Christmas tree. • White Spruce essential oil is useful in
cleansing a home of negative energy. • Keep a branch of
White Spruce in the home to attract the positive energy of
generous nature spirits.

Pimenta dioica 🍴🗡️🌳

Allspice Tree

Clove Pepper | Jamaica Pepper | Jamaican Pepper | Myrtle Pepper | Newspice

📍 **POTENTIAL MAXIMUM HEIGHT**
43 feet [13 meters]

✴️ **SYMBOLIC MEANINGS**
Compassion; Languishing; Love; Luck.

🌀 **POSSIBLE POWERS**
Accidents; Aggression; Anger; Carnal desire; Conflict; Create oxygen; Finding treasure; Fire element; Healing; Looking for hidden treasure; Love; Luck; Lust; Machinery; Mars; Masculine energy; Money; Rock music; Strength; Struggle; Treasure hunting; War.

🌿 **FOLKLORE AND FACTS**
The unripe dried fruit of the evergreen *Pimenta dioica* Allspice Tree is known as the culinary herb Allspice. The name of Allspice started being used around 1621 because the berry tastes like a combination of all the important spices of those days: Clove, Cinnamon, and Nutmeg. • Allspice is often added to herbal mixtures to attract money or luck. • Christopher Columbus encountered *Pimenta dioica* trees on his second New World voyage, back in the days when it grew wild and could only be found in Jamaica. • Birds are responsible for spreading the Allspice Tree in the wild. • When searching for treasure, wear an amulet of Allspice to assist in the hunt. • As a culinary herb, Allspice is used in both sweet and savory dishes. • Allspice essential oil is often added to a light carrier oil used to massage the skin, giving it an exotic, warm fragrance.

Pimenta racemosa ☠️🏺🌳

Bay Rum Tree

Ciliment | Mycia | West Indian Bay Tree

📍 **POTENTIAL MAXIMUM HEIGHT**
40 feet [12 meters]

✴️ **SYMBOLIC MEANINGS**
Manly; Ready for love; Ready for work.

🌀 **POSSIBLE POWERS**
Alert; Aphrodisiac; Create oxygen; Inner calm; Love; Luck; Lust; Machinery; Mars; Masculine energy; Protection; Romantic; Sailors; Sea; Strength; War; Water element.

🌿 **FOLKLORE AND FACTS**
Reminiscent of the Caribbean, the evergreen *Pimenta racemosa* Bay Rum Tree is the contributor of the fragrant leaves at the base of the pleasant Bay Rum scent. This aroma dates back to 180 years of continual use as an aftershave, cologne, and hair tonic and has been the iconic scent of several generations of men, most especially the well-groomed sailors of World War II. • Bay Rum's essential oil for aromatherapy is beneficial to help calm the inner spirit while simultaneously increasing alertness. • Romantically, keep in mind that the aroma of Bay Rum could easily be imagined to be feasibly connected to the conception of at least the baby boomer generation of human beings, particularly those conceived during and after World War II.

No. 325

Pinus coulteri 🌳

Coulter Pine
Big-cone Pine

📍 POTENTIAL MAXIMUM HEIGHT
79 feet [24 meters]

☀ SYMBOLIC MEANING
More than expected.

🌀 POSSIBLE POWERS
Air element; Awakening;
Create oxygen; Dreaming;
Enlightenment; Eternal
life; Fertility; Harmony;
Immortality; Injury;
Light; Magic; Magnitude;
Masculine energy; Mass;
Peace; Regeneration; Resurrection; Spiritual consciousness;
Spirituality; Sudden damage; Sudden death; Volume; Weight.

🌙 FOLKLORE AND FACTS
The cone of the evergreen conifer *Pinus coulteri* Coulter
Pine tree is the heaviest pine cone of any *Pinus*. One cone
can weigh up to 11 pounds (5 kg)! The weight of it can cause
grave damage if it were to drop off the tree and hit someone
on the head. That sudden fatal misfortune has occurred
enough to give the cones the name of "widow maker."

No. 326

Pinus lambertiana 🍴 🌳

Sugar Pine
Sugar Cone Pine

📍 POTENTIAL MAXIMUM HEIGHT
269 feet [82 meters]

☀ SYMBOLIC MEANINGS
Generously sweet; Impressive largesse.

🌀 POSSIBLE POWERS
Air element; Awakening; Create oxygen; Dreaming;
Eternal life; Fertility; Harmony; Immortality; Light; Magic;
Masculine energy; Peace; Protection; Psychic rejuvenation;
Regeneration; Resurrection; Sizable offering; Spiritual
consciousness; Spirituality.

🌙 FOLKLORE AND FACTS
Of all the *Pinus* trees on Earth, the tallest and most massive
evergreen conifer that just happens to also produce
fabulously long cones is the *Pinus lambertiana* Sugar Pine.
The pine cones are epically sized, being approximately
24 inches (61 cm) long from end to end and weighing up to
almost 5 pounds (2 kg). • The sweet Sugar Pine seeds were
consumed both raw and roasted, as well as ground into a
flour and enjoyed by many Native
Americans. • The grain of the
Sugar Pine wood is straight
and has made it a choice
material for the construction
of pipe organs.

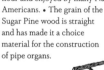

P

Pinus longaeva

Great Basin Bristlecone Pine Tree

Intermountain Bristlecone Pine | Western Bristlecone Pine

⊙ POTENTIAL MAXIMUM HEIGHT
65 feet [20 meters]

✲ SYMBOLIC MEANINGS
Long life; Longevity.

❀ POSSIBLE POWERS
Air element; Ancient
Earth; Awakening;
Cosmos; Create oxygen;
Dreaming; Earth energy;
Enlightenment; Immortality; Light; Live
beyond old age; Loneliness; Longevity; Magic;
Masculine energy; Peace; Regeneration; Resurrection;
Sadness; Spiritual consciousness; Spirituality.

❦ FOLKLORE AND FACTS
The longest-living tree on Earth is the *Pinus longaeva*
Great Basin Bristlecone Pine Tree. One specimen known as
Methuselah has been declared the oldest tree in existence
on the entire face of the Earth that has not taken advantage
of vegetative cloning. It regenerates via sprawling roots
and shoots. In 1957, core samples of the tree were taken and
scientists determined that its seed germinated and began
to grow in what is now California sometime back between
3051 and 2833 BCE. This precious, ancient tree is in a secret,
protected, remote area of the Inyo National Forest, located
somewhere between California and Nevada. Very cold
temperatures, along with high winds, are believed to have
slowed the tree's growth to the point that, in some years,
growth rings failed to develop. The slow growth has also
made the tree's wood extremely hard. The needles are
known to live and cling tenaciously to the tree's branches for
approximately thirty years before falling off. The nature of
the tree is that it is resistant to rot, fungus, and damage from
insects known to destroy plants. Even after all those years,
this Bristlecone Pine Tree has not grown much taller than
50 feet (15 m) upwards and approximately 13 feet (4 m)
around, which seems small for a nearly five thousand-year-
old tree. • A previous *Pinus longaeva* named Prometheus
was cut down in 1964. It was thought to be 4,862 years old
but was more likely over five thousand years old. Its felling,
for unfathomable quasi-valid reasons, remains a highly
controversial issue.

Pinus nigra 🖤🌰🍂

European Black Pine

Black Pine

⊙ POTENTIAL MAXIMUM HEIGHT
60 feet [18 meters]

✲ SYMBOLIC MEANING
Pity.

❀ POSSIBLE POWERS
Air element; Alleviate
feelings of guilt; Awakening;
Create oxygen; Dreaming;
Enlightenment; Eternal life; Fertility;
Harmony; Immortality; Light; Longevity;
Magic; Magical cleansing; Masculine energy; Peace;
Purification; Regeneration; Resurrection; Sanctification;
Spiritual consciousness; Spirituality.

❦ FOLKLORE AND FACTS
The conifer evergreen *Pinus nigra* European Black Pine
tree can live for a long time. Some specimens are over five
hundred years old. • Brush a branch on the ground to purify
and sanctify the area. • Run water over a pouch of Black
Pine needles to create a cleansing and purification bath.

Pinus pinea 🖤🍴🌰

Italian Stone Pine

Parasol Pine | Stone Pine | Umbrella Pine

⊙ POTENTIAL MAXIMUM HEIGHT
100 feet [30 meters]

✲ SYMBOLIC MEANING
Prosperity in life.

❀ POSSIBLE POWERS
Air element; Awakening; Create
oxygen; Dreaming; Enlightenment;
Eternal life; Fertility;
Harmony; Immortality; Light;
Magic; Mars; Masculine
energy; Peace; Regeneration;
Resurrection; Spiritual
consciousness; Spirituality.

P

FOLKLORE AND FACTS

Since prehistoric times, the evergreen conifer *Pinus pinea* Italian Stone Pine has been deliberately cultivated with the sole purpose of harvesting the edible seeds from its cones. The seeds are better known as pine nuts. • The Italian Stone Pine's pine nuts have been coveted trade items for more than six thousand years. • The Italian Stone Pine tree can live up to three hundred years.

No. 330

Pinus ponderosa

Ponderosa Pine

Blackjack Pine | Bull Pine | Filipinus Pine | Western Yellow-pine

POTENTIAL MAXIMUM HEIGHT

274 feet [84 meters]

SYMBOLIC MEANINGS

Heavy; Large; Ponderous; Weighty.

POSSIBLE POWERS

Air element; Awakening; Create oxygen; Dreaming; Enlightenment; Eternal life; Fertility; Harmony; Immortality; Light; Longevity; Magic; Masculine energy; Peace; Regeneration; Resurrection; Spiritual consciousness; Spirituality; Wisdom.

FOLKLORE AND FACTS

The quickly spreading evergreen conifer *Pinus ponderosa* Ponderosa Pine has invasively spread like a weed in some parts of Australia and across the highlands of New Zealand, which is forcing native plants to die out. • Many Native American peoples would gather the Ponderosa Pine seeds to roast and eat. • Ponderosa Pine bark is sweet, smells like butterscotch or vanilla, and has been brewed as a tea. • Ponderosa Pine trunks have been used by Native American peoples to carve out sturdy canoes. • Ponderosa Pine needles are a material that is used in pine needle basketry.

No. 331

Pinus rigida

Pitch Pine Tree

Northern Pitch Pine

POTENTIAL MAXIMUM HEIGHT

82 feet [25 meters]

SYMBOLIC MEANINGS

Faith; Philosophy; Time.

POSSIBLE POWERS

Air element; Awakening; Create oxygen; Dreaming; Enlightenment; Eternal life; Fertility; Harmony; Healing; Immortality; Light; Longevity; Magic; Masculine energy; Peace; Protective; Regeneration; Resurrection; Spiritual consciousness; Spirituality; Water-proofing.

FOLKLORE AND FACTS

In the past, due to its resinous sap, the evergreen conifer *Pinus rigida* Pitch Pine Tree was useful for producing pitch and short timbers for shipbuilding and railroad ties. • Many Native  American peoples often used Pitch Pine logs for canoe construction, with the resin used for sealing and waterproofing. • The resin from the Pitch Pine has been used as an emergency field bandage by many Native American peoples.

No. 332

Pinus strobus

White Pine Tree

Eastern White Pine | Northern White Pine | Soft Pine | Tree of Peace | Weymouth Pine

POTENTIAL MAXIMUM HEIGHT

80 feet [24 meters]

SYMBOLIC MEANINGS

Air element; Awakening; Boldness; Create oxygen; Courage; Daring; Dreaming; Endurance; Enlightenment; Eternal life; Fertility; Harmony; Hope; Immortality; Light; Longevity; Loyalty; Magic; Masculine energy; Peace; Pity; Regeneration; Resurrection; Spiritual consciousness; Spirituality; Time.

COMPONENT MEANING

Cone: Conviviality.

◉ POSSIBLE POWERS

Accidents; Aggression; Anger; Aphrodisiac; Carnal desire; Conflict; Create oxygen; Exorcism; Fertility; Healing; Lust; Machinery; Money; Peace; Protection; Purification; Rock music; Spiritual energy; Strength; Struggle; War.

✿ FOLKLORE AND FACTS

Because the conifer *Pinus strobus* White Pine Tree is an evergreen, in Japan it was once the custom to place a White Pine branch over the entrance door to the home to provide joy within it. • Make a cross using White Pine needles and place it near the fireplace to prevent evil entering the home from down the chimney. • White Pine is considered to be the Tree of Peace to the Iroquois. • When burned, White Pine needles are believed to have the power to return a malicious spell back to its sender. • Cones from White Pine trees are thought to provide a more vigorous energy in old age. At one time, a cone would be placed under the pillow with the hope that would be so. • Cones from White Pine trees are carried to increase fertility.

No. 333

Pinus sylvestris ☠ ♂ ☙ ♨

Scots Pine

Scotch Fir | Scotch Pine | Scottish Pine | Scot's Pine

◉ POTENTIAL MAXIMUM HEIGHT

60 feet [18 meters]

✹ SYMBOLIC MEANING

Elevation.

◉ POSSIBLE POWERS

Air element; Awakening; Charity; Christmas celebration; Create oxygen; Dreaming; Enlightenment; Eternal life; Excitement; Family gathering; Fertility; Generosity; Good cheer; Happiness; Harmony; Immortality; Joy; Light; Longevity; Love; Magic; Mars; Masculine energy; Peace; Regeneration; Resurrection; Spiritual consciousness; Spirituality; Triggers depression; Uplifting; Venus.

✿ FOLKLORE AND FACTS

The evergreen ornamental *Pinus sylvestris* Scots Pine is the most common choice for a Christmas tree in the United States. • The Scots Pine is native to the United Kingdom. • As a tall, straight tree, the fast-growing Scots Pine's soft wood has been very useful as sawn timber as well as for pulp. • Scots Pine essential oil used for aromatherapy can bring the fragrance of the outside inside.

No. 334

Pinus taeda ♂ ☙

Loblolly Pine

Bull Pine | North Carolina Pine | Oldfield Pine | Rosemary Pine | Taeda

◉ POTENTIAL MAXIMUM HEIGHT

160 feet [49 meters]

✹ SYMBOLIC MEANINGS

Mire; Mud hole.

◉ POSSIBLE POWERS

Air element; Awakening; Charity; Create oxygen; Dreaming; Enlightenment; Eternal life; Excitement; Fertility; Generosity; Harmony; Immortality; Light; Longevity; Magic; Masculine energy; Peace; Regeneration; Resurrection; Spiritual consciousness; Spirituality.

✿ FOLKLORE AND FACTS

Grown from seed, the evergreen conifer *Pinus taeda* Loblolly Pine tree is the second most prolifically common tree in North America (the *Acer rubrum* Red Maple Tree is the first). • When the Apollo 14 space flight blasted off, it had Loblolly Pine tree seeds onboard. When the mission returned to Earth, the seeds were planted in various places in the USA, including the White House Garden. Many of these moon tree Loblolly Pines are still growing. • Loblolly Pine needles will produce a green or tan dye.

No. 335

Piper methysticum

Kava Tree

Ava | Ava Pepper | Ava Root | Awa | Awa Root | Intoxicating Pepper | Kava-kava | Sakau | Yaqona

POTENTIAL MAXIMUM HEIGHT
15 feet [5 meters]

SYMBOLIC MEANINGS
Fidelity; Hex breaking; Love.

POSSIBLE POWERS
Addictive; Astral projection; Create oxygen; Escapism; Euphoria; Luck; Lust; Numbing; Protection while traveling; Visions.

FOLKLORE AND FACTS
The small evergreen *Piper methysticum* Kava Tree is sacred in the Pacific Islands, most particularly in Fiji, where Kava root is a regular part of the daily life and communal culture of Fijians. • A beverage made from the dried powdered root is mixed with water, then strained into a communal bowl that is shared in a ritualistic ceremonial fashion. The Kava beverage is consumed by drinking it from hollowed coconut shells in one long gulp rather than by sipping it. Then those present relax while the effect of the Kava supposedly smooths out their anxieties and other physical tensions.

No. 336

Piscidia erythrina

Jamaican Dogwood

Fish Poison Tree | Fishfuddle | Florida Fishpoison Tree | Jamaica Dogwood | Piscidia

POTENTIAL MAXIMUM HEIGHT
49 feet [15 meters]

SYMBOLIC MEANINGS
Fish killer; Little fish; Keeps secrets.

POSSIBLE POWERS
Create oxygen; Fish poison; Protection; Wishes.

FOLKLORE AND FACTS
The deciduous *Piscidia erythrina* Jamaican Dogwood can be found growing along coastal zones. The white flowers are tinged with either pink or red and blossom as pendulous pea-like clusters. • Indigenous peoples living in these coastal areas extract a toxin from any part of the tree to easily catch fish by stunning them with the poison.

No. 337
Pistacia lentiscus 🝆🍴🌿

Mastic Tree
Chios Tears | Gum Mastic | Masticke

🔍 POTENTIAL MAXIMUM HEIGHT
25 feet [8 meters]

☀ SYMBOLIC MEANINGS
Chew; Gnashing of teeth.

🌀 POSSIBLE POWERS
Abundance; Advancement; Air element; Chewing gum;
Conscious will; Create oxygen; Energy; Friendship; Growth;
Healing; Joy; Leadership; Life; Light; Lust; Masculine energy;
Natural or psychic power; Success; Sun.

🜸 FOLKLORE AND FACTS
An ivory-colored, aromatic resin has been collected from
the evergreen *Pistacia lentiscus* Mastic Tree for over two
thousand years. The Mastic resin is collected on the ground,
dripping from slashes made in the bark that force the tree
to bleed sap. • Mastic is a vital ingredient in myron, the
sacred holy oil used in the sacred rituals of some Orthodox
churches. • Mastic is also used as a flavoring for cakes and
pastries in Middle Eastern cuisine, and is an ingredient in
Greek cuisine. • The ancient Greeks enjoyed Mastic resin as
an early type of chewing gum.

No. 338
Pistacia vera 🝆🍴🌿🥜

Pistachio Tree
Pistacchio | Pistacia

🔍 POTENTIAL MAXIMUM HEIGHT
33 feet [10 meters]

☀ SYMBOLIC MEANINGS
Good fortune; Happiness.

🌀 POSSIBLE POWERS
Air element; Breaking
love spells; Create oxygen;
Masculine energy; Mercury.

🜸 FOLKLORE AND FACTS
Around 700 BCE, the deciduous *Pistacia
vera* Pistachio Tree was supposedly
included among the other plants showcased in
ancient Babylon's Hanging Gardens. • The Pistachio was
brought to Europe by the Romans in the first century CE.
• The shell of a Pistachio is so hard that to bite on it in an
attempt to open it can hurt your teeth. • When high-quality
Pistachio fruits ripen on the tree, the shell will change from
green to a natural yellowish-red and will suddenly split
partly open with an audible popping sound. • It takes around
seven years for a Pistachio to start producing a good yield of
fruit. Once it is established, it will produce for one hundred
years or more. • One year the Pistachio Tree will produce a
bountiful crop, and the following year it may not be as much.
Then the year after that it most likely will be bountiful again.
On and on it grows and goes. • Pistachio fruits grow in
clusters just like grapes do. • The ripened fruit surrounding
the Pistachio nut must be removed and the shells dried
within twenty-four hours of their harvest to prevent them
becoming moldy. • There is a myth that the Queen of Sheba
forbade peasants from eating a Pistachio because she claimed
they were for royalty only. • Dyeing Pistachio nut shells red
was for the purpose of hiding blemishes on the shell.
• To bring a zombie out of its trance and allow it to pass into
death, give it Pistachio nuts that have been dyed red.

No. 339

Platanus occidentalis ☠ ✇ ☠

American Sycamore Tree

American Plane | American Planetree | Buttonwood Tree | Occidental Plane |
Water Beech | Western Plane

🔍 POTENTIAL MAXIMUM HEIGHT
90 feet [27 meters]

✴ SYMBOLIC MEANING
Matrimony.

✸ POSSIBLE POWERS
Agreement; Create oxygen; Harmony; Love; Marriage;
Protection; Shelter.

✦ FOLKLORE AND FACTS
The wood of the deciduous *Platanus occidentalis* American
Sycamore Tree has been useful for wood crafting and in
making such things as barber poles, wooden baskets, pails,
organ cases, vintage wooden washing machines, trunks,
flooring, and a wide variety of other useful wooden items.
• In 1792, the New York Stock Exchange terms of formation
was signed by twenty-four stockbrokers under a *Platanus
occidentalis* American Sycamore Tree that was located at
68 Wall Street, New York City, NY. That document has
since been called the Buttonwood Agreement. • During
the long-ago pioneer days, a hollow, extremely wide, living
American Sycamore Tree could be used as an emergency
shelter and housing for livestock. Between 1764 and 1767,
two brothers named John and Samuel Pringle lived
inside a hollow American Sycamore Tree that was located
near present-day Upshur County, Texas. The tree was
reported to have been so huge that an 8-foot-long (2.4 m)
fence rail could be turned 90 degrees inside the tree.
• A 129-foot-high (39 m) American Sycamore Tree in
Jeromesville, Ohio, is reported to have a trunk diameter of
50 feet (15 m) around
at the bottom. At
approximately 5 feet
(1.5 m) up from the
bottom, the tree is
approximately
48 feet (15 m)
around. The
canopy spreads out
approximately
105 feet (32 m) wide.
Now, that is an
incredibly huge tree!

No. 340

Pleroma semidecandrum

Purple Glory Tree

Glory Bush | Lasiandra | Princess Flower Tree

🔍 POTENTIAL MAXIMUM HEIGHT
20 feet [6 meters]

✴ SYMBOLIC MEANINGS
Glorious beauty; Glory.

✸ POSSIBLE POWERS
Beautification; Create oxygen.

✦ FOLKLORE AND FACTS
The sprawling evergreen *Pleroma semidecandrum* Purple
Glory Tree can be easily tamed with pruning to be a lovely,
upright ornamental tree. • The blossoms are purple, measure
up to 5 inches (13 cm) across, and have long wispy white
stamens. • The Purple Glory Tree is impressive when the
tree is in full bloom. • Because the branches are somewhat
brittle, the tree cannot survive when planted in an area that
suffers from strong winds.

No. 341

Plinia cauliflora ✇ ⬥ ☠

Brazilian Grape Tree

Jaboticaba | Jabuticaba | Yvapurũ

🔍 POTENTIAL MAXIMUM HEIGHT
50 feet [15 meters]

✴ SYMBOLIC MEANINGS
Crunchy fruit; Fat tortoise.

✸ POSSIBLE POWERS
Create oxygen; Oddity; Unusual conditions.

✦ FOLKLORE AND FACTS
It takes eight years for the tropical evergreen *Plinia
cauliflora* Brazilian Grape Tree to mature enough to produce
fruit. The way the plump, purplish-black, grape-size fruit
grows is the fascinating part of this extremely unusual tree.
The fruit berries grow all over the surface of the trunk, and
when they are ripe, they are edible fresh or can be made
into jams, juice, and wine. If the conditions are just right, it
can bloom and then produce fruit multiple times during the
course of a year.

P

No. 342

Plumeria rubra ☠ 🗡 🍄

Plumeria Tree

Araliya | Calachuchi | Champa | Egg Yolk Flower Tree | Frangipani Tree | Gaai Daan Fa | Graveyard Flowers | Melia | Plumieria | Temple Tree

🔍 **POTENTIAL MAXIMUM HEIGHT**
25 feet [8 meters]

✴ **SYMBOLIC MEANINGS**
New; Perfection; Springtime; Star.

🌼 **POSSIBLE POWERS**
Celestial magic; Create oxygen; Emotions; Feminine energy; Fertility; Future messages; Generation; Inspiration; Intuition; Love; Psychic ability; Sea; Subconscious mind; Tides; Travel by water; Venus; Water element; Worship.

☘ **FOLKLORE AND FACTS**
Across Asia, people have thought that the evergreen *Plumeria rubra* Plumeria Tree provides shelter for demons and ghosts. • Malaysian folklore makes mention of the scent of Plumeria in association with a type of vampire known as Pontianak, which are supposedly undead women who have died in childbirth and are out and about seeking revenge. • In the Pacific Islands, Plumeria flowers are worn over the ear by women as a symbol of their eligibility. It will be over the right ear if the wearer is available and over the left ear if not. • Fragrant Plumeria flowers are frequently used to make exquisite leis in colors of either pink, red, white, or light yellow blossoms. • Plumeria is often associated with cemeteries and graves.

No. 343

Polyscias fruticosa ☠ 🗡 🍴 🍄 🌿

Ming Aralia Tree

Ming Tree

🔍 **POTENTIAL MAXIMUM HEIGHT**
7 feet [2 meters]

✴ **SYMBOLIC MEANING**
Golden popularity.

🌼 **POSSIBLE POWERS**
Accomplishment; Common sense; Create oxygen; Impressive; Popularity; Venus.

☘ **FOLKLORE AND FACTS**
When the interior light is just right, the small but mighty evergreen *Polyscias fruticosa* Ming Aralia Tree is a tropical tree with slender small leaves that has become a favorite indoor potted plant. Pruning this attractive tree can encourage it to grow even more gnarly looking and interesting. • In Thailand, the leaves of the Ming Aralia are eaten raw with a spicy condiment dip. It is also cooked and prepared as a curry.

No. 344

Populus alba ☠ 🗡 🌿 🌰 🎋

Silver Poplar Tree

Abeel | Abele | Albellus | Aubel | Silver-leaf Poplar | White Poplar

🔍 **POTENTIAL MAXIMUM HEIGHT**
100 feet [30 meters]

✴ **SYMBOLIC MEANINGS**
Conquer; Courage; Time.

🌼 **POSSIBLE POWERS**
Astral projection; Create oxygen; Divine inspiration; Earth element; Endurability; Flying; Language; Money; Past life connection; Speech; Wind.

☘ **FOLKLORE AND FACTS**
The deciduous *Populus alba* Silver Poplar Tree has a strong Earth element vibration. • It is believed by some that tuning into the rustling of Silver Poplar leaves is a method of receiving messages sent from a past life, our higher self, and even the divine. • Make and carry a sachet of Silver Poplar

buds and leaves to attract money. • Silver Poplar buds and leaves on the bed or on the body will supposedly promote astral projection. • Make, then wear a sachet of Silver Poplar buds and leaves to help one astral project. • The pith of a Silver Poplar stem is star-shaped. • Silver Poplar wood was used to make battle shields.

No. 345
Populus balsamifera 🗳🌱

Balsam Poplar
Bam | Bamtree | Eastern Balsam-poplar | Hackmatack | Tacamahac Poplar | Tacamahaca

🔘 POTENTIAL MAXIMUM HEIGHT
98 feet [30 meters]

✳ SYMBOLIC MEANINGS
Resilience; Security.

🌼 POSSIBLE POWERS
Create oxygen; Divine inspiration; Earth element; Finance; Insect repellent; Money; Overcome blockades and blockages of all types; Past life connection.

🌿 FOLKLORE AND FACTS
The deciduous *Populus balsamifera* Balsam Poplar is a fragrant tree with fine, short wood fibers that have made it useful for making tissue paper. • An extract of the Balsam Poplar shoots can be used as a rooting hormone for starting cuttings of other plants • The resin on the Balsam Poplar buds can be used as an insect repellent. • Bits of Balsam Poplar bark can be burned for use as a mosquito repellent. • The wood pulp of the Balsam Poplar is useful in the manufacture of cardboard boxes. • It is believed by some that tuning into the rustling of the Balsam Poplar leaves is a method of receiving messages sent from a past life, our higher self, and even the divine.

No. 346
Populus deltoides 🗳🍴🌱🌰🌱

Eastern Cottonwood Tree
Necklace Poplar | Pioneer of the Prairie | Plains Cottonwood | Rio Grande Cottonwood

🔘 POTENTIAL MAXIMUM HEIGHT
195 feet [59 meters]

✳ SYMBOLIC MEANING
Sun.

🌼 POSSIBLE POWERS
Afterlife; Create oxygen; Divine inspiration; Funerals; Longevity; Nourishment; Past life connection; Sun.

🌿 FOLKLORE AND FACTS
The deciduous *Populus deltoides* Eastern Cottonwood Tree leaves are known to be protein-rich with more amino acids than barley, corn, rice, or wheat. It is possible, with further research, the leaves can be processed and utilized as a viable food source that can provide more protein than meat. • When conditions are favorable, an Eastern Cottonwood Tree can live to be four hundred years old. • Ceremonial objects, such as kachina dolls and masks, have been carved from Eastern Cottonwood Tree roots. Sacred poles and other ritual artifacts have been made from the branches, and in some instances, the long trunks.

No. 347
Populus nigra 🗳🌱

Black Poplar
Lombardy Poplar

🔘 POTENTIAL MAXIMUM HEIGHT
98 feet [30 meters]

✳ SYMBOLIC MEANINGS
Affliction; Courage.

🌼 POSSIBLE POWERS
Create oxygen; Divine inspiration; Earth element; Grounding; Past life connection; Resiliency; Security.

🌿 FOLKLORE AND FACTS
The deciduous *Populus nigra* Black Poplar has shiny heart-shaped leaves. • Due to the destruction of its natural habitat, the tree is now endangered. • The Black Poplar subspecies known as *Populus nigra* subsp. *betulifolia* is one of the rarest trees in all of Great Britain. • In the 1960s the

𝒫

Black Poplar was a favorite planting that was extensively used in the design of golf courses. However, when it became obvious that drainage systems were being destroyed by the tree's highly invasive roots, the courses did whatever they could to remove the trees. • After around fifty years of growth, the Black Poplar weakens to the degree that a strong wind can knock it over and somewhat of a domino effect can take place as one tree knocks over another. • As a *Populus* tree the Black Poplar has a very strong Earth vibration. • It is believed by some that tuning into the rustling of Black Poplar leaves is a method of receiving messages sent from a past life, our higher self, and even the divine. • Black Poplar can produce vegetable fabric dyes that range in color from a yellow to a yellowish-brown.

No. 348

Populus tremuloides 🌰 🍶

Quaking Aspen

Aspen | Aspen Poplar | Common Aspen | Eurasian Aspen | European Aspen

📷 POTENTIAL MAXIMUM HEIGHT
98 feet [30 meters]

✳ SYMBOLIC MEANINGS
Advantage; Air element; Alteration; Awareness; Connectivity; Divine inspiration; Earth element; Eloquence; Fear; Focus; Groan; Lamentation; Manipulation; Masculine energy; Mercury; Opportunity; Past life connection; Purity; Sighing; Transformation; Transition.

🌱 COMPONENT MEANINGS
Leaf: Lamentation; Sighing.

🌐 POSSIBLE POWERS
Ancient Earth; Anti-theft; Astral projection; Binding; Building; Create oxygen; Death; Eloquence; Feminine energy; Flying; History; Knowledge; Limitations; Messages; Obstacles; Saturn; Time; Water element.

☘ FOLKLORE AND FACTS
As a *Populus* tree, the deciduous *Populus tremuloides* Quaking Aspen has a very strong Earth vibration. It is also believed by some that tuning into the rustling of Quaking Aspen leaves is a method of receiving messages sent from a past life, our higher self, and even the divine. • The attributes of all *Populus* trees are increased in the Quaking Aspen because of the naturally resonating sound of the trees' leaves as they move with the slightest movement of air passing over them. • Quaking Aspen leaves can produce a yellow dye for fabric. • Quaking Aspen is fast-growing and wind-resistant, making it useful for planting a protective shelter-belt. • Quaking Aspen wood is particularly useful for making paper as well as charcoal. • Carry a Quaking Aspen bud or leaf to attract money to you. • Utilize a Quaking Aspen bud or leaf in a sachet and wear it to help one make it easier to project the spirit self outside the body for astral flight. • Plant a Quaking Aspen tree on the property to protect the land and the buildings on it against the ill intent of thieves. • The oldest cloned cluster of trees that grows and spreads as a single stand is a phenomenal Quaking Aspen by the name of Pando. Pando means "I spread" in Latin, and that is precisely what the incredible Pando has done. Pando is comprised of approximately 47,000 Quaking Aspen clones that make only the one male *Populus tremuloides* Quaking Aspen that Pando botanically is. All the approximately 46,999 other trees in the cluster are just that much more of Pando. Extensions of Pando are expressed in the great many Quaking Aspen tree clones spreading and sprawling around it. Pando is approximately 108 acres (44 ha) wide. For a frame of reference, one regulation American football field is only 1.32 acres (0.5 ha)! So, Pando is approximately eighty-three football fields in a cluster! Pando is estimated to be between fourteen thousand and one million years old.

No. 349
Populus trichocarpa ⚱

Western Balsam Poplar
Aspen | Black Cottonwood | Cottonwood | Poplar

⬤ **POTENTIAL MAXIMUM HEIGHT**
225 feet [69 meters]

✴ **SYMBOLIC MEANINGS**
Eloquence; Flying; Lamentation; Money; Wealth.

✺ **POSSIBLE POWERS**
Anti-theft; Astral projection; Create oxygen; Divine
inspiration; Money; Past life connection; Perfumery;
Protection.

✹ **FOLKLORE AND FACTS**
The deciduous *Populus trichocarpa* Western Balsam Poplar
is the tallest *Populus* tree in both North and South America.
• In 2006, the Western Balsam Poplar was the first tree
that had its DNA fully sequenced. • As a *Populus* tree, the
Western Balsam Poplar has a strong Earth vibration. •
The wood of the Western Balsam Poplar has been used for
structures, canoe making, wooden woven baskets, and fish
traps. The gummy sap has been useful for waterproofing and
glue. • Essential oil extracted from the fragrant buds of the
Western Balsam Poplar is commercially used in cosmetics
and perfume. • The fragrance of the Western Balsam Poplar
can be perceived over 325 feet (99 m) away. • It is believed
by some that tuning into the rustling of Western Balsam
Poplar leaves is a method of receiving messages sent from a
past life, our higher self, and even the divine.

No. 350
Pouteria campechiana ⚱ 🍴 ❦

Canistel Tree
Cây Trứng Gà | Chicken Egg Plant | Cupcake Fruit |
Danhuang Guo | Eggfruit | Egg Yolk Fruit |
Khmer Peach | Peach of the Immortals |
Sawo Mentega | Yolk Fruit

⬤ **POTENTIAL MAXIMUM HEIGHT**
49 feet [15 meters]

✴ **SYMBOLIC MEANING**
Family comes first.

✺ **POSSIBLE POWERS**
Create oxygen; Harmonious home life; Love;
Love of family.

✹ **FOLKLORE AND FACTS**
The ripe fruit of the evergreen *Pouteria campechiana*
Canistel Tree is edible when it is bright orange-yellow. Its
texture is similar to a hard-boiled egg yolk with a flavor
reminiscent of egg custard. • When ripe, the Canistel Tree
fruit can be eaten raw, made into jam and confections,
blended into smoothies, milkshakes, and custards for pies,
puddings, and ice cream. • The wood of any *Pouteria* tree is
so hard that even power tools have difficulty cutting into it.

P

Prosopis cineraria 🗡🍴🌱🕯

Ghaf Tree
Banni Mara | Chhonkara | Jammi | Kalpavriksha of the Desert | Khejri | King of the Desert | Shami Tree | Tree of Life | Wonder Tree

◉ POTENTIAL MAXIMUM HEIGHT
49 feet [15 meters]

✳ SYMBOLIC MEANINGS
Peace; Stability; Tolerance.

✹ POSSIBLE POWERS
Balance; Create oxygen; Encourage tolerance; Inspire peacefulness; Stability; Unity.

✷ FOLKLORE AND FACTS
A remarkable evergreen *Prosopis cineraria* Ghaf Tree has survived in the extreme heat of a Bahraini desert for approximately four hundred years. There is no visible source of water anywhere near it. Its existence is a marvel and an inspiration, as well as a symbol of peace and stability. • The *Prosopis cineraria* tree root can penetrate approximately 115 feet (35 m) into the ground to find deep water in an extremely dry area. • The *Prosopis cineraria* tree is religiously significant to the Hindu faith. The tree is celebrated during the Dasara Festival, when princely *marathas* will shoot arrows into the top of a Ghaf Tree to gather the leaves that fall. • The pods of the tree are edible and often consumed as a vegetable.

No. 352
Prosopis glandulosa 🗡🍴

Honey Mesquite Tree
Mesquite

◉ POTENTIAL MAXIMUM HEIGHT
60 feet [18 meters]

✳ SYMBOLIC MEANINGS
Forgiveness; Self-blessing.

✹ POSSIBLE POWERS
Create oxygen; Healing.

✷ FOLKLORE AND FACTS
The tall, thorny, deciduous *Prosopis glandulosa* Honey Mesquite Tree will grow to be no taller than a shrub when water is scarce. • When a *Prosopis glandulosa* tree that has a single trunk is cut down, the tree that regrows

in place of it will be one with multiple trunks. • The seeds of the Honey Mesquite Tree have been dried and ground into flour by Native Americans in southwestern North America. • Native Americans in what is now known as California once used Honey Locust thorns and ash for tattooing. The wood was used to fashion simple tools and points for arrows. • Honey Mesquite wood is a favorite fuel to burn for cooking and to smoke foods barbecue-style.

No. 353
Prunus americana ☠🗡🍴🌱

Wild Plum Tree
American Plum | Common Wild Plum | Marshall's Large Yellow Sweet Plum

◉ POTENTIAL MAXIMUM HEIGHT
25 feet [8 meters]

✳ SYMBOLIC MEANINGS
Independence; Independent.

✹ POSSIBLE POWERS
Create oxygen; Feminine energy; Healing; Venus; Water element.

✷ FOLKLORE AND FACTS
The ripe fruit of the deciduous *Prunus americana* Wild Plum Tree can be used for making jelly, jam, and homemade wine. • The kernel of the Wild Plum seed is toxic, as it is with any other fruit of the *Prunus* genus. The only exception is the Sweet Almond *Prunus dulcis* var. *dulcis*. • The Dakota people have used Wild Plum Tree sprouts to create prayer sticks. • Wild Plum can be used to create dye to produce dark gray, green, and even red colors.

No. 354

Prunus armeniaca 🕷 🍷 🍴 ⚕

Apricot Tree
Abrecock | Abricot | Ansu Apricot | Apricot | Armenian Plum

📷 **POTENTIAL MAXIMUM HEIGHT**
20 feet [6 meters]

✴ **SYMBOLIC MEANINGS**
Beautiful woman; Beauty; Good fortune; Spring; Timid love.

🌱 **COMPONENT MEANINGS**
Blossom: Distrust; Doubt; Timid love.

🌸 **POSSIBLE POWERS**
Aphrodisiac; Attract love; Create oxygen; Feminine energy;
Love; Venus; Water.

🌿 **FOLKLORE AND FACTS**
The deciduous *Prunus armeniaca* Apricot Tree has been
cultivated in Armenia since prehistoric times as indicated by
seeds found at a Chalcolithic-era excavation site at Garni,
Armenia. • There are indications that the Apricot was
domesticated in regions that are now part of China, whereas
others believe that the Apricot was first cultivated in India
around 3000 BCE. • The kernel of the Apricot seed is toxic,
as it is with any other fruit of the *Prunus* genus. The only
exception is the Sweet Almond *Prunus dulcis* var. *dulcis*. •
The edible part of the *Prunus armeniaca* Apricot is the ripe,
fleshy drupe fruit. • The Apricot fruit is eaten fresh, and it
can also be juiced, made into preserves and jams, or dried. It
is also added to or made entirely into liqueurs and wine.
• Dried Apricot is a common ingredient in Middle Eastern
and Mediterranean cuisine. • Put Apricot leaves and flowers
in a pouch that is made to attract love to someone who is shy.
• It is supposedly lucky for an Apricot to appear in a dream.
• There are some who think it is possible
that the forbidden fruit in
the Garden of Eden may
have been an Apricot.
• The seed kernels of
any variety of Apricot are
considered highly toxic
due to the presence of
a poisonous compound
called amygdalin. Apricot
kernels are an especially
real threat for children,
who tend to bite open the seeds
and innocently ingest the
poisonous kernel. There have
been several disconcerting cases

of extreme illness in and death of children who ingested
Apricot pit kernels. If there is an Apricot Tree growing
in the neighborhood where children play, be aware of
this, especially around the time when the luscious fruit is
ripening. Children will be children.

No. 355

Prunus avium 🕷 🍷 🍴 ⚕ ♀

Sweet Cherry Tree
Cherry | Gean | Mazzard | Red Cherry | Wild Cherry

📷 **POTENTIAL MAXIMUM HEIGHT**
30 feet [9 meters]

✴ **SYMBOLIC MEANINGS**
Ascetic beauty; Education; Faith;
Feminine beauty; Gentle; Good
education; Honor of graceful
resignation; Insincerity; Intelligence; Kind;
Love; Peace; Power; Sexuality; Spiritual
beauty; Transience of life.

🌸 **POSSIBLE POWERS**
The Arts; Attraction; Beauty; Create oxygen;
Deception; Divination; Education; Feminine energy;
Friendship; Gifts; Harmony; Joy; Love; Pleasure; Sensuality;
Venus; Water element.

🌿 **FOLKLORE AND FACTS**
The deciduous *Prunus avium* Sweet Cherry Tree is
considered sacred. • The edible part is the ripe fruit, which
grows in pairs. • Sweet Cherry fruit can be eaten fresh or
cooked. It can also be puréed, juiced, candied, made into jam,
jelly, and syrup, dried, or baked into an iconic pie as well
as in a wide assortment of other baked goods and pastries.
Lastly, it can be made into wine and liqueur. • The kernel
of the seed is toxic. • To find love, tie one strand of your
own hair to a Sweet Cherry Tree that is in blossom. • One
particularly macabre divination is that when a Sweet Cherry
Tree is full of ripe fruit, run around the tree and shake it
hard. Count the number of cherries that fall to the ground.
That is how many years you will live. • Sweet Cherry Tree
wood is coveted by cabinetmakers all around the world
because it is reddish-brown and the grain is straight. • The
Sweet Cherry has flavored some medicinal syrups for many
generations. • An old English superstition is that the singing
cuckoo in the Sweet Cherry Tree must eat three meals of
cherries before it can stop singing. • Sweet Cherry Tree
leaves, especially the wilted ones, are extremely toxic to
livestock animals that forage the perimeter of a field and find
them along the fence lines.

No. 356

Prunus cerasifera 🕱 ⚰ 🏮 ♣

Myrobalan Plum Tree

Cherry Plum

◉ POTENTIAL MAXIMUM HEIGHT
30 feet [9 meters]

✳ SYMBOLIC MEANING
Privation.

❀ POSSIBLE POWERS
Create oxygen; Healing; Love.

❦ FOLKLORE AND FACTS
In the British Isles, the deciduous *Prunus cerasifera*
Myrobalan Plum Tree is one of the first trees to flower in the
spring. It is an attractive ornamental tree that comes with
flowers of several colors, mostly purple, pink, or white.
• Myrobalan Plum Tree bears edible drupe fruit that is a vital
ingredient in Georgian and Russian cuisine,
most notably in a sauce known as *tkemali* that
is used much like how ketchup is in
the USA. Tkemali sauce is liberally
used on grilled and fried poultry or
other meats, as well as with some
potato dishes. • The Myrobalan
Plum fruit is also used in some
stews and soups. Although some
of the fruits might be sweet
enough to eat fresh, most are tart
and would be best used to make
sugar-sweetened jam.

No. 357

Prunus cerasus 🕱 ⚰ 🏮 ♣

Sour Cherry Tree

Amarelle Cherry | Dwarf Cherry | Morello Cherry |
Tart Cherry

◉ POTENTIAL MAXIMUM HEIGHT
20 feet [6 meters]

✳ SYMBOLIC MEANINGS
Kindness; New beginnings;
Revival; Youth.

❀ POSSIBLE POWERS
Beginnings; Create oxygen;
Kindness; Love; Youthfulness.

❦ FOLKLORE AND FACTS
The tart ripe fruit of the deciduous
Prunus cerasus Sour Cherry Tree was more popular
before World War II, whereas nowadays it is usually the
generic Morello variety that is most often planted and
harvested. • Dried Sour Cherries are added to soups and
pork dishes, or made into confections, jams, pies, syrups,
beers, and wines. • The *Prunus cerasus* seed kernel is toxic.
• Unlike other *Prunus* cherry trees, *Prunus cerasus* is
self-reproductive, requiring only bees to move pollen from
flower to flower. • Make, then carry, dried Sour Cherries in a
sachet when starting something over.

No. 358

Prunus domestica 🕱 ⚰ 🏮 ♣

Plum Tree

Common Plum | Damson | European Plum | Greengage

◉ POTENTIAL MAXIMUM HEIGHT
39 feet [12 meters]

✳ SYMBOLIC MEANINGS
Beauty; Fidelity; Genius; Keep your promises; Longevity;
Promise.

❀ POSSIBLE POWERS
Create oxygen; Love; Protection; Venus;
Water element.

❦ FOLKLORE AND FACTS
The drupe fruit of the deciduous *Prunus domestica* Plum
Tree is edible when ripe. • A Plum fruit will continue
ripening after it has been picked from the tree. • Plum fruit
is eaten fresh or made into jam and confections. They can be
partially dried to a sticky softness that are then called prunes,

P

which are used in pastry fillings and are also juiced. • The pit of the Damson Plum clings to the pulp so tenaciously that when using it for jam-making it is usually cooked with the pit intact, which is then removed after cooking, before adding the sugar. • Damson Plums are sometimes pickled. • Hang a Plum branch over the home's doors and windows to protect it from evil. • Plum can produce a yellow dye for fabric. • The kernel of the Plum seed is toxic, as it is with any other fruit of the *Prunus* genus. The only exception is the Sweet Almond, *Prunus dulcis* var. *dulcis*.

No. 359

Prunus dulcis var. *amara* ☠☠

Bitter Almond Tree
Greek Nuts | Poison Almond Tree | Wild Almond Tree

◐ POTENTIAL MAXIMUM HEIGHT
33 feet [10 meters]

✳ SYMBOLIC MEANINGS
Fruitfulness; Giddiness; Heedlessness; Hope; Indiscretion; Promise; Prosperity; Stupidity; Thoughtlessness; Union; Virginity; Wisdom.

✿ POSSIBLE POWERS
Air element; Ambition; Attitude; Clear thinking; Create oxygen; Harmony; Higher understanding; Logic; Manifestation in material form; Masculine energy; Mercury; Money; Overcoming alcohol dependency; Prosperity; Spiritual concepts; Success in business ventures; Thought processes; Wisdom.

☙ FOLKLORE AND FACTS
The nut kernels of the deciduous *Prunus dulcis* var. *amara* Bitter Almond Tree are always poisonous. • Cultivation of the Sweet Almond Tree commenced when the sweet variety was able to be determined apart from the toxic bitter variety. • A divining rod made from Bitter Almond Tree wood will lead to successful treasure hunting just as well as one made from Sweet Almond wood. At any rate, treasure is treasure. Use whatever divining rod you have to start looking to find it. • A magic wand made of Bitter Almond wood corresponds to elemental Air, making it highly valued. • If you are not absolutely certain whether a tree is a Sweet Almond or a Bitter Almond, do not eat any of the nuts.

Prunus dulcis var. *dulcis* ☙🍴🍾🌰🍴

Sweet Almond Tree
Almendra Dulce | Almond Tree

◐ POTENTIAL MAXIMUM HEIGHT
33 feet [10 meters]

✳ SYMBOLIC MEANINGS
Fruitfulness; Giddiness; Heedlessness; Hope; Indiscretion; Promise; Prosperity; Stupidity; Thoughtlessness; Union; Virginity; Wisdom.

⚘ COMPONENT MEANINGS
Blossom: Hope; Watchfulness.

✿ POSSIBLE POWERS
Abundance; Air element; Ambition; Attitude; Clear thinking; Create oxygen; Fruitfulness; Harmony; Higher understanding; Logic; Luck; Manifestation in material form; Masculine energy; Mercury; Money; Overcoming alcohol dependency; Prosperity; Spiritual concepts; Success in business ventures; Thought processes; Wisdom.

☙ FOLKLORE AND FACTS
The domestication of the Sweet Almond Tree dates back to the Bronze Age. • The edible part of the deciduous *Prunus dulcis* var. *dulcis* Sweet Almond Tree is the seed of the fruit, which is actually

a drupe, the same as Peaches and other drupes. The seed within that fruit is what we know to be the part that we refer to as the "nut," even though it is not a nut at all. The seed kernels of a domesticated Sweet Almond Tree are not toxic. • Cultivation of the Sweet Almond Tree commenced when the sweet variety was able to be determined apart from the toxic bitter variety. • If you are not absolutely certain whether an almond tree is the edible safe Sweet Almond or the deadly poisonous Bitter Almond, do not eat any of the nuts. • When you go out on a job hunt, carry a Sweet Almond in your pocket for good luck. • It was believed that one can guarantee a successful business venture by climbing a Sweet Almond Tree. • A magic wand made from Sweet Almond Tree wood is highly valued for its correspondence to elemental Air. • In Hebrew, the word for "almond" and for "tonsil" is the same. • Almonds were discovered in Tutankhamen's tomb. • Hold a Sweet Almond when calling upon divine healing energy. • Many Hebrew scholars believe they have found evidence in the Talmud that Moses's staff was made of Sweet Almond. As the story goes, the staff was made of the Sweet Almond wood by God at midnight at the start of the first sabbath and given to Adam in the Garden of Eden. • Carry or wear a Sweet Almond amulet when attempting to overcome any type of addiction, whether physical or emotional.

No. 361

Prunus laurocerasus 💀🌿

English Laurel Tree

Almond Laurel | Cherry Laurel | Common Laurel

◉ POTENTIAL MAXIMUM HEIGHT
26 feet [8 meters]

✹ SYMBOLIC MEANING
Perfidy.

🌿 COMPONENT MEANING
Flower: Perfidy.

✿ POSSIBLE POWERS
Create oxygen; Ward off plague; Witchcraft.

✷ FOLKLORE AND FACTS
The foliage of the evergreen *Prunus laurocerasus* English Laurel Tree is commonly used as a leafy green element in commercially designed floral arrangements.

No. 362

Prunus padus 💀🌿

Bird Cherry Tree

Asian Bird Cherry | European Bird Cherry

◉ POTENTIAL MAXIMUM HEIGHT
50 feet [15 meters]

✹ SYMBOLIC MEANING
Perfidy.

✿ POSSIBLE POWERS
Create oxygen; Ward off plague; Witchcraft.

✷ FOLKLORE AND FACTS
During medieval times, the deciduous *Prunus padus* Bird Cherry Tree bark was placed at the door to ward off plague. • In some parts of northern Scotland, Bird Cherry Tree wood is particularly avoided as a Bird Cherry Tree is considered a "witch's tree."

No. 363

Prunus persica 💀✦🍴🌿✦

Peach Tree

Fuzzless Peach | Fuzzy Peach | Nectarine | *Prunus persica* var. *nectarina* | Shaved Peach | Smooth-skinned Peach | Velvety Skinned Peach

◉ POTENTIAL MAXIMUM HEIGHT
25 feet [8 meters]

✹ SYMBOLIC MEANINGS
Bridal hope; Divine fruit of the gods; Generosity; Gentleness; Happiness; Honors; Long life; Peace; Riches; Young brides; Your qualities and charms are unequaled.

🌿 COMPONENT MEANINGS
Blossom: Captive; I am your captive; I am yours; Long life; Longevity; My heart is yours; Unequaled qualities; Vitality.

✿ POSSIBLE POWERS
Create oxygen; Exorcism; Feminine energy; Fertility; Immortality; Longevity; Love; Protection against invisible evil; Repels a spirit; Tranquility; Venus; Vitality; Water element; Wishing.

✷ FOLKLORE AND FACTS
In China, the deciduous *Prunus persica* Peach Tree is the Tree of Immortality from which every three thousand years an immortal fruit is believed to ripen. The event is celebrated with an ethereal banquet attended by the Eight Immortals of Daoist mythology. The Chinese Peach of Immortality, or *pántáo*, is believed to have the power to allow people to remain young forever. • The first written English reference

to the Nectarine was in 1616. • Velvety-skinned Peach seeds can grow into trees that produce smooth Nectarines. A smooth Nectarine seed can grow into a tree that can produce either smooth Nectarines or velvety Peaches. There is no way of knowing what kind of tree the seeds of either will produce. Because of this anomaly, a Nectarine cutting, known as a scion, is grafted onto Peach Tree rootstock to guarantee Nectarine fruit. • The kernel of both the Peach and Nectarine fruits is toxic. • Because Peach blossoms will appear before the leaves, there are many who consider that the Peach Tree exhibits more vitality than other fruit trees. • Because Peaches are believed to repel spirits, they are never put on tables arranged to revere the spirits of the ancestors. • Peach wood magic wands are cut personally by whoever intends to use it, on the night before the first New Moon after the

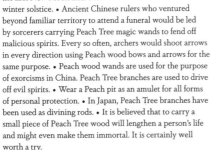

winter solstice. • Ancient Chinese rulers who ventured beyond familiar territory to attend a funeral would be led by sorcerers carrying Peach Tree magic wands to fend off malicious spirits. Every so often, archers would shoot arrows in every direction using Peach wood bows and arrows for the same purpose. • Peach wood wands are used for the purpose of exorcisms in China. Peach Tree branches are used to drive off evil spirits. • Wear a Peach pit as an amulet for all forms of personal protection. • In Japan, Peach Tree branches have been used as divining rods. • It is believed that to carry a small piece of Peach Tree wood will lengthen a person's life and might even make them immortal. It is certainly well worth a try.

Prunus serotina ☠ 🐄 🍽 ♣

Black Cherry Tree

Capuli | Cerezo | Rum Cherry | Wild Black Cherry

🔲 **POTENTIAL MAXIMUM HEIGHT**

100 feet [30 meters]

☀ **SYMBOLIC MEANING**

Tenacious beauty.

🐚 **POSSIBLE POWERS**

Create oxygen; Danger; Longevity.

🌰 **FOLKLORE AND FACTS**

The deciduous *Prunus serotina* Black Cherry Tree is considered to be an old, native pioneer *Prunus* species that can be found growing in fields in the midwestern USA with other pioneer tree species, such as the Hackberry, Black Walnut, and Black Locust. • Black Cherry branches falling from long, dense, hedgerow lines along fences are extremely difficult to monitor and have proven time and time again to be the cause of many livestock deaths when the animals graze on the highly toxic wilted leaves. • The kernel of the Black Cherry seed is toxic, as it is with any other fruit of the *Prunus* genus. The only exception is the Sweet Almond, *Prunus dulcis* var. *dulcis*. • The only edible part of the *Prunus serotina* Black Cherry tree is the ripe, pitted berry. The berry can be eaten raw, made into jelly, juiced, fermented into wine, or it can be made into a flavoring added to brandy, rum, ice cream, or carbonated soda. The berries are also used as an ingredient in recipes and go especially well with pork. Due to its unique flavor, Black Cherry is used as a seasoning. • High-quality Black Cherry lumber is used in the finest cabinetry.

No. 365

Prunus spinosa 🕱 ⚔ 🍶 🐾 🍶

Blackthorn Tree

May Tree | Sloe Berry Tree | Sloe Tree

◉ POTENTIAL MAXIMUM HEIGHT

16 feet [5 meters]

✷ SYMBOLIC MEANINGS

Austerity; Blessing after a challenge; Challenges ahead; Constraint; Difficulty; Fate; Inevitability; Strife.

✸ POSSIBLE POWERS

Banishes negative energy; Banishes negative entities; Combat anger; Create oxygen; Dark Moon magic; Exorcism; Fend off depression; Inner grounding; Outside influences; Preparation; Protection; Purification; Relieve fear; Remove negative energy; Retention of dark magic secrets; Waning Moon magic; Winter magic.

❦ FOLKLORE AND FACTS

The edible part of the deciduous *Prunus spinosa* Blackthorn Tree is the hard, grainy, astringently tart sloe berry, which will be slightly less so if collected within a few days after the first frost. This can also be accomplished by freezing the sloes after they have been picked, which will alleviate the arduous task of pricking each berry before adding to gin to make homemade "sloe gin" or "sloe vodka." By freezing the berries first, they will split perfectly for the infusion process. Sloes can also be preserved in vinegar or added to chutneys and jams. • Hang Blackthorn over doorways to ward off evil, calamity, negative vibrations, and to banish demons from the home. • A forked branch of Blackthorn will make an effective divining rod or wishing rod if it is cut in the spring by the individual who intends to use it. • Blackthorn wood will make a good magic wand for fending off malicious fairies. • Blackthorn Tree wood is very hard and takes a high polish, so it was a favorite for walking sticks and clubs. • Blackthorn walking sticks and shillelaghs are carried by officers of the Royal Irish Regiment. The shillelagh was originally used as a sturdy weapon for self-defense. • In Ireland during the nineteenth century,

it was a common practice to bury Blackthorn branches in the fields to help with drainage. • Blackthorn can produce vegetable dyes for fabrics that range in color from yellow, green, to dark gray. • The kernel of the Blackthorn seed is toxic, as it is with any other fruit of the *Prunus* genus. The only exception is the Sweet Almond, *Prunus dulcis* var. *dulcis*. • A charm made from a Sloe berry seed, a leaf, a sliver of bark, and a thorn can be fixed over the interior of all the entryways into the house to combat anger, fear, and depression away from all within the home. It can also offer protection and help everyone who resides there to assess their inner selves. It will also be an aid for all to ground themselves as well as help them recognize the influence of fate when its influence might be an energy to consider and, perhaps, accept.

No. 366

Prunus virginiana 🕱 ⚔ 🍶 🐾

Chokecherry Tree

Bitter-berry | Black Chokeberry | Virginia Bird Cherry | Western Chokecherry

◉ POTENTIAL MAXIMUM HEIGHT

30 feet [9 meters]

✷ SYMBOLIC MEANING

Better days to come.

✸ POSSIBLE POWERS

Calm; Create oxygen; Healing; Venus; Water element.

❦ FOLKLORE AND FACTS

Because the tree is notorious for harboring the threatening tent caterpillar, the deciduous *Prunus virginiana* Chokecherry Tree is also considered to be an invasive pest. • For many Native American tribes of the Northern Plains, the *Prunus virginiana* Chokecherry berries are an important part of a traditional, nutritious, high-energy staple food called pemmican. It is a combination of dried meats and particular tallow fats mixed with dried Chokecherries, and perhaps other dried berries and varying ingredients. The knowledge of the different ways to make it has been passed down from generation to generation, although there is no official recipe. • The kernel of the Chokecherry seed is toxic, as it is with any other fruit of the *Prunus* genus. The only exception is the Sweet Almond, *Prunus dulcis* var. *dulcis*.

P

No. 367

Pseudotsuga menziesii 🌿🌳

Douglas Fir Tree

British Columbian Pine | Columbian Pine | Douglas Spruce | False Hemlock | Oregon Pine |
Red Fir | Red Pine

📷 POTENTIAL MAXIMUM HEIGHT
330 feet [101 meters]

✳ SYMBOLIC MEANINGS
Determination; Durability; Perseverance; Protector;
Resistance.

🌐 POSSIBLE POWERS
Air element; Create oxygen; Dreaming; Eternal life; Fertility;
Harmony; Immortality; Light; Magic; Masculine energy;
Peace; Protection; Psychic rejuvenation; Regeneration;
Resurrection; Sizable offering; Spiritual consciousness;
Spirituality.

🍃 FOLKLORE AND FACTS
Contrary to the misleading names, the towering evergreen
conifer *Pseudotsuga menziesii* Douglas Fir Tree is neither an
Abies fir, nor a *Picea* spruce, nor a *Pinus* pine. • Douglas Fir
essential oil has a wintery, Christmas-like fragrance that can
be an effective pick-me-up and mood enhancer. • Native
Hawaiians would build double-hulled canoes called *wa'a
kaulua* from suitable Douglas Fir Tree
logs that had made their way to shore.
• The pitch obtained from the Douglas
Fir has been used for centuries to
seal boat hulls, roofs, and anything
else that has needed protection
from nature's elements. • A
talisman hand-carved from a
small piece of Douglas Fir can
be carried or worn to help
remember and fully appreciate
the past gifts granted by life, so
as to not take them for granted
in the future.

No. 368

Psidium guajava 🌿🍴🌳

Guava Tree

Apple Guava | Common Guava | Guayaba | Lemon Guava | Strawberry Guava |
Yellow-fruited Cherry Guava | Yellow Guava

📷 POTENTIAL MAXIMUM HEIGHT
33 feet [10 meters]

✳ SYMBOLIC MEANINGS
Fruit of success; Reap rewards of hard work.

🌐 POSSIBLE POWERS
Create oxygen; Success; Venus; Water element.

🍃 FOLKLORE AND FACTS
The evergreen *Psidium guajava* Guava Tree was cultivated
in Peru for its fruit as far back as 2500 BCE. • The ripe fruit
is edible raw or cooked. Guava fruit is often made into jams,
cooked in sauces, or used in condiments for pork, chicken, or
fish. It is also enjoyed juiced and, more often, blended in with
other fruit juices. • A delectable, very thick, jellied Guava
paste known as *guayabate* or *goiabada* was widely popular
in Colombia before it became increasingly enjoyed in other
parts of South America and the USA. • In most places, a
Guava is cut into quarters and eaten like an apple, either
plain, or with a pinch of salt, sugar, masala seasoning blend,
or ground cayenne pepper sprinkled
over it. • Guava wood and leaves
are often used to smoke meat.
• Guava wood is resistant to
fungus and insects, and is
strong enough to be used as
roof trusses in Nigeria.
• A rinse made of boiled,
cooled, and strained Guava
leaves in water is believed to
help thwart hair loss and aid new
growth. • Under the right conditions
and a little manual human intervention to
pollinate the flowers, the Guava plant can bear fruit
while growing in an indoor pot. • Guava has become an
invasive species in the Galápagos Islands. • The Guava is
used in shampoo products for its fragrance.

P

No. 369

Pterocarpus santalinus 🐚🌿

Red Sandalwood

Chandan | Chandanam | Ciwappuccantanam | Raktachandana | Rakta Chandana |
Red Sanders | Red Saunders | Saunderswood | Tzu-t'an Wood Tree | Yerra Chandanam |
Zitan Wood Tree

🔍 POTENTIAL MAXIMUM HEIGHT

26 feet [8 meters]

✳ SYMBOLIC MEANINGS

Desire; Fleshly desire; Sensual desires; Worldly desires.

🌸 POSSIBLE POWERS

Accidents; Aggression; Anger;
the Arts; Attraction; Beauty;
Carnal desires; Conflict;
Create oxygen;
Friendship gifts;
Harmony; Incense; Joy;
Love; Lust; Machinery;
Pleasures; Rock music;
Sensuality; Strength;
Struggle; Sound
resonance; War.

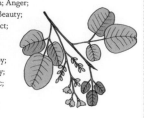

🜨 FOLKLORE AND FACTS

The wood of the deciduous *Pterocarpus santalinus* Red
Sandalwood tree is not considered to be particularly fragrant.
It should not be confused with Southern India's *Santalum*
Sandalwood trees that are richly aromatic and the primary
component of genuine Sandalwood incense. • As a prized
wood in China for thousands of years, it was during China's
Qing dynasty in the 1600s that Red Sandalwood was used
to fashion immensely ornate beautiful furniture that is now
rare to find and extremely costly. • Red Sandalwood has
traditionally been used to make the neck and bridge of the
Japanese musical instrument known as the shamisen.

No. 370

Punica granatum 🐚🍴🌿🌱🍷

Pomegranate Tree

Carthaginian Apple | Jnhm

🔍 POTENTIAL MAXIMUM HEIGHT

30 feet [9 meters]

✳ SYMBOLIC MEANINGS

Abundance; Ambition; Compassion; Conceit; Conceited;
Elegance; Fertility; Foolishness; Foppery; Fruitfulness;
Fullness; Good luck; Good things; Housewarming gift;
Kabbalah; Marriage; Mysteriousness; Mystical experience;
Offspring; Paradise; Prosperity; Resurrection; Righteousness;
Suffering; Suffering and resurrection; Summer; Sweetness of
the heavenly kingdom.

🌸 POSSIBLE POWERS

Abundance; Ancient Earth; Aphrodisiac; Attracts love;
Binding; Create oxygen; Creative power; Divination;
Elegance; Fertility; Fire element; Immortality; Incarceration;
Intellectual ability; Love; Luck; Masculine energy; Mature
elegance; Passion; Sensuous love; Unreciprocated love magic;
Venus; Wealth; Wishing.

🜨 FOLKLORE AND FACTS

The deciduous *Punica granatum*
Pomegranate Tree has been
cultivated in the Mediterranean
region for thousands of years.
• The fleshy, juicy,
membrane-encased,
finger-staining seeds of the
Pomegranate fruit are edible
fresh or juiced. The seeds
are often added to smoothies
or made into wines and
liqueur. Both fresh and
dried Pomegranate seeds
are widely used in Middle
Eastern cuisine as both an
ingredient and as a seasoning. As a

seasoning, ground dried Pomegranate seeds are known as
anar dana. • Grenadine syrup, popular for use in several
different cocktails, and Pomegranate molasses are both
made from Pomegranates. • Make a sachet filled with bits of
Pomegranate husk, then carry to increase fertility.
• Use a forked branch from a Pomegranate Tree as a divining
rod to search for and find hidden wealth. • Pomegranates
symbolize the Kabbalah as the mystical entryway into
the Garden of Pomegranates. • It is traditional to eat
Pomegranate seeds on Rosh Hashanah because the many

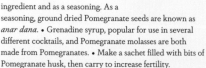

seeds represent fruitfulness. • In Greece, it is customary to give a Pomegranate as a housewarming gift, which is placed on or under the home's altar as a blessing of abundance, good luck, and fertility. • In the Book of Exodus, the robe worn by the Hebrew high priest had decorative Pomegranates embroidered all around the bottom near the hem. • According to Jewish law, the Pomegranate is one of the Seven Species that require a blessing before it is eaten. • A fun divination for a girl to try in order to find out how many children she might have is to throw a Pomegranate fruit onto the ground, hard enough to break it open. The number of seeds that fall out of the fruit equals the number of children she will someday have.

No. 371

Pyrus communis

Pear Tree
Common Pear | European Pear

POTENTIAL MAXIMUM HEIGHT
30 feet [9 meters]

SYMBOLIC MEANINGS
Affection; Hope.

POSSIBLE POWERS
Comfort; Create oxygen; Feminine energy; Long life; Love; Lust; Temptation; Venus; Water element.

FOLKLORE AND FACTS
A deciduous *Pyrus communis* Pear Tree will continue ripening after it has been picked from the tree. • There is archaeological evidence of Pears in several European Neolithic and Bronze Age sites. • Pear fruit is eaten fresh and can be cooked by poaching, or as an ingredient in baking. • Like Apple seeds, Pear seeds are toxic. • An iconic Pear Tree is included in the Christmas song, "The Twelve Days of Christmas," as the tree with the perched partridge. • Pear wood is desirable for constructing a magic wand. • Pear wood is one of the woods favored for use in the construction of

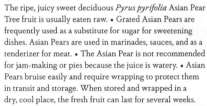

higher-quality woodwind instruments. • Make, then carry, a sachet of Pear blossom and leaf to encourage a long, loving, comfortable life. • Fabric dye made using Pear leaves and twigs can produce an attractive, yellowish-tan color.

No. 372

Pyrus pyrifolia

Asian Pear Tree
Apple Pear | Chinese Pear | Chinese White Pear | Japanese Pear | Korean Pear | Nashi Pear | Papple | Pearple | Sand Pear

POTENTIAL MAXIMUM HEIGHT
40 feet [12 meters]

SYMBOLIC MEANINGS
Gracefully special; Noble.

POSSIBLE POWERS
Create oxygen; Fertility; Love; Luck; Sex; Specialness; Water element.

FOLKLORE AND FACTS
The ripe, juicy sweet deciduous *Pyrus pyrifolia* Asian Pear Tree fruit is usually eaten raw. • Grated Asian Pears are frequently used as a substitute for sugar for sweetening dishes. Asian Pears are used in marinades, sauces, and as a tenderizer for meat. • The Asian Pear is not recommended for jam-making or pies because the juice is watery. • Asian Pears bruise easily and require wrapping to protect them in transit and storage. When stored and wrapped in a dry, cool place, the fresh fruit can last for several weeks. • Asian Pears are very often treated as a special gift with decorative wrapping and ribbon. It is also special enough to be appreciated by guests when served, or enjoyed eaten with family.

No. 373
Quassia amara ☠ ⚱ 🍽

Quassia Tree

Bitter Quassia | Hombre Grande | Quassia Bark | Quassia Wood

📷 POTENTIAL MAXIMUM HEIGHT
20 feet [6 meters]

✳ SYMBOLIC MEANINGS
Bitter; Bitterness.

🌼 POSSIBLE POWERS
Create oxygen; Healing.

📖 FOLKLORE AND FACTS
The bitterness extracted
from the evergreen
Quassia amara Quassia
Tree bark is used to make
bitters. • In beer making,
it is possible to substitute
Quassia bark extract
for hops.

No. 374
Quercus alba ⚱ ☠ 🍽 🌱 🌰

White Oak

Eastern White Oak | Forked-leaf White Oak | Northern White Oak | Ridge White | Stave Oak

📷 POTENTIAL MAXIMUM HEIGHT
100 feet [30 meters]

✳ SYMBOLIC MEANINGS
Endurance; Fine tree; Hospitality; Liberty; Noble presence;
Personal finances; Regal power; Wealth.

🌱 COMPONENT MEANINGS
Acorn: Fruition of long, hard labor; Good luck; Immortality;
    Life; Patience.
Leaves: Bravery; Strength; Welcome.
Sprig: Hospitality.

🌼 POSSIBLE POWERS
Abundance; Advancement; Air element; Aphrodisiac; Attract
love; Autumn; Business; Conscious will; Create oxygen;
Earth element; Energy; Expansion; Female energy; Fertility;
Fire element; Friendship; the Four Winds; Growth; Healing;
Honor; Insight; Joy; Leadership; Life; Light; Lightning; Love;
Luck; Masculine energy; Money; Natural power; Politics;
Potency; Power; Protection; Public acclaim; Responsibility;
Royalty; Spring; Success; Summer; Thunder; Water element;
Wealth; Winter.

📖 FOLKLORE AND FACTS
For a deciduous *Quercus alba* White Oak tree, any tree
that is aged over four hundred years is considered ancient.
• The White Oak Tree has been known to live for hundreds
of years. Although many have been cut for lumber, one
White Oak specimen has been dated to be six hundred years
old. • Since prehistoric times, White Oak and English Oak
trees have been revered to the degree of sacred holy worship.
• Although there were many other Oak trees, the Druids
would *only* perform rituals under a White Oak tree, most
particularly if there was mistletoe growing on its branches.
• The White Oak's wood is very hard and well suitable for
furniture. • Although it is called White Oak, bark that is
lighter than the usual light gray is a rare find. Even so, the
finished wood is a light color. • The only edible parts of the
Quercus alba White Oak are the acorns after they have been
processed by roasting or by boiling and drying. At that point,
they are best used ground into flour. • There was a time
when the best cure for a toothache was believed to hold a
magical splinter, whittled off a White Oak tree that had been
struck by lightning, between the teeth. • The ancient Greeks
once believed that stirring water with a White Oak branch
would make it rain. • If in autumn you happen to catch any
falling Oak leaf, the divination is that you will not have a
cold for all of winter. • A magic wand that has been lovingly
fashioned by its intended user from a length of White
Oak wood, then properly charged before putting it into
service, will provide powerful magic that offers tremendous
protection from evil, supported by strength, endurance, and
great luck. • Wearing an acorn as an amulet is thought to
have a number of positive effects. It will offer protection
against aches, pains, and illnesses. It is also believed it
can promote youthfulness and encourage longevity, even
immortality. Lastly, it is thought to improve sexual powers
and increase fertility.

No. 375

Quercus petraea 🐿 ☠🍽🐿🕯

Sessile Oak

Cornish Oak | Durmast Oak | Irish Oak | Welsh Oak

🔍 **POTENTIAL MAXIMUM HEIGHT**

131 feet [40 meters]

✹ **SYMBOLIC MEANINGS**

Endurance; Fine tree; Hospitality; Liberty; Noble presence;
Personal finances; Regal power; Wealth.

🌱 **COMPONENT MEANINGS**

Acorn: Fruition of long, hard labor; Good luck; Immortality;
Life; Patience.
Leaves: Bravery; Strength; Welcome.
Sprig: Hospitality.

🌀 **POSSIBLE POWERS**

Abundance; Advancement; Air element; Aphrodisiac; Attract
love; Autumn; Business; Conscious will; Create oxygen;
Earth element; Energy; Expansion; Female energy; Fertility;
Fire element; Friendship; the Four Winds; Growth; Healing;
Honor; Insight; Joy; Leadership; Life; Light; Lightning; Love;
Luck; Masculine energy; Money; Natural power; Politics;
Potency; Power; Protection; Public acclaim; Responsibility;
Royalty; Spring; Success; Summer; Tanning leather;
Thunder; Water element; Wealth; Winter.

🜃 **FOLKLORE AND FACTS**

Charles Darwin wrote about the large, deciduous *Quercus
petraea* Sessile Oak tree in his work *On the Origin of Species*
to differentiate it from the *Quercus robur* English Oak.
• Sessile Oak wood has been important for use in roof
beams, shipbuilding, furniture, barrels, paneling, and
decorative wood veneers. • If in autumn you happen to catch
any falling Oak leaf, the divination is that you will not have
a cold for all of winter. • Sessile Oak acorns are edible after
processing them for consumption
by roasting, boiling, and drying
them. • Sessile Oak has been
used for tanning
leather. • Wearing
an acorn as an amulet
is thought to have a
number of positive
effects, including
offering protection
against illnesses and
promoting youthfulness.

No. 376

Quercus robur 🐿 ☠🍽🕯

English Oak Tree

Common Oak | European Oak | King of the Forest | Pedunculate Oak

🔍 **POTENTIAL MAXIMUM HEIGHT**

100 feet [30 meters]

✹ **SYMBOLIC MEANINGS**

Endurance; Fine tree;
Hospitality; Liberty;
Love; Noble presence;
Personal finances; Regal
power; Supreme being;
Wealth.

🌱 **COMPONENT MEANINGS**

Acorn: Fruition of long, hard labor; Good luck; Immortality;
Life; Patience.
Leaves: Bravery; Strength; Welcome.
Sprig: Hospitality.

🌀 **POSSIBLE POWERS**

Abundance; Advancement; Ancient Earth; Aphrodisiac;
Attract love; Autumn; Business; Conscious will; Create
oxygen; Earth element; Energy; Expansion; Female energy;
Fire element; the Four Winds; Friendship; Growth; Healing;
Honor; Joy; Jupiter; Leadership; Life; Light; Lightning; Luck;
Masculine energy; Money; Natural power; Politics; Potency;
Power; Protection; Public acclaim; Responsibility; Royalty;
Spring; Success; Summer; Sun; Thunder; Wealth; Winter.

🜃 **FOLKLORE AND FACTS**

The deciduous *Quercus robur* English Oak Tree has been
revered, even worshipped, as an emblem of the Supreme
Being by significant cultures and people since prehistoric
times. • The most ancient Oak trees in all of Europe can
be found still growing in Blenheim Park, Oxfordshire, in
the UK. One of the English Oaks has been estimated to be
around 1,050 years old. A massive tree in Nottinghamshire's
Sherwood Forest known as the Major Oak is said to be
over one thousand years old, as well as the shelter of Robin
Hood and his Merry Men. • The Druids would listen to the
sound of the English Oak leaves rustling as a way to obtain
divinatory messages. • The word "druid" means "oak man."
• A very powerful protector against evil is a cross whittled
from English Oak wood into equal lengths that are tied
together in the center with red thread and hung in the house.
The resulting cross is known as the equal-armed cross, the
balanced cross, the Greek cross, and the peaceful cross that
predates Christianity. The symbol of that cross represents the
Earth, male and female, the four winds, the four seasons, and

the four elements. Sometimes it is found in a circle, and when it is, the cross represents the Earth, as it is on an astrological natal birth chart. • Carry a small piece of English Oak wood as protection from harm and as a good luck charm. • If in autumn you happen to catch a falling English Oak leaf, the divination is that you will not have a cold for all of winter. • Wear an English Oak acorn amulet for protection against aches, pains, and illnesses. • Wear an English Oak acorn as an amulet to promote youthfulness. • Wear an English Oak acorn as an amulet to encourage longevity and even immortality. • Wear an English Oak acorn as an amulet to increase fertility and to improve sexual powers. • With the proper mordant, English Oak can produce a rich, dark gray dye for fabric. • The only edible parts of the English Oak tree are the acorns after they have been processed by roasting or by boiling and drying. At that point, they are best used after grinding into flour.

No. 377

Quercus suber 🌰🌳

Cork Oak

Cork Tree

◙ POTENTIAL MAXIMUM HEIGHT
75 feet [23 meters]

✹ SYMBOLIC MEANING
Resilience.

🌼 POSSIBLE POWERS
Ancient Earth; Create oxygen; Masculine energy; Recoverability; Resiliency.

☙ FOLKLORE AND FACTS
The thick bark of the evergreen *Quercus suber* Cork Oak is the material source for bottle corks, bulletin boards, cricket ball cores, flooring, wall-coverings, and cork veneer. • There are *Quercus suber* fossils that date back several millions of years. • The Cork Oak is a drought-resistant tree that can age up to several hundred years old. The oldest living tree was planted in 1783 and has been named The Whistler, because of the many songbirds that perch on its branches. It grows in the Alentejo Region of Portugal. • Throughout its lifetime, Cork bark is harvested by hand several times, with nine to twelve years between harvests. The raw stripped bark is cured outdoors for at least six months before processing begins.

No. 378

Quercus virginiana 🌰🌳

Southern Live Oak

Bay Live Oak | Escarpment Live Oak | Live Oak | Plateau Live Oak | Plateau Oak | Roble | Scrub Live Oak | Texas Live Oak | Virginia Live Oak

◙ POTENTIAL MAXIMUM HEIGHT
80 feet [24 meters]

✹ SYMBOLIC MEANINGS
Fine tree; Hills.

🌼 POSSIBLE POWERS
Create oxygen; Feminine energy; Fertility; Liberation; Masculine energy; Shade; Spiritual nourishment; Union.

☙ FOLKLORE AND FACTS
The hardy evergreen *Quercus virginiana* Southern Live Oak tree has a long taproot that deeply anchors the tree into the ground, making it highly resistant to strong wind. • The Southern Live Oak acorns are pointy and longer than the other Oaks. The leaves are smaller and the trees, overall, can slowly grow to become quite large and beautiful. • When conditions suit it just right, the iconic, entirely non-parasitic epiphyte bromeliad known as *Tillandsia usneoides* or Spanish moss might be found draping the branches of Live Oak trees.

No. 379

Radermachera sinica ♂ ♣

Emerald Tree

Asian Bell Tree | China Doll | Serpent Tree

🔍 **POTENTIAL MAXIMUM HEIGHT**
90 feet [27 meters]

✸ **SYMBOLIC MEANING**
From China.

⊕ **POSSIBLE POWER**
Create oxygen.

❦ **FOLKLORE AND FACTS**
The pleasantly fragrant flowers of the deciduous.
Radermachera sinica Emerald Tree are large white trumpets
that will open once only at night, and then die when the sun
begins to shine. • Under optimal conditions, a much smaller
version of the Emerald Tree can be grown in a container
indoors, although it will most likely never bloom.

No. 380

Raphia farinifera ☠ ♂

Raffia Palm

Raffia

🔍 **POTENTIAL MAXIMUM HEIGHT**
82 feet [25 meters]

✸ **SYMBOLIC MEANING**
Binding.

⊕ **POSSIBLE POWERS**
Bindings; Create oxygen;
Sociability.

❦ **FOLKLORE AND FACTS**
The ripe fruit of the evergreen
Raphia farinifera Raffia Palm is edible
after it has been boiled. The sap, too, can
be extracted and processed into a palm
wine that is a highly crucial element of
West African social gatherings for men.
• The leaves of the Raffia Palm provide
the sturdy raffia fiber that is used
in a multitude of crafts, such as
weaving, thatching, as well as rope
making. An oil extracted from the seed kernel is used in soap
making. A fish poison can be extracted from Raffia Palm
stem bark.

No. 381

Ravenala madagascariensis ☠ ♂

Travelers Palm

East-West Palm | Fan Palm | Traveler's Tree

🔍 **POTENTIAL MAXIMUM HEIGHT**
30 feet [9 meters]

✸ **SYMBOLIC MEANING**
Forest leaves.

⊕ **POSSIBLE POWER**
Create oxygen;
Provide drinking
water to travelers in
the bush.

❦ **FOLKLORE AND FACTS**
Native to Madagascar, the exotic
evergreen *Ravenala madagascariensis*
Travelers Palm has enormous, beautiful,
highly distinctive fronds that widely fan
outward to each side towards the east and the west.
• The rainwater that accumulates in the cupped sheaths
of the stems, which is where the stem meets the trunk, can
be used as emergency drinking water. • As it is not a true
Palm and is related to the genus *Strelitzia*, the flowers of the
Travelers Palm look like bird-of-paradise flowers that emerge
high up in the tree at the base of the fronds.

No. 382

Rauvolfia tetraphylla ☠ ♂

Be Still Tree

Devil Pepper

🔍 **POTENTIAL MAXIMUM HEIGHT**
13 feet [4 meters]

✸ **SYMBOLIC MEANING**
Be still.

⊕ **POSSIBLE POWERS**
Create oxygen; Healing; Luck.

❦ **FOLKLORE AND FACTS**
The evergreen *Rauvolfia tetraphylla* Be Still Tree is often
grown as an ornamental, but it has also been used in
traditional medicine to obtain the hypertensive medication
known as deserpidine.

R

No. 383
Rhamnus cathartica 🕱 ⚙ 🌳

Buckthorn Tree
Buckthorn | Common Buckthorn | European Buckthorn | Hart's Thorn | Hartsthorn | Highwaythorn | Purging Buckthorn | Rams Thorn | Ramsthorn

🜨 POTENTIAL MAXIMUM HEIGHT
25 feet [8 meters]

☀ SYMBOLIC MEANINGS
Branch of thorns; Thorn branch; Thorny branch.

🌳 POSSIBLE POWERS
Create oxygen; Elf magic; Exorcism; Feminine energy; Force away an enchantment; Legal matters; Luck in a legal matter in court; Magical working; Protection; Saturn; Water element; Wishing.

🜨 FOLKLORE AND FACTS
To drive away all sorceries and all enchantments from the home and occupants, place branches of the deciduous *Rhamnus cathartica* Buckthorn Tree near the windows and doors. • Carry or wear a Buckthorn sachet made of leaves and pieces of bark for general good luck, most especially when undertaking legal matters. • Carry or wear a leafy sprig from the Buckthorn Tree to create good luck. • Buckthorn will produce a vegetable dye color ranging from pink to a rusty shade of red. • To make a strong wish, first make an infusion of Buckthorn Tree bark mixed with rainwater, natural spring water, or distilled water. Face the east, sprinkle a bit of the infusion, and concentrate on the wish. Turn left to face the north, repeat. Turn left again to face the west, repeat. Turn left again to face the south, repeat. Turn left again to face the east, sprinkle the infusion once more, and wish the wish one last time. Believe the wish will come true in good time.

No. 384
Rhamnus purshiana 🕱 ⚙ 🌳 🌰 ♦

Cascara Sagrada Tree
Bitter Bark | Cascara | Cascara Buckthorn | Chittam | Chittam Bark | Chitticum | Cittim Bark | Ecorce Sacrée | Sacred Bark | Yellow Bark

🜨 POTENTIAL MAXIMUM HEIGHT
33 feet [10 meters]

☀ SYMBOLIC MEANINGS
Patience; Providence.

🌳 POSSIBLE POWERS
Create oxygen; Legal matters; Money; Money spell; Protection; Protection against a hex.

🜨 FOLKLORE AND FACTS
A vase or bowl with leafy stems from the deciduous *Rhamnus purshiana* Cascara Sagrada Tree on the desk placed near where thoughtful work is done can help with well-focused concentration. • Make, then carry or wear a sachet of Cascara Sagrada to help concentrate. • To help win a court case, make, then carry or wear a sachet of Cascara Sagrada leaves and bits of bark to court to invite a positive outcome of the case. Then, before going to court, sprinkle an infusion of Cascara Sagrada leaves that have been mixed with rainwater, natural spring water, or distilled water around the home. • Carry or wear Cascara Sagrada to fend off hexes and evil.

No. 385
Rhapis excelsa ⚙ 🌳

Broadleaf Lady Palm
Dwarf Lady Palm | Fan Tufted Palm | Lady Palm | Bamboo Palm

🜨 POTENTIAL MAXIMUM HEIGHT
13 feet [4 meters]

☀ SYMBOLIC MEANING
Delicate beauty; Tall needle.

🌳 POSSIBLE POWERS
Cleansing; Create oxygen; Happiness; Interior decoration; Versatility.

🜨 FOLKLORE AND FACTS
The small, slow-growing evergreen *Rhapis excelsa* Broadleaf Lady Palm is unknown in the wild. • The Broadleaf

R

Lady Palm has thin stems and grows in snug clumps. • The Broadleaf Lady Palm was cultivated for use within the castles of the Japanese elite during the 1600s. • It has become a popular potted tree that is an ornamental favorite, as it is easily managed and requires little light to thrive. As a live potted tree grown in the home, offices, and shopping malls, it will adapt to whatever light conditions are available and will require very little care and no special attention.

Rhizophora mangle 🝛🌺

Red Mangrove
American Mangrove | Apareiba | Mangle | Mangle Dulce | Mangle Rojo | Mangrove | Red Mangle | Tiri Wai

◉ POTENTIAL MAXIMUM HEIGHT
75 feet [23 meters]

☀ SYMBOLIC MEANING
Sturdy root bearing.

🌼 POSSIBLE POWERS
Create oxygen; Create an island; Creation; Growth; Protection; Shelter; Tan leather.

🜚 FOLKLORE AND FACTS
The best known of the Mangroves is the evergreen *Rhizophora mangle* Red Mangrove with its reddish-colored, multi-stemmed, stilt-like roots. • As a true Mangrove, the Red Mangrove can densely grow together to form tightly matted islands to rise up in brackish waters. These small islands become crucial and advantageous in erosion protection and coastline stabilization. Catching and trapping sand and sediments in the extensive root systems can evolve to become a large enough island to be developable and eventually entirely habitable, such as the upscale Sanibel and Captiva Islands in southwest Florida. • The tangled roots of the Red Mangrove reach down into the water to provide a nursery shelter that is a perfect hideaway

for the defenseless and still developing tiny fish fry, baby seahorses, young mollusks, and infant crustaceans. • As the Red Mangrove Tree develops, it will become large and the wood will be hard. It has been used as a construction lumber in some areas of Southeast Asia. • Red Mangrove bark has also been used to tan leather.

Rhododendron maximum ☠🝛🌺🌰🜚

Great Rhododendron
American Rhododendron | Bigleaf Laurel | Big Rhododendron | Deertongue Laurel | Great Laurel | Late Rhododendron | Mountain Laurel | Rhododendron | Rose Bay | Summer Rhododendron

◉ POTENTIAL MAXIMUM HEIGHT
33 feet [10 meters]

☀ SYMBOLIC MEANINGS
Agitation; Ambition; Ambitious; Beware; Danger.

🌼 POSSIBLE POWERS
Banishing; Create oxygen; Learning who is against you; Power; Power to overcome enemies; Stirring up agitation.

🜚 FOLKLORE AND FACTS
A flowering evergreen *Rhododendron maximum* Great Rhododendron that has grown to be a tree can stop someone passing by just to look at it for a while and take a photo. The flower will not last longer than approximately three weeks. • The Great Rhododendron is a cold-hardy species that protects itself from the drying cold air below freezing temperatures by curling up its foliage *very* tightly and folding it downwards.

Rhopalostylis sapida 🝛

Nīkau Palm
Feather Duster Palm | Nikau | Shaving Brush Palm

◉ POTENTIAL MAXIMUM HEIGHT
50 feet [15 meters]

☀ SYMBOLIC MEANINGS
Coconut leaf; Pleasant; Without nuts.

🌼 POSSIBLE POWERS
Basketry; Create oxygen; Thatching; Weaving.

FOLKLORE AND FACTS

The slow-growing *Rhopalostylis sapida* Nīkau Palm is the only palm tree that is native to New Zealand's mainland. • It will readily grow from a seed. • Some trees of this species are believed to be at least two hundred years old. • The Nīkau Palm's fruit is a favorite food of the native New Zealand pigeon which is also known as the kererū. The kiwi will also eat the fruit, using the seeds as gizzard stones. • The Nīkau Palm flower begins as a gorgeous magenta-colored clustered spray that opens into hundreds of tiny, sweetly-fragranced, mauve flowers. The fragrance attracts insects, birds, and geckos that pollinate the flowers while feeding on the rich nectar. The flowers develop into bright red long-lasting fruit berries that will take almost a year to fully ripen. • The Māori have used the young inner leaves and flower clusters, both cooked and raw. For example, older leaves are used to thatch waterproof roofs. The raw fibers of the fibrous old leaves are woven into rope, floor mats, and traditional Māori baskets called *kete*. The red berries can be strung and worn as necklaces and bracelets. The berries have also been used as ammunition for blow-guns and slingshots.

No. 389

Rhus coriaria 💀 🎒 🍴 🌿 🌳

Sumac Tree

Sicilian Sumac | Sumak | Tanner's Sumach

🔵 POTENTIAL MAXIMUM HEIGHT

10 feet [3 meters]

☀ SYMBOLIC MEANINGS

Intellectual excellence; Splendid; Splendor.

🌐 POSSIBLE POWERS

Addresses difficulty; Create oxygen; Elemental fire energy; Energy of wild nature; Facilitates harmony among people; Intellect; Life; Movement; Tan leather.

📛 FOLKLORE AND FACTS

Tangy ripe fruit of the deciduous *Rhus coriaria* Sumac Tree, which is dried, crushed, then used as an herb, was introduced to Europeans long before the Lemon was. • Nine Sumac berries in the pocket will help get a lighter sentence if found guilty in a court trial. • A 3-foot-long (1 m) branch of Sumac Tree wood that is approximately ½ inch (12 mm) thick with a puff of downy eagle feathers attached on one end will suffice as a suitable Navajo shamanistic healing wand called a *nahikái*. • The toxic *Rhus coriaria* Sumac leaves have been used since ancient times to tan leather.

No. 390

Rhus typhina 🎒 🍴 🌳

Staghorn Sumac

Antler Tree | Stag's Horn Sumac | Velvet Sumac | Vinegar Tree

🔵 POTENTIAL MAXIMUM HEIGHT

25 feet [8 meters]

☀ SYMBOLIC MEANINGS

Sour; Velvety antlers.

🌐 POSSIBLE POWERS

Create oxygen; Colorizing; Endurance; Fire element; Fire energy; Healing; Natural wild energy; Peace; Resilience; Vitality.

📛 FOLKLORE AND FACTS

The deciduous *Rhus typhina* Staghorn Sumac is native to eastern North America and is the largest of the North American sumacs. It can be found all throughout the Appalachian Mountains. Staghorn Sumac is also cultivated around the world in areas with temperate climates. • It has a habit of widely spreading by cloning via aggressive root suckers from the base of the trunk, which, in the wild, will produce large colonies. Although the Staghorn Sumac is relatively unsuitable in a small garden because it grows very quickly, diligent pruning of its emerging suckers will help keep expanding growth under control. Even in a large, open garden or park setting, pruning the root suckers is crucial to maintain control over rampant growth, which is considered invasive in some areas. • The stems are covered completely with rust-colored, soft hair-like bristles that give it a velvety texture. As the branches also have a fork-like appearance, they evoke a stag's new velvety antlers. • Flowers are very tiny, greenish-yellow, and grow very densely in panicles that develop into fuzzy covered, deeply reddish, tiny berries that are a favorite winter food for songbirds. • The Staghorn Sumac fruit berries are edible, high in vitamin C, and are sometimes used to make a tart lemony-tasting beverage, as well brewed into wine. • In fall, the Staghorn Sumac becomes especially showy when its green leaves will turn to bright shades of yellow, gold, orange, and dark red • The dried tufts are

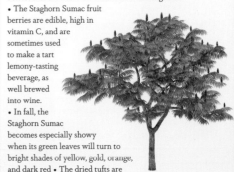

R

sometimes used in bee smokers used by beekeepers. • The leaves, tufts, and bark can be used to make both a natural dye and a mordant for dying that contributes to colorfastness. • A young Staghorn Sumac stem's pith is very soft and can be pushed out of the stem to make it completely hollow. Cut into pieces, the hollowed stem bits can be used to make beads and other decorations. • Carrying nine Staghorn Sumac berries in the pocket might help the wearer receive a lighter sentence in a losing court case.

No. 391

Robinia pseudoacacia 🕱 ◎ ♣ ◉

Black Locust Tree

False Acacia | Locust | Locust Rose | Robinia

📷 **POTENTIAL MAXIMUM HEIGHT**
82 feet [25 meters]

✷ **SYMBOLIC MEANINGS**
Concealed love; Elegance; Friendship; Platonic love.

◉ **POSSIBLE POWERS**
Create oxygen; Endurance; Ultimate strength.

🜏 **FOLKLORE AND FACTS**
The flowers of the deciduous *Robinia pseudoacacia* Black Locust Tree grow as long, pendulous, thick clusters of pink or white blossoms. • Jesuit missionaries arriving in the New World used to believe and tell others that Black Locust is the same species of Locust tree that sustained Saint John the Baptist's life in the wilderness. But it could not have been, because at that time the Black Locust Tree only grew in North America. • Black Locust flowers are a major source of pollen for the renowned Acacia honey. • Black Locust wood can resist rot for up to one hundred years. • Due to the strength of Black Locust wood, many Native Americans would often fashion their best bows from the wood.

• It was once written that Black Locust Tree wood was as long-lasting and strong as most brick walls, making it a desirable building material and one of the earliest lumber exports from North America to Europe.

No. 392

Roystonea regia ◎ ◉

Royal Palm

Cuban Royal Palm | Florida Royal Palm | Palma Criolla | Palma Real | Sla Barang | Vakka

📷 **POTENTIAL MAXIMUM HEIGHT**
112 feet [34 meters]

✷ **SYMBOLIC MEANINGS**
Most beautiful; Regal; Royalty; Special.

◉ **POSSIBLE POWERS**
Communication with the gods; Create oxygen; Moon; Rain; Shelter; Spiritual protection; Water element.

🜏 **FOLKLORE AND FACTS**
Throughout the subtropical and tropical parts of the world, the evergreen *Roystonea regia* Royal Palm tree has been strategically planted to achieve the most positive attention as an ornamental plant. • The Royal Palm is a magnificently tall, straight, and regally royal-looking palm tree that routinely towers over its surroundings. The trunk is an ashen, light-brown color before the smooth green leaf sheath begins to rise straight up above it. The tree's roots are fibrous, as witnessed by the narrowly matted portion that is visible where the tree meets the soil. • In places where it is plentiful, Royal Palm leaves are used for roof, wall, and furniture thatching. The wood is used for construction. • High above, under the canopy of the long, wide fronds, the tree's flower pollen is collected by bees. • The Royal Palm is slowly grown from seed, which is wildly distributed by birds and bats that enjoy the ripe berry-like fruit. • In the Catholic faith, the fronds are often used when celebrating Palm Sunday. • The Royal Palm has a spiritually symbolic importance to the Santería and Palo faiths. Believers leave offerings and perform ceremonies at the particular tree or trees that their followers favor. • In Panama, yellow-crowned parrots will commonly nest in the Royal Palm trees.

No. 393

Sabal palmetto 🌵🍄🌿

Sabal Palm

Blue Palmetto | Cabbage Palm | Cabbage Palmetto | Carolina Palmetto | Common Palmetto | Garfield's Tree | Palmetto Palm | Swamp Cabbage

POTENTIAL MAXIMUM HEIGHT
65 feet [20 meters]

SYMBOLIC MEANINGS
Courage; Strength.

POSSIBLE POWERS
Courageousness;
Create oxygen; Strength.

FOLKLORE AND FACTS
The evergreen *Sabal palmetto* Sabal
Palm tree is highly tolerant of sea
salt spray and seawater wash, but not
saltwater flooding. It is also resistant to
drought, high winds, and fire. • The Sabal Palm fruit is an
edible drupe. Its seeds can be ground into a flour. However,
for the Miccosukee and Seminole people, as well as the
early colonists of Florida, the choice part of the Sabal Palm
has been the terminal bud, which is harvested to obtain the
delicious and nutritious heart of palm. The harvesting of the
terminal bud will kill the tree.

No. 394

Salix alba 🌿🌳🌰

White Willow

English Willow | Osier | Pussy Willow | Saille | Salicyn Willow | Saugh Tree | Tree of Enchantment | Witches' Aspirin | Withe | Withy

POTENTIAL MAXIMUM HEIGHT
30 feet [9 meters]

SYMBOLIC MEANINGS
Bendable but not breakable; Enchantment; Immortality;
Prosperity.

POSSIBLE POWERS
Binding; Blessing; Create oxygen; Enchantments; Feminine
energy; Healing; Love; Love divination; Mercury; Moon;
Prosperity; Protection; Water element.

FOLKLORE AND FACTS
The overall look of the long-hanging branches of the
deciduous *Salix alba* White Willow tree are such an
intensely romantic vision that it is no surprise that the tree
attracts love. • Some ancient British burial mounds were

found lined with White Willow
branches. • White Willow
branches in the home will
offer protection against
evil. • The flexibility of the
White Willow branches
made it useful for basketry,
sculpture, and woven
furniture. • White Willow
wood has been used to make
cricket bats. • White Willow
can be used to make a yellow dye for fabric.
• White Willow is often used in wands that are particularly
used for Moon magic. • If you absolutely *need* to "knock on
wood," do it on White Willow tree wood.

No. 395

Salix babylonica 🌿🌳🌰

Weeping Willow

Babylon Willow | Chuí Liǔ | Napoleon Willow | Peking Willow

POTENTIAL MAXIMUM HEIGHT
60 feet [18 meters]

SYMBOLIC MEANINGS
Bendable but not breakable; Ebb and flux; Forsaken;
Melancholy; Metaphysics; Sadness; Tenacity.

POSSIBLE POWERS
Create oxygen; Cycles; Divination; Eloquence; Enchantment;
Feminine energy; Femininity; Fertility; Friendship; Healing;
Inspiration; Joy; Love; Moon magic; Mourning; Peace;
Prophecies; Protection; Romantic love; Rhythm; Unlucky
love; Wishing; Women's magic.

S

FOLKLORE AND FACTS

The forerunner of modern-day aspirin was found in the leaves of the deciduous *Salix babylonica* Weeping Willow tree that had been used medicinally for pain relief for over 2,400 years. • Weeping Willow wood is sacred to all the goddesses of the Moon. • Weeping Willow wood will make a powerful magic wand, which should be cut and properly fashioned by the intended user. After it has been charged under the light of the Moon, the wand's strength will greatly increase. • Use a pliable piece of Weeping Willow to make a wish while tying it into a loose knot. After the wish has been fulfilled, untie the knot, thank the tree, and leave it a gift. • Weeping Willow can be used to produce a yellow dye. • The flexibility of the Weeping Willow branches make it useful for basketry, sculpture, and woven furniture. • There was a time when a feverish person would be directed to send their affliction into a Weeping Willow tree by going to the tree with a handful of thick mud, without crossing over water or speaking a word. Then, they would make a gash in the bark, breathe deeply into the gash three times, and close it over quickly with the mud poultice and a prayer of gratitude for taking on the fever, before hurrying away from the tree without looking back at it.

No. 396

Salix caprea 🥀 🌰 ▮

Pussywillow

Goat Willow | Great Sallow | Osier | Rods of Life | Sallow | Willow

POTENTIAL MAXIMUM HEIGHT
32 feet [10 meters]

SYMBOLIC MEANINGS
Enchantment; Illness recovery; Immortality; Motherhood; Prosperity; Receiving a blessing; Spring.

POSSIBLE POWERS
Binding; Blessing; Create oxygen; Healing; Love; Love divination; Prosperity; Protection.

FOLKLORE AND FACTS
In ancient Rome, women were initiated into the role of motherhood by being flogged with deciduous *Salix caprea* Pussywillow branches in a ritual that intended to wish fertility upon them. • Dyngus Day, or Śmigus-dyngu, is a Slavic holiday following Lent. It is a celebration that includes parades, polkas, and pierogis, along with a peculiar tradition where single boys splash water on single girls to show their interest. The water represents cleansing, purification, and fertility, and the tradition dates back to when the first Polish monarch was baptized as a prince, bringing Christianity into Poland in 966 CE. The single girls who are intrigued by the boys will playfully slap them on their heads with the soft, furry, silvery-gray, catkin-covered stems of a Pussywillow branch. The use of the Pussywillow is a substitute for palm branches that were never available in Poland for church on Palm Sunday. The stems are very often kept within the home in a place of honor, throughout the year. • Using the blessed Pussywillow branches as whips refers back to Palm Sundays past, when after church the parishioners would go outside and whip one another with the branches for good luck. • Pussywillows were believed to be magical charms that could protect the home from lightning, protect livestock, and increase the amount of honey that bees would produce. • In China, Pussywillow branches are often placed on gates and front doors to ward off evil spirits that wander about during the Qingming Festival, or Tomb-Sweeping Day. • In old English folklore, a Pussywillow tree can be malicious because it has the ability to uproot and move about to stalk travelers. • It is believed by some that if a Pussywillow tree is growing anywhere near a cemetery, any spirits near it will not be able to depart the world of the living to move into the peaceful afterlife. • It is believed by some that communication with the spirits of the dead can be achieved by carving an image into *Salix caprea* wood, then sending a spiritual image of the carving into the netherworld, where a spirit can magically enter the wood and provide the information requested back to the sender.

No. 397

Sambucus canadensis ☠ 🥀 🌀 ▮

Common Elder

American Black Elderberry | Black Elder | Canada Elderberry | Common Elderberry | Elderberry | Ellhorn | Lady Elder

POTENTIAL MAXIMUM HEIGHT
12 feet [4 meters]

SYMBOLIC MEANINGS
Compassion; Creativity; Cycles; Death; Endings; Good health; Humility; Kindness; Prosperity; Protection against evil dangers; Rebirth; Regeneration; Renewal; Transformation; Zeal; Zealousness.

POSSIBLE POWERS
Aphrodisiac; Attract love; Create oxygen; Death; Exorcism; Feminine energy; Good luck; Healing; Kills a serpent; Magic; Midsummer solstice; Prosperity; Protection against a witch or evil spirit; Sends away a thief; Sleep; Sound resonance; Venus; Water element.

❧ FOLKLORE AND FACTS

Planting a deciduous *Sambucus canadensis* Common Elder tree near a home's entrance will protect the home and keep evil from entering. • Stone Age arrowheads were shaped to look like Elder leaves. • Elder is associated with witches. Elder leaves gathered on April 30th can be attached to doors and windows to keep witches from entering the home. • On the Isle of Man, in the British Isles, the Common Elder is considered to be a fairy tree. • Once the dead were buried, Elder branches were planted with the body to protect them from evil spirits. • Attaching a cross made of Elder wood to livestock stables is supposed to keep evil away from the animals. • Cradles were never to be made of Elder wood because it was believed the baby would fall out of it, not be able to sleep, or be pinched by fairies. • The English believe that burning Elder wood logs will bring the Devil into the house. • An amulet made from a piece of Elder wood on which the sun has never directly shone, tied inside a small pouch held between two knots, can be worn around the neck as a pendant to protect against evil. • Someone standing under an Elder tree at Midsummer might see fairies. • To the Druids, Elder indicated the beginning at the end and the end at the beginning. Perhaps for that reason, it was common that the Druids used an Elder wand for both curses and blessings. • An Elder wand can also force away evil spirits and negative or malicious thoughts. • The pith can be forced out of a young Elder stem. The hollow stem can be fashioned into a flute. Several single flutes can be bound together with a piece of string to make into a pan flute. Music played on a pan flute made of Elder will have the same power as that provided by a magic wand. • Before pruning an Elder tree, one must ask the tree's permission, then spit three times before making the first cut. • Elder essential oil aromatherapy might be able to help alleviate anxiety and calm irritability. It may even help lift one up from depression.

No. 398

Sambucus nigra ☠ ✿ 🍴 ◉

Black Elder

Black Elderberry | Elderberry | European Black Elderberry | Tramman

◐ POTENTIAL MAXIMUM HEIGHT

30 feet [9 meters]

✸ SYMBOLIC MEANINGS

Death in Life; Life in Death; Protection against evil dangers.

❀ POSSIBLE POWERS

Create oxygen; Death; Exorcism; Good luck; Healing; Magic; Prosperity; Protection; Protection against evil spirits; Protection against witches; Kill serpents; Send away thieves; Sleep; Venus; Water element.

❧ FOLKLORE AND FACTS

The English believe that burning logs of the deciduous *Sambucus nigra* Black Elder tree will bring the Devil into the house. • Before pruning a Black Elder tree, one must ask the tree's permission. Once permission has been granted, spit three times before making the first cut. • Black Elder leaves gathered on the last day of April can be attached to the doors and windows to keep witches from entering the home. • An amulet made from a piece of Black Elder wood on which the sun has never shone can be tied between two knots on a piece of string that are then worn around the neck as protection against evil. • Once the dead were buried, branches of Black Elder were planted with the body to protect them from evil spirits. • According to Norse mythology, the goddess Freya chose the Black Elder tree for her home.

Santalum album 🫖🌱🍶

Sandalwood Tree

Indian Sandalwood Tree | Sandal | Santal | White Sandalwood | White Saunders | Yellow Sandalwood

◉ POTENTIAL MAXIMUM HEIGHT
65 feet [20 meters]

☀ SYMBOLIC MEANING
Deep meditation.

⚘ POSSIBLE POWERS
Business; Caution; Cleverness; Communication; Create oxygen; Creativity; Emotions; Exorcism; Faith; Feminine energy; Fertility; Generation; Healing; Illumination; Incense; Initiation; Inspiration; Intelligence; Intuition; Learning; Love; Memory; Moon; Prayer; Protection; Protection against a dog bite; Protection against a ghost; Protection against a snake bite; Protection against drunkenness; Protection against sorcery; Prudence; Psychic ability; Purification; Science; Sea; Self-preservation; Sound judgment; Spirituality; Subconscious mind; Thievery; Tides; Transactions; Travel by water; Water element; Wisdom; Wishing.

⚗ FOLKLORE AND FACTS
Although the evergreen *Santalum album* Sandalwood Tree is an overharvested and threatened species in the wild, they can live to be over one hundred years old. • Wooden beads made of Sandalwood are believed to be protective and facilitate spiritual awareness whenever they are worn. • Sandalwood is one of the most expensive woods in the world. • When you enter into a temple, it will most likely smell like fragrant sacred Sandalwood. • Sandalwood essential oil used in aromatherapy does much to calm agitations and relieve tension.

Santalum spicatum 🫖🍴🌱

Australian Sandalwood

Dutjahn | Uilarac | Waang | Wolgol | Wollgat

◉ POTENTIAL MAXIMUM HEIGHT
13 feet [4 meters]

☀ SYMBOLIC MEANINGS
Calm; Meditation.

⚘ POSSIBLE POWERS
Awakens libido; Calm; Create oxygen; Incense; Inner peacefulness; Spiritual awareness.

⚗ FOLKLORE AND FACTS
Overharvesting during the 1800s for the purpose of manufacturing incense pushed wild evergreen *Santalum spicatum* Australian Sandalwood very close to extinction. • Beads made of Australian Sandalwood are protective and facilitate a calm, inner peacefulness and a spiritual awareness whenever they are worn. • Using Australian Sandalwood essential oil for aromatherapy can help lift the vibration of a low libido to be higher. • The fruit and seed of the *Santalum spicatum* Australian Sandalwood tree have been an important resource as both bush food and medicine for many First Nations peoples in western Australia for thousands of years.

Sapium glandulosum ☠🫖

Milktree

Gumtree | Leche de Olivo | Olivo Macho

◉ POTENTIAL MAXIMUM HEIGHT
115 feet [35 meters]

☀ SYMBOLIC MEANING
Cover over.

⚘ POSSIBLE POWER
Create oxygen.

⚗ FOLKLORE AND FACTS
The latex that can be obtained in large amounts from the evergreen *Sapium glandulosum* Milktree is thick, and of a high enough quality to process into rubber. However, because harvesting the tree is so difficult, it is not used in that way.

S

No. 402

Sassafras albidum ☠ 🗹 🍴

White Sassafras

Gumbo Filé | Red Sassafras | Sassafras | Silky Sassafras

📷 **POTENTIAL MAXIMUM HEIGHT**
98 feet [30 meters]

✳ **SYMBOLIC MEANING**
Lucky wood.

🌀 **POSSIBLE POWERS**
Create oxygen; Fire element; Healing; Jupiter;
Masculine energy; Money.

🜨 **FOLKLORE AND FACTS**
Cajun cuisine's filé powder is made from the tiny, newly
growing leaves of the deciduous *Sassafras albidum* White
Sassafras tree, which are dried and ground into a fine
powder. Filé powder was first devised by the Choctaw
people, who used it to thicken stews. • Make a sachet of
White Sassafras using a leaf or a few pinches of filé powder,
then carry it in the purse or wallet to attract money.

No. 403

Schefflera actinophylla ☠

Australia Umbrella Tree

Amate | *Heptapleurum actinophyllum* | Octopus Tree |
Queensland Umbrella Tree | Umbrella Tree

📷 **POTENTIAL MAXIMUM HEIGHT**
50 feet [15 meters]

✳ **SYMBOLIC MEANING**
Protective covering.

🌀 **POSSIBLE POWERS**
Covering; Create oxygen; Protection.

🜨 **FOLKLORE AND FACTS**
The evergreen *Schefflera actinophylla* Australia Umbrella
Tree flowers develop at the top of the tree as racemes that
are up to 6 feet (1.8 m) long and covered with almost
1,000 tiny red flowers. • The leaves, nectar-rich flowers,
and fruit provide food for wildlife and nectar-eating birds
for months. • When started from seed in a pot, the
Australia Umbrella Tree can be grown as a houseplant.
• The *Schefflera actinophylla*, although a freestanding tree,
may also spend part of its growth cycle clinging to a host
tree for support and to assist it in pulling itself upward as an
epiphyte. • When conditions are ideal, the tree will produce
aerial roots that will fully root into the ground.

No. 404

Schefflera arboricola ☠ 🌳

Dwarf Schefflera Tree

Dwarf Umbrella Tree | Ézhǎng Téng | Hawaiian Elf | Hawaiian Elf Schefflera |
Miniature Schefflera | Miniature Umbrella Tree

📷 **POTENTIAL MAXIMUM HEIGHT**
40 feet [12 meters]

✳ **SYMBOLIC MEANING**
Protective covering.

🌀 **POSSIBLE POWERS**
Covering; Create oxygen;
Protection.

🜨 **FOLKLORE AND FACTS**
The evergreen *Schefflera arboricola* Dwarf Schefflera Tree
is one of the trees most often potted and brought inside to
be grown as impressive houseplants. The height and width
of an interior tree is limited by available space and careful
pruning. Gracing a room from a small, tidy table-top size to
grow tall and wide requires a location near a bright window.
• If planted outside, the Dwarf Schefflera Tree will grow to
its full potential to flower, fruit, and provide some food for
nectar-eating birds and other wildlife.

No. 405

Schinus terebinthifolia ☠ 🗹 🌳

Brazilian Pepper Tree

Aroeira | Broadleaved Pepper Tree | California Pepper Tree | Christmasberry Tree | Duvaua |
Florida Holly | Jesuit's Balsam | Pepper Tree |
Peruvian Mastic Tree | Peruvian Pepper Tree |
Piru | Rose Pepper

📷 **POTENTIAL MAXIMUM HEIGHT**
49 feet [15 meters]

✳ **SYMBOLIC MEANINGS**
Marriage; Religious enthusiasm.

🌀 **POSSIBLE POWERS**
Create oxygen; Healing; Protection;
Purification.

🜨 **FOLKLORE AND FACTS**
Also known as Florida Holly, the evergreen *Schinus
terebinthifolia* Brazilian Pepper Tree has invasively spread
all over Florida since its introduction sometime around or
before 1891. It has forced out the growth of native plants and
thousands of acres of Mangroves. • Mexican folk healers
have used *Schinus terebinthifolia* branches in healing by

brushing the branch over the sick individual with the expectation that the branch will absorb the sickness. Then the branch is burned, with the intent to destroy the disease.
• The medicinal properties of the *Schinus terebinthifolia* fruit berries continue to be researched with great interest in its bacteria control. With that comes the potential to someday effectively treat antibiotic-resistant MRSA infections in human beings.

No. 406

Sciadopitys verticillata 🌿

Japanese Umbrella-Pine
Kōyamaki | Umbrella Pine

🔘 **POTENTIAL MAXIMUM HEIGHT**
40 feet [12 meters]

🌟 **SYMBOLIC MEANING**
Whorled.

🌐 **POSSIBLE POWERS**
Ancient Earth; Create oxygen; Longevity; Perseverance.

🜨 **FOLKLORE AND FACTS**
Since it evidently exists in the fossil record as being approximately 230 million years old, the near-threatened evergreen conifer *Sciadopitys verticillata* Japanese Umbrella-Pine is considered to be a living fossil.

No. 407

Senegalia senegal 🜨 ⚰ 🍴 🌿

Gum Arabic Tree
Acacia Gum | Arabic Gum | Cape Gum | Egyptian Thorn | Gum Acacia | Gum Arabic | Gum Senegal Tree | Hashab Gum Tree | Shittah Tree | Sudan Gum Arabic

🔘 **POTENTIAL MAXIMUM HEIGHT**
20 feet [6 meters]

🌟 **SYMBOLIC MEANING**
Platonic love.

🌐 **POSSIBLE POWERS**
Air element; Create oxygen; Masculine energy; Money; Platonic love; Protection; Psychic powers; Purification; Purity; Purifies evil or negativity; Spiritual enhancement; Spirituality; Sun; Wards off evil.

🜨 **FOLKLORE AND FACTS**
A leafy sprig of the deciduous *Senegalia senegal* Gum Arabic Tree placed over a bed or worn on a hat will purify the area and ward off evil. • The term "Gum Arabic" dates back to when it was used in the Middle East, from around the ninth century. • The highest-quality Gum Arabic resin is from Sudan. • The thick, gummy sap is harvested by cutting slashes into a branch, stripping out the bark in the wound, then waiting several weeks for the resinous gum to collect in the gash and harden. • Among its many uses, Gum Arabic acts as a binder, thickening agent, stabilizer, or emulsifier in the manufacturing of certain food products, confections, and beverage syrups. • Because it is water soluble, Gum Arabic is a valuable binder used with watercolor paints. • Gum Arabic is used to anoint and consecrate all the accoutrements used in carrying out magical rituals of all types.

No. 408

Sequoia sempervirens ⚰ 🌿

Coast Redwood
California Redwood | Coastal Redwood

🔘 **POTENTIAL MAXIMUM HEIGHT**
381 feet [116 meters]

🌟 **SYMBOLIC MEANING**
Immense height.

🌐 **POSSIBLE POWERS**
Abundance; Air element; Ancient Earth; Awakening; Create oxygen; Dreaming; Enlightenment; Fertility; Harmony; Immortality; Light; Longevity; Luck; Magic; Masculine energy; Protection; Regeneration; Renewal; Resurrection; Spiritual consciousness; Spiritual life; Spiritual love; Spirituality; Survival.

🜨 **FOLKLORE AND FACTS**
Among the oldest living things on all of the Earth, the fast-growing evergreen conifer *Sequoia sempervirens* Coast Redwood is iconic among the tallest living trees as well. Even so, due to uncontrolled harvesting in the past, currently in the wild the Coast Redwood is thought to age closer to only over six hundred years. Having naturally grown along the coastal areas of the states of California and Oregon, the Coast Redwood trees once covered over 2 million acres

S

(809,371 ha) of land until the early 1900s, when commercial logging began to remove the tallest, most ancient of the trees. • An interesting thing about the Coast Redwood is that it is highly dependent upon the presence of fog to hydrate the uppermost parts of the tree. The more fog, the better the ability to reach tall heights. • At one time the railroad ties and train trestles throughout the state of California were primarily made of Coast Redwood because it is highly resistant to decay. The old Coast Redwood railroad ties are highly desirable to recycle into a wide variety of creative uses, from garden borders to tabletops. • The Coast Redwood tree has also been naturalized in New Zealand, where because of the availability of ample rainwater, it has a higher rate of growth than the Coast Redwood trees of California and elsewhere in the world where this tree is cultivated. • The impressive height and longevity of the Coast Redwood trees have garnered identifying names to distinguish one tree from another. • The Coast Redwood is large enough to drive through a hole tunneled through the trunk in parks located in California. There is a huge drive-thru tree, located near Leggett, California, that is called the Chandelier Tree. • Oddly, as large as the *Sequoia sempervirens* Coast Redwood tree is, it will produce very small cones that measure to be approximately only 1 inch (2.5 cm) long! • This majestically tall tree is grown from a seed approximately the size of a tomato seed.

No. 409

Sequoiadendron giganteum 🌳

Giant Sequoia
Big Tree | Giant Redwood | Hea-Mi-Withic | Sierra Redwood | Sierran Redwood | Toos-Pung-Ish | Wawona | Wellingtonia Giant Sequoia | Wellingtonia gigantea

🔘 POTENTIAL MAXIMUM HEIGHT
311 feet [95 meters]

✳ SYMBOLIC MEANINGS
Enormity; Follow; Majesty.

🌼 POSSIBLE POWERS
Abundance; Air element; Ancient Earth; Awakening; Create oxygen; Dreaming; Enlightenment; Fertility; Harmony; Immortality; Inspire awe; Light; Longevity; Luck; Magic; Masculine energy; Protection; Regeneration; Renewal; Resurrection; Spiritual consciousness; Spiritual life; Spiritual love; Spirituality; Survival.

🌿 FOLKLORE AND FACTS
Growing natively on the west side of the Sierra Nevada mountains in California, the endangered evergreen conifer *Sequoiadendron giganteum* Giant Sequoia is the most massive tree on all the Earth. Since the destruction of thousands of these trees during three major forest fires between 2020 and 2021, the Giant Sequoia species is critically endangered. • The Giant Sequoia trees are also known to be one of the oldest living plants on Earth. Estimating the age of living trees by dating felled trees of a similar size, living Giant Sequoia trees are well over three thousand years old. • As tall and wide as the trunks of the Giant Sequoia are, the trunk of an ancient tree is very brittle. Loggers of the past took their chances and felled trees anyway. Some of the routinely felled trees shattered to pieces when they hit the ground. Any wood that remained usable ended up as roof shingles. Or, the inconceivably worst thing for a Giant Sequoia to end up as–matchsticks! The hideous visual devastation of what remained as clear cut or broken Giant Sequoia groves spurred the public to vehemently object to the continuous felling and to advocate for the protection of what groves remained. The Giant Sequoia National Monument was finally proclaimed as late as 2000, to provide 328,000 acres (132,737 ha) of protection. • Looking up at one of these magnificent trees, it is hard to comprehend that each one of them was grown from a seed. The Giant Sequoia tree cones are very small and tight, being no more than 3 inches (8 cm) in length. They can remain closed for twenty years, until insect damage can cause the cone to open enough to release some of the seeds from within it. An actual seed is no larger than 0.2 x 0.04 inch (5 x 1 mm) in size! From such a small but mighty seed a great tree can grow. For the past two centuries, the Giant Sequoia trees have been cultivated from seed to grow in other parts of the world wherever the growing conditions are suitable. As a result of this effort, there are Giant Sequoia trees successfully growing in the United Kingdom, Canada, France, Australia, New Zealand, Poland, Denmark, Germany, Serbia, and the Czech Republic. • When the Giant Sequoia was first introduced to Great Britain in 1853 it began to be called *Wellingtonia gigantea*. It was so named to honor the recently deceased Duke of Wellington. However, there was already a plant named *Wellingtonia*, so it could not be a replacement scientific name. But *Wellingtonia gigantea* has been legitimately recognized as a synonym and another of its common names in Great Britain. • In California's Sequoia National Park stands a Giant Sequoia named the General Sherman Tree, which is the largest tree in the world by volume. The second largest is also in the same park; its name is the General Grant Tree.

No. 410
Shorea faguetiana 🗡️ 🍴
Yellow Meranti Tree
Bangkirai Guruk | Damar Hitam | Damar Hitam Siput | Gelbes Seraya | Gele Seraya | Gul Seraya | Kalo | Karambuku Lahung | Kunyit | Lun Gajah | Lun Kuning | Lun Merat | Lun Siput | Menara | Meranti Damar Hitam | Meranti Kelim | Meranti Kuning | Meranti Telepok | Paramuku | Selangan Kacha | Selangan Kuning | Seraya Amarilla | Seraya Gialla | Seraya Jaune | Seraya Kuning | Seraya Kuning Siput | Ulu Tupai | Yellow Meranti | Yellow Seraya

📷 **POTENTIAL MAXIMUM HEIGHT**
331 feet [101 meters]

✳️ **SYMBOLIC MEANINGS**
Tower; Towering above.

🌼 **POSSIBLE POWERS**
Beauty; Confidence; Create oxygen.

🍀 **FOLKLORE AND FACTS**
The world's tallest tropical flowering tree, the evergreen *Shorea faguetiana* Yellow Meranti Tree can be found growing in Tawu Hills National Park, in Borneo. Unfortunately, it is also highly endangered and threatened with the very real possibility of extinction in Borneo, the Malay Peninsula, and Thailand. • Resin drippings from the upper branches of the Yellow Meranti Tree resemble dark icicles. The resin is used in some varnishes. • The seeds are rich with oils that can substitute for cocoa butter in cosmetics as well as in cooking. • *Shorea faguetiana* wood is a choice alternative to Teak for use in manufacturing outdoor furniture. • The tallest tropical tree in the entire world is a Yellow Meranti Tree named Menara. In comparison, Menara is 16 feet (5 m) taller than London's Big Ben. It is also 26 feet (8 m) taller than the Statue of Liberty.

No. 411
Sida fallax 🗡️ 🌿
Yellow Ilima Tree
Ilima

📷 **POTENTIAL MAXIMUM HEIGHT**
10 feet [3 meters]

✳️ **SYMBOLIC MEANING**
Love.

🌼 **POSSIBLE POWERS**
Create oxygen; Love magic.

🍀 **FOLKLORE AND FACTS**
The evergreen *Sida fallax* Yellow Ilima Tree has small, pretty, yellow flowers that resemble the Hibiscus flower. At one time, the flowers were used to make beautiful leis that were only worn by royalty because when completed, they would resemble the yellow-feathered lei that only chiefs could wear. That has changed, and since then, the pretty yellow flower leis have become very popular.

No. 412
Simmondsia chinensis 🗡️ 🌿
Jojoba
Coffeeberry | Dear Nut | Goat Nut | Gray Fox Bush | Hohowi | Jojoba Bean | Pignut | Quinine Nut | Wild Hazel

📷 **POTENTIAL MAXIMUM HEIGHT**
19 feet [6 meters]

✳️ **SYMBOLIC MEANING**
Soothe.

🌼 **POSSIBLE POWERS**
Cleansing; Conditioning; Create oxygen; Healing; Moisturizing; Smoothing; Softening; Soothing.

🍀 **FOLKLORE AND FACTS**
The deciduous *Simmondsia chinensis* Jojoba can be trained and pruned to be a small ornamental tree. • Of all the seed oils, it is believed that the oil extracted from the Jojoba seed is the closest to human sebum that nature can provide. • Jojoba oil is very often used to condition dry hair and dry skin. • Scientific study has determined that Jojoba oil is rare in that it is more similar to whale oil than it is to vegetable oil.

No. 413
Sophora chrysophylla ☠️ 🗡️ 🌿
Māmane Tree
Mamani

📷 **POTENTIAL MAXIMUM HEIGHT**
50 feet [15 meters]

✳️ **SYMBOLIC MEANING**
Gold leaf.

🌼 **POSSIBLE POWERS**
Authority; Create oxygen; Ward off evil.

🍀 **FOLKLORE AND FACTS**
The brightly yellow-flowering, evergreen *Sophora chrysophylla* Māmane Tree can be found on every Hawaiian Island except Kahoʻolawe and Niʻihau. • Māmane Tree wood is hard, durable, and was the main source of building

S

materials for constructing houses. The wood was also used to make digging sticks, spears, sled runners, scrapers, adze handles, and fencing posts, as well as for firewood. • A piece of Māmane Tree wood wrapped in a special handwoven dark plant fiber fabric called kapa cloth, which was held overhead to symbolize authority, was religiously used by Hawaiian high priests to ward off evil.

No. 414
Sorbus americana 💀 🗡️ 🍴 ⚘

American Mountain Ash
American Mountain-Ash | Rowan

◉ POTENTIAL MAXIMUM HEIGHT
30 feet [9 meters]

✳ SYMBOLIC MEANINGS
Prudence; With me you are safe.

❀ POSSIBLE POWERS
Create oxygen; Healing; Love; Prosperity; Protection.

❦ FOLKLORE AND FACTS
The deciduous *Sorbus americana* American Mountain Ash berries are a favorite food of the birds. But, after the first full winter freeze they can be eaten raw by humans, although they are better enjoyed when used as a filling in a pie.

No. 415
Sorbus aucuparia 💀 🗡️ 🍴 ⚘ 🌰

European Rowan Tree
Rowan

◉ POTENTIAL MAXIMUM HEIGHT
49 feet [15 meters]

✳ SYMBOLIC MEANINGS
Balance; Connection; Courage; Harmony; Mystery; Prudence; Transformation; With me you are safe.

❀ POSSIBLE POWERS
Abundance; Communication with the spirit world; Create oxygen; Defiance; Determination; Divination; Divining metals; Fends off malicious fairy magic; Fends off malicious witchcraft; Fertility; Fire element; Healing; Inner strength; Intuition; Love; Lucky; Masculine energy; Power; Prosperity; Protection; Psychic power; Resilience; Strength when facing adversity; Success; Sun; Visions; Wards off evil or sorcery; Wisdom.

❦ FOLKLORE AND FACTS
The deciduous *Sorbus aucuparia* European Rowan is the tree of the Queen of the Fairies. • The European Rowan is closely associated with the spirit world, offering its protection to anyone journeying there. • European Rowan wood is the traditional wood of choice to use for carving a set of divination runes. • A magic wand made from European Rowan wood can bring about success when used for divination, healing, and aiding psychic power. • To the ancient Celts, the European Rowan Tree is believed to be the most powerful of all trees and is the Tree of Life; any that grow near a stone circle will be the most potent of all.
• Carry European Rowan wood to increase psychic powers.
• It is believed that European Rowan is sacred to Thor, Norse god of lightning, and that lightning will only rarely ever strike it. • An effective divining rod can be made using a forked European Rowan branch. • In Europe, for hundreds of years protective crosses have been made from European Rowan twigs that have been tied together with red thread and then carried. • European Rowan Trees growing near a house can often be found with branches pinned to grow over doorways in order to ward off evil and sorcery from entering the dwelling. • On the day of the winter solstice and again on the summer solstice, branches of European Rowan were often placed across the door and window lintels to bring good fortune to the home. • A European Rowan Tree grows in most of the oldest Welsh churchyards as a defense against evil spirits. • The Druids planted circles of European Rowan around their encampments to offer protection against the dark powers that threatened all within them. • During the winter solstice, the sparkly frost on the clustered branches of the European Rowan tree can sometimes give the illusion of twinkling stars.
• The berries of the European Rowan tree are plentiful and edible once they have been frozen in the first frost, then cooked. European Rowan berries are used to make jellies, jams, syrup, chutney, wine, liqueur, and tea.

No. 416

Sorbus domestica

Service Tree

Sorb | Sorb Tree | True Service Tree | Whitty Pear

POTENTIAL MAXIMUM HEIGHT

65 feet [20 meters]

SYMBOLIC MEANINGS

Harmony; Prudence.

POSSIBLE POWERS

Create oxygen; Healing; Love; Prosperity.

FOLKLORE AND FACTS

The fruit of the long-living deciduous *Sorbus domestica* Service Tree resembles an apple, but as it is extremely tart with a somewhat grainy pulp, it tastes nothing like one. The fruit is edible, but more pleasant to eat when it becomes a bit overripe. Then it can be used to make jam, juiced to make a fruit cider beverage, or distilled into brandy. • Plato used the metaphor of a halved Service Tree fruit to explain the halving of the original humans by Zeus, originating the concept of "twin flames," who Plato claimed originally had four arms, four legs, two faces on one head, and two separate sets of genitalia. • Service Trees can live up to four hundred years.

No. 417

Spondias purpurea

Jocote Tree

Hog Plum | Purple Mombin | Red Mombin | Sineguela

POTENTIAL MAXIMUM HEIGHT

82 feet [25 meters]

SYMBOLIC MEANINGS

Privation; Sour fruit.

POSSIBLE POWERS

Adhesion; Create oxygen; Healing.

FOLKLORE AND FACTS

The evergreen *Spondias purpurea* Jocote Tree fruit is edible raw and is high in vitamin C when it is fully ripe and soft. The fruit will ripen to a red color, be very sweet, and taste like a cross between the Plum and Mango. • Jocote Tree pulp can be mashed and used in beverages and cocktails, as well as cooked down to make a syrup that is enjoyed as a topping for ice cream. Boiled fruits can also be dried for later use in dessert recipes and curries. Underripe fruits are very tart and can be pickled along with the flower buds or made into spicy sauces. The young leaves can be cooked and eaten as a leafy vegetable. • Jocote sap can sometimes be used as a type of glue.

No. 418

Staphylea pinnata

European Bladdernut Tree

Bladder Nut Tree | Herball | Jonjoli

POTENTIAL MAXIMUM HEIGHT

15 feet [5 meters]

SYMBOLIC MEANINGS

Amusement; Frivolity.

POSSIBLE POWERS

Chase away demons; Create oxygen; Healing; Prayer.

FOLKLORE AND FACTS

The deciduous *Staphylea pinnata* Bladdernut Tree produces extremely pretty, white, bell-shaped drooping flower panicles that have five to fifteen flowers each. After flowering, they develop into attractive, papery, bladder-like, puffed egg-shaped seed pods. The seeds within have a distinctive cut-nose end. The pistachio-tasting seeds are edible. Unfortunately, the flower nectar is toxic to honeybees. • In archaeological sites located in South Moravia and Italy, loose Bladdernut seeds that were punched out to form beads have been discovered. In other ancient European archaeological sites, these types of seeds have also been discovered strung on wires to form bracelets or necklaces. Some of this jewelry includes other beads, such as those fashioned from amber. In all cases, they appear to have been adornments worn in the grave. • In Poland, Bladdernut seeds have been found included in rosaries.

No. 419

Strychnos nux-vomica ☠ ⚗

Strychnine Tree

Kuchla | Nux Vomica | Poison Fruit | Quaker Buttons | Semen Strychnos

◉ POTENTIAL MAXIMUM HEIGHT

82 feet [25 meters]

✳ SYMBOLIC MEANING

Poisonous nut.

✾ POSSIBLE POWERS

Create oxygen; Death;
Rodent poison.

❦ FOLKLORE AND FACTS

The deciduous *Strychnos
nux-vomica* Strychnine Tree is poisonous,
even though monkeys and birds are known to eat the large
apple-shaped fruit. • The disk-shaped seeds within the fruit
are not a nut. The seeds contain strychnine and are intensely
poisonous. They have been used to produce a deadly
arrow-tip poison. • Simply breathing around the tree can be
poisonous because the fruit will fall, then rot under the tree
to expose the seeds that can dry out to a dusty powder.

No. 420

Styphnolobium japonicum ☠ ⚗ ❧

Pagoda Tree

Chinese Scholar Tree | Japanese Pagoda Tree | Zuihuai

◉ POTENTIAL MAXIMUM HEIGHT

100 feet [30 meters]

✳ SYMBOLIC MEANING

Scholarly.

✾ POSSIBLE POWERS

Create oxygen; Education; Studiousness.

❦ FOLKLORE AND FACTS

The flowers and leaves of the evergreen *Styphnolobium
japonicum* Pagoda Tree are one of the fifty essential herbs
used in traditional Chinese medicine. • Since Emperor
Chongzhen, the last emperor of the Chinese Ming dynasty,
hanged himself from a Pagoda Tree in 1644, the tree
became known as the Guilty Chinese Scholar Tree. The
tree itself is now a Chinese national landmark and tourist
attraction in Jingshan Park, located in Beijing. It has been
replaced many times since its day of infamy. And yet the
current Pagoda Tree is already over 150 years old. • Well

known as one of the original Old Lions, a Pagoda Tree that
is still standing was planted in Kew Gardens in 1762. This
tree was the first of its species in England. • The name
"pagoda" might have been originally inspired because they
were often planted around Buddhist temples. • A yellow
and a grey vegetable dye can be made from its bark
and leaves.

No. 421

Styrax benzoin ☠ ⚗

Gum Benjamin Tree

Ben | Benjamen | Benzoin | Gum Benjamin | Gum Benzoin | Kemenyan | Loban | Onycha |
Siam Benzoin | Siamese Benzoin | Sumatra | Storax

◉ POTENTIAL MAXIMUM HEIGHT

82 feet [25 meters]

✳ SYMBOLIC MEANINGS

Good luck; Protection.

✾ POSSIBLE POWERS

Abundance;
Advancement;
Aphrodisiac; Astral
travel; Attract love;
Binding; Building;
Business transactions;
Calming anger; Caution;
Cleverness; Communication; Conscious will;
Create oxygen; Creativity; Death; Energy; Enhances
concentration; Faith; Friendship; Growth; Healing;
History; Illumination; Incense; Initiation; Intelligence; Joy;
Knowledge; Leadership; Learning; Life; Light; Limitations;
Manifestation of spirits; Memory; Natural power; Obstacles;
Perfumery; Promote generosity; Prosperity; Protect the
flying spirit during astral travel; Provides focus; Prudence;
Purification; Relaxing irritability and stress; Relief from
depression; Relief from resentment; Relieve sexual fears;
Science; Self-preservation; Shape-shifting; Sound judgment;
Success; Thievery; Time; Travel; Wisdom.

❦ FOLKLORE AND FACTS

The aromatic evergreen *Styrax benzoin* Gum Benjamin
Tree is cultivated in parts of Asia for its resin, which was
once used in the ancient Egyptian mummification process.
The resin is also known as *sambrami*, *loban*, or benzoin
resin. It is collected after piercing the bark to allow the
sap to accumulate. • The Gum Benjamin Tree resin is used
in some cosmetics and is also used as a stabilizing fixative
in perfumery. It is a vital ingredient in incense that is
commonly burned in Asia. • *Styrax benzoin* essential oil is
helpful in aromatherapy in lifting depression and helping

with relaxation. • If burned on charcoal, *Styrax benzoin* could bring peace and good luck. • The combined scents of Cinnamon, basil, and benzoin incense or essential oils could attract customers to a place of business.

No. 422
Swietenia mahagoni ☠ ✇ ♣

West Indies Mahogany Tree
American Mahogany | Cuban Mahogany | Mahogany | Small-leaved Mahogany

◉ POTENTIAL MAXIMUM HEIGHT
75 feet [23 meters]

✴ SYMBOLIC MEANINGS
Beauty; Strength.

✿ POSSIBLE POWERS
Beauty; Construction; Create oxygen; Sound resonance; Strength.

✷ FOLKLORE AND FACTS
The deciduous *Swietenia mahagoni* West Indies Mahogany Tree is classified as a threatened tree and protected by law in Florida. • A Mahogany wood cross with the year 1514 carved into it was found in a cathedral in tropical Santo Domingo. That church is now considered the oldest church in the West Indies. The cross was placed as a blessing at the commencement of its construction. • By the eighteenth century in Europe, Mahogany was the primary material used in shipbuilding due to its ability to resist gunshots. • Mahogany has also been a favorite for use in fine cabinetry. Its favor rose to such a high degree that Mahogany wood was considered to be a vital material in eighteenth-century British fine furniture during the Age of Mahogany. From then onward, Mahogany was favored for a vast array of uses, which included the manufacture of delicate scientific instruments and sturdy protective cases for such devices as microscopes. • Mahogany wood is used to construct the striking bars of the marimba.

No. 423
Syringa vulgaris ✇ ♣

Lilac Tree
Common Lilac | Field Lilac | French Lilac | Lilak | Nila | Nilak | Paschalia

◉ POTENTIAL MAXIMUM HEIGHT
16 feet [5 meters]

✴ SYMBOLIC MEANINGS
Disappointment; Do you still love me? First emotion of love; Fraternal love or sympathy; Humility; Love; Love's first emotions; Memory; Remember me; Reminder of young love; Youthful innocence.

✿ COLOR MEANINGS
Pink: Acceptance; Youth.
Purple: First emotions of love; First love; Infatuation; Obsession.
White: Candor; Children; First dream of love; Youth; Youthful innocence; Youthful looks.

✿ POSSIBLE POWERS
Create oxygen; Exorcism; Feminine energy; Protection; Purification; Venus; Water element.

✷ FOLKLORE AND FACTS
In New England, the small deciduous *Syringa vulgaris* Lilac Tree was originally planted to fend off evil from properties. • Fresh Lilac flowers can help clear out a haunted house of ghosts and haunted energies. • Lilac wood is feminine and ruled by Venus, so it is associated with love, beauty, balance, and harmony in all things. • A well-charged Lilac-wood magic wand will do a fine job of driving away evil and unwanted lurking ghosts from a home.

No. 424
Syzygium aromaticum ✇ ❶ ☘ ♣

Clove Tree
Cengkih

◉ POTENTIAL MAXIMUM HEIGHT
60 feet [18 meters]

✴ SYMBOLIC MEANINGS
Dignity; Lasting friendship; Love; Love spells; Money; Restraint.

S

Abundance; Advancement; Aphrodisiac; Conscious will; Create oxygen; Energy; Exorcism; Fire element; Friendship; Growth; Healing; Incense; Joy; Jupiter; Leadership; Legal issues; Life; Light; Love; Masculine energy; Mental clarity; Money; Natural power; Protection; Purification; Success.

FOLKLORE AND FACTS

The seventeenth-century trade wars between European nations and the Maluku Islands of Indonesia inspired the planting of the deciduous *Syzygium aromaticum* Clove Tree wherever in the world it would grow. • A Clove is the edible dried flower bud of the *Syzygium aromaticum* tree. Clove is used as a fragrant culinary seasoning in cooking with meats, curries, and fruits as well as in baking in the cuisines of India, East Asia, Africa, the Middle East, Peru, the Mediterranean, and North America. A little bit of the intensely flavored and scented Clove goes a long way. • Worn or carried tucked in a pocket, the magical properties and fragrance of a whole Clove will attract the opposite sex as well as comfort someone who has suffered an emotional loss and is bereaved. • If Clove is burned as incense, it will stop people gossiping, attract riches, drive away hostility, turn away negative energies, and produce positive spiritual energy. All the while it will also purify wherever its fragrance goes. • Clove essential oil mixed in a spray bottle of distilled water can make a good cleaner for the home when there is illness. • A time-honored home remedy found in the spice cabinet is a whole Clove to chew on to offer some relief from the pain of a toothache. • During the winter holiday celebrations, the aromatherapy of the warm, spicy fragrance of essential Clove oil can bring the nature of the holidays into the home. • Completely cover a Sweet Orange by puncturing the peel with whole Cloves and allow it to dry to create a fragrant good luck charm that is also protective against illness. • Stud a red wax candle with whole Cloves while imagining the gossip that you believe might be around you. Burn the candle for the willpower, strength, and energy to protect yourself from gossip's damage. • In ancient Rome, Cloves were more valuable than gold.

No. 425

Syzygium jambos 🍴 🌱 🌰

Rose Apple Tree

Chom Pu | Cloud Apple | Malabar Plum | The Golden Fruit of Immortality

POTENTIAL MAXIMUM HEIGHT

26 feet [8 meters]

SYMBOLIC MEANING

The Golden Fruit of Immortality.

POSSIBLE POWERS

Calmness; Create oxygen; Immortality; No aggression; No combat; Peace of mind; Peacefulness.

FOLKLORE AND FACTS

Looking so much like a Guava, the fruit of the deciduous *Syzygium jambos* Rose Apple Tree is very often mistaken for one. There the similarity stops, as the Rose Apple fruit contains one or two seeds within a somewhat hollow cavity of the fruit, while the Guava snugly holds dozens of them in its pulp. • A ripe Rose Apple fruit is often determined by shaking it. When you hear a rattle, you know it is ripe enough to eat its fragrant pulp raw or to use as an ingredient in Chinese cuisine. • It is believed that the Rose Apple is the Golden Fruit of Immortality and that the young Buddha received enlightenment after meditating under the tree while he was still a young prince. • The Rose Apple flowers are fanciful tasseled tufts, while the blossom end of the fruit looks like a crown.

No. 426
Taiwania cryptomerioides 🌿🌱

Coffin Tree
Formosan Redwood | Taiwania

🌏 **POTENTIAL MAXIMUM HEIGHT**
300 feet [91 meters]

✷ **SYMBOLIC MEANING**
Hidden parts.

🌀 **POSSIBLE POWERS**
Air element; Ancient Earth; Awakening; Create oxygen; Masculine energy; Protection; Spiritual consciousness; Spirituality; Spiritual life; Spiritual love; Survival.

🜂 **FOLKLORE AND FACTS**
The endangered evergreen conifer *Taiwania cryptomerioides* Coffin Tree is one of the largest trees in all of Asia. • In the past, the fragrant spicy scented wood was a favorite for the construction of coffins and temples.

No. 427
Tamarindus indica 🌿🍯🌱

Tamarind Tree
Ma-Kham | Tamarandi | Tambran

🌏 **POTENTIAL MAXIMUM HEIGHT**
60 feet [18 meters]

✷ **SYMBOLIC MEANINGS**
Love; Romance; Sex.

🌀 **POSSIBLE POWERS**
Attract negative energy; Bad luck; Create oxygen; Feminine energy; Ghosts; Healing; Love; Protection; Saturn; Sex magic; Water element.

🜂 **FOLKLORE AND FACTS**
Explorer Marco Polo referenced the evergreen *Tamarindus indica* Tamarind Tree in his writings. • The pulp of a

ripe Tamarind fruit is edible, tart, and becomes sweeter as it ripens. It has a wide variety of uses after it has been processed into a paste. For example, it is used in chutneys and sauces, added as a savory component in meat dishes, made into sweets, and added as a flavoring in baked goods, as well as being transformed into beverages, stews, and soups. • Make, then carry a pink and red sachet of Tamarind seeds to attract romantic love. • Hindu legend tells that the Tamarind Tree symbolizes the wife of the creator, Brahma. • Tamarind was believed to attract ghosts. • Some people believe that a house should never be built anywhere near a Tamarind Tree. This is because they believe ghosts congregate around the tree, and the tree also pulls negative energy and evil spirits towards it. • Tamarind wood is used to make common useful household objects such as mortars and pestles, but also for artistically carving small boxes all the way to large cabinets. • The Tamarind fruit can also be used as a metal polish for brass, copper, and bronze.

No. 428
Tamarix aphylla 🌿🌱🌰🌱

Athel Tamarisk
Athel Pine | Athel Tree | Messenger of Yama | Salt Cedar | Tamarisk | Tree of Yama | Yamadruma

🌏 **POTENTIAL MAXIMUM HEIGHT**
60 feet [18 meters]

✷ **SYMBOLIC MEANING**
Crime.

🌀 **POSSIBLE POWERS**
Attract honeybees; Create oxygen; Exorcism; Feminine energy; Funerals; Protection; Saturn; Water element.

🜂 **FOLKLORE AND FACTS**
As the largest of the *Tamarix* trees, the evergreen *Tamarix aphylla* Athel Tamarisk is considered to be a deeply rooted invasive species because the profuse flowers attract and provide nectar for their honeybees. • The use of Athel Tamarisk in exorcism rituals to drive away evil and demons dates back to more than four thousand years ago. • In the Bible's Genesis 21:33, it is written that Abraham planted the eshel tree in Beersheda as a memorial to honor God, which is believed by scholars to be the Athel Tamarisk. • In India, the Athel Tamarisk tree is considered to be a funeral tree.

T

No. 429

Tasmannia lanceolata ☠ ✝ ⚕ ↯

Tasmanian Pepper Tree
Mountain Pepper

◉ POTENTIAL MAXIMUM HEIGHT
33 feet [10 meters]

✳ SYMBOLIC MEANING
Dodgy.

✸ POSSIBLE POWERS
Create oxygen; Quickness.

✦ FOLKLORE AND FACTS
The stems of the evergreen *Tasmannia lanceolata* Tasmanian Pepper Tree are a crimson color. • The berries have a sweetly fruity flavor at first, followed by the peppery taste for which it has been used as a bush substitute for any peppering. • Tasmanian Pepper berries are imported into Japan to flavor wasabi. • Tasmanian Pepper has been used by many First Nations Australians as a fish poison.

No. 430

Taxodium distichum ✝ ❀ 🌰

Bald Cypress
Gulf Cypress | Red Cypress | Swamp Cypress | Tidewater Red Cypress | White Cypress |

◉ POTENTIAL MAXIMUM HEIGHT
150 feet [46 meters]

✳ SYMBOLIC MEANINGS
Hope; Immortality.

✸ POSSIBLE POWERS
Ancient Earth; Create oxygen; Deeper meaningfulness; Longevity; Moon; Water element.

✦ FOLKLORE AND FACTS
Knobby "knees" growing up from the roots of the deciduous *Taxodium distichum* Bald Cypress surround the trees, emerging sporadically from the water where the trees grow along the marshes and in the swamps of southern North America, such as the Florida Everglades and Georgia's Okefenokee. • An ancient Bald Cypress that grows in North Carolina along the Black River is estimated to be at least 2,624 years old. Another ancient tree that is growing in High Springs, Florida, is estimated to be over 2,704 years old. • When conditions suit it just right, the iconic, entirely non-parasitic epiphyte Bromeliad known as *Tillandsia usneoides* Spanish Moss might be found draping all over and down from the branches of Bald Cypress.

No. 431

Taxodium mucronatum ✝ ❀ 🌰

Montezuma Cypress
Ahuehuete | Āhuēhuētl | Montezuma Bald Cypress | Sabino

◉ POTENTIAL MAXIMUM HEIGHT
80 feet [24 meters]

✳ SYMBOLIC MEANINGS
Nobility; Old man of the water.

✸ POSSIBLE POWERS
Create oxygen; Girth; Moon; Strength; Water element.

✦ FOLKLORE AND FACTS
The ancient Aztecs generously planted the deciduous *Taxodium mucronatum* Montezuma Cypress along their processional paths and canals. • The Montezuma Cypress is part of the creation story of the ancient Zopotec people who once dwelled in Oaxaca, Mexico. • The tree is commonly found growing along the very edges of riversides, marshes, and springs in Mexico. • Unlike other species of Bald Cypress trees, the Montezuma Cypress only rarely ever grows as tall as other Cypress tree species. Rather than for height, the Montezuma Cypress is known for how stout of a tree it can develop into. El Árbol del Tule, found growing in Oaxaca, Mexico, is widely known to be the stoutest tree in the entire world. It measures 37½ feet (11 m) around! • A Montezuma Cypress wand is for one who is brave, bold, and unafraid to face their own dark nature.

No. 432
Taxus baccata ☠ 🍂 🌰 🍃

English Yew

Common Yew | European Yew | Ewen | Iubhar | Iúr | Ivinenn | Ywen

📷 POTENTIAL MAXIMUM HEIGHT
25 feet [8 meters]

✳ SYMBOLIC MEANINGS
Change; Death; Eternal life; Honor; Illusion; Immortality;
Introspection; Leadership; Longevity; Mortality; Mystery;
Penitence; Power; Rebirth; Regeneration; Reincarnation;
Repentance; Sadness; Sanctity; Silence; Sorrow; Strength;
Victory; Worship.

🌀 POSSIBLE POWERS
Ancient Earth; Cancer-fighting; Create oxygen; Enhance
magical ability; Enhance psychic ability; Feminine energy;
Healing; Induce visions; Introspection; Mortality; Raising
the dead; Reincarnation; Runes; Saturn; Silence; Strength;
Transformation; Victory; Water element; Winter solstice;
Worship.

🍂 FOLKLORE AND FACTS
In medieval times, the evergreen *Taxus baccata* English
Yew was consistently planted in churchyards because it was
believed that the roots would grow down and through the
eyes of the dead so that they would stop seeing into the world
of the living. This was to prevent the dead from trying to
return to the world as ghostly spirits. • A fungus that doesn't
kill the tree but will cause it to develop a hollow trunk makes
it impossible to date some of the oldest trees. Even so, some
English Yew trees have grown to quite enormous diameters,
with some being as much as 13 feet (4 m) around. Using
another mathematical method to calculate a tree's age via its
diameter, a conservative estimate dates some of these trees
to be two thousand years old. One known in the United
Kingdom as the Ashbrittle Yew Tree is estimated to be four
thousand years old.

No. 433
Taxus brevifolia ☠ 🍂 🌰

Pacific Yew

Western Yew | Yŏĭ′-Kō

📷 POTENTIAL MAXIMUM HEIGHT
60 feet [18 meters]

✳ SYMBOLIC MEANINGS
Honor; Illusion; Immortality; Introspection; Leadership;
Longevity; Mortality; Mystery; Penitence; Power;
Repentance; Sadness; Sanctity; Silence; Sorrow; Strength;
Victory; Worship.

🌀 POSSIBLE POWERS
Cancer-fighting; Create oxygen; Feminine energy; Healing;
Introspection; Mortality; Raising the dead; Repentance;
Sadness; Sanctity; Saturn; Silence; Strength; Victory; Water
element; Worship.

🍂 FOLKLORE AND FACTS
The wood of the evergreen *Taxus brevifolia* Pacific Yew
has been a favorite of Native Americans in what is now
called the Pacific Northwest, who favored it for making
canoes, paddles, and bows. • The Pacific Yew is the source of
a drug called taxol or paclitaxel, which is used to treat lung,
ovarian, and breast cancers. • The Pacific Yew was deemed
threatened even before the cancer-fighting drug
was discovered.

No. 434
Tectona grandis 🍂 🌰

Teak Tree

Sagwan Tree | Teca

📷 POTENTIAL MAXIMUM HEIGHT
156 feet [48 meters]

✳ SYMBOLIC MEANING
High-class luxury.

🌀 POSSIBLE POWERS
Create oxygen; Durability;
Insect resistance; Luxuriousness;
Water resistance.

🍂 FOLKLORE AND FACTS
The deciduous and very slow-growing *Tectona grandis* Teak
Tree can live for one hundred years. Teak wood is termite-,
rot-, and water-resistant. It is a long-lasting tree outdoors.
• Teak wood is a preferred hard strong wood for boat
building, wooden boat decks, indoor and outdoor furniture,

as well as flooring and veneer. • Boiling Teak Tree wood shavings produces a red dye that has been used to color Easter eggs.

No. 435
Terminalia anogeissiana 🐮 🌿

Axlewood Tree
Axle Wood | Baajhi | Baklee | Bakli | Buttontree | Chakwa | Chirimanu Dawu | Dhaora | Dhau | Dhaura | Dhavada | Dhavado | Dhavaha | Dhawa | Dhawra | Dhurandhara | Dindiga | Dindiga-Tree | Dohu | Ghattitree | Indian Gum Tree | Indian Sumac | Indravruksha | Korattikkaanjiram | Mazhukkaanjiram | Namai | Njaama | Raam | Shakataaya | Takhian-Nu | Vekkaali | Vella Nava | Vellainakai | Vet-Kali

🌑 POTENTIAL MAXIMUM HEIGHT
118 feet [36 meters]

🌼 SYMBOLIC MEANING
Revolve.

🌀 POSSIBLE POWERS
Anti-aging; Aphrodisiac; Create oxygen; Healing; Snakebite and scorpion sting antidote; Stabilizing; Tan leather.

🜸 FOLKLORE AND FACTS
As one of the most useful trees growing in India, the deciduous *Terminalia anogeissiana* Axlewood Tree's leaves feed the *Antheraea paphia* silk moth which produces wild tussar silk. • The leaves can also be used to make a black dye that is widely used in India. • The trunk of the Axlewood Tree produces a resin that provides Indian gum, or gum-ghatti, which is used, among others, in the inks used for printing calico fabric. • Axlewood bark is useful for tanning light soft leather. • Axlewood flowers are an important source of pollen for bees.

No. 436
Terminalia superba 🐮 🌿

Afara Tree
African Limba Wood | Frake | Korina | Limba | Ofram | Superb Terminalia

🌑 POTENTIAL MAXIMUM HEIGHT
131 feet [40 meters]

🌼 SYMBOLIC MEANING
Risen from the dust.

🌀 POSSIBLE POWERS
Create oxygen; Sound resonance.

🜸 FOLKLORE AND FACTS
The wood of the deciduous *Terminalia superba* Afara Tree is a favorite for manufacturing table tennis paddles and guitars.

No. 437
Theobroma cacao 🐮 🌿 🍴

Cacao Tree
Cacahuatl | Cocoa | Cocoa Tree | Food of the Gods

🌑 POTENTIAL MAXIMUM HEIGHT
25 feet [8 meters]

🌼 SYMBOLIC MEANINGS
Food of the gods; Love; Sensual.

🌀 POSSIBLE POWERS
Aphrodisiac; the Arts; Attract love; Attraction; Awakens creativity; Awakens the inner self; Beauty; Clarifies thoughts; Create oxygen; Develops creativity; Enhances energy; Friendship; Gifts; Harmony; Healing; Joy; Love; Meditation; Opening the heart; Peace; Peacefulness; Pleasures; Sensuality; Vibrancy; Wisdom.

🜸 FOLKLORE AND FACTS
Long before there was an effort to transform the bean seeds found in the pods of the evergreen *Theobroma cacao* Cacao Tree into what is known and loved as chocolate, Cacao beans were used in religious and cultural Maya and Aztec ceremonial rituals. • According to mythology, it was the Maya deity named the Plumed Serpent who gave Cacao to the Maya. The discovery that there was something inside of the Cacao pod that was edible on the Cacao Tree was made by indigenous peoples who lived deep in the tropical rainforests in Central America over two thousand years ago. God bless them for their curiosity. • Processing a Cacao bean requires multiple steps, which include fermentation, roasting, and grinding. • The fatty cocoa butter is extracted and used in cosmetics. • Unsweetened, dried, powdered Cacao is a flavoring known as cocoa powder, which holds the potential for an endless variety of desserts and treats of all kinds, including chocolate baked delicacies, pastries, glossy frostings, puddings, silky mouthwatering confections, sweet beverages, fragrant liqueurs, *and* the comfort of a cup of hot cocoa topped with a slowly melting marshmallow! • In some areas of Mexico, such as the Yucatán, Cacao beans were used as currency until as recently as the late 1800s. • What is known as "white" chocolate contains cocoa butter but no cocoa. • When feeling down and needing a lift, eat some chocolate.

No. 438

Theobroma grandiflorum

Cupuaçu Tree
Copoasu | Cupuassu | Cupuaçú

📷 POTENTIAL MAXIMUM HEIGHT
32 feet [10 meters]

☀ SYMBOLIC MEANING
Food for the gods.

🌀 POSSIBLE POWERS
Create oxygen; Moisturizing.

🌿 FOLKLORE AND FACTS
Although it is difficult to
determine, the fruit of the
tropical evergreen *Theobroma*

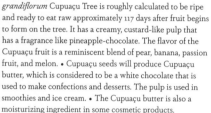

grandiflorum Cupuaçu Tree is roughly calculated to be ripe
and ready to eat raw approximately 117 days after fruit begins
to form on the tree. It has a creamy, custard-like pulp that
has a fragrance like pineapple-chocolate. The flavor of the
Cupuaçu fruit is a reminiscent blend of pear, banana, passion
fruit, and melon. • Cupuaçu seeds will produce Cupuaçu
butter, which is considered to be a white chocolate that is
used to make confections and desserts. The pulp is used in
smoothies and ice cream. • The Cupuaçu butter is also a
moisturizing ingredient in some cosmetic products.

No. 439

Thuja occidentalis ☠ 🌱 🌿 🌰

Arborvitae
American Arborvitae | American Arbor-Vitae | Arbor Vitae | Eastern Arborvitae |
Eastern White Cedar | Northern White Cedar | Swamp Cedar | Thuja | Tree of Life

📷 POTENTIAL MAXIMUM HEIGHT
60 feet [18 meters]

☀ SYMBOLIC MEANINGS
Everlasting friendship; Friendship; Live
for me; True friendship; Unchanging;
Unchanging affection or friendship.

🌀 POSSIBLE POWERS
Banishing; Cleansing; Create oxygen;
Exorcism; Good fortune; Happiness;
Harmony; Healing; Justice; Luck;
Money; Peace; Privacy; Protection;
Psychic power; Purification;
Releasing; Riches.

🌿 FOLKLORE AND FACTS
Interestingly, it seems that
the evergreen conifer, *Thuja
occidentalis* Arborvitae originated
in North America. It later reached
East Asia via its seeds manually
crossing over the Bering Land
Bridge that existed during the Miocene
Age. • Arborvitae is frequently planted in
front of residence windows to provide some privacy. • An
Arborvitae tree named Manidoo-Giizhikens, also known
as the Little Cedar Spirit Tree or the Witch Tree, is a *Thuja
occidentalis*. This tree grows on the edge of an undisclosed
lake in Minnesota and is sacred among the Ojibwe people.
Documentation regarding this tree was recorded in 1731. The
tree is estimated to be close to or over four hundred years
old. The land on which the tree grows was purchased by the
Ojibwe people to protect the tree.

No. 440
Tilia americana 🐝☠️🦷🌳

American Basswood Tree
Americanbasswood | American Basswood | American Linden | Basswood | Carolina Basswood

◉ POTENTIAL MAXIMUM HEIGHT
130 feet [40 meters]

❋ SYMBOLIC MEANING
Wings.

❀ POSSIBLE POWERS
Create oxygen; Healing; Sound resonance.

❦ FOLKLORE AND FACTS
The relatively fast-growing, deciduous *Tilia americana* American Basswood Tree can be expected to live for two hundred years, only producing flowers and seeds between age fifteen and one hundred. • The American Basswood Tree is considered to be one of the most difficult trees to grow from seed since the seeds need to be very freshly planted to successfully germinate. This requires planting the seeds before they dry and develop a hard coating that greatly hinders their germination. • American Basswood wood is not particularly strong, and does not bend well when steamed, but it has other attributes that make it a favorite to use in the manufacture of wooden boxes, smoking pipes, and economy furniture. • American Boxwood wood is also a favorite for the manufacture of some opaque-painted, solid-body, hard-rock-style electric guitars. • The Ojibwe people ate the young tree buds and leaves raw or cooked. They would also tap the sweet sap, then boil it into syrup. • The Iroquois would sometimes use the American Basswood bark to bandage wounds in an emergency.

No. 441
Tilia × europaea 🐝☠️🌳

Linden Tree
Basswood | Common Lime | Common Linden | Lime | Lime Tree | Linnflowers

◉ POTENTIAL MAXIMUM HEIGHT
114 feet [35 meters]

❋ SYMBOLIC MEANINGS
Conjugal affection or love; Love; Luck; Marriage; Matrimony.

❧ COMPONENT MEANING
Sprig: Conjugal love.

❀ POSSIBLE POWERS
Air element; Create oxygen; Fire element; Healing; Immortality; Jupiter; Love; Luck; Masculine energy; Prevents intoxication; Protection; Sleep; Sun; Venus.

❦ FOLKLORE AND FACTS
A magic wand fashioned from the deciduous *Tilia × europaea* Linden Tree wood is very strongly connected to medicine, healing, and justice. Properly charged for a useful service, a Linden-wood wand is a positive magical wand full of light that is perfectly suited for white magic. • It is believed that one can prevent intoxication by having a few Linden leaves in the pocket. • Effective good luck charms can be carved from Linden wood.

No. 443
Toxicodendron vernix ☠ ⬚ 🎍

Poison Sumac Tree
Swamp-sumac | Thunderwood

🔲 **POTENTIAL MAXIMUM HEIGHT**
25 feet [8 meters]

✹ **SYMBOLIC MEANING**
Poison varnish.

🌀 **POSSIBLE POWERS**
Create oxygen; Painful rash.

🜨 **FOLKLORE AND FACTS**
The highly poisonous *Toxicodendron vernix* Poison Sumac Tree will leave a terrible burning, itching rash from simply brushing past it. • Every part of the tree is poisonous, even after the tree has died. If the plant is burned, the smoke is so highly toxic that even just inhaling it can be fatal.

No. 442
Torreya taxifolia ☠ ⬚

Florida Torreya Tree
Florida Nutmeg | Foetid Yew | Gopher Wood | Mountain Yew | Polecat Wood | Savin | Stinking Cedar | Stinking Yew | Yew-leaved Torreya

🔲 **POTENTIAL MAXIMUM HEIGHT**
40 feet [12 meters]

✹ **SYMBOLIC MEANING**
Stinky.

🌀 **POSSIBLE POWERS**
Ancient Earth; Create oxygen; Tenaciousness.

🜨 **FOLKLORE AND FACTS**
The rarest conifer in the world is the evergreen *Torreya taxifolia* Florida Torreya Tree. Primarily due to a rare fungus that persistently killed off the mature trees, the Florida Torreya Tree has been on the critically endangered list since 1998. • When the tree is bruised or burnt, it emits a peculiar odor which inspired the common name of Stinking Cedar. • Although Florida Torreya has not been harvested since the 1950s, prior to that time, one of the insect-resistant wood's common uses was in building fences. Those fences were still solid sixty years later. Another use was as fuel to power riverboats traveling on Florida's Apalachicola River.

No. 444
Tsuga canadensis ⬚ 🎍 🌰

Eastern Hemlock Tree

🔲 **POTENTIAL MAXIMUM HEIGHT**
175 feet [53 meters]

✹ **SYMBOLIC MEANINGS**
Heat; Warmth.

🌀 **POSSIBLE POWERS**
Air element; Awakening; Create oxygen; Dreaming; Enlightenment; Eternal life; Fertility; Harmony; Immortality; Light; Magic; Masculine energy; Regeneration; Resurrection; Spiritual consciousness; Spirituality; Tan leather; Warmth.

🜨 **FOLKLORE AND FACTS**
No part of the evergreen *Tsuga canadensis* Eastern Hemlock Tree is poisonous. There are specimens of the slow-growing Eastern Hemlock Tree that are nearly one thousand years old. • Its bark has been used for tanning leather. • A wand fashioned from Eastern Hemlock wood is best used in the hands of a quick-thinking practitioner.

T

No. 445

Ulmus americana 🪴🌳🌰

American Elm
Water Elm | White Elm

🔘 **POTENTIAL MAXIMUM HEIGHT**
100 feet [30 meters]

✹ **SYMBOLIC MEANING**
Clear vision.

🌀 **POSSIBLE POWERS**
Attract love; Balance the mind; Bring order to chaos;
Courage; Create oxygen; Divination; Divine feminine;
Dreams; Earth; Earth goddesses; Feminine energy; Fertility;
Friendship; Liberation; Love; Mother; Protects the loving
heart; Romantic love; Platonic love; Prophecy; Saturn;
Solutions to difficult situations; the Underworld.

📖 **FOLKLORE AND FACTS**
When the deciduous *Ulmus americana* American Elm was
catastrophically infected by a fungus known as Dutch Elm
Disease, one hundred thousand trees died, at the very least.
Trees in areas that were not affected managed to survive and
have the capacity to live for several hundred years. • During
the nineteenth century it was common to plant the American
Elm along streets and in city parks. Those along streets grew
quickly to create gorgeous wide-spreading bowers overhead.
However, because the American Elm is not a natural
grove-producing tree, their close proximity to each other
created an unnatural situation which made them susceptible
to the devastating infectious fungus. Had it not been for the
American Elm's wind dispersed seeds, which carried seeds to
grow trees in more open areas, the species could have been
completely wiped out. • The wood of the American Elm
tree has been used for boxes, barrels, baskets, caskets, and
furniture, as well as for fuel. • An Elm wand is believed to
have the power to stabilize and ground a magic spell.

No. 446

Ulmus glabra 🪴🌳🌰

Wych Elm
Scotch Elm | Scots Elm

🔘 **POTENTIAL MAXIMUM HEIGHT**
25 feet [8 meters]

✹ **SYMBOLIC MEANING**
Tree of Justice.

🌀 **POSSIBLE POWERS**
Attract love; Balance
the mind; Bring order to
chaos; Courage; Create
oxygen; Divination;
Divine feminine; Dreams;
Feminine energy; Fertility;
Friendship; Liberation;
Love; Protects the
loving heart; Platonic love;
Prophecy; Romantic love;
Saturn; Solutions to difficult
situations; the Underworld.

📖 **FOLKLORE AND FACTS**
Having grown abundantly in Scotland, the deciduous
and very commonly growing *Ulmus glabra* Wych Elm
is considered to be the only completely British Elm
tree species. • The wood of the Wych Elm is incredibly
interesting to woodcrafters because of its distinctive grain
and markings. When it is worked, it can sometimes present
an interesting, greenish iridescent sheen.

No. 447

Ulmus parvifolia 🪴🌳🌰

Chinese Elm Tree
Lacebark Elm

🔘 **POTENTIAL MAXIMUM HEIGHT**
59 feet [18 meters]

✹ **SYMBOLIC MEANING**
Harmony.

🌀 **POSSIBLE POWERS**
Attract love; Balance; Calm; Create
oxygen; Inner strength; Intuition; Love;
Peaceful energy; Protection; Sharpen
psychic skills and powers; Wisdom.

U

The wood of the deciduous *Ulmus parvifolia* Chinese Elm Tree is considered the hardest wood of any Elm tree. It is used to make archery bows, tool handles, and baseball bats.
• The mottled trunk bark is likely the most interestingly attractive bark of any tree, with colors of varying greys, tans, and reds.

No. 448

Ulmus procera 💀🏴‍☠️🌳

English Elm Tree

Atinian Elm | Common Elm | Elm | Elven | European Elm | Field Elm | Horse May | Vanishing Elm | Water Elm | White Elm

POTENTIAL MAXIMUM HEIGHT
114 feet [35 meters]

SYMBOLIC MEANINGS
Achievement of a goal; Death; Dignity; Dignity and grace; Life; Patriotism; Rebirth; the Underworld; Victory.

POSSIBLE POWERS
Attract love; Balance the emotions; Coffins; Create oxygen; Energize the mind; Feminine energy; Love; Protection; Rebirth; Saturn; Tune psychic powers; Water element.

FOLKLORE AND FACTS
The deciduous *Ulmus procera* English Elm Tree was among the fast-growing and tallest trees in all of Europe, before the Dutch Elm disease began infecting them in the 1960s.
• English Elm is known to be a favorite tree of elves who diligently guard burial mounds. • Carry bits of English Elm bark or leaves in a pink and red sachet to attract love.
• The English Elm Tree has been associated with the Underworld. • The wood of the English Elm Tree has been used for making baskets as well as coffins.

No. 449

Ulmus rubra 💀🏴‍☠️🍽🌳

Slippery Elm Tree

Gray Elm | Indian Elm | Moose Elm | Red Elm | Soft Elm

POTENTIAL MAXIMUM HEIGHT
65 feet [20 meters]

SYMBOLIC MEANINGS
Independence; Smooth and silky.

POSSIBLE POWERS
Air element; Create oxygen; Feminine energy; Halt gossip; Invisibility; Saturn.

FOLKLORE AND FACTS
Packaged medicinal herbal teas for the treatment of sore throats often contain the deciduous *Ulmus rubra* Slippery Elm Tree bark. • To stop idle gossip, tie knots along a length of yellow thread, then tie the thread around a few rolled Slippery Elm leaves before tossing the small bundle into a fire. • Women who are pregnant or think they might be pregnant should not use Slippery Elm in any form. • There was a time in the past when baseball pitchers would chew Slippery Elm tablets with the intention their saliva would improve their spitballs' curve. • The wooden yoke that supported the Liberty Bell was made from Slippery Elm. • A rainwater powder to sprinkle upon oneself and anything else needing to disappear can supposedly be made by grinding together a mix of magically prescribed equal amounts of dried powdered Slippery Elm, Myrrh, marjoram, poppyseed, and maidenhair fern.

U

No. 450

Umbellularia californica ☠ �]️ ⓞ 🔥

California Bay Laurel
California Bay | California Laurel | Headache Tree | Myrtlewood Tree | Sô-ê'-bâ

🔍 **POTENTIAL MAXIMUM HEIGHT**
175 feet [53 meters]

☀️ **SYMBOLIC MEANINGS**
Agitation; Ambition; Ambitious; Beware; Danger.

🌀 **POSSIBLE POWERS**
Banishing; Create oxygen; Learning who is against you; Power; Power to overcome enemies; Stirring up agitation; Sound resonance.

🜨 **FOLKLORE AND FACTS**
The leaf of the more intensely pungent evergreen *Umbellularia californica* California Bay Laurel is used to flavor soups, stews, and casseroles in the same way as a spicier *Laurus nobilis* Bay Leaf. However, it is the inner pit of the fruit that is sought out, as it will easily split in half, and can be roasted to a dark brown color that will indicate it is ready to be eaten whole or ground into a powder. As a powder, it resembles and somewhat tastes like cocoa powder. It can then be made into a beverage or used in cooking as a flavoring ingredient. • The fine-grained hard California Bay Laurel wood is a known tonewood that is also known as Myrtlewood, and is used to make the backs and the sides of acoustic guitars. • In North Bend, Oregon, coins that were made from California Bay Laurel wooden discs were printed during a banking emergency in 1933 when the only bank in town, the First National, was forced to temporarily close down. The bank printed coins to pay their employees, with the promise of redeeming them as soon as possible, which did occur after a few months. However, many people kept their wooden coins as a keepsake. Those coins are still considered legal tender in North Bend. One full set is preserved in a collection held by the Chase Manhattan Bank in New York City.

No. 451

Ungnadia speciosa ☠ ⓞ

Mexican Buckeye Tree
Ungnadia

🔍 **POTENTIAL MAXIMUM HEIGHT**
30 feet [9 meters]

☀️ **SYMBOLIC MEANING**
Showy.

🌀 **POSSIBLE POWERS**
Create oxygen; Divination; Gambling; Good luck; Money; Wealth.

🜨 **FOLKLORE AND FACTS**
The deciduous *Ungnadia speciosa* Mexican Buckeye Tree is very beautiful when pruned and trained to grow as a flowering ornamental tree. It has gorgeous orchid-like blossoms and is native to Mexico and Texas. The seeds resemble those of other Buckeye trees and are poisonous, but have been strung to be like beads for a necklace as well as played with as marbles.

U

No. 452

Vachellia farnesiana

Sweet Acacia Tree

Huisache | Needle Bush

POTENTIAL MAXIMUM HEIGHT
25 feet [8 meters]

SYMBOLIC MEANINGS
Chaste love; Concealed love;
Decrease of love; Elegance;
Endurance of the soul;
Friendship; Immortality;
Let us forget; Platonic love;
Poetry; Pure and platonic
love; Purity; Resurrection;
Secret love; Sensitiveness.

POSSIBLE POWERS
Abundance; Advancement;
Air element; Ancient Earth;
Architects; Banishing;
Business transactions;
Caution; Cleverness;
Communication; Conscious will; Create oxygen;
Creativity; Divination; Energy; Exorcism; Faith; Feminine
energy; Friendship; Growth; Healing; Illumination; Incense;
Initiation; Intelligence; Joy; Leadership; Learning; Life;
Light; Love; Masculine energy; Memory; Money; Natural
power; Perfumery; Prophetic dreams; Protection; Prudence;
Purification; Repel demons or ghosts; Saturn; Science;
Self-preservation; Sound judgment; Success; Thievery;
Water element; Wisdom.

FOLKLORE AND FACTS
A leafy sprig from the evergreen *Vachellia farnesiana*
Sweet Acacia Tree placed over a bed or worn on a hat will
supposedly ward off evil. • Use Sweet Acacia incense to
consecrate boxes and cabinets where magical ritual tools
are to be stored. • Sweet Acacia has been used in perfumery
for thousands of years. • The Sweet Acacia Tree has been
associated with Egyptian mythology's Tree of Life. Legend
tells that the Sweet Acacia Tree could have been the burning
bush that Moses encountered in Exodus 3:2 of the Bible.
• It is also thought that the Ark of the Tabernacle was
constructed of Sweet Acacia wood. • Jesus Christ's crown of
thorns is thought to have been fashioned from thorny Sweet
Acacia stems. • Sweet Acacia will purify an area of evil and
negativity. • Sweet Acacia wood is sacred in India and the
Middle East. • Sacred ritual fires will burn Sweet Acacia
wood. • Many temples in India are built using Sweet Acacia
wood. • Burn Sweet Acacia wood with Sandalwood to raise

psychic vibrations and increase psychic perception and
reception. • Sweet Acacia bark smoke is believed by some to
have the power to repel ghosts, demons, and all manners of
evil spirits.

No. 453

Vernicia fordii

Tung Tree

China Wood-oil Tree | Kalo Nut Tree | Tóng Tree | Tung Oil Tree | Tungoil Tree

POTENTIAL MAXIMUM HEIGHT
23 feet [7 meters]

SYMBOLIC MEANINGS
Management; Supervision.

POSSIBLE POWERS
Ancient Earth; Create oxygen; Paint and varnish additive;
Preservative; Wood finish.

FOLKLORE AND FACTS
Originally, the
oil extracted
from the seeds
of the beautifully
flowering deciduous
Vernicia fordii Tung Tree
was used in China as fuel
for lamps. But for thousands
of years, it has since been
used as an ingredient in
paints and varnishes, as well
as a wood finishing oil for fine
furniture and other decorative wooden objects

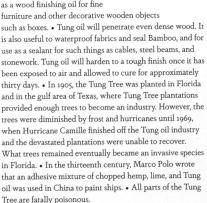

such as boxes. • Tung oil will penetrate even dense wood. It
is also useful to waterproof fabrics and seal Bamboo, and for
use as a sealant for such things as cables, steel beams, and
stonework. Tung oil will harden to a tough finish once it has
been exposed to air and allowed to cure for approximately
thirty days. • In 1905, the Tung Tree was planted in Florida
and in the gulf area of Texas, where Tung Tree plantations
provided enough trees to become an industry. However, the
trees were diminished by frost and hurricanes until 1969,
when Hurricane Camille finished off the Tung oil industry
and the devastated plantations were unable to recover.
What trees remained eventually became an invasive species
in Florida. • In the thirteenth century, Marco Polo wrote
that an adhesive mixture of chopped hemp, lime, and Tung
oil was used in China to paint ships. • All parts of the Tung
Tree are fatally poisonous.

No. 454
Viburnum prunifolium 🕱 🐚 🍴 🌳

Black Haw Tree

American Sloe | Blackhaw | Blackhaw Viburnum | Devil's Shoestring | Stagberry | Stag Bush | Stagbush | Sweet Haw

🌑 **POTENTIAL MAXIMUM HEIGHT**
15 feet [5 meters]

☀ **SYMBOLIC MEANINGS**
Coolness; Retain.

🌼 **POSSIBLE POWERS**
Calm hysterics; Create oxygen; Employment; Exorcism; Fire element; Gambling; Good luck; Luck; Mars; Masculine energy; Power; Protection.

🜨 **FOLKLORE AND FACTS**
Carry or wear a sachet or pouch of the deciduous *Viburnum prunifolium* Black Haw Tree leaves, flowers, or bark to increase luck when job seeking. • Carry or wear a sachet or pouch of Black Haw when speaking to an employer regarding any work-related issue or when requesting a raise. • Carry or wear a sachet or pouch of Black Haw to increase positive results when collecting money that is owed to you. • After the first frost, the sloe berries are edible.

No. 455
Vitellaria paradoxa 🐚 🍴 🌳

Shea Butter Tree

Karité | Shea Tree | Shi Tree | Vitellaria

🌑 **POTENTIAL MAXIMUM HEIGHT**
49 feet [15 meters]

☀ **SYMBOLIC MEANING**
Butter seed.

🌼 **POSSIBLE POWERS**
Condition; Create oxygen; Healing; Lubricate; Smooth; Soften.

🜨 **FOLKLORE AND FACTS**
An edible, thick, fatty, rich emollient or "butter" is extracted from the seed kernel of the deciduous *Vitellaria paradoxa* Shea Butter Tree's plum-like fruit and is used in several African pastries and confections • Even though the smooth fat is sometimes used in cooking, especially baking, this emollient is most often jarred as a specific cosmetic to soften the skin and is also potentially blended with myriad other ingredients intended for other cosmetic products that would not be edible at all. • The Shea Butter Tree blossoms and fully develops only after the tree has been growing for ten to fifteen years.

No. 456
Vitex agnus-castus 🕱 🐚 🌳 🌰 🕯

Chaste Tree

Abraham's Balm | Agnos | Chaste Berry | Chasteberry | Lilac Chastetree | Mediterranean Chaste Tree | Monk's Pepper | Vitex

🌑 **POTENTIAL MAXIMUM HEIGHT**
20 feet [6 meters]

☀ **SYMBOLIC MEANINGS**
Coldness; Indifference; Life without love.

🌼 **POSSIBLE POWERS**
Anaphrodisiac; Aphrodisiac; Attract love; Contrariness; Create oxygen; Suppression.

Unfortunately, apparently a common side effect of consuming an herbal supplement containing the dried fruit and leaves of the deciduous *Vitex agnus-castus* Chaste Tree is hair loss. Then again, it later claimed to be a possible remedy for baldness. The name of the Chaste Tree originated in a folk belief that it suppressed the libido. And *then* it was thought to be an aphrodisiac. Convoluted trickery indeed! That is where the contrariness shows itself so clearly. Perhaps it is best to entirely avoid the Chaste Tree and simply admire it from a safe distance. Why tempt fate? • When it is in bloom with its lovely lilac flowers, it is a pretty tree to look at.

No. 457
Vitex negundo ☠ ☷

Chinese Vitex

Banna | Begunia | Bili nekki | Chinduvaram | Chinese Chaste Tree | Cut Leaf Vitex | Cut-leaf Chastetree | Dabtan | Dangla | Five-leaved Chaste Tree | Horseshoe Vitex | Huáng Jīng | Huang Ping | Indrani | Jommokhyeong | Lagundi | Lekkali | Lingad | Liñgei | Marwan | Maura | Mawa | Mewri | Nagoda | Nalla-vavili | Nika | Nirgudi | Nirgundi | Nirnochchi | Nishinda | Nisinda | Nochchi | Notchi | Posotiya | Samalu | Sambhalu | Sawbhalu | Sephalika | Shamalic | Simali | Sindhuvara | Sumbaloo | Svetasurasa | Swanjan | Tella-vavili | Torbanna | Vavili | Vellai-nochchi | Vrikshaha

POTENTIAL MAXIMUM HEIGHT
9 feet [3 meters]

SYMBOLIC MEANING
Defender.

POSSIBLE POWERS
Create oxygen; Healing; Pest control.

FOLKLORE AND FACTS
The deciduous *Vitex negundo* Chinese Vitex is often used to keep pests away from dried garlic bulbs being kept in warehouse storage. • Chinese Vitex is being studied more intensely as a potential remedy for extreme coughing.

No. 458
Volkameria glabra ☷ ♣

Volkamenia

Bittrblaar | Cat's Whiskers | Ifamu | Mohlokohloko | Motlhokutlhoku | Munukha-tshilongwe | Smooth Tinderwood | Stinkboom | Tontelhout | Truijie-Roer-My-Nie | Uluvethe | Umnukalembiba | Umphehlacwatsi | Umphehlavatsi | Umqaqonga | Umqaqongo | Umqawaqu | Umqwaqwanam | Uphehlecwathi | Uqangazane | Uqangazani | Verbena Tree | Weeping Tree | White Cat's Whiskers | Xinhun'welambeva

POTENTIAL MAXIMUM HEIGHT
39 feet [12 meters]

SYMBOLIC MEANINGS
Dignity; Dignity and grace; May you be happy; Patriotism.

POSSIBLE POWERS
Create oxygen; Love; Protection.

FOLKLORE AND FACTS
There is an unproven, legendary belief that the deciduous *Volkameria glabra* Volkameria can prevent hair from turning white. • The common name of Munukha-tshilongwe is from the South African Venda language and means "smells of cattle dung."

No. 459
Warburgia ugandensis 🌿🍴🌳

Ugandan Greenheart
East African Greenheart | Muthiga | Pepper Bark Tree

🔵 POTENTIAL MAXIMUM HEIGHT
138 feet [42 meters]

✴ SYMBOLIC MEANINGS
Health giving; Wholesome.

🌀 POSSIBLE POWERS
Create oxygen; Healing; Luck.

🍃 FOLKLORE AND FACTS
Early immigrants to Kenya used the leaves of the evergreen *Warburgia ugandensis* Ugandan Greenheart tree to add flavor and a fierce heat to curries before chili plants were introduced to Africa. The bark is also peppery. • The wood of the Ugandan Greenheart tree is very hard and so strong that it is commonly used to make ox yokes for ox-pulled wagons. • Medicinally, it is the bark of the Ugandan Greenheart tree that is the most potent.

No. 460
Warszewiczia coccinea ☠🌿

Wild Poinsettia
Chaconia | Cuetlaxochitl | Pride of Trinidad and Tobago

🔵 POTENTIAL MAXIMUM HEIGHT
30 feet [9 meters]

✴ SYMBOLIC MEANINGS
Celebration; Good cheer; Imperishability of life; Mirth; Purity.

🌀 POSSIBLE POWERS
Aphrodisiac; Attract love; Celebration; Create oxygen; Wishing.

🍃 FOLKLORE AND FACTS
The evergreen *Warszewiczia coccinea* Wild Poinsettia was considered to be a symbol of purity to the ancient Aztecs.

• Botanist Joel Roberts Poinsett was the first us Ambassador to Mexico who recognized something special about the plants. Poinsett brought the first Wild Poinsettia plants to South Carolina in the 1820s. • During the fourteenth through the sixteenth centuries, Wild Poinsettia bracts were used to make a reddish dye. • Because Wild Poinsettia could not be grown in the high altitude of Mexico City, the last ancient Aztec king, Moctezuma II, would have the flowers brought to him by caravan.

No. 461
Washingtonia robusta ☠🌿🍴

Mexican Fan Palm
Abanico | Mexican Washingtonia | Palma Blanca | Palma Colorado | Palma Negra | Palma Real | Skyduster | Zamij Ctam

🔵 POTENTIAL MAXIMUM HEIGHT
100 feet [30 meters]

✴ SYMBOLIC MEANINGS
Eternal life; High; Peace; Triumph; Victory.

🌀 POSSIBLE POWERS
Create oxygen; Longevity.

🍃 FOLKLORE AND FACTS
The evergreen *Washingtonia robusta* Mexican Fan Palm's fronds flutter atop what seems like an impossibly tall, much too skinny trunk, which draw the eyes far upward, attracting attention to the most iconic tree in Los Angeles, California. Their extreme height inspired their common name of Skyduster. Some of the oldest Mexican Fan Palms date back to around 1875. • *Washingtonia robusta* palms can potentially live to be over five hundred years old.

No. 462
Wodyetia bifurcata ☠

Foxtail Palm
Fox Tail Palm Tree | Wodyetia

🔵 POTENTIAL MAXIMUM HEIGHT
50 feet [15 meters]

✴ SYMBOLIC MEANING
Twice divided.

🌀 POSSIBLE POWERS
Create oxygen; Desire to possess.

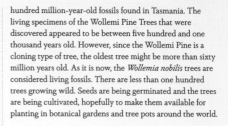

FOLKLORE AND FACTS

The spectacular evergreen *Wodyetia bifurcata* Foxtail Palm's fronds look like the fluffy tail of a fox, which inspired its common name. • The beautiful tall Foxtail Palm was not introduced to the world until 1983 when a First Nations Australian man named Wodyetia brought attention to its special beauty. • As word spread about the loveliness of the Foxtail Palm, the seeds became a commodity on the black market. So much so that the naturally wild trees were illegally stripped of seeds, with poachers actually felling trees just to reach the seeds. This uncontrolled behavior nearly obliterated the natural groves. It has long since become one of the most popularly grown Palm trees in the world. And yet, even as late as 1996, in the Cape Melville National Park where the Foxtail Palm grew naturally, the trees were still a target for unconscionable and highly destructive seed poachers who stopped at nothing to get their hands on the seeds so they could be smuggled to palm tree growers for mutual financial reward. • The seeds of the Foxtail Palm have also been used to fashion bodhi beads.

No. 463
Wollemia nobilis 🌲

Wollemi Pine Tree
Wollemi

POTENTIAL MAXIMUM HEIGHT
131 feet [40 meters]

SYMBOLIC MEANING
Survival.

POSSIBLE POWERS
Ancient Earth; Create oxygen; Longevity; Survival.

FOLKLORE AND FACTS
It was not until September 1994 that a living specimen of the flat-leaved evergreen conifer *Wollemia nobilis* Wollemi Pine Tree was discovered. The Wollemi Pine was previously believed to be extinct, present only in two

hundred million-year-old fossils found in Tasmania. The living specimens of the Wollemi Pine Trees that were discovered appeared to be between five hundred and one thousand years old. However, since the Wollemi Pine is a cloning type of tree, the oldest tree might be more than sixty million years old. As it is now, the *Wollemia nobilis* trees are considered living fossils. There are less than one hundred trees growing wild. Seeds are being germinated and the trees are being cultivated, hopefully to make them available for planting in botanical gardens and tree pots around the world.

No. 464
Xanthoceras sorbifolium 🌱🍴🌳🌿

Yellowhorn Tree
Chinese Flowering Chestnut | Goldenhorn | Shiny Leaf Yellowhorn | Yellowhorn

POTENTIAL MAXIMUM HEIGHT
26 feet [8 meters]

SYMBOLIC MEANING
Good luck.

POSSIBLE POWERS
Create oxygen; Fire element; Luck; Money; Prosperity.

FOLKLORE AND FACTS
The seed of the hardy deciduous *Xanthoceras sorbifolium* Yellowhorn Tree is smaller than the Horse Chestnut. • The showy white flowers that are yellow in the center are abundant and very fragrant when the tree is in full bloom. The flowers transition from creamy-white to greenish petals with orange centers. The seeds, flowers, and leaves of the Yellowhorn Tree are all edible. • Carry a seed in a pocket for luck in encouraging money to go into it.

No. 465
Xanthocercis madagascariensis 🌱🍴

Haraka Tree
Andraidriala | Antendriala | Kilioty | Manaritoloha | Sakoanala | Sandrazy | Somotratsangy | Vavanga | Voankazomeloka

POTENTIAL MAXIMUM HEIGHT
100 feet [30 meters]

SYMBOLIC MEANING
Yellow.

POSSIBLE POWERS
Create oxygen; Provide.

The deciduous *Xanthocercis madagascariensis* Haraka Tree is only found in Northern Madagascar. • The wood is highly valued for making luxury furniture as well as many other things, while the ripe brown berry fruit's pulp is edible and enjoyed locally.

No. 466
Xanthocercis zambesiaca 🪒 🍴

Nyala Tree
Hoenderspoor | Mshatu | Mutshato | Njalaboom | Umhlwati

POTENTIAL MAXIMUM HEIGHT
100 feet [30 meters]

SYMBOLIC MEANING
Thorny fruit.

POSSIBLE POWERS
Beautify; Create oxygen.

FOLKLORE AND FACTS
The evergreen *Xanthocercis zambesiaca* Nyala Tree flowers are small, creamy-white and smell like roses. • The ripe fruit can be eaten fresh, but they are mostly enjoyed by monkeys, baboons, and birds. The fruit grows in grape-like clusters. Each of the berry fruits is tipped with a thorn. • Elephants and giraffes enjoy eating the leaves.

No. 467
Ximenia americana 🍴

Hog Plum
Yellow Mombin | Yellow Plum

POTENTIAL MAXIMUM HEIGHT
32 feet [10 meters]

SYMBOLIC MEANING
Retain.

POSSIBLE POWERS
Create oxygen; Venus;
Water element.

FOLKLORE AND FACTS
The fruit of the evergreen *Ximenia americana* Hog Plum is one of the world's most valued wild foods. • Ripe Hog Plum fruit is juicy and can be eaten raw, but it is more often used to make jam, juice, liqueurs, and a type of beer. The fruit and the flower buds are sometimes pickled in vinegar or used in curries. The seed is large, and its kernel is pressed to produce an oil that is used as a butter substitute in recipes

and as an ingredient in cosmetics. The nuts are purgative and the leaves are toxic unless they are young and have been thoroughly cooked. Even then, they should not be consumed in any large quantity. • Hog Plum flowers smell like lilacs.

No. 468
Xylia xylocarpa 🪒 🍴 🌳

Burma Ironwood
Căm Xe | Jambu | Pyinkado | Sokram

POTENTIAL MAXIMUM HEIGHT
120 feet [37 meters]

SYMBOLIC MEANINGS
Strong; Sturdy.

POSSIBLE POWERS
Create oxygen; Strength.

FOLKLORE AND FACTS
The evergreen *Xylia xylocarpa* Burma Ironwood tree's flowers are bright yellow, making the tree very showy. • The wood of the Burma Ironwood tree was used to make sturdy carts. • The leaves of the Burma Ironwood are used as poultices to help wounded elephants. • The ripe cooked Burma Ironwood seeds are edible.

No. 469
Xylopia aethiopica 🪒 🍴

Ethiopian Pepper Tree
Africa Pepper | African Grains of Selim | Erinje | Erunje | Grains of Selim | Guinea Pepper | Hwentia | Kimba | Moor Pepper | Spice Tree | Uda

POTENTIAL MAXIMUM HEIGHT
100 feet [30 meters]

SYMBOLIC MEANING
Bitter wood.

POSSIBLE POWER
Create oxygen; Purification.

FOLKLORE AND FACTS
During the Middle Ages, the seeds of the fragrant evergreen *Xylopia aethiopica* Ethiopian Pepper Tree were used in Europe as another type of pepper. • In Africa, the fruit is used in water for purification. • The dried aromatic edible seeds of the *Xylopia aethiopica* Ethiopian Pepper Tree are used as a seasoning to flavor food or soups. • In Senegal, the fruit is used to flavor a spiritual coffee drink widely known as café Touba.

No. 470
Xylosma hawaiiense 🌿

Maua Tree
A'e | Hawai'i Brushholly | Xylosma

◉ POTENTIAL MAXIMUM HEIGHT
40 feet [12 meters]

☀ SYMBOLIC MEANINGS
Belongs to Hawaii; Belonging to us; Ours.

❀ POSSIBLE POWERS
Create oxygen; Perfumery; Pounding.

❦ FOLKLORE AND FACTS
The young leaves of the deciduous *Xylosma hawaiiense* Maua Tree are an attractive coppery color before turning green. • When the small clusters of flowers fruit, the ornamental berries are green, then ripen to a reddish purple. • The Maua Tree grows wild on every Hawaiian Island except Kaho'olawe and Ni'ihau. • The Maua Tree wood is used to perfume coconut oil. • The Maua Tree wood is hard and dense. So much so that at one time, early Hawaiians used poi pounders known as *pōhaku ku'i 'ai* that were made from Maua Tree wood.

No. 471
Yucca brevifolia ☠

Joshua Tree
Humwichawa | Hunuvat Chiy'a | Jaeger's Joshua Tree | Palm Tree Yucca | Tree Yucca | Yucca Palm

◉ POTENTIAL MAXIMUM HEIGHT
40 feet [12 meters]

☀ SYMBOLIC MEANINGS
Perseverance; Resilience; Survival; Useful.

❀ POSSIBLE POWERS
Ancient Earth; Beauty; Create oxygen; Resiliency; Tenaciousness; Usefulness.

❦ FOLKLORE AND FACTS
The existence of the evergreen *Yucca brevifolia* Joshua Tree goes back approximately three million years ago. • In all the world, they only grow in Arizona, California, Nevada, and Utah. • Its splaying limbs on the desert landscape have given the Joshua Tree an iconic identity as a resilient, persevering tree. • The deeply-rooted Joshua Tree has long been considered a productive tree to Southwestern Native American tribes. The leaves have been woven into sandals and baskets. Its ripe seeds are eaten raw or roasted. The flower buds can also be eaten. • As pioneers began arriving in the western part of North America, the Joshua Tree's limbs and trunks were used to make corrals for livestock and to make fence posts. The wood was also burned for fuel for cooking and heating. • Miners used Joshua Tree wood to stoke the fires of the steam-powered machines they use to process their excavated ore. • The Joshua Tree does not have growth rings. • It is believed that the Joshua Tree can live approximately 150 years, although it could be longer. • Researchers have surmised that in order for branching to commence development, there needs to be a flowering first, one that has been initiated by a winter freeze. Also, if and when blooming conditions are ever perfect it would have to include a spring rain. Then, long-stalked clusters of greenish-white flowers *may* bloom. When flowering does not occur, a Joshua Tree will continue to grow, but it will tend to look like an upright branchless stalk.

No. 472
Yucca rostrata ☠ 🌿 🍴

Beaked Yucca
Big Bend Yucca

◉ POTENTIAL MAXIMUM HEIGHT
15 feet [5 meters]

☀ SYMBOLIC MEANINGS
New opportunities; Options.

❀ POSSIBLE POWERS
Create oxygen; Loyalty; New opportunities; Protection; Purity.

❦ FOLKLORE AND FACTS
The white flowers of the hardy, very slow-growing evergreen *Yucca rostrata* Beaked Yucca are very showy when the tree is in full bloom. • Since the Beaked Yucca is extremely attractive, it is a choice ornamental tree. • Because of its thorny leaf tips, the Beaked Yucca can be accidentally treacherous when working around the garden. Take care to avoid eye injuries, or consequential sudden injuries to ears.

No. 473

Zanthoxylum piperitum ☠ 🌿 🍴 🍂 🌳

Szechuan Pepper

Chinese Pepper | Chopi | Japanese Pepper | Japanese Pepper Tree | Japanese Prickly-ash | Mala Pepper | Sanshō | Sichuan Pepper

◉ POTENTIAL MAXIMUM HEIGHT
15 feet [5 meters]

✳ SYMBOLIC MEANING
Numbing.

❀ POSSIBLE POWERS
Create oxygen; Fire element; Healing; Mars; Masculine energy; Numbing spiciness.

❦ FOLKLORE AND FACTS
The dried lemony-tasting berry of the deciduous *Zanthoxylum piperitum* Szechuan Pepper tree is a common seasoning in Chinese cuisine, but it is not actually a pepper. • Szechuan Pepper is one of the main ingredients in the Japanese multi-spice blend known as *shichimi togarashi* and can also be found in Chinese five-spice powder. • Szechuan Pepper leaves a tingly sensation in the mouth that can be followed by a sense of numbness. • The Szechuan Pepper has been used in traditional Chinese medicine for many centuries.

No. 474

Zelkova serrata 🌳 🌰

Keyaki Tree

Japanese Elm | Japanese Zelkova | Keyaki | Neutinamu Tree | Tsuki | Zelkova Tree

◉ POTENTIAL MAXIMUM HEIGHT
100 feet [30 meters]

✳ SYMBOLIC MEANINGS
Protector; Thrust.

❀ POSSIBLE POWERS
Ancient Earth; Create oxygen; Longevity; Monument; Protection; Shade; Sound resonance.

❦ FOLKLORE AND FACTS
Since ancient times, the long-living deciduous *Zelkova serrata* Keyaki Tree has been considered a tree of protection for villages, towns, and cities throughout South Korea. • In South Korea, beneath the shade of the Keyaki Tree is considered a gathering place as well as a location for prayerful rituals and ceremonies as offerings to the tree. • There is a living Keyaki Tree in South Korea that is over one thousand years old. • Keyaki wood has often been used to make Japanese taiko drums and finely crafted pieces of heirloom furniture.

No. 475

Ziziphus mauritiana 🌿 🍴 🌳

Indian Jujube Tree

Chinese Date

◉ POTENTIAL MAXIMUM HEIGHT
32 feet [10 meters]

✳ SYMBOLIC MEANING
Bear.

❀ POSSIBLE POWERS
Air element; Calming; Create oxygen; Fertility; Induce sleep; Prosperity; Relax the mind; Sun; Wealth.

❦ FOLKLORE AND FACTS
Crisp and somewhat juicy, the ripe fruit of the evergreen *Ziziphus mauritiana* Indian Jujube Tree is edible, exceptionally high in vitamin C, and resembles an apple with a pit that contains two seeds. The fruit can be eaten raw or stewed, used in beverages, or pickled.

A FOREST

There are extensive forests of magnificent trees reaching for the heavens all around the world. Most of them are relatively inaccessible, to be experienced only by the adventurous few determined to photograph and film them from every possible angle. It is to their credit, as well as their adept skills and tenacity, that we have such colorful, vivid panoramic impressions of these fabulous forests.

On the other hand, there are some extraordinary forests that are relatively easy to access. They can be experienced by hiking, biking, or on horseback along specific, relatively predictable mapped-out directions along the still wild, but familiar forest paths. Several forest trails are paved or planked to make it possible for those in wheelchairs or other personal mobility devices to travel along with relative ease. Other forests can be experienced by car, taking a simple slow drive in one's own vehicle, enjoying the passing scenery by looking out through the car windows, pulling over to stop and take a photo from time to time. One forest can even be explored by kayak!

A forest of one's choosing is dependent on proximity, true. But, once you get near enough to any one of the forests listed below, you won't require a helicopter to get there. Some forests you can discover are worthy of a day trip, and others are worth a well-planned, long-distance journey to get close enough to enter like every other tourist. A visit might be something to tick off your bucket list.

It really doesn't take more than a very short walk and a gazing, contemplative look around us and upward to the sky when we are surrounded by towering trees and soft filtered light.

Within minutes, one may recognize that it is an opportunity to temporarily remove ourselves from our absorbing connection to our phones or other electronics, so we can focus on the sounds of Nature encircling us. We may *choose* to listen, not just *hear*, the tweets of birds perched nearby in the trees. We breathe in the scent of what's discreetly growing and going on around us. And then we may realize that, we, our own selves, are vital components in the pulse of a forest. Our steps send out a vibration. The sounds of our own breathing are magnified to the sensitive ears of the wildlife. We may find a sprig of pine and bring it to our nose to take in its predictable fragrance. No matter how magnificent or mundane, we have connected.

As we breathe, we are expelling the carbon dioxide that the trees are actively taking in, while in turn we are actively taking in the oxygen that the trees generate. This temporary hyper-intimate relationship between ourselves and the trees in a forest clearly illustrates the symbiotic relationship we have with it and with all the trees growing on the planet. Our worries dissipate a little. Maybe entirely. Just wafting away, rising upward into the treetops and out to the sky. We are blessedly connected to the persistent pulse of the living Earth, itself, by way of a forest. Any forest. Every forest. There is sure to be a forest that is accessible to you—*somewhere.*

Amazon Rainforest

LOCATION
Mainly Brazil, but spans throughout South America

GEOGRAPHIC COORDINATES
Longitude 3.4653° S
Latitude 62.2159° W

The largest tropical rainforest in all the world awaits, calling to the inner adventurer in so many people. It is on the bucket list. There are many trail locations and hiking tours for the energetic explorer, as well as days-long paddling excursions for those who want to see the trees from a different perspective. Amazon River cruises are ideal for those who would prefer to just look at whatever they happen to pass by. At any rate, the Amazon Rainforest is the kind of place that calls for the service of an experienced guide before stepping out into any part of the rainforest or heading down the river with paddle in hand. Though true of every forest highlighted in this section, but especially with the Amazon, it is prudent to know where one is going and how to return safely.

Once those details are sorted, there are so many possibilities of exploring the Amazon Rainforest to see first-hand a mere few of the 12,000 species of the 400 *billion* individual trees that compose this tremendously important forest. Palm trees abound. The *Hevea brasiliensis* Rubber Tree and the peculiar *Socratea exorrhiza* Walking Palm, with its unusual stilt-like roots, can also be spotted.

Arashiyama Bamboo Forest

LOCATION
Japan

GEOGRAPHIC COORDINATES
Longitude 35.0093° N
Latitude 135.7788° E

Only thirty minutes northwest from the bustling city center of Kyoto, Japan, two sections of a massive natural Bamboo forest can be found in the Arashiyama district, covering approximately 6 miles (10 km). Magical, surreal, and towering extremely high overhead, this serenely green forest consists of thousands of erect *Phyllostachys edulis* Mōsō Bamboo trees. Mōsō Bamboo is a species of a giant timber Bamboo that can grow up to 92 feet (28 m) overhead. The sound of the thickly dense, swaying, creaking, knocking Bamboo is an acoustic wonderment that has the ability to imbue a one-of-a-kind auditory calm. The unique sounds

of the Arashiyama Bamboo Forest is such that the Japanese government has deemed the forest to be one of the "100 Soundscapes of Japan."

A paved walkway, known as Bamboo Alley, runs through the center of the forest, making it accessible to everyone who is fortunate to visit this special forest. If one walks without stopping, the walk can take approximately one hour. But the stroll can take anywhere from three to four hours instead, if one's pace slows down to fully embrace the experience.

If one is able to find themselves in the forest before the crowd of meandering tourists fills the pathway, one's internal response to the natural music performed by the Arashiyama Bamboo Forest trees can be profound.

Baobab Avenue

LOCATION
Madagascar

GEOGRAPHIC COORDINATES
Longitude 20.2505° S
Latitude 44.4197° E

Looking like it was planted upside down to grow to a large size and to live to be as ancient as three thousand years old is the iconic Baobab tree, the symbol of Madagascar. Referred to as the Reniala or "mother of the forest," Baobab trees were once tucked into dense forests of other trees that covered huge areas of the island. When these areas were cleared for lumber, crop planting, and other such endeavors, the Baobab trees were left standing. Of the eight species of Baobab trees in the world, six of them only grow in Madagascar.

The Baobab tree has large white flowers that bloom at night. During the dry season, it flowers to also produce a fruit that is considered among the most nutritious in the entire world. During the rainy season, due to the spongy nature of its bark, a Baobab tree can store up to 26,000 gallons (98,421 L) of water in its huge trunk, making a fully grown Baobab tree quite drought resistant.

In Morondava, Madagascar, there is a grove of endangered, majestically ancient, tall *Adansonia grandidieri* Giant Baobab trees along a public dirt road that is commonly known as "Baobab Avenue." This picturesque grove of iconic Baobab trees is Madagascar's first protected natural monument. In the late of the day, when the sun is not as hot overhead, tourists can be seen meandering along the road with their cameras pointing in every direction, snapping photographs of the surreal scene surrounding them.

The Black Forest

📍 LOCATION
Germany

✣ GEOGRAPHIC COORDINATES
Longitude 48.2775° N
Latitude 8.1860° E

The Black Forest can be found in the state of Baden-Württemberg, home to the cuckoo clock and located in the southwest corner of Germany. More commonly known in German as Schwarzwald, the Black Forest is full of legends and myths about witches and wizards, fairies and gnomes, and fairy princes and princesses. It is the original and ultimate enchanted forest of fairytales, such as nearly all of those written by the Brothers Grimm, who may have been inspired by the forest's mysterious character. In fact, it is said that the name "Black Forest" was bestowed by the Romans because of the density of conifers that grow in abundance.

The Black Forest has five airports within it, and is extremely accessible via car, train, and bus. Once there, many roads and trails that are the favorites of hikers, bikers, and wintertime's cross-country skiers begin in different parts of the forest. One easily and immensely pleasurable tourist trail can be explored by car year-round. It is known as the Schwarzwaldhocstrasse, or the Black Forest High Road. It is the oldest tourist trail in the Black Forest. It is wisely focused on the panoramic views and the scenery of the northern Black Forest. Another trail in the southern part of the Black Forest is the Schwarzwald Panoramastraße, or the Black Forest Scenic Road, where one can enjoy spectacular views of the wide variety of tree species that are predominant. These include Alder, Ash, Beech, Douglas Fir, Elm, Hazel, Juniper, Larch, Linden, Maple, Oak, Scots Pine, Silver Fir, Spruce, and Walnut. One may also find Apple, Cherry, Peach, and Plum trees.

The Crooked Forest

📍 LOCATION
Poland

✣ GEOGRAPHIC COORDINATES
Longitude 53.2141° N
Latitude 14.4758° E

A small wooden sign on the edge of the Gryfino forest points out which direction to walk 984 feet (300 m) towards Krzywy Las, which is the Polish name for the Crooked Forest. What is intriguing about this particular small forest is

that sometime in the late 1920s or early 1930s, four hundred Pine trees were planted in a grove found in northwestern Poland, in the town of Nowe Czarnowo. All four hundred of these trees face north. They all have a curving ninety-degree bend at the base of their trunks, giving the trees the appearance of fishhooks hovering atop the land. And they all carry the mystery of who, what, why, and how they were bent that way.

Speculation runs rampant! It was once believed that it is the result of a strong wind or a damaging snowstorm. However, there is no evidence of any such thing having occurred. Some believe that they were tugged into that shape by the gravitational pull of the Earth. That theory cannot be proven either. It is also thought that the foresters who planted the trees intentionally bent them for whatever reasons. Some think it was as folly for their amusement, or the trees were intended to be someday used by the foresters to make furniture. Either way, their tree-bending project was apparently abandoned at the start of World War II, leaving us to only speculate on the how or the why.

We can allow ourselves to thoroughly enjoy the whimsical nature of these crooked Pine trees that make for a delightful grove of trees while we ponder the ongoing mystery of their existence.

The Daintree Rainforest

📍 LOCATION
Australia

✣ GEOGRAPHIC COORDINATES
Longitude 16.1700° S
Latitude 145.4185° E

The Daintree Rainforest is located on the northeast coast of Queensland, Australia. It is rightfully listed as a UNESCO World Heritage site. Thought to be at least 135 million years old, it is the oldest tropical rainforest in the world, with one of the most complex ecosystems on Earth.

It is, perhaps, the most fun of anywhere to explore, with its forest boardwalks, high-up aerial skywalks, and even an 82-foot-high (25 m) observation tower providing wide panoramic views of the vast forest! Great care is taken to protect the forest floor by preventing visitors from setting foot upon it. While exploring the flora from one of those unique vantage points, one will likely have an opportunity to view the majestic cassowary birds, as they wander about foraging, drinking, and bathing in the pure forest rainwater.

From all different points of view one can discover that among the forest's many rainforest tree species, there can also be found the treacherous, painful Australian Stinging Tree that must always be avoided, wherever it may be. Another is the rare *Idiospermum australiense* Idiot Fruit or Ribbonwood tree. It dates to over 110 million years old and is considered the most primitive of flowering plants. Since there is no animal or bird that can eat its fruit, gravity is the tree's only means of dispersal. Its discovery in 1970 brought to light how ancient this Australian rainforest really is.

Sequoia National Forest

📍 **LOCATION**
United States

✤ **GEOGRAPHIC COORDINATES**
Longitude 36.0233° N
Latitude 118.4968° W

Located in the Sierra Nevada Mountains, the Sequoia National Forest in California is also known as the Land of the Giants because it contains all the naturally growing groves of *Sequoiadendron giganteum* Giant Sequoia trees in the world. The endangered Giant Sequoia is the most massive tree on all the Earth and is thought to be one of the oldest living plants. Estimating the age of living trees by dating felled trees of similar size, living Giant Sequoia trees are well over 3,000 years old. Due to the destruction of thousands of these trees during three major forest fires between 2020 and 2021, the Giant Sequoia species is critically endangered.

This is also the home of the General Sherman Sequoia, which is one of the largest trees in the world. Several trails lead the way to the gigantic tree from the entrance, including the aptly named General Sherman Trail, a wide paved path that is an easy ½ mile (805 m) long. There are many more trails to explore via footpaths and driving trails, including those that are off-road.

Considering the Sequoia National Forest's location in the Sierra Nevada, it is prudent to specifically keep in mind that during the especially changeable seasons of autumn and spring, the weather is so fickle it can suddenly and quite quickly transition from blissfully idyllic to treacherously deadly without warning.

Sherwood Forest

📍 **LOCATION**
England

✤ **GEOGRAPHIC COORDINATES**
Longitude 53.2059° N
Latitude 1.0861° W

Sherwood Forest was once a former royal hunting ground. What woodland remains of it today is located just 17 miles (27 km) north of Nottingham, England.

Sherwood Forest covered a much larger area when it was known for being the stomping grounds of the legendary medieval outlaw, the elusive and stealthy Robin Hood, who, during the 1200s, supposedly "stole from the rich to give to the poor." According to the stories about them, Robin Hood and his group of Merry Men committed themselves to defending the defenseless poor by fooling the law of the land while they hid among the huge Oak trees of the forest. More specifically, as the legends go, the tree that was the favored forest shelter for Robin Hood and his merry men was a *Quercus robur* English Oak which is still standing and is at least one thousand years old. This enormously large hollow tree is known as England's largest, most famous, and most well protected English Oak tree, the Major Oak.

The Major Oak can be seen along the way of a 3.7-mile (6 km) looping hiking trail that imbues a magical atmosphere, where one can see hundreds of ancient English Oak, Birch, Sweet Chestnut, and Beech trees, in addition to all the wildlife and birds.

WORKS
CONSULTED

Acamovic, T., C.S. Stewart and T.W. Pennycott, Eds., *Poisonous Plants and Related Toxins* (Cabi, 2004)

Alexander, Courtney, "Berries as Symbol and in Folklore," https://cpb-us-e1.wpmucdn.com/blogs.cornell.edu/dist/0/7265/files/2016/12/berryfolklore-2ljztoq.pdf

American Botanical Council, http://herbalgram.org

American University of Beirut, *AUB Landscape Plant Database*, https://landscapeplants.aub.edu.lb

Ancient Trees Forum, "Ancient Trees," https://www.ancienttreeforum.org.uk/ancient-trees

Ancient Wisdom Foundation, "Herbs: A-Z List: The Medicinal, Spiritual and Magical Uses," http://www.ancient-wisdom.com/herbsaz.htm

Arbor Day Foundation, "Tree Facts," https://www.arborday.org/trees/treefacts/

Arbor Day Foundation, *Tree Guide Database*, https://shop.arborday.org/treeguide

Arrowsmith, Nancy, Calantirniel, et al., *Llewellyn's 2010 Herbal Almanac* (Llewellyn Publications, 2010)

Atlas Obscura, "El Árbol del Tule (The Tule Tree): The stoutest tree in the world," https://www.atlasobscura.com/places/el-arbol-del-tule-tule-tree

Atlas of Florida Plants, https://florida.plantatlas.usf.edu

Australian Tropical Rainforest Plants, https://apps.lucidcentral.org/rainforest/text/intro/index.html

Bailey, L.H., Ethel Zoe Bailey, Staff of Liberty Hyde Bailey Hortotorium, and David Bates, *Hortus Third: A Concise Dictionary of Plants Cultivated in the United States and Canada* (Macmillan, 1976)

Balcony Garden Web, "40 Best Trees for Bonsai," https://balconygardenweb.com/best-trees-for-bonsai-best-bonsai-plants

Barrow, Mandy, "What Did the Romans Eat?" https://www.primaryhomeworkhelp.co.uk/romans/food.html

Bathroom Readers' Institute, *Uncle John's New & Improved Briefs: Fast Facts, Terse Trivia & Astute Articles* (St. Martin's Press, 1988)

Baynes, Thomas Spencer, Day Otis Kellogg, and William Robertson Smith, *The Encyclopedia Britannica* (Encyclopaedia Britannica, 1897)

Behind the Name, *The Etymology and History of First Names*, https://www.behindthename.com

Bender, David A., *A Dictionary of Food and Nutrition, 4th Edition* (Oxford University Press, 2013)

Beyerl, Paul, *A Compendium of Herbal Magick* (Phoenix Publishing Inc., 1998)

Biodiversity Heritage Library, https://www.biodiversitylibrary.org

Bios, "The Fascinating Cultural Trend of 'Wish Trees'," https://urnabios.com/the-fascinating-cultural-trend-of-wishing-trees/

Black Forest Germany, "The Black Forest," https://www.blackforestgermany.com

Bonsai Empire, "Care guides for the common Bonsai tree species," https://www.bonsaiempire.com/tree-species

Bremness, Lesley, *Herbs* (DK Smithsonian Handbooks, 1994)

Brickell, Christopher, *The Royal Horticultural Society A–Z Encyclopedia of Garden Plants*, (Dorling Kindersley Publishers Ltd., 1996)

Buhner, Stephen Harrod, *Sacred Plant Medicine: The Wisdom in Native American Herbalism* (Bear & Company, 2006)

California Department of Food & Agriculture, http://www.cdfa.ca.gov

Charles Darwin Foundation, https://www.darwinfoundation.org/en/datazone

Citrus Pages, http://citruspages.free.fr/index.php

Coats, Alice M. and John L. Creech, *Garden Shrubs and Their Histories* (Simon & Schuster, 1992)

Coombes, Allen J., *The Collingridge Dictionary of Plant Names* (Hamlyn, 1985)

Cowie, Ashley, "Ancient Highland Clootie Well Has Been Stripped of Its Cloots!" https://www.ancient-origins.net/news-general/clootie-well-0016345

Culpepper, Nicholas, *The Complete Herbal* (A. Cross, 1652)

Cunningham, Scott, *Cunningham's Encyclopedia of Magical Herbs* (Llewellyn Publications, 1985)

Cunningham, Scott, *Magical Herbalism: The Secret Craft of the Wise* (Llewellyn's Practical Magick, 1986)

Cunningham, Scott, *The Magic in Food: Legends, Lore & Spellwork* (Llewellyn Publications, 1991)

Daintree Discovery Centre, https://www.discoverthedaintree.com

Dammann's Lawn, Garden & Landscaping Centers, "Ornamental Tree List," https://www.dammanns.com/2017/01/10/dammanns-ornamental-tree-list-2013/

de Abreu, Kristine, "Natural Wonders: Poland's Crooked Forest," https://explorersweb.com/natural-wonders-polands-crooked-forest

Delaware Valley Unit of the Herb Society of America, https://www.delvalherbs.org

Designer Trees, "Bottle Trees: Not All the Same," https://www.designertrees.com.au/bottle-trees-not-all-the-same/

Dobelis, Inge N., *Magic and Medicine of Plants* (Reader's Digest, 1986)

Duke, James A., Peggy-Ann K. Duke, and Judith L. duCellie, *Duke's Handbook of Medicinal Plants of the Bible* (CRC Press, 2007)

Ebben Nurseries, "Trees," https://www.ebben.nl/en/treeebb/

eFloras.org, https://www.efloras.org

Encyclopedia, https://encyclopedia.com

Fairchild Tropical Botanic Garden, https://www.fairchildgarden.org

Fielding, Robert O., *Spices: Their Histories* (The Trade Register, 1910)

Flowers of India, http://www.flowersofindia.net

Folkard, Richard Jr., *Plant Lore, Legends, and Lyrics: Embracing Myths, Traditions, Superstitions, and Folk-Lore of the Plant Kingdom* (R. Folkard and Son, 1884)

Forest Service, U.S. Department of Agriculture (USDA), "Sequoia National Forest," https://www.fs.usda.gov/sequoia

Forestry Focus, "Sacred and Magical Trees," https://www.forestryfocus.ie/social-environmental-aspects/cultural-heritage/trees-and-folklore/sacred-and-magical-trees/

Gardeners' World, https://www.gardenersworld.com/plants/

Gardenia, "Plant Types: Trees," https://www.gardenia.net/plants/plant-types/trees

Gardening Channel, "List of Herbs from A to Z," https://www.gardeningchannel.com/list-of-herbs-from-a-to-z/

Gardening Know How, "Ornamental Trees," https://www.gardeningknowhow.com/ornamental/trees

Garland, Sarah, *The Complete Book of Herbs and Spices* (Viking Press, 1979)

Global Trees Campaign, "Threatened Trees," https://globaltrees.org/threatened-trees

Grieve, Maud, Mrs., *A Modern Herbal*, https://botanical.com (online, originally published 1931)

Growables, "Grow Florida Edibles," https://www.growables.org/index.html

Gunther, Shea, "9 of the World's Most Amazing Trees," https://www.treehugger.com/worlds-most-amazing-trees-4869240

Gymnosperm Database, https://www.conifers.org

Harvard University Herbaria & Libraries, https://kiki.huh.harvard.edu/databases/botanist_index.html

Hazlitt, William Carew, and John Brand, *Faiths and Folklore and Facts: A Dictionary* (Charles Scribner's Sons, 1905)

Holl, Karen D., "How would planting 8 billion trees every year for 20 years affect Earth's climate?" https://www.weforum.org/agenda/2021/08/planting-trees-combat-climate-change

Hopman, Ellen Evert, *A Druid's Herbal of Sacred Tree Medicine*, (Destiny Books, 2008)

Howard, Michael, *Traditional Folk Remedies: A Comprehensive Herbal* (Century, 1987)

Humboldt County Visitors' Center, "Redwoods," https://www.visitredwoods.com/explore-the-redwoods/

Hutchens, Alma R., *Indian Herbalogy of North America: The Definitive Guide to Native Medicinal Plants and Their Uses* (Shambhala, 1991)

Ingram, Simon, "What makes Glastonbury so mystical?" https://www.nationalgeographic.co.uk/history-and-civilisation/2019/06/what-makes-glastonbury-so-mystical

International Dendrology Society, *Trees and Shrubs Online: Plant Index*, https://treesandshrubsonline.org/articles/

James Cook University, *Australian Tropical Herbarium*, https://www.ath.org.au/australian-tropical-herbarium/about-the-herbarium/databases

Japan National Tourism Organization (JNTO), "Arashiyama Bamboo Grove," https://www.japan.travel/en/spot/1141

Japan-Guide, "Tanabata," https://www.japan-guide.com/e/e2283.html

Keating, Helen, "British trees: folklore and mythology," https://www.woodlandtrust.org.uk/blog/2021/04/tree-folklore/

Kepler, Angela Kay, *Hawaiian Heritage Plants* (University of Hawaii Press, 1998)

Kew Royal Botanic Gardens, *Plants of the World Online*, https://wcsp.science.kew.org/home.do

Knight, Sophie, and Olivia Morelli, "The most amazing and unusual trees in the world in pictures," https://www.cntraveller.com/gallery/unusual-trees

Kuhns, Michael, "What is a tree?" https://forestry.usu.edu/tree-identification/what-is-a-tree

Lad, Vasant K., *Ayurveda: The Science of Self-Healing* (Lotus Press, 1985)

Land 8, "Top 10 Sacred Trees," https://land8.com/top-10-sacred-trees

Local Tree Estimates, "How Many Trees Are in the World?" https://localtreeestimates.com/how-many-trees-are-in-the-world/

Lust, John, *The Herb Book: The Most Complete Catalog of Herbs Ever Published* (Bantam Books, 1979)

Madagascar Treasure Island, "The Baobab: A Malagasy Tree," https://madagascar-tourisme.com/en/what-to-do/fauna-and-flora/baobab

Magical Plants, https://www.tphta.ws

Mangroves, http://www.mangrove.at/mangrove.html

McGuffin, Michael, *American Herbal Products Association's Botanical Safety Handbook* (American Herbal Products Association, 2013)

Michelle, Omaya, "Where, When, Why: Oud Fragrance," https://www.moderneast.com/life/where-when-why-oud-fragrance-217383.html

Minnesota Stormwater Manual, "Tree species list—morphology," https://stormwater.pca.state.mn.us/index.php/Tree_species_list_-_morphology

Missouri Botanical Garden, http://www.missouribotanicalgarden.org/plantfinder/plantfindersearch.aspx

Moore, Peter, "Timber! The world's 7 most famous trees," https://www.wanderlust.co.uk/content/world-s-most-famous-trees/

Mount, Harry, "Britain's mightiest oak: A staggering 1,046 years old, it's still going strong (even if it is getting a bit stout around the middle)," https://www.dailymail.co.uk/news/article-3685614/Britain-s-mightiest-oak-staggering-1-046-years-old-s-going-strong-getting-bit-stout-middle.html

Myths and Legends, "Encyclopedia of Myths," http://www.mythencyclopedia.com

National Capital Poison Center Poison Control, "Poisonous and Non-poisonous Plants," https://www.poison.org/articles/plant

National Gardening Association, *Plants Database*, https://garden.org/plants/

National Parks of Singapore, *Flora and Fauna Web*, https://www.nparks.gov.sg/florafaunaweb

Nations Online, http://www.nationsonline.org

Native Hawaiian Garden, "Flowering Plants," https://www.nativehawaiiangarden.org/flowering-plants

Natural Medicinal Herbs, http://www.naturalmedicinalherbs.net/herbs/natural/

Nature & Garden, "Trees and Shrubs," https://www.nature-and-garden.com/gardening/shrub

New Zealand Plant Conservation Network, "New Zealand's Flora," https://www.nzpcn.org.nz/flora/

Next Travel Sri Lanka, "All About Jaya Sri Maha Bodhi, The Miracle Sacred Tree in Sri Lanka," https://nexttravelsrilanka.com/sri-maha-bodhi/

North Carolina State University, "Extension Gardener Plant Toolbox," https://plants.ces.ncsu.edu/find_a_plant

Northcote, Lady Rosalind, *The Book of Herbs*, (Turnbull & Spears, 1903)

Ody, Penelope, *The Complete Medicinal Herbal* (Dorling Kindersley, 1993)

Okakura, Kakuzo, *The Book of Tea* (Fox, Duffield & Company, 1906)

Mercado, Jocelyn, "People and Trees: Intimately Connected Through the Ages," https://blog.pachamama.org/people-and-trees-intimately-connected-through-the-ages

Pennisi, Elizabeth, "Earth home to 3 trillion trees, half as many as when human civilization arose," https://www.science.org/content/article/earth-home-3-trillion-trees-half-many-when-human-civilization-arose

Petruzzello, Melissa, "How Can Some Trees Survive for Thousands of Years?" https://www.britannica.com/story/how-can-some-trees-survive-for-thousands-of-years

Plant List, http://www.theplantlist.org

Plants for a Future, https://pfaf.org

Premier Tree Solutions, "Weird Tree Tour: Trees So Toxic You Can't Even Stand Under Them," https://chopmytree.com/weird-tree-tour-trees-so-toxic-you-cant-even-stand-under-them/

Princeton Tree Care, "Enchanted Forests: Mystical Powers of Different Trees," https://www.princetontreecare.com/tree-of-knowledge/mystical-powers-of-different-trees

Regional Conservation, *Floristic Inventory of South Florida*, https://regionalconservation.org/ircs/database/plants/SFPlantListByL.asp?Letter=A

Rohde, Eleanour Sinclair, *The Old English Herbals*, (Longmans, Green and Co., 1922)

Royal Society for the Protection of Birds (RSPB), "Sherwood Forest," https://www.visitsherwood.co.uk

San-Miguel-Ayanz, J., de Rigo, D., Caudullo, G., Houston Durrant, T., and Mauri, A., Eds., *European Atlas of Forest Tree Species*, https://forest.jrc.ec.europa.eu/en/european-atlas (European Commission, 2016, reprinted 2021)

Science Direct, https://www.sciencedirect.com

Sentient Metaphysics, "Metaphysical Plants And Trees," https://sentientmetaphysics.com/category/plants-trees

Shoot, "Plant Identification & Finder," https://www.shootgardening.co.uk/plant/identify

Simonetti, Gualtiero and Stanley Schuler, Eds., *Simon & Schuster's Guide to Herbs and Spices*, (Simon & Schuster, 1990)

Simons, Frederick J., *Plants of Life, Plants of Death* (University of Wisconsin Press, 1998)

Song of the Woods, "Index of Plants," https://www.songofthewoods.com/index-of-plants/

South African National Biodiversity Institute, https://sanbi.org

South Regional Network of Expertise and Collections, SERNEC Data Portal, https://sernecportal.org/portal/index.php

Spells of Magic, "Magical Properties of Wood for Wands," https://www.spellsofmagic.com/coven_ritual.html?ritual=3300&coven=510

Spirit Lodge, "Spiritual Element of Trees," http://www.spiritlodge.itgo.com/libsym13.html

Spirited, "Portugal's Oldest Producing Cork Tree," https://www.spiritedbiz.com/portugals-oldest-producing-cork-tree/

Stuntz, Dylan, "Sacred Roots: Trees in Folklore," https://www.americanforests.org/blog/sacred-roots-trees-in-folklore/

Theoi Project, "Flora 1: Plants of Greek Myth," https://www.theoi.com/Flora1.html

Thiselton-Dyer, T.F., *The Folk-Lore of Plants* (D. Appleton and Company, 1889)

Tisserand, Robert B., *The Art of Aromatherapy: The Healing and Beautifying Properties of the Essential Oils of Flowers and Herbs* (Healing Arts Press, 1978)

Torreya Guardians, http://www.torreyaguardians.org

Tree Names, "Bonsai Tree Names with Pictures," https://www.treenames.net/types/bonsai bonsai_tree_names_pictures.html

Tree Names, "Lists of Common Tree Names or List of Latin Botanical Tree Names," https://www.treenames.net

Trees of South Africa, *Tree Database*, https://treesa.org/search/

University of Arizona, "Campus Arboretum," https://apps.cals.arizona.edu/arboretum/browse.aspx

University of California, "Safe and Poisonous Garden Plants," https://ucanr.edu/sites/poisonous_safe_plants/

University of California Riverside, "Citrus Variety Collection," https://citrusvariety.ucr.edu/index.html

University of Connecticut, *Plant Database*, https://plantdatabase.uconn.edu

University of Florida, Environmental Horticulture, "680 Tree Fact Sheets," https://hort.ifas.ufl.edu/database/trees/trees_scientific.shtml

University of Rochester Medical Center, "A Guide to Common Medicinal Herbs," https://www.urmc.rochester.edu/encyclopedia/content

University of Texas at Austin, Lady Bird Johnson Wildflower Center, "Plant Lists," https://www.wildflower.org/collections

U.S. Forest Service, "Plants of Mind and Spirit," https://www.fs.fed.us/wildflowers/ethnobotany/Mind_and_Spirit/index.shtml

USDA, "Plants," https://plants.usda.gov/home

USDA Natural Resources Conservation Service, https://www.nrcs.usda.gov/wps/portal/nrcs/site/national/home

Westover, Robert Hudson, USDA, "Methuselah, a Bristlecone Pine is Thought to be the Oldest Living Organism on Earth," https://www.usda.gov/media/blog/2011/04/21/methuselah-bristlecone-pine-thought-be-oldest-living-organism-earth

Valnet, Jean, *The Practice of Aromatherapy*, translated from the French by Robin Campbell and Libby Houston (Random House, 1982; Vermilion, 2011)

Vaughan, J.G. and Judd, P.A., *The New Oxford Book of Health Foods* (Oxford University Press, 2003)

Vaughan, John, and Geissler, Catherine, *The New Oxford Book of Food Plants* (Oxford University Press, 2009)

Ward, Lyn, "The fascinating culture of Wishing Trees," https://www.fethiyetimes.com/magazine/23357-wishing-trees-wonderful-example-similarities-many-cultures.html

Welch, Craig, "What's the oldest tree on Earth—and will it survive climate change?" https://www.nationalgeographic.com/environment/article/whats-the-oldest-tree-on-earth-and-will-it-survive-climate-change

Wichtl, Max, Ed., *Herbal Drugs and Phytopharmaceuticals: A Handbook for Practice on a Scientific Basis* (Medpharm, 2004)

Woodland Trust, *Ancient Tree Inventory*, https://ati.woodlandtrust.org.uk/

Your Irish Culture, "Folklore of Fairy Trees in Ireland," https://www.yourirish.com/folklore/irish-fairy-trees

Zich F.A., Hyland B.P.M., Whiffin T., and Kerrigan R.A., *Australian Tropical Rainforest Plants, Edition 8*, https://apps.lucidcentral.org/rainforest/text/intro/index.html (Centre for Australian National Biodiversity Research, 2020)

ACKNOWLEDGMENTS

A s soon as I began researching this book about trees I have wanted to especially dedicate it to my dear friend, Robert, who, over the years, would engage in delightfully meaningful and fascinating discussions with me about the mystically magical nature of a forest. Also in mind have been my tree-loving family and friends, as well as the protective tree-huggers, hopeful tree-planters, and energetic tree-climbers everywhere in the world.

Special thanks to Wellfleet Press and all things Quarto Publishing Group USA. Everyone I have worked with has been outstanding. Millions of my heartfelt thanks goes to Wellfleet's fabulous Editor, Elizabeth You, for her easy accessibility, profound wisdom, guidance, and much appreciated suggestions throughout the development of my books.

Thank you to Quarto's brilliant Publisher, Rage Kindelsperger, and wonderful Managing Editor, Cara Donaldson, for their overall vision and ongoing encouragement. Thank you to my Copyeditor, Helena Caldon, for her careful attention to the text. Thank you to Creative Director Laura Drew and the entire Art Team for skillfully and conscientiously creating absolutely gorgeous books that I am very proud to have my name on. Thank you to Senior Editor Katie Moore, who offered me the opportunity to take on this especially interesting project. I wish each of you incredibly talented people all the very best in every way imaginable.

Thank you to God for the trees, and for an endless ongoing list of seriously good reasons.

Peace and love to everyone.

ABOUT THE AUTHOR

Spring, summer and autumn container gardening on a small apartment's balcony is all the more appreciated during the short growing season in the Enchanted Mountains of Western New York State, where eclectic artist and writer S. Theresa Dietz makes her home. Her fascination with all things magical and mysterious, along with a deep abiding love of trees, plants, and flowers, motivates her to continue learning more about them.

PHOTO CREDITS

Unless otherwise listed below, all images © Shutterstock.com

© Alamy Stock Photo: Frontis, page 2

© Alamy Stock Photo: 273 (*Malus sylvestris*)

© GettyImages: 380 (*Raphia farinifera*)

© GettyImages: 030 (*Araucaria araucana*)

© GettyImages: 444 (*Tsuga canadensis*)

© GettyImages: 236 (*Kigelia africana*)

© Alamy Stock Photo: 302 (*Nothofagus betuloides*)

© Alamy Stock Photo: 373 (*Quassia amara*)

© Alamy Stock Photo: 235 (*Kalopanax septemlobus*)

© Alamy Stock Photo: 385 (*Rhapis excelsa*)

© Alamy Stock Photo: 452 (*Vachellia farnesiana*)

Index of
COMMON TREE NAMES

Elephant Apple, *162*
Emerald Tree, *379*
Engkala Tree, *258*
English Elm Tree, *448*
English Hawthorn Tree, *150*
English Holly Tree, *223*
English Laurel Tree, *361*
English Oak Tree, *376*
English Walnut, *231*
English Yew, *432*
Ethiopian Pepper Tree, *469*
European Beech Tree, *190*
European Black Pine, *328*
European Bladdernut Tree, *418*
European Crabapple Tree, *273*
European Hornbeam Tree, *074*
European Larch, *243*
European Privet, *252*
European Rowan Tree, *415*
European Smoketree, *148*
European Spindle Tree, *183*
Everglades Palm, *009*

F

Feijoa Tree, *191*
Fig Tree, *194*
Florida Torreya Tree, *442*
Floss Silk Tree, *094*
Flowering Dogwood, *144*
Foxtail Palm, *462*
Fragrant Screw-Pine, *314*

G

Garcinia Cambogia Tree, *201*
Garjan Tree, *166*
Geiger Tree, *143*
Ghaf Tree, *351*
Giant Chinkapin Tree, *107*
Giant Fishtail Palm, *078*
Giant Sequoia, *409*
Giant Thorny Bamboo, *044*
Giant Tree Aloe, *020*
Ginkgo Tree, *207*
Golden Rain Tree, *237*
Golden Shower Tree, *081*

Golden Spoon Tree, *064*
Grapefruit Tree, *123*
Great Basin Bristlecone Pine Tree, *327*
Great Rhododendron, *387*
Greenheart Tree, *105*
Grey Bark Tree, *173*
Guava Tree, *368*
Guayusa Tree, *224*
Guinep, *280*
Gum Arabic Tree, *407*
Gum Benjamin Tree, *421*
Gutta-Percha Tree, *312*

H

Hackberry Tree, *095*
Hand-Flower Tree, *104*
Handkerchief Tree, *159*
Haraka Tree, *465*
Hawaiian Cotton Tree, *238*
Hawaiian Gardenia, *204*
Hazel Tree, *146*
Henna Tree, *247*
Hibiscus, *215*
Hinoki Cypress Tree, *101*
Hog Plum, *467*
Honey Locust Tree, *208*
Honey Mesquite Tree, *352*
Horse Chestnut Tree, *012*
Houpu Magnolia, *266*
Hyuganatsu Tree, *129*

I

Ichang Papeda Tree, *115*
Incense Cedar, *065*
Indian Jujube Tree, *475*
Ironwood Tree, *281*
Italian Cypress, *152*
Italian Stone Pine, *329*
Ixora, *228*

J

Jacaranda Tree, *229*
Jackfruit Tree, *038*
Jaggery Palm, *079*
Jamaican Dogwood, *336*
Japanese Camellia, *067*

Japanese Flowering Crabapple Tree, *272*
Japanese Maple, *006*
Japanese Raisin Tree, *220*
Japanese Umbrella-Pine, *406*
Jellyfish Tree, *276*
Jelly Palm, *062*
Jocote Tree, *417*
Jojoba, *412*
Joshua Tree, *471*
Judas Tree, *100*
Juniper Tree, *232*

K

Kabosu Papeda Tree, *126*
Kapok Tree, *093*
Karoi Tree, *017*
Katsura Tree, *099*
Kauri Tree, *014*
Kava Tree, *335*
Keyaki Tree, *474*
Key Lime Tree, *112*
Khat Tree, *088*
King Sago Palm, *154*
Kinkeliba Tree, *138*
Koa Tree, *004*
Kokum Tree, *202*
Kola Nut Tree, *137*
Kumquat Tree, *198*

L

Laurel Magnolia, *268*
Lebanese Cedar Tree, *092*
Lemon Myrtle, *042*
Lemon Tree, *118*
Lenga Beech Tree, *304*
Lilac Tree, *423*
Linden Tree, *441*
Loblolly Pine, *334*
Logwood, *212*
Loquat Tree, *178*
Lychee Tree, *256*

M

Macadamia Tree, *260*
Magellan's Beech, *302*
Makrut Lime Tree, *116*

Malabar Chestnut Tree, *310*
Māmane Tree, *413*
Manchineel Tree, *217*
Mandarin Orange Tree, *124*
Mangosteen Tree, *203*
Mango Tree, *274*
Manna Ash Tree, *200*
Mānuka Tree, *249*
Mastic Tree, *337*
Maua Tree, *470*
May Chang Tree, *257*
Me'ee Tree, *262*
Melaleuca Tree, *277*
Melinjo Tree, *209*
Mexican Buckeye Tree, *451*
Mexican Fan Palm, *461*
Mexican Rubber Tree, *085*
Milktree, *401*
Mimosa, *003*
Ming Aralia Tree, *343*
Monkey Puzzle Tree, *030*
Montezuma Cypress, *431*
Moringa Tree, *286*
Mountain Laurel, *234*
Myrobalan Plum Tree, *356*
Myrrh Tree, *140*

N

Nectandra Tree, *298*
Neem Tree, *041*
Nikau Palm, *388*
Norfolk Island Pine, *032*
North American Beech Tree, *189*
Northern Bayberry Tree, *293*
North Indian Rosewood Tree, *158*
Norway Spruce, *321*
Nutmeg Tree, *295*
Nyala Tree, *466*

O

Oleander, *299*
Olive Tree, *309*
Oriental Persimmon, *164*
Osage Orange Tree, *261*

Index of
REPRESENTED TREES
ACCORDING TO HEIGHT

No. 107 *Chrysolepis chrysophylla* Giant Chinkapin
150 feet [46 meters]

No. 166 *Dipterocarpus turbinatus* Garjan Tree
150 feet [46 meters]

No. 430 *Taxidium distichum* Bald Cypress
150 feet [45 meters]

No. 296 *Myroxylon balsamum* var. *pereirae*
Balsam of Peru 148 feet [45 meters]

No. 014 *Agathis australis* Kauri Tree 148 feet [45 meters]

No. 151 *Cratoxylum formosum* Pink Mampat Tree
148 feet [45 meters]

No. 303 *Nothofagus dombeyi* Dombey's Beech Tree
148 feet [30 meters]

No. 199 *Fraxinus excelsior* Ash Tree 141 feet [43 meters]

No. 459 *Warburgia ugandensis* Ugandan Greenheart
138 feet [42 meters]

No. 028 *Aquilaria malaccensis* Agar-Agar Tree
131 feet [40 meters]

No. 085 *Castilla elastica* Mexican Rubber Tree
131 feet [40 meters]

No. 463 *Wollemia nobilis* Wollemi Pine Tree
131 feet [40 meters]

No. 214 *Hevea brasiliensis* Rubber Tree
131 feet [40 meters]

No. 219 *Hopea odorata* White Thingan Tree
131 feet [40 meters]

No. 244 *Larix gmelinii* Dahurian Larch
131 feet [40 meters]

No. 375 *Quercus petraea* Sessile Oak 131 feet [40 meters]

No. 436 *Terminalia superba* Afara Tree
131 feet [40 meters]

No. 058 *Brosimum guianense* Snakewood Tree
130 feet [40 meters]

No. 230 *Juglans nigra* Black Walnut 130 feet [40 meters]

No. 440 *Tilia americana* American Basswood Tree
130 feet [40 meters]

No. 076 *Carya illinoinensis* Pecan Tree
130 feet [40 meters]

No. 090 *Cedrela odorata* Spanish Cedar
130 feet [40 meters]

No. 105 *Chlorocardium rodiei* Greenheart Tree
130 feet [40 meters]

No. 221 *Hura crepitans* Dynamite Tree
130 feet [40 meters]

No. 243 *Larix decidua* European Larch
130 feet [40 meters]

No. 019 *Alnus glutinosa* Common Alder
121 feet [37 meters]

No. 092 *Cedrus libani* Lebanese Cedar Tree
120 feet [37 meters]

No. 231 *Juglans regia* English Walnut 120 feet [37 meters]

No. 282 *Metasequoia* glyptostroboides Dawn Redwood
120 feet [37 meters]

No. 468 *Xylia xylocarpa* Burma Ironwood
120 feet [37 meters]

No. 435 *Terminalia anogeissiana* Axlewood Tree
118 feet [36 meters]

No. 057 *Brachylaena huillensis* Silver Oak
115 feet [35 meters]

No. 401 *Sapium glandulosum* Milktree 115 feet [35 meters]

No. 008 *Acer saccharum* Sugar Maple 115 feet [35 meters]

No. 059 *Broussonetia papyrifera* Paper Mulberry Tree
115 feet [35 meters]

No. 149 *Couroupita guianensis* Cannonball Tree
115 feet [35 meters]

No. 441 *Tilia* × *europaea* Linden Tree
114 feet [35 meters]

No. 448 *Ulmus procera* English Elm Tree
114 feet [35 meters]

No. 072 *Carapa guianensis* Crabwood Tree
114 feet [35 meters]

No. 259 *Lodoicea maldivica* Coco de Mer Palm
112 feet [34 meters]

No. 392 *Roystonea regia* Royal Palm 112 feet [34 meters]

No. 420 *Styphnolobium japonicum* Pagoda Tree
100 feet [30 meters]

No. 044 *Bambusa bambos* Giant Thorny Bamboo
100 feet [30 meters]

No. 069 *Cananga odorata* Ylang-Ylang Tree
100 feet [30 meters]

No. 086 *Casuarina equisetifolia* Whistling Pine Tree
100 feet [30 meters]

No. 445 *Ulmus americana* American Elm
100 feet [30 meters]

No. 461 *Washingtonia robusta* Mexican Fan Palm
100 feet [30 meters]

No. 135 *Cocos nucifera* Coconut Palm
100 feet [30 meters]

No. 274 *Mangifera indica* Mango Treew
100 feet [30 meters]

No. 304 *Nothofagus pumilio* Lenga Beech Tree
100 feet [30 meters]

No. 321 *Picea abies* Norway Spruce 100 feet [30 meters]

No. 322 *Picea laxa* White Spruce 100 feet [30 meters]

No. 329 *Pinus pinea* Italian Stone Pine
100 feet [30 meters]

No. 344 *Populus alba* Silver Poplar Tree
100 feet [30 meters]

No. 374 *Quercus alba* White Oak Tree
100 feet [30 meters]

No. 376 *Quercus robur* English Oak Tree
100 feet [30 meters]

No. 465 *Xanthocercis madagascariensis* Haraka Tree
100 feet [30 meters]

No. 466 *Xanthocercis zambesiaca* Nyala Tree
100 feet [30 meters]

No. 469 *Xylopia aethopica* Ethiopian Pepper Tree
100 feet [30 meters]

No. 474 *Zelkova serrata* Keyaki Tree 100 feet [30 meters]

No. 281 *Mesua ferrea* Ironwood Tree 99 feet [30 meters]

No. 141 *Conocarpus lancifolius* Qalab 99 feet [30 meters]

No. 158 *Dalbergia sissoo* North Indian Rosewood Tree
99 feet [30 meters]

No. 163 *Diospyros ebenum* Ebony Tree 99 feet [30 meters]

No. 319 *Phoenix dactylifera* Date Palm 99 feet [30 meters]

No. 224 *Ilex guayusa* Guayusa Tree 98 feet [30 meters]

No. 018 *Aleurites moluccanus* Candlenut Tree
98 feet [30 meters]

No. 070 *Canarium luzonicum* Elemi Canary Tree
98 feet [30 meters]

No. 193 *Ficus benjamina* Benjamin Fig Tree
98 feet [30 meters]

No. 210 *Grevillea robusta* Silky Oak Tree
98 feet [30 meters]

No. 345 *Populus balsamifera* Balsam Poplar
98 feet [30 meters]

No. 402 *Sassafras albidum* White Sassafras
98 feet [30 meters]

No. 004 *Acacia koa* Koa Tree 98 feet [30 meters]

No. 053 *Borassus flabellifer* Palmyra Palm
98 feet [30 meters]

No. 082 *Castanea dentata* American Chestnut Tree
98 feet [30 meters]

No. 083 *Castanea sativa* Sweet Chestnut
98 feet [30 meters]

No. 174 *Durio zibethinus* Durian Tree 98 feet [30 meters]

No. 195 *Ficus religiosa* Bodhi Tree 98 feet [30 meters]

No. 208 *Gleditsia triacanthos* Honey Locust Tree
98 feet [30 meters]

No. 222 *Hymenaea courbaril* West Indian Locust
98 feet [30 meters]

No. 248 *Lecythis pisonis* Paradise Nut Tree
98 feet [30 meters]

No. 275 *Manilkara zapota* Sapodilla Tree
98 feet [30 meters]

No. 278 *Melaleuca leucadendra* Cajeput Tree
98 feet [30 meters]

No. 306 *Nothotsuga longibracteata* Bristlecone Hemlock
98 feet [30 meters]

No. 308 *Ochroma pyramidale* Balsa Wood Tree
98 feet [30 meters]

No. 347 *Populus nigra* Black Poplar 98 feet [30 meters]

No. 348 *Populus tremuloides* Quaking Aspen
98 feet [30 meters]

No. 095 *Celtis occidentalis* Hackberry Tree
95 feet [29 meters]

No. 245 *Larix laricina* Tamarack Tree 95 feet [29 meters]

No. 007 *Acer rubrum* Red Maple 90 feet [27 meters]

No. 339 *Platanus occidentalis* American Sycamore Tree
90 feet [27 meters]

No. 379 *Radermachera sinica* Emerald Tree
90 feet [27 meters]

No. 001 *Abies balsamea* Balsam Fir 89 feet [27 meters]

No. 258 *Litsea garciae* Engkala Tree 85 feet [26 meters]

No. 315 *Pausinystalia yohimbe* Yohimbe Tree
82 feet [25 meters]

No. 017 *Albizia procera* Karoi Tree 82 feet [25 meters]

No. 056 *Brachychiton rupestris* Queensland Bottle Tree
82 feet [25 meters]

No. 185 *Euterpe oleracea* Açaí Palm 82 feet [25 meters]

No. 417 *Spondias purpurea* Jocote Tree 82 feet [25 meters]

No. 421 *Styrax benzoin* Gum Benjamin Tree
82 feet [25 meters]

No. 010 *Adansonia digitata* Baobab Tree
82 feet [25 meters]

No. 045 *Banksia integrifoli* Coast Banksia Tree 82 feet [25 meters]

No. 088 *Catha edulis* Khat Tree 82 feet [25 meters]

No. 089 *Cecropia peltata* Trumpet Tree 82 feet [25 meters]

No. 159 *Davidia involucrata* Handkerchief Tree 82 feet [25 meters]

No. 173 *Drypetes deplanchei* Grey Wood Tree 82 feet [25 meters]

No. 188 *Fagraea fragrans* Tembusa Tree 82 feet [25 meters]

No. 192 *Ficus benghalensis* Banyan Tree 82 feet [25 meters]

No. 200 *Fraxinus ornus* Manna Ash Tree 82 feet [25 meters]

No. 203 *Garcinia mangostana* Mangosteen Tree 82 feet [25 meters]

No. 235 *Kalopanax septemlobus* Prickly Castor Oil Tree 82 feet [25 meters]

No. 302 *Nothofagus betuloides* Magellan's Beech 82 feet [25 meters]

No. 331 *Pinus rigida* Pitch Pine Tree 82 feet [25 meters]

No. 380 *Raphia farinifera* Raffia Palm 82 feet [25 meters]

No. 391 *Robinia pseudoacacia* Black Locust Tree 82 feet [25 meters]

No. 419 *Strychnos nux-vomica* Strychnine Tree 82 feet [25 meters]

No. 301 *Nothofagus antarctica* Antarctic Beech Tree 80 feet [25 meters]

No. 016 *Ailanthus altissima* Tree of Heaven 80 feet [24 meters]

No. 030 *Araucaria araucana* Monkey Puzzle Tree 80 feet [24 meters]

No. 038 *Artocarpus heterophyllus* Jackfruit Tree 80 feet [24 meters]

No. 077 *Carya ovata* Shagbark Hickory Tree 80 feet [24 meters]

No. 431 *Taxodium mucronatum* Montezuma Cypress 80 feet [24 meters]

No. 012 *Aesculus hippocastanum* Horse Chestnut Tree 80 feet [24 meters]

No. 074 *Carpinus betulus* Hornbeam Tree 80 feet [24 meters]

No. 283 *Metrosideros excelsa* Pōhutukawa Tree 80 feet [24 meters]

No. 332 *Pinus strobus* White Pine Tree 80 feet [24 meters]

No. 378 *Quercus virginiana* Southern Live Oak 80 feet [24 meters]

No. 043 *Bactris gasipaes* Peach Palm Tree 79 feet [24 meters]

No. 049 *Betula lenta* Black Birch 79 feet [24 meters]

No. 325 *Pinus coulteri* Coulter Pine 79 feet [24 meters]

No. 268 *Magnolia splendens* Laurel Magnolia 76 feet [23 meters]

No. 051 *Betula pendula* Silver Birch 75 feet [23 meters]

No. 101 *Chamaecyparis obtusa* Hinoki Cypress 75 feet [23 meters]

No. 132 *Cladrastis kentukea* American Yellowood Tree 75 feet [23 meters]

No. 189 *Fagus grandifolia* North American Beech Tree 75 feet [23 meters]

No. 254 *Liquidambar styraciflua* Sweetgum 75 feet [23 meters]

No. 298 *Nectandra membranacea* Nectandra Tree 75 feet [23 meters]

No. 377 *Quercus suber* Cork Oak 75 feet [23 meters]

No. 386 *Rhizophora mangle* Red Mangrove 75 feet [23 meters]

No. 422 *Swietenia mahagoni* West Indies Mahogany Tree 75 feet [23 meters]

No. 289 *Morus rubra* Red Mulberry Tree 72 feet [22 meters]

No. 266 *Magnolia officinalis* Houpu Magnolia 70 feet [21 meters]

No. 037 *Artocarpus altilis* Breadfruit Tree 70 feet [21 meters]

No. 050 *Betula papyrifera* Paper Birch 70 feet [21 meters]

No. 109 *Cinnamomum camphora* White Camphor Tree 70 feet [21 meters]

No. 265 *Magnolia grandiflora* Southern Magnolia 70 feet [21 meters]

No. 310 *Pachira aquatica* Malabar Chestnut 70 feet [21 meters]

No. 034 *Areca catechu* Betel Nut Tree 66 feet [20 meters]

No. 041 *Azadirachta indica* Neem Tree 66 feet [20 meters]

No. 196 *Ficus sycomorus* Sycomore Fig Tree 66 feet [20 meters]

No. 262   *Madhuca longifolia* Me'ee Tree
66 feet [20 meters]

No. 236   *Kigelia africana* Sausage Tree 66 feet [20 meters]

No. 024   *Amentotaxus hatuyenensis* Catkin-Yew
65 feet [20 meters]

No. 035   *Arenga pinnata* Sugar Palm 65 feet [20 meters]

No. 036   *Argania spinosa* Argan Tree 65 feet [20 meters]

No. 312   *Palaquium gutta* Gutta-Percha Tree
65 feet [20 meters]

No. 137   *Cola acuminata* Kola Nut Tree
65 feet [20 meters]

No. 327   *Pinus longaeva* Great Basin Bristlecone Pine
65 feet [20 meters]

No. 393   *Sabal palmetto* Sabal Palm 65 feet [20 meters]

No. 399   *Santalum album* Sandalwood Tree
65 feet [20 meters]

No. 416   *Sorbus domestica* Service Tree
65 feet [20 meters]

No. 449   *Ulmus rubra* Slippery Elm Tree
65 feet [20 meters]

No. 084   *Castanospermum australe* Black Bean Tree
60 feet [18 meters]

No. 087   *Catalpa bignonioides* Southern Catalpa Tree
60 feet [18 meters]

No. 110   *Cinnamomum cassia* Cassia Tree
60 feet [18 meters]

No. 263   *Magnolia acuminata* Cucumber Magnolia
60 feet [18 meters]

No. 395   *Salix babylonica* Weeping Willow
60 feet [18 meters]

No. 066   *Calophyllum inophyllum* Beautyleaf Tree
60 feet [18 meters]

No. 424   *Syzygium aromaticum* Clove Tree
60 feet [18 meters]

No. 091   *Cedrus atlantica* Atlas Cedarwood
60 feet [18 meters]

No. 099   *Cercidiphyllum japonicum* Katsura Tree
60 feet [18 meters]

No. 104   *Chiranthodendron pentadactylon*
Hand-Flower Tree 60 feet [18 meters]

No. 152   *Cupressus sempervirens* Italian Cypress
60 feet [18 meters]

No. 295   *Myristica fragrans* Nutmeg Tree
60 feet [18 meters]

No. 328   *Pinus nigra* European Black Pine
60 feet [18 meters]

No. 333   *Pinus sylvestris* Scots Pine 60 feet [18 meters]

No. 352   *Prosopis glandulosa* Honey Mesquite
60 feet [18 meters]

No. 427   *Tamarindus indica* Tamarind Tree
60 feet [18 meters]

No. 428   *Tamarix aphylla* Athel Tamarisk
60 feet [18 meters]

No. 433   *Taxus brevifolia* Pacific Yew 60 feet [18 meters]

No. 439   *Thuja occidentalis* Arborvitae 60 feet [18 meters]

No. 202   *Garcinia indica* Kokum Tree 59 feet [18 meters]

No. 280   *Melicoccus bijugatus* Guinep 59 feet [18 meters]

No. 447   *Ulmus parvifolia* Chinese Elm Tree
59 feet [18 meters]

No. 246   *Laurus nobilis* Bay Laurel Tree
55 feet [17 meters]

No. 020   *Aloidendron barberae* Giant Tree Aloe
54 feet [17 meters]

No. 286   *Moringa oleifera* Moringa Tree 53 feet [16 meters]

No. 061   *Bursera graveolens* Palo Santo 50 feet [15 meters]

No. 078   *Caryota obtusa* Giant Fishtail Palm
50 feet [15 meters]

No. 094   *Ceiba speciosa* Floss Silk Tree 50 feet [15 meters]

No. 269   *Magnolia virginiana* Sweetbay Magnolia
50 feet [15 meters]

No. 307   *Nyssa sylvatica* Tupelo Tree 50 feet [15 meters]

No. 413   *Sophora chrysophylla* Māmane Tree
50 feet [15 meters]

No. 462   *Wodyetia bifurcata* Foxtail Palm
50 feet [15 meters]

No. 071   *Canella winterana* Cinnamon Bark Tree
50 feet [15 meters]

No. 093   *Ceiba pentandra* Kapok Tree 50 feet [15 meters]

No. 134   *Coccoloba uvifera* Sea Grape 50 feet [15 meters]

No. 170   *Dracaena draco* Canary Islands Dragon Tree
50 feet [15 meters]

No. 187   *Fagraea berteroana* Perfume Flower Tree
50 feet [15 meters]

No. 197   *Firmiana simplex* Chinese Parasol Tree
50 feet [15 meters]

No. 232   *Juniperus communis* Juniper Tree
50 feet [15 meters]

No. 233   *Juniperus virginiana* Virginian Juniper
          50 feet [15 meters]

No. 276   *Medusagyne oppositifolia* Jellyfish Tree
          50 feet [15 meters]

No. 287   *Morus alba* White Mulberry Tree
          50 feet [15 meters]

No. 341   *Plinia cauliflora* Brazilian Grape Tree
          50 feet [15 meters]

No. 362   *Prunus padus* Bird Cherry Tree
          50 feet [15 meters]

No. 388   *Rhopalostylis sapida* Nikau Palm
          50 feet [15 meters]

No. 403   *Schefflera actinophylla* Australia Umbrella Tree
          50 feet [15 meters]

No. 415   *Sorbus aucuparia* European Rowan Tree
          49 feet [15 meters]

No. 097   *Ceratonia siliqua* Carob Tree 49 feet [15 meters]

No. 225   *Ilex paraguariensis* Yerba Mate
          49 feet [15 meters]

No. 300   *Newbouldia laevis* Boundary Tree
          49 feet [15 meters]

No. 336   *Piscidia erythrina* Jamaican Dogwood
          49 feet [15 meters]

No. 318   *Persea americana* Avocado Tree
          49 feet [15 meters]

No. 455   *Vitellaria paradoxa* Shea Butter Tree
          49 feet [15 meters]

No. 015   *Agonis flexuosa* Peppermint Tree
          49 feet [15 meters]

No. 033   *Arbutus unedo* Strawberry Tree
          49 feet [15 meters]

No. 079   *Caryota urens* Jaggery Palm 49 feet [15 meters]

No. 111   *Cinnamomum verum* Cinnamon Tree
          49 feet [15 meters]

No. 162   *Dillenia indica* Elephant Apple
          49 feet [15 meters]

No. 176   *Elaeis guineensis* African Oil Palm
          49 feet [15 meters]

No. 186   *Excoecaria agallocha* Blinding Tree
          49 feet [15 meters]

No. 209   *Gnetum gnemon* Melinjo Tree 49 feet [15 meters]

No. 249   *Leptospermum scoparium* Mānuka Tree
          49 feet [15 meters]

No. 285   *Mimusops elengi* Tanjong Tree 49 feet [15 meters]

No. 294   *Myrica rubra* Yangmei Tree 49 feet [15 meters]

No. 320   *Phyllanthus emblica* Amla Tree
          49 feet [15 meters]

No. 350   *Pouteria campechiana* Canistel Tree
          49 feet [15 meters]

No. 351   *Prosopis cineraria* Ghaf Tree 49 feet [15 meters]

No. 405   *Schinus terebinthifolia* Brazilian Pepper Tree
          49 feet [15 meters]

No. 025   *Anacardium occidentale* Cashew Tree
          46 feet [14 meters]

No. 323   *Pimenta dioica* Allspice Tree 43 feet [13 meters]

No. 217   *Hippomane mancinella* Manchineel Tree
          40 feet [12 meters]

No. 252   *Ligustrum vulgare* European Privet
          40 feet [12 meters]

No. 442   *Torreya taxifolia* Florida Torreya Tree
          40 feet [12 meters]

No. 470   *Xylosma hawaiiense* Maua Tree
          40 feet [12 meters]

No. 471   *Yucca brevifolia* Joshua Tree 40 feet [12 meters]

No. 081   *Cassia fistula* Golden Shower Tree
          40 feet [12 meters]

No. 160   *Delonix regia* Royal Poinciana Tree
          40 feet [12 meters]

No. 229   *Jacaranda mimosifolia* Jacaranda Tree
          40 feet [12 meters]

No. 234   *Kalmia latifolia* Mountain Laurel
          40 feet [12 meters]

No. 237   *Koelreuteria paniculata* Golden Rain Tree
          40 feet [12 meters]

No. 261   *Maclura pomifera* Osage Orange Tree
          40 feet [12 meters]

No. 324   *Pimenta racemosa* Bay Rum Tree
          40 feet [12 meters]

No. 372   *Pyrus pyrifolia* Asian Pear 40 feet [12 meters]

No. 404   *Schefflera arboricola* Dwarf Schefflera Tree
          40 feet [12 meters]

No. 406   *Sciadopitys verticillata* Japanese Umbrella-Pine
          40 feet [12 meters]

No. 048   *Betula alleghaniensis* Yellow Birch
          39 feet [12 meters]

No. 064   *Byrsonima crassifolia* Golden Spoon Tree
          39 feet [12 meters]

No. 256   *Litchi chinensis* subsp. *chinensis* Lychee Tree
          39 feet [12 meters]

No. 458   *Volkameria glabra* Volkamenia
39 feet [12 meters]

No. 073   *Carica papaya* Papaya Tree 39 feet [12 meters]

No. 100   *Cercis siliquastrum* Judas Tree 39 feet [12 meters]

No. 128   *Citrus tachibana* Tachibana Orange
39 feet [12 meters]

No. 147   *Corymbia ficifolia* Red Flowering Gum Tree
39 feet [12 meters]

No. 164   *Diospyros kaki* Oriental Persimmon Tree
39 feet [12 meters]

No. 279   *Melia azedarach* Chinaberry Tree
39 feet [12 meters]

No. 358   *Prunus domestica* Plum Tree 39 feet [12 meters]

No. 067   *Camellia japonica* Japanese Camellia
36 feet [11meters]

No. 241   *Lagerstroemia indica* Crape Myrtle
35 feet [11 meters]

No. 250   *Libidibia punctata* Bridalveil Tree
35 feet [11 meters]

No. 238   *Kokia drynarioides* Hawaiian Cotton Tree
35 feet [10 meters]

No. 062   *Butia odorata* Jelly Palm 33 feet [10 meters]

No. 387   *Rhododendron maximum* Great Rhododendron
33 feet [10 meters]

No. 138   *Combretum apiculatum* Kinkeliba Tree
33 feet [10 meters]

No. 142   *Copernicia prunifera* Brazilian Wax Palm
33 feet [10 meters]

No. 169   *Dracaena cinnabari* Dragon's Blood Tree
33 feet [10 meters]

No. 183   *Euonymus europaeus* European Spindle Tree
33 feet [10 meters]

No. 313   *Pandanus edulis* Bakong 33 feet [10 meters]

No. 338   *Pistacia vera* Pistachio Tree 33 feet [10 meters]

No. 359   *Prunus dulcis* var. *amara* Bitter Almond Tree
33 feet [10 meters]

No. 360   *Prunus dulcis* var. *dulcis* Sweet Almond Tree
33 feet [10 meters]

No. 368   *Psidium guajava* Guava Tree 33 feet [10 meters]

No. 384   *Rhamnus purshiana* Cascara Sagrada
33 feet [10 meters]

No. 429   *Tasmannia lanceolata* Tasmanian Pepper
33 feet [10 meters]

No. 098   *Cerbera odollam* Pong-Pong Tree
32 feet [10 meters]

No. 251   *Ligustrum lucidum* Chinese Glossy Privet
32 feet [10 meters]

No. 288   *Morus nigra* Black Mulberry Tree
32 feet [10 meters]

No. 011   *Aegle marmelos* Bael 32 feet [10 meters]

No. 212   *Haematoxylum campechianum* Logwood Tree
32 feet [10 meters]

No. 220   *Hovenia dulcis* Japanese Raisin Tree
32 feet [10 meters]

No. 260   *Macadamia integrifolia* Macadamia Tree
32 feet [10 meters]

No. 396   *Salix caprea* Pussywillow
32 feet [10 meters]

No. 438   *Theobroma grandiflorum* Cupuaçu Tree
32 feet [10 meters]

No. 467   *Ximenia americana* Hog Plum 32 feet [10 meters]

No. 475   *Ziziphus mauritiana* Indian Jujube
32 feet [10 meters]

No. 026   *Annona cherimola* Cherimoya Tree
30 feet [9 meters]

No. 039   *Asimina triloba* Paw-Paw 30 feet [9 meters]

No. 040   *Averrhoa carambola* Star Fruit Tree
30 feet [9 meters]

No. 080   *Cascabela thevetia* Yellow Oleander
30 feet [9 meters]

No. 218   *Hippophae rhamnoides* Sea Buckthorn
30 feet [9 meters]

No. 273   *Malus sylvestris* European Crabapple
30 feet [9 meters]

No. 355   *Prunus avium* Sweet Cherry Tree
30 feet [9 meters]

No. 414   *Sorbus americana* American Mountain Ash
30 feet [9 meters]

No. 381   *Ravenala madagascariensis* Travelers Palm
30 feet [9 meters]

No. 006   *Acer palmatum* Japanese Maple
30 feet [9 meters]

No. 366   *Prunus virginiana* Chokecherry Tree
30 feet [9 meters]

No. 009   *Acoelorrhaphe wrightii* Everglades Palm
30 feet [9 meters]

No. 046   *Beaucarnea recurvata* Ponytail Palm
30 feet [9 meters]

No. 096   *Cephalotaxus harringtonia* Plum Yew
30 feet [9 meters]

No. 102   *Chilopsis linearis* Desert Willow
30 feet [9 meters]

No. 133   *Clusia rosea* Autograph Tree 30 feet [9 meters]

No. 143   *Cordia sebestena* Geiger Tree 30 feet [9 meters]

No. 144   *Cornus florida* Flowering Dogwood
30 feet [9 meters]

No. 145   *Cornus mas* Cornelian Cherry Tree
30 feet [9 meters]

No. 153   *Cussonia spicata* Spiked Cabbage Tree
30 feet [9 meters]

No. 175   *Dypsis lutescens* Areca Palm 30 feet [9 meters]

No. 178   *Eriobotrya japonica* Loquat Tree
30 feet [9 meters]

No. 194   *Ficus carica* Fig Tree 30 feet [9 meters]

No. 213   *Hamamelis virginiana* Witch Hazel Tree
30 feet [9 meters]

No. 226   *Ilex vomitoria* Yaupon Holly 30 feet [9 meters]

No. 242   *Lagunaria patersonia* Pyramid Tree
30 feet [9 meters]

No. 309   *Olea europaea* Olive Tree 30 feet [9 meters]

No. 356   *Prunus cerasifera* Myrobalan Plum
30 feet [9 meters]

No. 370   *Punica granatum* Pomegranate Tree
30 feet [9 meters]

No. 371   *Pyrus communis* Pear Tree
30 feet [9 meters]

No. 394   *Salix alba* White Willow 30 feet [9 meters]

No. 398   *Sambucus nigra* Black Elder 30 feet [9 meters]

No. 451   *Ungnadia speciosa* Mexican Buckeye Tree
30 feet [9 meters]

No. 460   *Warszewiczia coccinea* Wild Poinsettia
30 feet [9 meters]

No. 113   *Citrus × aurantium* Bitter Orange Tree
29 feet [9 meters]

No. 223   *Ilex aquifolium* English Holly Tree
29 feet [9 meters]

No. 055   *Bourreria succulenta* Bahama Strongbark Tree
29 feet [9 meters]

No. 125   *Citrus × sinensis* Sweet Orange Tree
29 feet [9 meters]

No. 165   *Diospyros lotus* Date Plum Tree 29 feet [9 meters]

No. 108   *Cinchona officinalis* Cinchona Tree
26 feet [8 meters]

No. 317   *Pennantia baylisiana*
Three Kings Kaikōmako Tree 26 feet [8 meters]

No. 361   *Prunus laurocerasus* English Laurel Tree
26 feet [8 meters]

No. 369   *Pterocarpus santalinus* Red Sandalwood
26 feet [8 meters]

No. 425   *Syzygium jambos* Rose Apple Tree
26 feet [8 meters]

No. 464   *Xanthoceras sorbifolium* Yellowhorn Tree
26 feet [8 meters]

No. 021   *Amborella trichopoda* Amborella Tree
25 feet [8 meters]

No. 029   *Aralia spinosa* Devil's Walking Stick
25 feet [8 meters]

No. 267   *Magnolia × soulangeana* Saucer Magnolia
25 feet [8 meters]

No. 272   *Malus × floribunda*
Japanese Flowering Crabapple 25 feet [8 meters]

No. 383   *Rhamnus cathartica* Buckthorn Tree
25 feet [8 meters]

No. 443   *Toxicodendron vernix* Poison Sumac Tree
25 feet [8 meters]

No. 446   *Ulmus glabra* Wych Elm 25 feet [8 meters]

No. 452   *Vachellia farnesiana* Sweet Acacia Tree
25 feet [8 meters]

No. 023   *Amelanchier canadensis* Shadblow Serviceberry
Tree 25 feet [8 meters]

No. 131   *Citrus tangerina* Tangerine Tree
25 feet [8 meters]

No. 150   *Crataegus laevigata* English Hawthorn Tree
25 feet [8 meters]

No. 292   *Myrica cerifera* Southern Wax Myrtle Tree
25 feet [8 meters]

No. 293   *Myrica pensylvanica* Northen Bayberry Tree
25 feet [8 meters]

No. 337   *Pistacia lentiscus* Mastic Tree 25 feet [8 meters]

No. 342   *Plumeria rubra* Plumeria Tree 25 feet [8 meters]

No. 353   *Prunus americana* Wild Plum Tree
25 feet [8 meters]

No. 363   *Prunus persica* Peach Tree 25 feet [8 meters]

No. 432   *Taxus baccata* English Yew 25 feet [8 meters]

No. 437   *Theobroma cacao* Cacao Tree 25 feet [8 meters]

No. 390   *Rhus typhina* Staghorn Sumac 25 feet [8 meters]

No. 155   *Cydonia oblonga* Quince Tree 24 feet [7 meters]

No. 156   *Cytisus scoparius*   Scotch Broom
24 feet [7 meters]

No. 172   *Drimys winteri*   Winter's Bark Tree
2 4 feet [7 meters]

No. 123   *Citrus × paradisi*   Grapefruit Tree
23 feet [7 meters]

No. 154   *Cycas revoluta*   King Sago Palm   23 feet [7 meters]

No. 257   *Litsea cubeba*   May Chang Tree   23 feet [7 meters]

No. 453   *Vernicia fordii*   Tung Oil Tree   23 feet [7 meters]

No. 054   *Boswellia sacra*   Sacred Boswellia Tree
20 feet [6 meters]

No. 103   *Chionanthus virginicus*   White Fringe Tree
20 feet [6 meters]

No. 240   *Laburnum anagyroides*   Common Laburnum
20 feet [6 meters]

No. 299   *Nerium oleander*   Oleander Tree
20 feet [6 meters]

No. 354   *Prunus armeniaca*   Apricot Tree
20 feet [6 meters]

No. 357   *Prunus cerasus*   Sour Cherry Tree
20 feet [6 meters]

No. 407   *Senegalia senegal*   Gum Arabic Tree
20 feet [6 meters]

No. 456   *Vitex agnus-castus*   Chaste Tree
20 feet [6 meters]

No. 003   *Acacia dealbata*   Mimosa   20 feet [6 meters]

No. 005   *Acacia tortilis*   Umbrella Thorn Acacia
20 feet [6 meters]

No. 063   *Buxus sempervirens*   Boxwood   20 feet [6 meters]

No. 117   *Citrus × latifolia*   Persian Lime Tree
20 feet [6 meters]

No. 118   *Citrus × limon*   Lemon Tree   20 feet [6 meters]

No. 119   *Citrus × limonia*   Rangpur Tree   20 feet [6 meters]

No. 120   *Citrus maxima*   Pomelo Tree   20 feet [6 meters]

No. 201   *Garcinia gummi-gutta*
Garcinia Cambogia Tree   20 feet [6 meters]

No. 204   *Gardenia brighamii*   Hawaiian Gardenia
20 feet [6 meters]

No. 247   *Lawsonia inermis*   Henna Tree   20 feet [6 meters]

No. 290   *Murraya koenigii*   Curry Leaf Tree
20 feet [6 meters]

No. 291   *Musa acuminata*   Banana Tree   20 feet [6 meters]

No. 340   *Pleroma semidecandrum*   Purple Glory Tree
20 feet [6 meters]

No. 373   *Quassia amara*   Quassia Tree   20 feet [6 meters]

No. 042   *Backhousia citriodora*   Lemon Myrtle
19 feet [6 meters]

No. 112   *Citrus × aurantiifolia*   Key Lime Tree
19 feet [6 meters]

No. 116   *Citrus hystrix*   Makrut Lime Tree
19 feet [6 meters]

No. 277   *Melaleuca alternifolia*   Melaleuca Tree
19 feet [6 meters]

No. 412   *Simmondsia chinensis*   Jojoba   19 feet [6 meters]

No. 271   *Malus domestica*   Common Apple Tree
17 feet [5 meters]

No. 060   *Brugmansia aroborea*   Brugmansia Tree
16 feet [5 meters]

No. 052   *Bixa orellana*   Achiote Tree   16 feet [5 meters]

No. 114   *Citrus × bergamia*   Bergamot Orange Tree
16 feet [5 meters]

No. 140   *Commiphora myrrha*   Myrrh Tree
16 feet [5 meters]

No. 227   *Illicium verum*   Star Anise 16 feet [5 meters]

No. 297   *Myrtus communis*   True Myrtle Tree
16 feet [5 meters]

No. 365   *Prunus spinosa*   Blackthorn Tree 16 feet [5 meters]

No. 423   *Syringa vulgaris*   Lilac Tree   16 feet [5 meters]

No. 198   *Fortunella japonica*   Kumquat Tree
15 feet [5 meters]

No. 335   *Piper methysticum*   Kava   15 feet [5 meters]

No. 454   *Viburnum prunifolium*   Black Haw Tree
15 feet [5 meters]

No. 472   *Yucca rostrata*   Beaked Yucca   15 feet [5 meters]

No. 068   *Camellia sinensis*   Tea Tree   15 feet [5 meters]

No. 106   *Chrysobalanus icaco*   Cocoplum Tree
15 feet [5 meters]

No. 115   *Citrus cavaleriei*   Ichang Papeda Tree
15 feet [5 meters]

No. 121   *Citrus medica*   Citron Tree   15 feet [5 meters]

No. 122   *Citrus medica* var. *sarcodactylis*
Buddha's Hand Citron Tree   15 feet [5 meters]

No. 124   *Citrus × reticulata*   Mandarin Orange Tree
15 feet [5 meters]

No. 126   *Citrus sphaerocarpa*   Kabosu Papeda Tree
15 feet [5 meters]

No. 136   *Coffea arabica*   Arabica Coffee Tree
15 feet [5 meters]

No. 146 *Corylus avellana* Hazel Tree 15 feet [5 meters]

No. 148 *Cotinus coggygria* European Smoketree
15 feet [5 meters]

No. 168 *Dracaena arborea* Slender Dragon Tree
15 feet [5 meters]

No. 191 *Feijoa sellowiana* Feijoa Tree 15 feet [5 meters]

No. 228 *Ixora coccinea* Ixora 15 feet [5 meters]

No. 418 *Staphylea pinnata* European Bladdernut Tree
15 feet [5 meters]

No. 473 *Zanthoxylum piperitum* Szechuan Pepper
15 feet [5 meters]

No. 253 *Lindera benzoin* Spicebush Tree 13 feet [4 meters]

No. 314 *Pandanus odorifer* Fragrant Screw-Pine
13 feet [4 meters]

No. 400 *Santalum spicatum* Australian Sandalwood
13 feet [4 meters]

No. 022 *Amelanchier alnifolia* Saskatoon 13 feet [4 meters]

No. 139 *Commiphora gileadensis* Balm of Gilead
13 feet [4 meters]

No. 270 *Malpighia emarginata* Acerola Cherry
13 feet [4 meters]

No. 382 *Rauvolfia tetraphylla* Be Still Tree
13 feet [4 meters]

No. 385 *Rhapis excelsa* Broadleaf Lady Palm
13 feet [4 meters]

No. 130 *Citrus × tangelo* Tangelo Tree
12 feet [4 meters]

No. 215 *Hibiscus rosa-sinensis* Hibiscus
12 feet [4 meters]

No. 397 *Sambucus canadensis* Common Elder
12 feet [4 meters]

No. 216 *Hibiscus syriacus* Rose of Sharon
12 feet [4 meters]

No. 205 *Gardenia jasminoides* Common Gardenia
10 feet [3 meters]

No. 389 *Rhus coriaria* Sumac Tree 10 feet [3 meters]

No. 179 *Erythrina crista-galli* Cockspur Coral Tree
10 feet [3 meters]

No. 206 *Gaultheria shallon* Salal Tree 10 feet [3 meters]

No. 311 *Paeonia × suffruticosa* Tree Peony
10 feet [3 meters]

No. 411 *Sida fallax* Yellow Ilima Tree
10 feet [3 meters]

No. 161 *Dendrocnide moroide*s Stinging Tree
10 feet (3 meters)

No. 171 *Dracaena reflexa* Song of India Tree
10 feet (3 meters)

No. 184 *Euphorbia pulcherrima* Poinsettia Tree
10 feet (3 meters)

No. 457 *Vitex negundo* Chinese Vitex 9 feet [3 meters]

No. 127 *Citrus sudachi* Sudachi Tree 9 feet [3 meters]

No. 129 *Citrus tamurana* Hyuganatsu Tree
9 feet [3 meters]

No. 343 *Polyscias fruticosa* Ming Aralia Tree
7 feet [2 meters]

Index of
COMMON MEANINGS